W9-ABZ-346

NATIVE AMERICAN BIBLIOGRAPHY SERIES

Advisory Board: Brenda Child, University of Minnesota, Minneapolis • R. David Edmunds, Texas Christian University • Arlene B. Hirschfelder, Teaneck, N.J. • Karl Kroeber, Columbia University • A. Lavonne Ruoff, University of Illinois, Chicago • Emory Sekaquap-tewa, University of Arizona • Virginia Driving Hawk Sneve, Flandreau, S.D. • Clifford E. Trafzer, University of California, Riverside

General Editor: Jack W. Marken, South Dakota State University

1. *Bibliography of the Sioux*, by Jack W. Marken and Herbert T. Hoover. 1980
2. *Biobibliography of Native American Writers, 1772–1924*, by Daniel F. Littlefield Jr., and James W. Parins. 1981
3. *Bibliography of the Languages of Native California*, by William Bright. 1982
4. *A Guide to Cherokee Documents in Foreign Archives*, by William L. Anderson and James A. Lewis. 1983
5. *A Biobibliography of Native American Writers, 1772–1924: Supplement*, by Daniel F. Littlefield Jr., and James W. Parins. 1985
6. *Bibliography of the Osage*, by Terry P. Wilson. 1985
7. *A Guide to Cherokee Documents in the Northeastern United States*, by Paul Kutsche. 1986
8. *In Pursuit of the Past: An Anthropological and Bibliographic Guide to Maryland and Delaware*, by Frank W. Porter III. 1986
9. *The Indians of Texas: An Annotated Research Bibliography*, by Michael L. Tate. 1986
10. *Bibliography of the Catawba*, by Thomas J. Blumer. 1987
11. *Bibliography of the Chickasaw*, by Anne Kelley Hoyt. 1987
12. *Kinsmen through Time: An Annotated Bibliography of Potawatomi History*, by R. David Edmunds. 1987
13. *Bibliography of the Blackfoot*, by Hugh A. Dempsey and Lindsay Moir. 1989
14. *The Upstream People: An Annotated Research Bibliography of the Omaha Tribe*, by Michael L. Tate. 1991
15. *Languages of the Aboriginal Southeast: An Annotated Bibliography*, by Karen Booker. 1991

16. *Yakima, Palouse, Cayuse, Umatilla, Walla Walla, and Wanapum Indians: An Historical Bibliography*, by Clifford E. Trafzer. 1991
17. *The Seneca and Tuscarora Indians: An Annotated Bibliography*, by Marilyn Haas. 1994
18. *The Native American in Long Fiction: An Annotated Bibliography*, by Joan Beam and Barbara Branstad. 1996
19. *Indigenous Languages of the Americas: A Bibliography of Dissertations and Theses*, by Robert Singerman. 1996
20. *Health of Native People of North America: A Bibliography and Guide to Resources*, by Sharon A. Gray. 1996
21. *A Bibliography of the Indians of San Diego County: The Kumeyaay, Diegueño, Luiseño, and Cupeño,* by Phillip M. White and Stephen D. Fitt. 1998
22. *Indian Slavery, Labor, Evangelization, and Captivity in the Americas: An Annotated Bibliography,* by Russell M. Magnaghi. 1998
23. *Diné Bibliography to the 1990s: A Companion to the Navajo Bibliography of 1969*, by Howard M. Bahr. 1999
24. *Native Americans in the* Saturday Evening Post, by Peter G. Beidler and Marion F. Egge. 2000
25. *The Native American in Short Fiction in the* Saturday Evening Post: *An Annotated Bibliography*, by Peter G. Beidler, Harry J. Brown, and Marion F. Egge. 2001
26. *The Shawnee Indians: An Annotated Bibliography*, by Randolph Noe. 2001
27. *The Native American in Long Fiction: An Annotated Bibliography, supplement 1995–2002,* by Joan Beam and Barbara Branstad. 2003.

The Native American in Long Fiction

An Annotated Bibliography: Supplement, 1995–2002

Joan Beam and Barbara Branstad

Native American Bibliography Series, No. 27

The Scarecrow Press, Inc.
Lanham, Maryland, and Oxford
2003

PS
374
.I49
B42
2003

SCARECROW PRESS, INC.

Published in the United States of America
by Scarecrow Press, Inc.
A wholly owned subsidiary of the Rowman & Littlefield Publishing Group, Inc.
4501 Forbes Boulevard, Suite 200, Lanham, Maryland 20706
www.scarecrowpress.com

PO Box 317, Oxford, OX2 9RU, UK

Copyright © 2003 by Joan Beam and Barbara Branstad

All rights reserved. No part of this publication may be reproduced, stored in a retrieval system, or transmitted in any form or by any means, electronic, mechanical, photocopying, recording, or otherwise, without the prior permission of the publisher.

British Library Cataloguing in Publication Information Available

Library of Congress Cataloging-in-Publication Data

Beam, Joan.
The Native American in long fiction : an annotated bibliography: supplement, 1995–2002 / Joan Beam and Barbara Branstad.
p. cm.—(Native American bibliography series ; no. 27)
Includes bibliographical references and indexes.
ISBN 0-8108-4841-4 (alk. paper)
1. American fiction—Bibliography. 2. Indians in literature—Bibliography. 3. American fiction—Indian authors—Bibliography. I. Branstad, Barbara. II. Title. III. Series.
Z1231.F4B42 2003 [PS374.I49]
016.813008'03520397—dc21 2003008245

∞™ The paper used in this publication meets the minimum requirements of American National Statndard for Information Sciences—Permanence of Paper for Printed Library Materials, ANSI/NISO Z39.48-1992.
Manufactured in the United States of America.

52085914

Contents

Series Editor's Foreword

This book by Joan Beam and Barbara Branstad is a supplement to their compilation published in 1996 by Scarecrow Press as No. 18 in the Native American Bibliography Series. The Supplement follows the same format as the original edition, containing the same useful indices, though with the addition of a new section of Authors' Choice to provide guidance to readers to help them choose the best and most significant recent novels. The novels included in the Supplement are those which, as the authors stated in the original edition, have as a central them "either Native American characters, events in Native American history, or a depiction of Native American social life and culture, whether historic or contemporary.

As in their first book, "this work is suitable for educators of all levels from junior high through graduate school. It will be useful to librarians and will inform the general reader about fiction that exists relating to individual tribes, particularly Native American authors of long fiction from these tribes. Another good feature is the annotations to each entry, which are not only critical but include citations to reviews of these novels found in standard journals." This book is a valuable sort of compilation that ought to be updated every decade or so.

Jack W. Marken
Professor of English Emeritus
South Dakota State University
Brookings, South Dakota

Introduction

Today when someone in the United States hears the term Indian or American Indian or Native American, what image arises unbidden in their imagination? A well-dressed small business owner, a school teacher, accomplished artist, computer technician or a member of a university faculty? Or perhaps is it the image of a Navaho rug weaver, a Sioux chief in full headdress, a chanting medicine man over a smoky fire, a rodeo cowboy, or a quiet Hopi woman selling turquoise jewelry on a blanket? More likely the immediate mental image is of people in a time, culture and dress of the past, rather than to a current member of society. Should the immediate image of the Indian be contemporary, even here stereotypes abound. Is the contemporary image of a poverty-stricken reservation dweller, or of a wealthy casino owner, or of a New Age shaman in braids and beads? Do contemporary images always immediately include farmers and authors, lawyers and teachers? How have our images of Native Americans been formed over time by books, movies, newspapers and other forms of media? How have U.S. history, politics, literature and media shaped our image of a people who have had their cultural, social, economic and political fate controlled by the federal government centuries longer than any other ethnic group in the United States? Is it unreasonable to assume that the immediate mental image of American Indians might not be a positive one, when the wealthiest nation on the earth also is the home of one of the poorest of the world's ethnic peoples? When reservations are occupied by so many living far below the poverty level and unemployment is the norm? The indigenous peoples once "owned" this nation before the arrival of any Europeans or Asians and yet the Indians' concept of shared governance and ownership ultimately contributed to the loss of their traditional lands. The loss of land brought a loss of power and thus diminished the social standing and image of the American Indian in the U.S. consciousness for many years.

During the course of collecting and reading novels for our first volume of *The Native American in Long Fiction* (1996) and recently for the second bibliography of fictional works published primarily since 1995, it has become obvious that there are definite roles into which Native Americans have been placed by white U.S. society over time. It is also apparent that these roles are recently undergoing dramatic and welcome changes.

We are all familiar with the concept of the Noble Savage, first revered by eighteenth-century Romantic European writers who heard of the uncorrupted native peoples of newly discovered territories in the western hemisphere. Tales of kindly, generous, child-like naked people welcoming Spanish explorers without guile or warfare, spread throughout Europe. French philosophers and authors, such as Jean-Jacques Rousseau, saw "Indians" as exemplifying the pure life of truly natural living. During the time of initial benign white contact between the natives and European invaders, the Noble Savage was a safe and uplifting image to describe the native peoples. The natives represented the purity that Europeans had lost in their decadent and overly-sophisticated societies. Later, when conflict arose between the native peoples that traditionally lived in the new lands and those foreign invaders who wanted to take over the land and resources, this noble image abruptly altered. Soon the images of native peoples, fighting for their lives, homes and cultures, altered to that of pagan uncivilized heathens, raping and torturing innocent hard-working settlers. Unless the European intruders accepted their own guilt and responsibility for removing or killing the traditional dwellers of the rich seashores and forests, blame for the conflict had to be placed upon the people who resisted. To Europeans, these natives were not Christian, but worshipped an undefined spirit, if anything at all. They had no written language or body of literature and white men did not understand their languages or their oral histories. American Indians did not adhere to the proper civilized European rules of warfare, but kidnapped women and children and killed peaceful farmers in surprise attacks. Never mind that European invaders did the same to sleeping native villages. The Indians did not own private land, but lived in communal societies usually without individual ownership of their small plots of corn, beans or squash. Much of their food came from hunting and gathering. They did not have the domesticated beasts of burden necessary to turn land into large productive farms. Clearly they did not appear to be industrious, nor did they utilize the natural resources the way the colonist thought they ought to. The land would be better used by newly arrived European immigrants with their long histories of farming, domesticated animals and industrialization. Native Americans now became the savage enemy, who needed to be driven out, subdued, Christianized or killed. For the European immigrants to live in harmony and accept the native peoples as equals would be to recognize the Native American's civil and property rights, which immigrating people cannot do if they plan on consistent violation of these rights. The Noble Savage had deserved respect, fairness and justice. The Uncivilized Heathen could deserve suppression or death.

Several centuries of warfare, beginning in the sixteenth century and lasting until the end of the nineteenth century, between European arrivals and the native inhabitants, cemented the concept in the U.S. consciousness that Native Americans had to be conquered and forced to accept the mainstream culture of Christianity, English language and private ownership of land. There was no room in this European/U.S. concept of civilization and religion for native culture or language, native religions or mythology, or tribal communal ownership of land and property. As Walking Buffalo (1871-1967) said: "You whites assumed we were savages. You didn't understand our prayers. You didn't try to understand. When we sang our praises to the sun or moon or wind, you said we were worshipping idols. Without understanding, you condemned us as lost souls just because our form of worship was different from yours." (Strickland. *Tonto's Revenge*. p. 85) Communal ownership of land and farms, which had worked well for the American Indian for centuries, was in conflict with the capitalistic model of the U.S. economy. One owner, one farm was the model, and the Dawes Act of 1887 attempted to force Indians to become individual landowners. The net result was a loss of tribal lands, from an estimated 113 million acres in 1887 to approximately 47 million acres in 1932 (Weston. *Native Americans in the News*. p. 20).

Subdued, defeated and usually consigned to the most barren and unproductive lands in the United State, the Native American became an object of pity and scorn, derision and ridicule. Wards of the State, recipients of government subsidies for food, clothing and housing, stripped of their language and culture or a reason to work, the time around the turn of the twentieth century was the lowest point of the American Indian's social standing and consequently their image in the American mind. This was the time of the Vanishing American, thought to be gone from the plains and the coasts, the forests and the mountains. Restricted to reservations, they disappeared from the social consciousness. Native Americans, the first people on these lands, were not even granted citizenship until 1924. Robbed of much of their ancestral lands, forbidden their language, culture and religious practices, and lacking in any political power, the Native American should have quietly disappeared, should have become the Vanished American. That was the unspoken intention of the dominant society. But hidden on those remote reservations were the seeds of rebirth and resurrection. By being isolated, the native people and their tribal cultures and languages were protected and could secretly be maintained and could later flourish.

By the 1920's changes were happening. American anthropologists led by Franz Boas began to study the indigenous people of this land, rather than foreign exotic cultures. They discovered complex rich cultures of people. The first books, Wissler's *The American Indian: An Introduction to the Anthropology of the New World,* (1917) and Parsons's *American Indian Life by Several of its Students*, (1922) raised awareness of the American Indian culture. Ruth Benedict's *Patterns of Culture* (1934), describing the Zuni and Kwakiutl societies, was a popular best seller reaching many laypersons. The one thing all the anthropologists did, however, was discuss the cultures as if they were frozen in time, and that time was set in the past. In the 1920's John Collier, a social worker and reformer, took up the Native American cause and made it his own. Through constant publicity in the press, Collier, the white artists' colonies of Taos and Santa Fe, and the Pueblo people were able to block the Bursum Pueblo Land Bill that legalized all "squatters' rights" claims to Pueblo land, especially to the irrigated acreage. Ultimately the Bill was killed by the Pueblo Indians and their white supporters, thus preventing the loss of these Pueblo lands. President Roosevelt appointed John Collier the Commissioner of Indian Affairs in 1933, a position he held until 1945. Collier was determined to preserve the American Indian tribal life and cultures and was dead set against forced assimilation. Responsible for the Indian Reorganization Act, Collier ended allotments and the shrinkage of tribal lands. The Act recognized tribal culture as something special to be preserved, not eradicated. Executive Orders and federal administrative decisions ordered that no interference with Indian religious practices would be allowed, infuriating Christian missionaries and Christian Indians, who considered these practices little better than paganism. Collier was able to revamp the educational system, eliminating distant boarding schools and setting up local day schools. The novel *Reservations* by Harold Meyers (U. Press of Colorado, 1999) describes one of these new schools on the Navajo reservation. Collier decentralized the Bureau of Indian Affairs and allowed more decision-making by the tribal governments, granting tribes more self-governance. During the Indian New Deal under Collier, the American Indian was finally recognized as a person with his own culture, own religion, own system of government, and own ability to teach Indian youth about their own artistic, religious and cultural ways.

By 1945 Collier's enemies forced him out of office and his successor changed the official federal policies to a philosophy of termination. After

World War II, American Indians were expected to become fully assimilated into society and no longer be wards of the federal government. Under the termination policy of the federal government, exemplified by Public Law 280 in 1953, local states were expected to take over financial responsibility and civil and criminal jurisdiction for their state's reservations. American Indians were encouraged by the Bureau of Indian Affairs to leave poor reservations and relocate to urban areas, where employment might be more available. Some tribes were completely disbanded, such as the Flathead, Menominee and the Klamath, by the 1953 House Concurrent Resolution 108 that passed both Houses unanimously. The Resolution also terminated all the federal agencies set up to serve the tribes in Texas, California, New York and Florida, "freeing" the American Indians from federal supervision. (Kilpatrick. *Celluloid Indians.* p. 56) In effect, this once again effectively forced the assimilation of Native Americans into mainstream white society. Congress terminated trust status of tribal lands, making them subject to taxes and ultimately causing more tribal lands to be lost due to unpaid taxes. By the 1950's the American Indian was once again in trouble. It is no surprise that the 1960's brought militancy to the reservations and urban ghettos where so many Indians lived in poverty and unemployment.

The 1960's and early 1970's in the U.S. were a time of civil unrest and a search for new ways to live by disaffected American youth. American Indians participated in the civil disobedience and provided a model for a new mode of spirituality and lifestyle. American Indian communal living became a model for the 1960's hippie commune. The Native American beliefs in spirituality, shamanism, religious peyote use, and sharing among members of a tribal society were all adopted by white middle class youth. The American Indian became someone to emulate. Not exactly the Noble Savage, but certainly the Revered and Honored Shaman. Obviously the circular philosophy of the Native American, that life is an endless cycle of birth, life, death and renewal, seemed to apply. Now the native philosophy, so adored by the French philosophers hundreds of years ago, of belief in a natural lifestyle tied to Mother Earth, was back. A new stereotype arose, that of the native environmentalist, someone more attuned to natural ecology than anyone could be in a White society. This was also a time period when American Indians assumed new roles in one of the major forms of influential media in the U. S., the Hollywood movie.

Hollywood is an industry that influences the globe. Movies from the United States are seen all over the world, exporting our culture and many of our social standards, both good and bad. A well-written novel may reach hundreds of readers, perhaps thousands. Even a poorly executed film can easily reach millions of viewers worldwide. A novel may take days to read, a film takes only hours to watch. The potential effect of any one movie is vastly greater than any one book. Therefore the depiction of Native Americans in film is extremely important when one is looking at how White American society views indigenous people.

For the most part, when a film was produced, its portrayal of Native Americans reflected the then prevailing attitudes of White society, as would be expected. The many westerns made by John Ford in particular often depicted grunting, howling, painted braves attacking wagon trains, killing settlers and stealing little girls (*The Searchers,* 1956). There were no definite tribal identities, no Lakota or Iroquois, just the generic "Indian." The time period most often used in westerns was the latter half of the nineteenth century and the fact American Indians have been interacting with Whites since the 1500's was rarely explored. Native American characters were rarely able to speak English except in broken sentences, even though White scouts and agents could often speak fluent Apache or Comanche. A not-so-subtle comment on the intelligence of Native Americans was being broadcast to American audiences. The American Indian in the American western was portrayed as an uncivilized savage, with no unique culture, no character or tribal affiliation, and certainly no justifiable cause for resisting White settlement. The fact that Native American lands were being stolen and their villagers slaughtered was immaterial to the plot of a Hollywood movie that championed the U.S. Army and the ranchers, cowboys and settlers moving west. It is unfortunate that the social consciousness of several generations of moviegoers was based upon these representations, repeated over and over and finally accepted as the truth of what it meant to be an American Indian during the settlement of the West.

If a movie western had sympathetic Indian characters, such as Chochise in Daves' *Broken Arrow* (1950), or Chingachgook and Uncas in Michael Mann's *The Last of the Mohicans* (1992), they were still subservient to the more intelligent, more powerful main White character. Nathanial Bumpo (what happened to Natty?) is stronger, wiser, more capable and more powerful than his Mohican friends, and must lead the charges and organize the rescues. In *A Man Called Horse* (1970), a severely flawed film with many incorrect tribal references, it is the Englishman Richard Harris who teaches the Lakota warrior tribesmen how to fight and win. One wonders how they had survived until his lucky arrival. Of course the well-recognized Lone Ranger and Tonto friendship was always predicated upon the American Indian playing a supportive role to the decisive masked leader of the fight against crime on the western frontier. Another not-so-subtle clue about just who is more intelligent, and therefore more capable of leading and making decisions, was constantly being conveyed to the movie theater audience.

Relationships between Indians and Whites could be friendships, with the natives of course in the supporting role, but could not be sexual. Marriage, should it occur, was never between Native American men and White women, only White men and Indian women, with the woman and any child soon killed, as Jack Crabb (Dustin Hoffman)'s Cheyenne wife Sunshine and their newborn are killed in the film *Little Big Man* (1970). Miscegenation was strictly forbidden by Hollywood and the social code. Even in the far more enlightened and sympathetic *Dances with Wolves* (1990) the marriage between Dunbar and Stands with a Fist really is a marriage of an Army lieutenant and a previously captured White woman. The obvious love between Uncas and Cora's younger sister, the pure and fair-haired Alice in *The Last of the Mohicans*, is never consummated. Instead the two potential lovers fall or leap to their mutual deaths before any such possibility can occur (Kilpatrick. *Celluloid Indians: Native Americans and Film.* 1999).

With the overwhelming effect that film has upon society, it is therefore no wonder that Native Americans were seen as less capable of determining their own fates and futures. The message was conveyed again and again that Native Americans had trouble with the English language, could not be allowed to make crucial decisions, and certainly could never be accepted as a new member of a White or non-Indian family through marriage. The best an Indian could be was a friend or supporter of the White main characters. One recent movie often held up as a good example of a film trying to truly represent American Indians in a positive and constructive way was *Dances with Wolves* (1990). The effort to give Native Americans their own voices and perspectives, spoken in their own language and using Native American actors, was commendable and the positive social effects were many. The Indian characters in the film filled many different roles in the Lakota society besides warrior and had fully developed personalities. For the first time audiences were exposed to the humor, the intelligence and the generosity of the Lakota Sioux —all safely set in the past and left there, as the ending implied the disappearance of those people under the harsh pursuit of the U.S. Army. Even when Hollywood intentions were good, the Native American was still seen as a resident of the distant and long-gone past, the Vanished American.

The tide is slowly changing with contemporary films such as *PowWow Highway* (1989), a film that shows young Cheyenne men searching for meaning and roles in life that are unique and valuable as part of their native culture. Although the movie does use some standard Hollywood scenarios, such as the road trip, it also shows real Native American diversity and conflicts, using Native American actors. Lately Native Americans themselves have begun writing, directing and producing films. Sherman Alexie's and Chris Eyre's film *Smoke Signals* (1998) was given critical acclaim, as it well deserved. Based upon his short stories in *The Lone Ranger and Tonto Fistfight in Heaven*, the characters of Victor and Thomas Builds-the-Fire, the storyteller no one wants to listen to, take over the film and the audience's heart. Alexie has recently released a new film, *The Business of Fancydancing* (2002). Chris Eyre has recently released *Skins* (2002) starring Graham Greene, about two very different Sioux brothers, based upon the Adrian C. Louis novel of the same name published in 1995.

How has the written literature changed over time? As the portrayal of Native Americans in films is changing and presenting viewpoints from the native perspective, using strong and identifiable native characters and actors, so too is the portrayal of Native Americans changing in literature. The most striking change between our first bibliography and this second compilation is the fact that more and more novels are set in contemporary times, rather than in the past. The Native American is no longer a character out of history, but instead a member of modern society. Fewer of the included works feature the historical characters of Sitting Bull or Tecumseh. Instead the main characters are men and women dealing with the problems and situations of today. Another major difference between the first bibliography and this second one is that more and more authors are Native Americans, writing about their own tribes, experiences and families. Some focus on reservation scenarios, others on the urban dwelling Indian, and many on the transition between the two worlds. Louise Erdrich's families live on the reservations of North Dakota and Minnesota, some of her characters try city life, and others prefer the traditional reservation. David Treuer's characters in *The Hiawatha* move to Minneapolis and St. Paul from the reservation, but flee back home when life falls apart. Greg Sarris's Pomo, a tribe that never had a reservation to call home, of *Grand Avenue* are city dwellers in Santa Rosa, California.

In the past many novels only contained American Indians as supporting players, while today they are often central to the plot. In "generic literature" westerns may still have cowboys in the main role, but oddly, it is the romance novel that now focuses upon the half-Cheyenne handsome and dashing male as the central character. Where Hollywood refused to ever allow a Native American man into a romantic role with a white woman, today's romance heroines often seek out the half-Indian male. Notice however, that it is usually a man of only partial Native heritage, with a solid white side to his background as well. While many of these romances are of poor literary quality and few are included in this bibliography, their existence in the publishing world is worth note. Using even half-Indian romantic leads in the written literature is a giant step away from the rule against miscegenation of the Hollywood movie.

It is the genre of the detective and mystery novel that really has incorporated the Native American as integral or central character more than any other genre. Gina and Andrew Macdonald's book *Shaman or Sherlock? The Native American Detective* (2002) fully explores this topic. They cover every section of the United States and detail the authors and Native American main characters of hundreds of mystery titles. Mardi Oakley Medawar's Tay Bodal or James Doss's Charlie Moon, may not be as familiar to readers as Tony Hillerman's Leaphorn and Chee, but they are no less strong or valid representations of their Native American cultures. Peter Bowen's Gabriel Du Pre is a Metis, with strong Native ancestors and offering another facet of Indian culture. J. F. Trainor's Angela Biwaban can be annoying in her self-absorption, but she is still strongly Anishinabe. The Thurlos' Ella Clah mysteries feature a Navaho policewoman who knows where she is needed; with her people. Kirk Mitchell has two Native American main characters, one BIA agent Emmett Parker, the other FBI agent Anna Turnipseed. For mysteries tied to archaeology and the Native American cultures that have evolved or mysteriously disappeared, try W. Michael and Kathleen Gear's First People series and their Anasazi mysteries. The Anasazi mysteries switch back and forth between Southwestern Indians of today and those of twelfth-century Chaco Canyon and other cliff dwellers and are excellent depictions of Anasazi culture. The more recent titles in the Gears' First People of North America series have also included the more historically relevant Native American cultures of the Mississippian Mound Builders, Eastern Algonquins and Southwestern Pueblo cultures, and these also usually include some mystery that must be solved.

The portrayal of Native Americans in fiction has definitely grown and evolved over time, with many dramatic changes occurring in the last decade or so. The list of American Indian authors has expanded from a handful to a long list of well-recognized names, such as Vizenor, Erdrich, Alexie, and Louis Owens. New authors such as David Treuer and Debra Magpie Earling are writing elegant, poetic novels with strong memorable characters. Who can ever forget characters such as Erdrich's Nanapush, or Alexie's Thomas Builds-the-Fire? American Indian authors come from a variety of tribal backgrounds; Spokane/Coeur d'Alene, Ojibwe, Miwok and Cherokee. Many of these authors are excellent, prize-winning writers and can stand alongside many other major American authors as peer, if not as superior. The novels these Native American authors compose are often stunning works of literature, able to join the best works by European or American authors. Entire courses at the university level can be based upon the wealth of literature by contemporary American Indian authors. In our collection of works for our bibliographies on Native Americans in fiction over the years, we have seen the evolution of the Indian from peripheral character, to strong supporting player, to central protagonist in published fictional works. Central themes and plots in fiction are increasingly concerned with more contemporary legal issues such as Indian gaming, the adoption of American Indian children by Whites and the Native American Graves Protection and Repatriation Act (NAGPRA). With American Indians as authors, writing of the Native experience in American society, we are finally hearing more of the truth of what Indians have experienced in our nation's history. It is a time that has been a long time coming—may it never be gone.

The Native American in fiction, in movies, and in our general social consciousness has held many roles over the decades. The Noble Savage went through some hard times, becoming the pagan savage, then the downtrodden reservation Indian, and eventually the wise shaman or the natural ecologist, believed to be inherently more aware of the spiritual and natural world than a white person could ever hope to be. But that is merely trading one stereotype for another. Until everyone stops "characterizing" ethnic groups as predominately one thing or another, we will have not achieved the true equality that our country presumably intends for all of its citizens. Each unique culture should make every attempt to retain its uniqueness, its own traditions and cultural identity. But that identity should be chosen and defined by those within the ethnic or cultural group, not assigned by those outside it. Hopefully we are achieving that status with the American Indian in contemporary U.S. society and social awareness.

In our second bibliography of annotated fictional works featuring Native Americans as central characters or Native American themes as central to the plot, we once again hope our collection to be of use to librarians, collection development staff, teachers and faculty at all instructional levels, and to readers seeking quality fictional works. We have read each work thoroughly and checked for obvious historical inaccuracies. Each work has been identified by time period covered, geographical location of the events, and tribes featured in the work. If an author is Native American, we have identified their tribal affiliation to the best of our ability. Once again, we have used the standardized terms for each tribe, although we recognize that individual tribes may prefer to use other terminology. Thus we use "Sioux" rather than "Lakota" and "Ojibwe" rather than "Anishinabe." Each critical annotation contains a brief plot summary and comments on the literary quality or historical accuracy of the work. In this second bibliography we have tended to consolidate series or novels with the same main character, set in the same location, and featuring similar content, together. Thus the Doss mysteries featuring Charlie Moon, the Thurlos' Ella Clah series, the Hillerman Jim Chee mysteries, and the Christopher Lane Ray Attla mysteries, among others, are all combined and placed under one entry for the author with a general synopsis following of the titles featuring the same main character. Once again, we have attempted to identify critical reviews of each entry in our bibliography in the standard reviewing sources and may also include monographs of criticism on particular authors, if able to identify titles. We also include a short, non-comprehensive, updated bibliography of works dealing with literary criticism of Native American fiction in the appendix. The appendices also contains a list of those works we rejected and the reasons why we did so. In addition, we have included a list of those novels that we especially found worthy of mention. This "Best Books" list arose from so many requests from readers as to our favorites in our first bibliography. As in our first bibliography, we have indexed the entire volume and include indexes by title, by historical persons, historical events, time periods and tribes.

This has been a labor of love, and has exposed us to some of the finest authors and literary efforts of the last few years. Our first work has been so well-received that we are confident this second updated bibliography will be equally welcome and fill a need among readers, teachers, and librarians in identifying novels by and about the Native American experience in American history and current social life.

BIBLIOGRAPHY OF SOURCES FOR INTRODUCTION

Adamson, Joni. *American Indian Literature, Environmental Justice, and Ecocriticism: the Middle Place.* Tucson: University of Arizona Press. 2001.

Berkhofer, Robert F. *The White Man's Indian: Images of the American Indian from Columbus to the Present.* New York: Knopf. 1978.

Churchill, Ward. *Fantasies of the Master Race: Literature, Cinema, and the Colonization of American Indians.* San Francisco: City Lights Books. c1998.

Kilpatrick, Jacquelyn. *Celluloid Indians: Native Americans and Film*. Lincoln: University of Nebraska Press. c1999.

Macdonald, Andrew, Gina Macdonald, and MaryAnn Sheridan. *Shape-shifting: Images of Native Americans in Recent Popular Fiction.* Westport, CT: Greenwood Press. 2000.

Macdonald, Gina, and Andrew Macdonald. *Shaman or Sherlock? The Native American Detective.* Westport, CT: Greenwood Press. 2002.

Native American Representations: First Encounters, Distorted Images, and Literary Appropriations. Edited by Gretchen M. Bataille. Lincoln: University of Nebraska Press. 2001.

Rollins, Peter C., and John E. O'Connor, editors. *Hollywood's Indian: The Portrayal of the Native American in Film*. Lexington: University Press of Kentucky. c1998.

Strickland, Rennard. *Tonto's Revenge: Reflections on American Indian Culture and Policy.* Albuquerque: University of New Mexico Press. c1997.

Weston, Mary Ann. *Native Americans in the News: Images of Indians in the Twentieth Century Press.* Westport, CT: Greenwood Press. 1996.

Annotated Bibliography

1. Alcalá, Kathleen. *The Flower in the Skull.* San Francisco: Chronicle Books. 1998. 180 p.

Time: 1890's to present
Tribe: Opata
Place: Sonoran Desert, Mexico and Arizona

In simple and charming language Alcalá has woven a tale that will stay with the reader long after this book is closed. In the 1890's Concha's father is taken away by the Mexican army and her mother flees with Concha, her twin sisters and little brother on a northern route away from the Mexicans, away from the Apaches. Her mother eventually abandons all the girls, Concha loses her twin sisters and arrives in Tucson alone and frightened. Befriended by the Morenos, a Mexican family, Concha works for them and becomes a part of their life. Concha never forgets her family and life in her Opata village. Raped by a White man, Concha bears his child, Rosa, who is raised with the Moreno girls but never accepted as one of them. Later Concha marries Dr. Martinez but the marriage fails when she is unable to produce more children. He leaves both Concha and Rosa to make their own way as best they can. Years later Rosa's great granddaughter Shelly, the victim of sexual harassment at work, comes to Arizona to do research for a book on the Opata and finds old photographs which are oddly familiar to her. Knowing nothing of her family's background, Shelly is at first confused, but then gathers the courage to report her boss's harassment. Shelly returns to Arizona and then to Mexico. The women of this family have come full circle. This novel can be read on many levels and is a delight for the reader.

Reviewed in: Multicultural Review 6/99; Library Journal 1/99; Booklist 6/1/99.

2. Alexie, Sherman. (Spokane/Coeur d'Alene). *Indian Killer*. NY: Atlantic Monthly Press. 1996. 420 p.

Time: Contemporary
Tribe: Spokane
Place: Seattle

Alexie's novels are usually full of humor which overlay a fundamental despair about the Native American condition. This novel, however, contains little humor, and a great deal of despair. John Smith was adopted into a wealthy, White Seattle family as an infant and is now suffering feelings of alienation. He fantasizes about what his real mother and family life on a reservation might have been like while he is a construction worker in Seattle. On the University of Washington campus, Marie Polatkin organizes the Native American students into protests and complains bitterly about the teaching of a course in Native American literature. A local mystery writer, Jack Wilson, tries to pretend he, too, is part Native American, but is ridiculed by them. All these disparate lives come together when someone starts killing White men and scalping them, creating local fear of an "Indian Killer." This fear, fueled by a radio talk-show host, results in attacks by Whites on Native Americans and vice versa. Prejudice is not far below the surface in our society and fear quickly brings it out. John Smith's parents search for him in vain after he disappears from work, the victim of his rapidly disintegrating mind. Is he the Indian Killer? Or is it Marie's angry cousin Reggie Polatkin, raised by an abusive White father? Or is it Jack Wilson, acting out a role as the Indian he wants to be? There are no easy answers, no clear roles. This is a deeply disturbing novel commenting with a heavy hand on the place of Native Americans in our society.

Reviewed in: Booklist 9/1/96; Library Journal 8/96; New York Times 11/24/96; Publishers Weekly 7/29/96.

3. Alexie, Sherman. (Spokane/Coeur d'Alene). *Reservation Blues.* NY: Atlantic Monthly Press. 1995. 306 p.

Time: Contemporary
Tribe: Spokane and Flathead
Place: Washington State

Thomas Builds-the-Fire meets an old Black man with a guitar at a crossroads on the reservation. Robert Johnson is looking for Big Mom, who lives up on the mountain. Thomas ends up with the magic guitar, gives it to Victor Joseph, and together with Junior Polatkin, they form the Coyote Springs rock band. Performing their own original songs, adding Chess and Checkers Warm Springs, two Flathead sisters, as singers, the band gets better and better. They get invited to audition for the Cavalry label by Phil Sheridan and George Wright, two record agents; or are they? Maybe not. The past intertwines with the present, old atrocities are remembered, history repeats itself. Big Mom has helped a lot of musicians in the past and tries to help this band too. Members of the band get sidetracked, fall in love with the wrong people, end their lives and the life of the band. Success is not something easily obtained by Native Americans. Alexie uses humor to convey impatience with New Age followers, distress at the effects of Christianity on native beliefs, and the disastrous effects of alcohol on reservations.

Reviewed in: Publishers Weekly 5/1/95; Booklist 6/1/95; Library Journal 6/1/95; New York Times 7/16/95.

4. Ammerman, Mark. *The Cross and the Tomahawk, Book 1. The Rain from God.* Camp Hill, PA: Horizon Books. 1997. 320 p.

Time: 1600–1675
Tribe: Narragansett, Pequot, Wampanoag, Mohegan
Place: Connecticut, Rhode Island

Few novels have dealt with the Eastern tribes during the time of the first English settlements in New England. While the conversion of the Native Americans to Christianity may be the ultimate outcome of the story, most of the action concerns the inter-tribal warfare between these peoples. The culture and practices are well portrayed and the history is accurately followed. Katanaquat is Rain from God and his best friends are Assoko the Fool, a simple but loyal and steadfast warrior, and Miantonomi, a leader of the Narragansett. His principle enemy is Uncas the Mohegan, a cousin but also an evil traitor who slays

Miantonomi. The historical events and characters include the deceptive Squanto, playing the English off against the Indians and finally abandoned by both; Massasoit, the leader of the Wampanoag; Canonicus, the principal sachem of the Narragansett; Roger Williams; King Philip's War; the Pequot War; and Miles Standish. One can learn a great deal about this historical time period, and the conflicts between the warring tribes and the Dutch and English settlers. The characters are well developed, although lack a certain depth. The conversion of Katanaquat to Christianity and his finally giving up his hatred for Uncas seem the actions of an aging man rather than a true believer. Overall the series is an approachable introduction to the seventeenth century in New England written by a descendent of Roger Williams.

Reviewed in: Library Journal 9/1/97.

5. Ammerman, Mark. *The Cross and the Tomahawk, Book 2. The Ransom.* Camp Hill, PA: Horizon Books. 1997. 392 p.

Time: 1600–1676
Tribe: Narragansett, Pequot, Wampanoag, Mohegan
Place: Connecticut, Rhode Island, Massachutsetts

The time period covered is the same as in Book 1, *Rain from God*, but here the protagonist is Job Kattenanit, Night Wind, the Narragansett son of Katanaquat, the Rain from God. Job is an early convert to Christianity and it weakens his resolve for battle. He prefers the quiet life of marriage and family, working with John Eliot to translate the Bible into Narragansett, which is accomplished by 1663. All the characters from Book 1 are here as well, including Assoko the Fool, Roger Williams, Uncas, Canonicus, and Miantonomi. The many historical events described are all factual as are the characters. This volume is the most religious of the three, with extensive coverage of the Praying Indians of New England. Unfortunately, King Philip's War, the chance for the New England tribes to join forces and fight back the English, is undermined by these very same Praying Indians. Job Kattenanit acts as a spy for the English against his own Narragansett people. It is hard to find honor in his actions, even if they were supported by his Christian beliefs. When King Philip is finally killed by a Christianized Indian, the last hope of freedom and independence for the Mohegan, Pequot, Narragansett and Wampanog is gone. It is hard to justify this loss with the introduction of Christianity to their lives. The book is extremely useful as an introduction to the tribes and historical events of the seventeenth century in New England, including King Philip's War. Little has been written in historical fiction about these tribes and their losses to the English.

6. Ammerman, Mark. *The Cross and the Tomahawk, Book 3. Longshot.* Camp Hill, PA: Horizon Books. 2000. 301 p.

Time: 1750–1751
Tribe: Narragansett, Susquehannock, Twigtwee (Miami)
Place: Rhode Island, Ohio Valley

In the third volume in the trilogy, Caleb Hobomucko is the great great grandson of Katanaquat, the Rain from God. Caleb is a follower of the old god, Cautantowwit, the Creator. His is angry at the loss of his Narragansett tribes' homelands and culture, overrun by the White men. Many of his people have turned to the Christian god, but Caleb hates the religion and the White men who brought it. However, he is Christopher Long's friend, and accompanies Long on a survey of the Ohio Valley for the Ohio Company. Long's journals are really a fictionalized account of the historical Christopher Gist, who was a surveyor in the mid-eighteenth century. Joining them on their travels is Connie Joe, a Susquehannock (Contestoga) Indian, now ancient, but once a fierce warrior. Connie Joe becomes Caleb's surrogate father, preaching the gospel of Christianity over the campfire every night. Their discourses take up much of the text, with perhaps many readers siding with Caleb in his anger at the encroachment of the whites on all Indian lands, destroying their native cultures and replacing them with European religions. The novels are extremely well researched, cover a time period not often encountered, and truly add to our knowledge of the displacement of the eastern seaboard tribes. In this third novel, it is the Miamis and the Wyandots (the tobacco Indians) and the Susquehannocks who are about to suffer as their rich Ohio lands are settled and they are pushed further west.

7. Armstrong, O. K., and Marjorie Moore Armstrong. *The Cherokee Trail 1838–1839.* Muskogee, OK: Indian University Press. Bacone College. 1994. 259 p.

Time: 1829–1839
Tribe: Cherokee
Place: Southeastern United States

A stilted and awkwardly written historical account of the events leading up to and through the Cherokee Trail of Tears, the novel is, however, based on solid research. Events are carefully reconstructed by the authors, but the narrative style is poor and difficult to read. As a source for the historical events, written in something of a fictional style, this book is excellent. As a form of entertainment, which fictional reading should be, it is not nearly so successful. Character development is lacking, but still one feels the pain and injustices suffered by the Cherokee as their battles are won in the legal system but lost in the real world. Better novels dealing with this theme are Stewart's *River Rising,* Wilkinson's *Oblivion's Altar* and the excellent book by Glancy, *Pushing the Bear.*

8. Assiniwi, Bernard. (Cree). *The Beothuk Saga.* Translated by Wayne Grady. NY: Thomas Dunne Books/St. Martin's Press. 1996/2000. 341 p.

Time: 1000 A.D. to early 1800's
Tribe: Beothuk and Micmac
Place: Newfoundland

In 1000 A.D. the young Beothuk, Anin, sails around his home island, encountering many adventures. He rescues a young Beothuk woman from attacking Ashwans of the northern cold country. He encounters *Bouguishamesh*, the Vikings who have recently landed. He rescues one of their women, Gudruide, and two Scottish slaves, and adds them all to his family. When he returns to his village, he is proclaimed a chief of all the clans. In 1500 John Cabot lands and meets the Beothuk, kidnapping some of them to take back to England. Since the Beothuks are covered in a paste of red ochre to fend off mosquitos, the English call them "Redskins," thought to be the origin of this designation for the New World's peoples. Jacques Cartier from France arrives and leaves behind a sailor, Jean Le Guellec, called *Wobee*, or White. He marries Ooish of the Seal Clan and becomes a valuable member of the tribe. Many years of encounters with Portuguese, French, and English decimate the Beothuk by the diseases and the muskets of the Europeans. The Beothuk are pushed inland, away from their homelands along the shores. The Beothuk hide in the forests, venturing out to harvest seafood, frequently being murdered or captured by the English. In 1758 a young woman is captured and sent to England. Her lexicon of the Beothuk language is included in an appendix of the novel. Finally in the late 1700's the Beothuk are reduced to only about five hundred desperate people. In 1790 a large group of unarmed Beothuk decide to approach the White men bravely and in peace. Four hundred of them are massacred on Hant's Harbour by fur trappers. The English King George III declares that the Beothuk should be treated kindly, but leaves a 100-pound bounty for their capture. The Beothuk always designate one of their elders as the Living Memory, entrusted with carrying on the traditions of their tribe. In the early 1800's the only Beothuk alive is

Shanawdithit, a young woman who becomes the last Living Memory and tells her tribe's story to her English master. Renamed Nancy April, she is a maid in an En-glish household until she dies of tuberculosis. The Beothuk are completely gone. The Mi'kmaq, or Micmac, survive on Newfoundland because they were willing to convert to Christianity and to work with the English in trapping the furs the Europeans desired. The Beothuk tried to stay separate and were exterminated. Based upon historical facts and characters, the novel is a sad rendition of the demise of a Newfoundland tribe at the hands of the same Europeans that negatively impacted the tribes of the United States.

Reviewed in: Booklist 1/1/02; Kirkus Reviews 11/15/01; Library Journal 11/15/01; Publishers Weekly 10/29/01; Quill & Quire 9/1/00.

9. Baker, Laura. *Broken in Two.* NY: St. Martin's Press. 1999. 308 p.

Time: Contemporary
Tribe: Hopi and Navajo
Place: Arizona

Ella Honanie has spent her life trying to control the people and world around her. Daughter of a Navajo mother and a Hopi father, Ella and her family were labeled "outcasts," belonging to neither culture. With her parents dead, Ella continues to operate their trading post and care for her niece Jenny. Jenny resists Ella's efforts and idealizes her father Eddie. When Eddie is murdered, FBI agent Frank Reardon arrives to investigate Eddie's connection with the flourishing trade in stolen Indian artifacts. Did Eddie really know where the two pieces of the Hopi tablet were, the sacred tablet that promised the reunification of its pieces would bring peace to the warring tribes? Frank had been at Red Earth where his wife was killed in a shootout between the FBI and AIRO, the militant Indian rights organization. Was Eddie also involved in this group? Although neither Frank nor Ella is looking for a new relationship, they are drawn to each other as they try and sort out the good guys from the bad in this better-than-average romance.

Reviewed in: Publishers Weekly 9/27/99.

10. Baker, Laura. *Legend.* NY: St. Martin's Press. 1998. 280 p.

Time: Contemporary
Tribe: Navajo
Place: Arizona

FBI profiler Jackson Walker has been called in to work on several brutal murders on the Navajo Reservation. A trader, a young girl, and a pseudo-medicine man have all been found severely slashed, almost as though an animal had done it. Walker usually works by feeling the last moments of the victim, but in these cases he is overwhelmed by the thoughts of the killer. Ainii Henio is the daughter of the last medicine man; she watched her father die as he tried to confront the *yenaldlooshi*, the shape-shifter in the form of a wolf. Ainii was not taught her father's secrets, those he imparted to her brother Arland, but Arland left the reservation to become a detective in Albuquerque. Now Ainii has no one to help her solve these murders except Walker and he, although born Navajo, refuses to believe any of the legends of the culture. While there are the obligatory love scenes, most of this novel deals with the legend of the shape shifters, the power they hold, and what can be done to defeat them. An ordinary reader may find the frequent use of the Navajo language distracting, but the story is definitely above the typical romance novel.

11. Baker, Laura. *Stargazer.* NY: St. Martin's Press. 1998. 310 p.

Time: Contemporary
Tribe: Navajo
Place: New Mexico

In 1863 Jacob Lonewolf sees the future of his Navajo people and tries to encourage them to make peace with the Whites before they are destroyed. The other leaders prefer to fight and exile him from the tribe; his grandfather tells him "Your future is not here." Indeed not, for Lonewolf is transported to contemporary New Mexico where Officer Willow Becenti is holding a gun on him. Has Lonewolf been brought forward in time to train the boy Manuelito, who lies unconscious in a hospital bed, as the next Starway Shaman? Or was he brought through time to teach Willow the ways of love and the ways of the Navajo? Willow has always rejected the spiritual, mystical side of her culture, believing only in logic and what she can see and hear. Does any of this relate to the theft of Navajo treasures from the caves where they have long been buried? There is not much made of the time-travel theme. Lonewolf doesn't seem terribly surprised by the twentieth century and logical Willow readily accepts that he has come across time to her. When Manuelito has been rescued from the hospital and the sacred ceremonies performed, Lonewolf tries to return to his own time. He is still hoping to save the Navajo people from their fate. Willow's grandfather convinces Jacob that the past cannot be changed and that the people, and Willow, need him more in this century. Baker writes well and gives the reader an intriguing look into another culture.

12. Bell, Betty Louise. (Cherokee). *Faces in the Moon.* Norman: University of Oklahoma Press. 1994. 193 p.

Time: Contemporary
Tribe: Cherokee
Place: Oklahoma

This deceptively simple novel tells the story of Lucie Evers, a contemporary Cherokee woman of the generation which "had a choice." It is also the story of her mother Gracie, her grandmother Helen, her great-aunt Lizzie, and all the other women whose stories are woven into Lucie's memories. There is little action, as a small child Lucie is sent to live with her great-aunt Lizzie and learns a little of her heritage. Only after her mother's death does Lucie start reconstructing that heritage, acknowledging that the stories have helped shaped who she is. "I am a follower of stories, a negotiator of histories, a wild dog of many lives. I am Quanah Parker swooping down from the hills into your bedroom in the middle of the night. And I am centuries of Indian women who lost their husbands, their children, their minds . . . I am your worst nightmare. I am an Indian with a pen." Bell writes simply and clearly, evoking a sense of character, of time and place, that stay with the reader.

Reviewed in: Booklist 3/1/94; Library Journal 3/1/94; NYTBR 5/29/94; Publishers Weekly 2/7/94.

13. Bird, Beverly. *Comes the Rain.* NY: Avon. 1990. 504 p.

Time: 1857–1868
Tribe: Navajo
Place: New Mexico

Gray Eyes is a young Navajo girl taught by Long Earrings to be a medicine woman during the time of warfare between General Carleton and the Navajo chiefs Manuelito, Barboncito, and Delgondito. Hawk is a young warrior in love with Gray Eyes who fights under these chiefs. This long novel covers the historical events of the time period; the misunderstandings and killings, the concerted effort by Kit Carson to burn and starve out the Navajo and their resistance. The events are wrapped around the love affair and marriage of Gray Eyes and Hawk. Gray Eyes leads the women and children to presumed safety at Canyon de Chelly, where the soldiers invade and shoot Hawk. The rest are led away to years of starvation at Bosque Redondo, Fort Sumner. At Fort Sumner Gray Eyes is protected by a soldier, Michaels, until he is killed when she tries to escape. General Carleton is in charge of the Navajo and Apache placed on that reservation and does such a poor job that the U.S. government finally intervenes. Fort Sumner is shut down and the Navajo are allowed to start the Long Walk back to their homelands in the north. On her way home again, Gray Eyes and her four-year-old son discover evidence that Hawk still lives and she vows to find him. Good coverage of the Navajo history and culture is sometimes overwhelmed by the love story, but overall this is a fine novel.

Reviewed in: Publishers Weekly 8/24/90.

14. Bird, Beverly. *The Pony Wife.* NY: Jove Books. 1995. 456 p.

Time: 1855–1877
Tribe: Nez Perce
Place: Idaho

A novel of Chief Joseph and the Nez Perce battle to evade the U.S. Army's attempts to send them to reservations, the tale uses the personal life of an orphan girl, Dark Moon, to tell the story. When Dark Moon achieves her vision, she becomes Kiye Kipi, the woman who can work with animals, specifically with the tribe's horse herds. Kiye Kipi is in love with Twelic, a warrior who believes he is impervious to any one woman's charms. He leads a life of freedom and hunting until Lawyer signs away the Nez Perce rights to their tribal hunting grounds in the name of all the chiefs. The historical personages are all included here: Joseph, Looking Glass, White Bird, Alokot, and Toolhoolhoolzote. They are well-rounded characters with strengths and weaknesses, but all are devoted to saving their lands and freedom. Kiye Kipi is instrumental in the success of the Nez Perce in their flight from General Howard through her years of breeding strong and hardy horses for warfare. During the battles with the Army, Kiye Kipi and Twelic recognize their mutual love and the strength of being united with each other. Basically a romance that could have used some editing in the romantic conflict, the novel is well written and full of accurate historical detail about the Nez Perce.

Reviewed in: Kliatt 9/95.

15. Bird, Beverly. *Touch the Sun.* NY: Berkley. 1994. 344 p.

Time: 1800's
Tribe: Cheyenne
Place: Western United States

Eagle Voice is a young Cheyenne woman growing up in Colorado in the 1800's. She lives through the Sand Creek massacre, the removal to the Indian Territory, the battles against the white settlers, and finally another attempt to return north with Dull Knife. Her first husband, Walks Far, is a Cheyenne Dog soldier and she lives with his band of warriors. Her true love is another Dog soldier, Fire Wolf, to whom she promises herself in a fertility ritual as part of a Sun Dance. The accuracy of this fertility ritual is questionable. Walks Far is killed in battle, but Eagle is so fixated on saving the life of her injured son, Broken Stick, that she cannot bring herself to marry Fire Wolf. Eventually after Stick gets better, Eagle allows herself to love Fire Wolf. More interesting for the historical details of Sioux alliances, battles with the U.S. Army, and the progress in the settling of the West than Eagle's agonizing personal life, the novel presents the Native American viewpoint in a sympathetic light.

16. Bissell, Sallie. *A Darker Justice.* NY: Bantam. 2002. 319 p.

Time: Contemporary
Tribe: Cherokee
Place: Georgia, North Carolina

In this sequel to *In the Forest of Harm*, Mary Crow is asked by the FBI to persuade her friend and mentor Judge Irene Hannah to accept federal protection. For the past year one judge in each of the federal judicial districts has died and it appears Judge Hannah may be next. When she adamantly refuses, Mary tries to protect her, but Irene is kidnapped almost before her very eyes. In trying to find out who kidnapped Irene and where she is being held, Mary encounters former military man Robert Wurth who runs a strange "camp" for wayward boys. She also finds papers of her mother's which seem to indicate that her father's death in Vietnam may not have been an accident after all. After being kidnapped herself, escaping the camp "castle" with Irene and one of the boys, Mary manages to blow up Russell Cave, their hiding place, killing almost all of the bad men, except Sheriff Logan. She learns he is her mother's murderer. Martha Crow was apparently getting too close to the truth of her husband's death. Mary also tries to renew her relationship with Jonathan Walkingstick, but Jonathan has become involved with a full-blooded Cherokee from Oklahoma. As that relationship ends, Mary finds herself attracted to FBI agent Daniel Safer. There is little of Cherokee lore or themes in this book, but the suspense keeps the pages turning.

Reviewed in: Publishers Weekly 11/19/01; Kirkus Reviews 11/15/01; Booklist 11/1/01.

17. Bissell, Sallie. *In the Forest of Harm.* NY: Bantam. 2001. 304 p.

Time: Contemporary
Tribe: Cherokee
Place: Tennessee, North Carolina

Prosecutor Mary Crow has just convicted Cal Whitman for a brutal murder and decides to go on a small camping trip with two girlfriends. She wants to show them some of the old Cherokee places and maybe exorcise some ghosts of her own. Mary has not been back to the place she grew up since her mother was murdered when Mary was eighteen. Martha Crow's murderer was never caught and Mary still feels guilty for making love to Jonathan Walkingstick instead of coming straight home from school that afternoon. Although neither Joan nor Alex are experienced campers, they manage fine until the madman Henry Brank rapes Joan and kidnaps Alex while Mary is absent from camp. Joan is badly hurt but Mary knows if she takes Joan back to the trailhead, she will lose all chance of rescuing Alex. So with only two sweatshirts, one pair of jeans and one pair of boots between them, Mary and Joan pursue Alex's trail through the Appalachian wilderness. Mary knows some Cherokee lore, but not enough to save them both. Alex manages to leave a trail as Brank takes her to his cabin where he has taken other victims before he tortures and kills them. While Mary and Joan are trailing Alex, Mitchell Whitman is trailing Mary for the conviction of his brother, and Jonathan Walkingstick is trailing him in hopes of saving Mary. Mary Crow is a contemporary Cherokee living easily in the white man's world, but her heritage is strong and the conclusion of the novel is brutal with bodies everywhere. The murderer of Mary's mother is still at large and the relationship between Jonathan and Mary is unsettled.

Reviewed in: Library Journal 1/1/01; Kirkus Reviews 11/15/00; Publishers Weekly 11/6/00.

18. Bittner, Rosanne. *Mystic Dreamers.* NY: Forge. 1999. 347 p.
Mystic Visions. NY: Forge. 2000. 316 p.
Mystic Warriors. NY: Forge. 2001. 366 p.

Reviewed in: Publishers Weekly 4/3/00.

Time: 1830's–1870's
Tribe: Sioux
Place: Western United States

In these three volumes Bittner has told the late 1800's history of the Sioux through the lives of Rising Eagle and Buffalo Dreamer. Rising Eagle had a vision which told him to seek Buffalo Dreamer as his wife. Although Rising Eagle wins Buffalo Dreamer with her father's approval, she did not love him at first and refused to be Rising Eagle's wife in all ways. Not until Buffalo Dreamer is taken prisoner by the Crow and then found by Rising Eagle riding on the back of a white buffalo, does she realize she has come to love him. The couple has children of their own and adopts children, both Sioux and White. They are happy raising their family, but the White tide cannot be stemmed. Smallpox decimates their band, kills two of their children and leaves Rising Eagle horribly scarred. After the Battle of the Little Bighorn, Rising Eagle and Buffalo Dreamer return to Medicine Mountain to die. While this series does contain a great deal of Sioux culture and legends, the novels are highly romanticized, are filled with implausible occurrences and the characters are flat and stilted.

19. Bittner, Rosanne. *Savage Destiny Series.*
Sweet Prairie Passion. NY: Zebra. 1983. 463 p.
Ride the Free Wind. NY: Zebra. 1984. 444 p.
River of Love. NY: Kensington. 1984. 413 p.
Embrace the Wide Land. NY: Kensington. 1984. 446 p.
Climb the Highest Mountain. NY: Kensington. 1985. 441 p.
Meet the New Dawn. NY: Kensington. 1986. 477 p.
Eagle's Song. NY: Zebra. 1996. 445 p.

Reviewed in: Booklist 9/15/98.

Time: 1846–1901
Tribe: Cheyenne
Place: Colorado and the West

This extensive series features Zeke Monroe, a Cheyenne half-breed who marries Abigail after her family dies on their way west. Together Abby and Zeke face numerous hardships and are involved in many historical events in Colorado and the west in the years between 1846 and 1900. They raise horses on their southern Colorado ranch in the Arkansas Valley. They have several children who must each face his or her own trials, although Zeke often is there to rescue them. Abby is a strong woman and lives through hardships of her own, but the love between herself and Zeke remains strong. The oldest son, Wolf's Blood, is a prominent character in the series, eventually dying at Wounded Knee. The series finally ends in 1901 with the death of Abby. Her grandchildren are thriving, wealthy and successful in the new Colorado that has grown up along with Abby's children. Bittner includes historically accurate characters and events such as William Bent, the Fort Laramie treaty, the Sand Creek Massacre, and Wounded Knee. The portrayal of the customs and decency of the Cheyenne people is accurate. All in all, this is a pleasant romance series with much information about the Cheyenne and historical times in Colorado.

20. Bittner, Rosanne. *Song of the Wolf.* NY: Bantam. 1992. 480 p.

Time: 1840's–1870's
Tribe: Northern Cheyenne
Place: Western U.S.

As a small girl, Medicine Wolf sees a vision of the future and is protected by wolves when she and her mother are captured by a Crow war party. She is to become a holy woman, protector of her tribe and can only marry Bear Paw. First she must spend two years with the Whites at Fort Laramie while they try to indoctrinate her in the ways of civilization. She learns English and many things about the Whites, but her heart remains Cheyenne. Only Tom Prescott, son of the missionaries who try to convert her, becomes her friend and wants to learn about the Cheyenne. Medicine Wolf and Tom become blood brothers before she returns to her people, who still believe that they can live free in the old ways. The novel then recounts all the terrible things that happened to the Cheyenne, from Sand Creek to Washita to Little Big Horn. The Whites continually break the treaties they make, the Cheyenne are continually hunted, the game is slaughtered, their way of life destroyed. The love Bear Paw and Medicine Wolf have for each other survives battles, alcoholism, and infertility, but they cannot survive against the onslaught of the Whites and after encouraging their people and the children to go to the reservation, they die, protected and surrounded by the sacred wolves. While the romance aspect of this novel gets rather tedious, Bittner does provide a clear history of the Cheyenne.

Reviewed in: Publishers Weekly 2/3/92.

21. Black, Michelle. *An Uncommon Enemy.* NY: Tom Doherty. 2001. 398 p.

Time: 1868
Tribe: Cheyenne
Place: Kansas

When Custer attacks the peaceful Black Kettle camp on the Washita, murdering more women and children than warriors, a white woman is found among the Cheyenne. Rescued against her will, Eden Murdoch is taken back to a small town in Kansas to await her father's arrival. Captain Brad Randall becomes her protector and listens to her tale of four years with the Cheyenne, whom she loved. Married to Hanging Road, with sister wives Red Feather Woman and Nightwalking, Eden is known as Ghost Woman, *Seota*. A nurse during the Civil War, Eden becomes a healer among the Cheyenne. She tells of her husband's peacefulness and his spirituality, a contrast to the vicious wife-beater, Lawrence Murdoch, she had been married to before her capture. Custer meanwhile is using Eden as the rationale for having attacked a peaceful camp, although there was no knowledge of her presence there before his attack. General Sheridan also uses her to justify Custer's actions since Washita is being compared in the press and in Washington D.C. to the massacre at Sand Creek four years before. Randall discovers that Hanging Road is still alive and Eden abandons white civilization to return to the Cheyenne with her husband. This is an excellent account of a white captive who prefers the life among the Cheyenne to any more years in white society. Custer did in fact find a White woman among the Cheyenne at Washita and Sheridan did try to use her "rescue" to excuse the massacre. A sequel to this novel, *Solomon Spring,* published by Forge in 2002 follows Eden as she returns to white society after Hanging Road dies. Brad Randall and Lawrence Murdoch vie for Eden's love and her children while the Cheyenne are mostly ignored in the story.

Reviewed in: Publishers Weekly 9/3/01.

22. Blake, Michael. *The Holy Road.* NY: Villard. 2001. 339 p.

Time: 1870–1880
Tribe: Comanche
Place: Texas

The characters from *Dances with Wolves* are all back in this sequel, set a decade later in Texas. The Comanche people are divided between Wind in his Hair's warrior philosophy and Kicking Bird's wish to make peace with the White men, following their "holy road" which is a combination of religion and progress. Smiles a Lot becomes a warrior and a member of the Hard Shields, the warrior society. Stands with a Fist is recaptured by Whites who return her to her White family, the Gunthers, where she is miserable until Dances with Wolves rescues her. Agent Lawrie Tatum bravely approaches the Comanche, attempting to bring them onto the reservation. Tatum and the U.S. Army prevail upon the important chiefs to visit Washington D.C. where Ten Bears dies. When Wind in his Hair and then Dances with Wolves are killed fighting the Army and the Comanche pony herds are destroyed, the renegades are forced to come into the reservation. Kicking Bird is headman there and is told to send twenty-five warriors and their families to prison in Florida, sending off Smiles a Lot and his family with the others. The slow, sad, decline of the free tribes in Texas—the Comanche, Kiowa and Southern Cheyenne—is portrayed in this novel with characters many are already familiar with, giving the facts added emotional impact. Kicking Bird is the wisest Chief, realizing that the coming of the white men has changed their traditional lives forever, and that the Comanche and Kiowa need to adapt to those changes rather than resist them. The trip of the principal chiefs to the east coast, where they see the polluted Potomac River and are given a tour of a slaughter house, is heavy handed, but otherwise the novel is very well written and sympathetic to the inevitable defeat of the southern plains tribes. Many of the historical events, such as the trip to Washington, and the selection by Kicking Bird of the men to send to prison, are true. Immediately after this, Kicking Bird, now considered a traitor, was poisoned by a tribal medicine man.

Reviewed in: Publishers Weekly 7/16/01; Booklist 7/1/01; Kirkus Reviews 6/15/01.

23. Blakely, Mike. *Comanche Dawn.* NY: Tom Doherty. 1998. 413 p.

Time: 1687–1720
Tribe: Shoshone, Comanche
Place: Plains

On the day of Horseback's birth his Shoshone father saw a horse for the first time as the frightened animal raced through their camp. Born-on-the-Day-of-the-Shadow-Dog became his first name and he would become a great warrior and horseman, leading his people, a branch of the Shoshones, from their poor hunting grounds in the north to rich land in the south in the early 1700's. There the Ute name of Comanche, meaning "our enemies," became the new name of this branch of Shoshone. Their oneness with the horse made them fierce fighters for they did not dismount in battle as did other tribes. It also enabled them to wage war on their traditional enemies, the Apache. The Comanche could cover long distances and kill many buffalo to feed their people and changed the traditions of the tribe. In his journeys Horseback encountered the Metal Men in Santa Fe, particularly Jean L'Archeveque who had been a boy on LaSalle's disastrous expedition up the Mississippi, had lived with the Raccoon-Eyed People, the Jumanos, and was now a trader with the Spanish. Jean and Horseback become friends, teaching each other their ways and languages, but Jean warns Horseback to be wary of the Black Robes who will try to enslave and convert him. Although he is caught, Horseback is quickly rescued and resumes his role as leader of his people. Blakely has presented a very interesting story of how the Shoshone became the Comanche, the encounters between the Metal Men and the Comanches and has done his historical research well. The story tends to become overly detailed in places but maintains its fascination for the reader.

Reviewed in: Publishers Weekly 9/14/98.

24. Blevins, Win. (Cherokee). *RavenShadow.* NY: Tom Doherty. 1999. 448 p.

Time: 1990 and 1890
Tribe: Sioux
Place: South Dakota

Essentially a novel of the 1890 massacre at Wounded Knee, Blevins tells the story from contemporary times. Joseph Blue Crow has gone through many hard stages in his life and is now looking for some real meaning to it. He is haunted by the dark spirit of RavenShadow which fills his life with pessimism and darkness. Blue's grandmother Unchee was a silent, hate-filled, difficult woman, born the day after Wounded Knee to her severely injured mother. Unchee picked Joseph to be the bearer of the family sacred pipe and gave him her father's name. Blue is approaching middle age and returns to the Pine Ridge reservation to join a commemorative winter ride to celebrate the memory of Wounded Knee. He meets a shaman who teaches Blue how to travel between this time and the past. Blue experiences the days up to and during the massacre again, seeing his relatives and the relatives of his contemporaries. Although Blue is powerless to change history, it changes him, and he assumes his role as one of the strong members of his family and of the tribe.

Reviewed in: Booklist 11/1/99; Kirkus Reviews 10/15/99; Publishers Weekly 9/27/99.

25. Blevins, Win. (Cherokee). *Stone Song: A Novel of the Life of Crazy Horse.* NY: Tom Doherty. 1995. 400 p.

Time: mid-1800's
Tribe: Sioux
Place: Great Plains

This nearly mystical novel reminds one of both Mari Sandoz's *Crazy Horse* and James Welch's *Fool's Crow.* The writing is sympathetic but factual. Blevins incorporates the warmth and humor of tribal life with the religious experiences all young men feel they must go through in order to grow. He emphasizes how different His Crazy Horse was from the other young men, distaining the wearing of honors, the taking of scalps, and the self-praise expected of all warriors. Blevins also stresses the deeply political nature of the disputes between His Crazy Horse and the Red Cloud band, vying for power among the Sioux. Blevins has used historical sources in writing his novel so the portrayals of the U.S. Army leaders and the Native American leaders ring very true. Throughout the novel he speaks from within His Crazy Horse and stresses the spiritual conflict this young leader felt. An excellent portrayal of one of the most important figures in Native American history, this could be considered the definitive biographical novel of the young man known to us as Crazy Horse.

Reviewed in: Booklist 7/95; Publishers Weekly 5/8/95; Library Journal 6/1/95.

26. Bogue, Lucile. *Blood on the Wind: The Memoirs of Flying Horse Mollie, A Yampa Ute.* Montrose, CO: Western Reflections. 2001. 142 p.

Time: 1878–1879
Tribe: Ute
Place: Colorado

The Yampa and White River Utes live on the White River Agency in Colorado, run by Nathan Meeker, his family and his assistants. Meeker is a harsh man, with no love for the Ute ways. He renames all the men with whom he must interact, calling the chiefs Quinket "Douglas," and Nicaagat "Jack" and the tribe medicine man Canalla, "Johnson." Flying Horse is a young girl who learns to speak and read English from Nathan's sweet daughter, Josie, and Meeker calls the Ute girl Mollie. Mollie is the narrator of this short novel, describing the events of 1878 which led up to the Meeker Massacre on September 29th. Utes love their ponies and love to race them, so when Meeker orders their pony race track put to the plow, they erupt and kill the men, kidnap the women, and flee south to Chief Ouray. Chased by the Army, finally a peace is negotiated by General Adams and Ouray. However the Utes suffer banishment from the state of Colorado and are sent off to the Uintah Reservation in Utah. All the principal characters are well depicted and sympathy clearly lies with the Utes. Colorado's Governor Pitkin had been declaring for years "the Utes must go" so the massacre played into his hands beautifully. Chief Ouray was truly a hero of his people, settling the problems and negotiating treaties all the while dying of kidney failure in his mid forties. One of the best novels on the Meeker Massacre, the novel is very suitable for Young Adult readers.

27. Bolton, Clyde. *Nancy Swimmer: A Story of the Cherokee Nation*. n.p.: Highland Press. 1999. 272 p.

Time: 1813–1838
Tribe: Cherokee
Place: Georgia

This is a thorough and accurate historical account of the legal battles the Cherokee faced to try and stay in their Georgia homelands. It is also extremely well written with well developed and sympathetic characters. Nancy Swimmer is a young girl when she marries Charley Marley, a part-Cherokee preacher who teaches her to read and write. Becoming close friends with Elias and Harriet Boudinet, publishers of the *Cherokee Phoenix* newspaper, exposes Nancy to such historical figures as Major and John Ridge, Stand Watie, John Ross, and others involved in the removal versus anti-removal factions. President "Chicken Snake" Jackson backs the Georgia government and its militia as they pass laws forbidding Cherokees to testify against Whites, allowing Cherokee lands to be sold off in lotteries to Whites, forbidding Cherokee from digging for gold on their own lands, and other legal efforts to disenfranchise the tribal people. Members of the ragtag Georgia militia attack a pregnant Nancy, causing her to lose her baby, and then kill Charley. They are never charged. Nancy agrees to marry a rich Cherokee plantation owner, Bartholomew Bramlett, if he will kill Charley's murderers, which his foreman, Pepper Rodman, does. Trapped in a loveless marriage, Nancy begins an affair with Strong Hickory, her childhood friend who has always loved her. Nancy's personal story is really the background for a complete account of the steps the state of Georgia and the U.S. federal government deliberately took to remove the Cherokee. Every Supreme Court decision that was ignored by Jackson and the Governor of Georgia is explained. The steps the Cherokee Treaty Party took to agree to removal and how it impacted the Nation and the John Ross followers is also covered in detail. Bramlett is killed by anti-removal men, Nancy marries Strong Hickory but he dies on the Trail of Tears. Arriving in "okla-homma," the Choctaw word for red people, Nancy marries her fourth and last husband, Pepper Rodham. Major Ridge, son John and nephew Elias are murdered by Ross's men for betraying the Cherokee people. Although this novel may not have seen wide distribution, it is an excellent account of the historical and legal events leading up to the Cherokee Removal.

28. Bond, Geoffrey. *Geronimo Rides Out.* London: Arco Publications. 1962. 190 p.

Time: 1800's
Tribe: Apache
Place: Arizona

This novel chronicles Geronimo's life from the time he was a young boy called "He Who Yawns" through his warrior feats against both the Mexicans and the Americans and culminates with his surrender. While the basic elements are true, the book is poorly written and full of clichés and stilted language. Although the definitive novel based on Geronimo is yet to be written, better books are available on the Apache wars. Two in this bibliography are Karl Schlesier's *Josanie's War: A Chiricahua Apache Novel* and Tim Simmons' *Brothers of the Pine.* Robert Conley's *Geronimo: An American Legend*, although something of a movie script, is also good.

29. Bowen, Peter. *Coyote Wind: A Gabriel Du Pre Mystery.* NY: St. Martin's Press. 1994. 154 p.

Reviewed in: Booklist 7/94; NYTBR 11/27/94; Publishers Weekly 6/27/94.

Specimen Song. NY: St. Martin's. 1995. 201 p.

Reviewed in: Booklist 3/15/95; Kirkus Reviews 3/15/95; Publishers Weekly 3/6/95.

Wolf, No Wolf. NY: St. Martin's. 1996. 213 p.

Reviewed in: Booklist 3/1/96; Publishers Weekly 2/5/96; Kirkus Reviews 2/1/96.

Notches. NY: St. Martin's. 1997. 196 p.

Reviewed in: Booklist 3/15/97; NYTBR 3/2/97; Publishers Weekly 12/2/96.

Thunder Horse. NY: St. Martin's. 1998. 243 p.

Reviewed in: NYTBR 4/19/98; Library Journal 3/1/98; Booklist 4/15/98; Publishers Weekly 2/2/98.

Long Son. NY: St. Martin's. 1999. 246 p.

Reviewed in: Library Journal 4/1/99; Publishers Weekly 3/29/99; Booklist 2/15/99.

The Stick Game. NY: St. Martin's. 2000. 282 p.

Reviewed in: Booklist 2/15/00; NYTBR 5/7/00; Library Journal 4/1/00; Publishers Weekly 3/6/00.

Cruzatte and Maria. NY: St. Martin's Minotaur. 2001. 264 p.

Reviewed in: Library Journal 4/1/01; Booklist 2/15/01; Publishers Weekly 2/12/01; Kirkus Reviews 1/15/01.

Ash Child. NY: St. Martin's Minotaur. 2002. 214 p.

Reviewed in: Booklist 4/1/02 and 3/1/02; Publishers Weekly 3/25/02; Kirkus Reviews 1/15/02; NYTBR 5/5/02.

Time: Contemporary
Tribe: Cree, Blackfeet, Assiniboine, Chippewa, Crow, Gros Ventre
Place: Montana

Gabriel Du Pre is a Metis, a descendent of the Cree, Chippewa and Ojibwe tribes mixed with French. His long time girlfriend is Madelaine Placquemines and his best friend is Bart Fascelli, a reformed alcoholic with lots of energy and lots of money for good causes. Du Pre is a brand inspector in Montana, living in the small town of Toussaint, playing his fiddle on the weekends in the Toussaint Bar, the local meeting place. Du Pre is a real local inhabitant, attuned to the realities of rural life in a cold and remote state, son of generations of Metis living along the U.S. and Canadian border. Du Pre also gets involved in local murders, rapes, mysterious happenings, serial killers, and other forms of crime and criminal behavior. The FBI are constantly being called in, only to find Du Pre way ahead of them, often taking justice into his own vigilante hands. Du Pre is good at solving crimes for one reason: his friend Benetsee, an ancient Cree shaman with a taste for cheap wine. Benetsee is so old he knows languages, songs and myths of peoples long gone from the area. Benetsee is not an attractive figure, being more of a smelly, alcoholic hermit with a strange sense of humor than a noble medicine man. But Benetsee can see the truth about people and he directs Gabriel Du Pre to the right places to find out the answers to horrible crimes. Benetsee is always accompanied by coyotes, "God's dogs" as he calls them, and perhaps sometimes turns into one of them. The mysteries are all fascinating. The discovery of a T. Rex vertebrae over the skeleton of an ancient Caucasian man, poisonous run-off from mines causing birth defects in animals, a serial killer moving across the state murdering young girls, the great great grandson of an abused Indian woman coming back to exact revenge upon the abuser's current family, and even city environmentalists trying to reintroduce wolves to a community that does not want them and promises to kill the animals and their human supporters. The FBI agent, Harvey Weasel Fat Wallace, is Blackfeet, which helps him be more accepted by Du Pre and the locals. Every book includes wonderful scenes of Du Pre playing his fiddle with his band, singing the old Voyager songs of the Metis. Life in Toussaint on a Saturday night at the Bar would be a great place to go and listen to Du Pre and his small band play. Toussaint is the kind of town where everyone knows everyone and cares about each other. The Metis are an important contribution to the Native American spectrum along the Canadian border and Du Pre is a perfect example of one of the Voyagers' descendents. He lives the culture and keeps the music alive.

30. Brand, Max. *The Legend of Thunder Moon.* Lincoln: University of Nebraska Press. c. 1927, 1996. 160 p.
Red Wind and Thunder Moon. Lincoln: University of Nebraska Press. c. 1927, 1996. 166 p.
Thunder Moon and the Sky People. Lincoln: University of Nebraska Press. c. 1927, 1996. 210 p.
Farewell, Thunder Moon. Lincoln: University of Nebraska Press. c. 1927, 1996. 82 p.

Time: 1830–1850
Tribe: Cheyenne
Place: Great Plains, Southern States

In 1927 Max Brand, the pseudonym for Frederick Faust, wrote the Thunder Moon stories for *Western Story Magazine*. These four compilations recently published by the University of Nebraska contain the original text, which is amazingly contemporary in its enlightened view of Cheyenne life and culture. Brand based his stories upon the anthropological books of Charles Grinnell on the Cheyenne and the portrayal of life in a Cheyenne village is quite accurate. Big Hard Face, a chief without a son, goes East to steal thoroughbred horses from a southern plantation to establish a notable herd. He also finds a White infant there and brings the child back as his son. Raised as a Cheyenne, Thunder Moon is nonetheless subtly different. He is afraid of torture and will not endure the Sun Dance ritual. He refuses to take scalps from the many Comanche and Pawnee he kills in battle. He refuses to believe in the medicine man's powers and only puts his faith in the Sky People. Showing great courage in battle, Thunder Moon is respected as a brave and intelligent leader of war parties. Another Cheyenne chief brings his beautiful half-White daughter Red Wind to Thunder Moon as a bride. Thunder Moon is completely blind to her love for him and refuses her which turns her angry and manipulative. Thunder Moon's best friend is Standing Antelope and together they share many adventures, until Red Wind reveals to Thunder Moon that he is a White man. Shocked and upset, Thunder Moon is determined to find his true parents and returns to the southern plantation from which he was stolen twenty years before. There he is welcomed as the long lost son, but resented by his younger brother, Jack, who thought to inherit it all. Thunder Moon, now William Sutton, falls in love with Charlotte Keene, until a rival for her affections turns the town against him. When Big Hard Face, Red Wind, and Standing Antelope come to bring him back to his tribe, Thunder Moon returns with them. Big Hard

Face is killed in the battle with the pursuing White men, but the other three escape. In the final volume Jack Sutton and Charlotte Keene come west with a wagon train to find William and convince him to return to his rightful place as the owner of a southern plantation raising chestnut thoroughbreds. Consumed with jealousy, Red Wind conspires against Thunder Moon, turning his best friends against him and causing them to attack Thunder Moon. The White men repel the attack, but this convinces Thunder Moon to leave the Cheyenne and return to being William Sutton. These stories flow easily from one to another, with fully developed and sympathetic characters. The complexities of social organization and warfare among the Cheyenne are very well portrayed as are the motivations for the characters' actions. As evil and manipulative as Red Wind is, one understands she has been driven to it by Thunder Moon's complete ignorance of her feelings. Charlotte Keene is a pretty flower, but nothing compared to Red Wind. Perhaps, however, she is who the insensitive Thunder Moon deserves. He turns his back on his Cheyenne village and joins the White world. Red Wind disappears and Standing Antelope is bereft. Brand is far more sympathetic to his Cheyenne characters, all of whom are far more fully developed with much more complex personalities, than he is to the shallow, ego-driven whites.

Reviewed in: Publishers Weekly 7/1/96.

31. Brashear, Charles. (Cherokee). *Killing Cynthia Ann.* Fort Worth: Texas Christian University Press. 1999. 209 p.

> **Time**: 1860–1870
> **Tribe**: Comanche
> **Place**: Texas

In 1836 nine-year old Cynthia Ann Parker was captured by the Comanche and was totally assimilated into the tribe. She married and bore three children and neither remembered nor wanted to remember any of her early White years. In 1860 she and her small daughter were recaptured by a party of Texas Rangers and she was returned against her will to her White relatives. This slim novel is the story of her last ten years as both she and her relatives struggled, and failed, to come to terms with her reintroduction to White society. When her daughter died in 1863, Cynthia Ann had nothing left to live for. She was prevented from trying to find her husband and sons and they, still at war with the Whites, could not come for her. After another seven years of despair, Cynthia Ann finally died. The jacket cover is a haunting picture of Cynthia

Ann and while the novel is full of footnotes and historical references, it still gives the reader a disturbing image of this tragic figure.

Reviewed in: Library Journal 9/1/99; Publishers Weekly 8/30/99.

32. Braun, Matt. *Bloody Hand.* NY: St. Martin's. 1975. 378 p.

Time: 1840's
Tribe: Crow
Place: Wyoming, Montana

Colonel Ashley of the Rocky Mountain Fur Company sends Jim Beckwourth to befriend the Crow tribe and to persuade them to allow beaver trapping in their lands. Jim passes himself off as half Crow, half Cheyenne, but is in fact a mulatto from the South. The Crow don't really care what his heritage is and he becomes a member of the tribe, adopted by Strikes-Both-Ways, an elderly bow maker. First Jim becomes a *biraxdeta,* a hunter who always fills the pot. Fighting for the Crow against their enemies, he then becomes Bloody Hand, a pipe carrier. Bloody Hand lives as *bacbapite*, or grandson to Strikes-Both-Ways, who teaches him the way of the *Apsahrokee*, the Sparrow Hawk People. Bloody Hand falls in love with Pine Leaf, an arrogant young woman who demands one hundred scalps to win her in marriage. Bloody Hand begins collecting these scalps and the novel degenerates into pages of bloody fighting, scalping, stabbing, shooting, and even torture. Finally Bloody Hand has his hundred scalps and wins Pine Leaf. What started off as an interesting novel about the Sparrow Hawk People turns into another violent western with little redeeming value. Braun knows a great deal about the Crow and it is unfortunate that is not the main focus of the western. See Hotchkiss: *The Medicine Calf* and *Ammahabas* in *The Native American in Long Fiction* (1996) for other treatments of Jim Beckwourth's life among the Crow Indians.

33. Brierley, Barry. *Wasichu.* Mesa, AZ: Bear Books. 1996. 360 p.

Time: Contemporary, 1970's, 1876
Tribe: Sioux
Place: South Dakota, Montana

Vietnam veteran Christopher Raven goes to the Black Hills to honor the memory of his fallen buddy Joe Spotted Horse, but is transported back in time during a lightning storm. Joe had taught him Lakota while they were in Vietnam, so he can speak haltingly to the people he encounters. Because he has a spotted horse tattooed on his chest, just as Joe had a raven tattooed on his, the tribe welcomes Chris and he quickly becomes a part of them as they prepare for war against the Bluecoats and fight General Crook's Army at the Battle of the Rosebud. Brierley obviously loves his subject and has done his research well, but there are too many plot lines going. Brierley and his wife find a pipestone carving of a horse in a South Dakota store, which leads him to manuscripts written by Christopher Raven. Chris's story is both that of Vietnam and of 1876. There is also the "journal" of Little Hawk, a young boy whom Raven befriends and who becomes his stepson when Chris marries his mother. The battle scenes are well done, but the story is contrived and does not read easily.

34. Brierley, Barry. *Wasichu's Return.* Mesa, AZ: Bear Books. 1996. 325 p.

Time: 1876, 1976
Tribe: Sioux
Place: Montana, South Dakota

Chris Raven, called Okute by the Sioux, is a respected member of the tribe, husband to Blue Feather and stepfather to Little Hawk. His best friends are Bear Foot, Wolf Spirit and Ptecila. Most of the novel is an account of the the Battle of the Little Bighorn. Historical figures from Gall to the horse Comanche, the only survivor from the U.S. Army, are depicted in their roles during the battle. Finally after the fighting is over, life returns somewhat to normal, only to have Little Hawk come down with appendicitis. Chris decides to time travel again and return to South Dakota, carrying Little Hawk on his back, to have him treated in a modern hospital. Chris is successful in his travel back and in his getting proper medical treatment for his stepson. Unfortunately there are unnecessary plot additions in the form of ugly Sturgis bikers, and evil time traveling Vietnam vets, which Chris must fight off too. However, he and Little Hawk finally return to life with the Sioux in the 1870's once again.

35. Brierley, Barry. *White Horse, Red Rider.* Mesa, AZ: Bear Books. 1996. 187 p.

Time: Early 1800's
Tribe: Sioux, Blackfeet
Place: Wyoming

A beaver trapper, Joshua Donner, finds a young Sioux boy with an injured ankle in the mountains, fleeing from pursing Blackfeet from whom the boy has stolen a horse. Joshua falls and cuts his head, temporarily blinding himself. Together the two join to save themselves, with Curly Hair riding on Joshua's shoulders and guiding him through the deep snow. Meanwhile Swift Runner, Joshua's Sioux wife, senses his danger and comes to find him, bringing their wolf pet, Heyoka. Joshua and Curly outsmart and defeat most of the Blackfeet, except for those with Makwi, a large wolf-dog. Heyoka kills Makwi, the final Blackfeet are driven off or killed, and Curly goes on his way. A slight western with no literary merit, the secret, if it is one, is that Curly Hair is the early name of Crazy Horse.

Reviewed in: Roundup 4/97.

36. Bruchac, Joseph. (Abenaki). *Long River.* Golden, CO: Fulcrum. 1995. 298 p.

Time: pre-1500
Tribe: Abenaki
Place: New England

In this sequel to *Dawn Land*, Young Hunter has returned to his village, married Willow Woman, and is becoming a storyteller and leader of his people. Although all seems well, Young Hunter feels a disturbance, a threat to the village, but he cannot tell what the threat is. There are chapters told from the point of view of Young Hunter's grandfather Rabbit Stick and other village members. There are also stories of Angry Face, a woman from upriver who was badly burned in a fire and who sees the destruction of her own village and tries to warn those downstream. The evil force is Walking Hill, a woolly mammoth who has been injured and seen his family die. In his pain and rage, he strikes out at all humans, destroying their villages and killing the inhabitants before moving on. The little people *Mikumwesu* and the giant Ancient Ones also play their parts as do Young Hunter's three dogs. As in *Dawn Land*, Bruchac has woven Abenaki legends into this novel, which gives it richness and depth.

Reviewed in: Publishers Weekly 7/31/95; Kirkus Reviews 7/15/95.

37. Bruchac, Joseph. (Abenaki). *The Waters Between.* Hanover, NH: University Press of New England. 1998. 291 p.

Time: pre-1500
Tribe: Abenaki
Place: New England

Although the threat of Walking Hill is over, the Only People are in danger from other sources. Some huge being swims in *Petonbowk,* the waters between. This bigger-than-big-snake kills and devours anything it encounters and Young Hunter must warn the peoples of the various villages they must avoid the lake. A dark-seer, Watches Darkness, has turned evil and in his twisted mind has determined to kill as many other dark-seers as he can find. His companion is a great white bear who also kills whatever he encounters. Young Hunter and his mentor Bear Talker seek Watches Darkness and the white bear, but it is his wife Willow Woman and his dog Pabesis who encounter them. There is little plot in this book, it is even more a stringing together of Abenaki legends than the first two in the trilogy.

Reviewed in: Publishers Weekly 8/17/98.

38. Cady, Jack. *Inagehi.* Seattle: Broken Moon Press. 1994. 258 p.

Time: 1957
Tribe: Cherokee
Place: North Carolina

When Harriette Johnson's mother dies, she decides to find out the truth about her father's murder which occurred when he was logging their forest land seven years earlier. This arouses fear and mistrust long hidden in her Cherokee community which wishes to keep the secrets buried and she begins to feel threatened. Dead animals are found in her car and hanging from her tree. Retired Sheriff Blaine reopens the case on his own and with the help of retired history professor Warwick, tracks down the man and legal history behind these harassing events. Harriette meets an *Inagehi*, a person who lives alone in the wilderness, and this woman, Molla, makes the events surrounding the death of Harriette's father clear. Johnnie Whitcomb, an old friend of her father's, becomes a new friend of Harriette's. She learns to accept the truth and believe in the *Nunnehi*, the secret warriors who protect and defend their lands and trees against intruders bent on their destruction. A mysterious novel full of Cherokee words and legends, Cady's story adds to the knowledge about these complex people.

Reviewed in: Booklist 4/15/94.

39. Calandro, Ed. *Skiriki.* Shelton, CT: Pierpont Publishing. 1990. 386 p.

Time: 1950's, 1860's and 1870's
Tribe: Cheyenne
Place: Oklahoma and Great Plains

Henry Belski is a thief who wants to rob a bank before he gets out of the robbery business. He finds the Cattleman's Bank in Skiriki, Oklahoma, just waiting to be robbed and takes a room in the town to look over the situation. Soon he finds himself involved in the life of his landlady Deb and her two daughters. To give himself a cover story, he claims to be a writer working on a project involving the Plains Indians and soon encounters a mysterious old Indian Hoovehe who appears to be able to change into a coyote. Alternate chapters tell the harrowing story of the Cheyenne from Sand Creek to the Washita to the Little Bighorn to the slaughter of Dull Knife's band. Is Belski also a time traveler? Was he the Cheyenne Backwards years ago and is Hoovehe Roaming Wolf or his spirit? The tragic story of the Cheyenne is always moving but it has been told better in Sandoz's *Cheyenne Autumn* and the contemporary story of Belski and the bank robbery is tedious.

Reviewed in: Publishers Weekly 2/14/94.

40. Canty, Kevin. *Nine Below Zero.* NY: Doubleday. 1999. 371 p.

Time: Contemporary
Tribe: Blackfeet
Place: Montana

Marvin Deernose has been around, living and working all over the United States, married, divorced, and now finally returned to his birthplace to work as a carpenter. He comes upon a car accident with ex-Senator Henry Neihart trapped in the car. Henry has suffered a stroke, is blinded, and asks Marvin to end his suffering. Marvin calls for the ambulance instead. When Henry's granddaughter Justine comes from Oregon to care for him, she also comes to Marvin with the same request to end her grandfather's suffering. Justine has been seriously depressed and on medication since her four-year-old son Will was killed in another car accident several years before. She has left her husband Neil and now becomes involved with Marvin. Marvin knows this is a mistake, that the town of Rivulet is too small and too full of gossiping people to hide this relationship. Events spiral out of control, Justine stops taking her medication, her husband comes from Oregon to claim her, and Henry suffers more pain from the tumors in his brain. Marvin feels overwhelmed and trapped. He spends time remembering hunting with his father for deer, being in the Montana wilderness, and how simple and clean life once was for him. A final confrontation between Marvin, Justine and Henry's ranch hands leaves Marvin with broken bones and a broken heart. He is fired from his carpenter job and forced to leave his hometown. Going home did not solve his problems because he brought them all with him. Beautiful descriptions of growing up and living in Montana are paired with tortured internal dialogues from Marvin, Henry and Justine in this complex and disturbing novel.

Reviewed in: Library Journal 2/1/99; Booklist 1/1/99; Publishers Weekly 11/16/98; NYTBR 3/7/99.

41. Carey, Dorothy. *Wau-mato.* Nashville, TN: Winston-Derek Publishers. 1992. 212 p.

Time: 1840's
Tribe: Winnebago
Place: Wisconsin

Wau-mato is a young girl when she accompanies her father Chief White Hawk on a trip to Washington to see President Pierce. White Hawk hopes to convince the President to return the land at the Wisconsin Dells to the Winnebagoes. Although a treaty was signed turning this land over to the whites, the tribal leaders did not understand what they were signing and wish to remain on their lands. Wau-mato wants to see the cities of the white men, but she also wants some time away from the tribe. Little Elk is pressuring her to marry him and while Wau-mato does not want to go against the opinions of all who favor this match, she knows she does not love him. While in Washington she meets a white surveyor Rolf Benson and feels for him what she has never felt for Little Elk. When Wau-mato and her father return to Wisconsin, with little hope from the President that their lands will be returned, Rolf arrives with a painter friend and gradually the friendship between them grows into love. The characters are not well developed and the theme is simplistic. Parties of Native Americans did travel to Washington, however, and it has been included for that aspect.

42. Carr, A. A. (Navajo and Laguna Pueblo). *Eye Killers.* Norman: University of Oklahoma Press. 1995. 344 p.

Time: Contemporary
Tribe: Navajo
Place: New Mexico

American Indian Literature and Critical Studies Series, v.13

When Albuquerque teenager Melissa Roanhorse is taken by Falke, it is not a simple abduction. Falke is one of the undead who has chosen Melissa as his next bride. His previous consort Hanna hates this and wants to kill Melissa, while his current wife Elizabeth, still with some remnant of humanity, tries to help Melissa who is attracted by Falke's promise of eternal life. Fighting for Melissa are her aged grandfather Michael Roanhorse and her teacher Diana Logan who join forces to try and win Melissa back. To do this, Michael must remember the old songs and chants, but it is Diana who is chosen to learn them and use them against Falke. Blending the cultures of Transylvanian vampires and Navajo skinwalkers, Carr has written an intriguing novel for those who like horror fiction.

Reviewed in: Booklist 3/1/95; NYTBR 4/30/95; Publishers Weekly 2/20/95; Bloomsbury Review 5/95.

43. Carroll, Margaret. (Copyright held by Carol A. Whitney). *Prairie Light.* NY: Harper. 1994. 311 p.

Time: Contemporary
Tribe: Crow
Place: Montana

Wealthy Katherine Norton has always known she was adopted, but had always assumed her heritage was Greek like her adoptive mother's. Stunned to learn her birth mother was Native American, Kat Kourolakis comes to Billings, Montana, to learn about her mother. With her strong art history background, she is a natural for a job in a local art gallery and quickly becomes intrigued by Western and Native American art and artists; subjects she had never previously considered. When Kat meets attorney Sam Strong, she is at first put off by his manner, but soon finds herself in love with him and planning a future in the East together. Sam wants nothing to do with his Native American heritage and the ways of the traditionalists. Each hides a secret from the other, which is almost the ending of their relationship. Eventually both Sam and Kat realize that their love is stronger than the secrets of the past. Although a typical romance, the strong art theme and both characters being Native American make it somewhat different.

44. Charbonneau, Eileen. (Huron and Metis). *Rachel LeMoyne.* NY: Forge. 1998. 317 p.

Time: 1832–1849
Tribe: Choctaw
Place: Ireland and Western United States

This book is based on an historical footnote: in the 1840's during the Great Famine in Ireland, the Choctaw Nation sent corn to feed the starving Irish people. Rachel LeMoyne was a child during the Choctaw Removal from Mississippi to Oklahoma and was educated by the missionaries. She was chosen to accompany the corn on its ocean journey to Ireland. There she convinced a hunted millwright to get the mill running again and had the corn ground so people could use it. The missionaries who accompanied her were very displeased by her actions, but more displeased when she spirited Dare Ronan out of prison, smuggled him aboard the ship returning to America, and married him. Dare and the Irish peasants were hated and hunted in their own land as the Choctaw and other tribes were in America. Deciding to go west to Oregon, Rachel, her brother Atoka, and Dare join a wagon train out of St. Louis where Dare has shot a man who attacked Rachel. The train they join has a family which is bringing four hundred young fruit trees west in their own special wagon. Through the hardships of the trail including Indian encounters, a near fatal snake bite, and the pursuit by the man Dare shot, Dare and Rachel make their way to Oregon. Although a "typical" Oregon Trail tale, this novel is enlivened by the author's use of historical occurrences and personages.

Reviewed in: Library Journal 5/15/98; Booklist 5/15/98; Publishers Weekly 4/27/98.

45. Chiaventone, Frederick J. *Moon of Bitter Cold.* NY: Tom Doherty. 2002. 398 p.

Time: 1866–1868
Tribe: Sioux, Cheyenne, Arapaho
Place: Wyoming

After the Civil War the Bozeman Trail through Wyoming and into Montana was supposed to be protected by a series of newly built Army forts. Poorly supplied and poorly manned, these small forts suffered under the forces combined by Red Cloud to keep whites out of the Sioux homelands. Admitting they had already stolen this territory from the Crow, Red Cloud still manages to forge a union of the Cheyenne and Arapaho along with the many factions within the Sioux nation to stand off the U. S. Army. This novel covers the only successful Native American campaign, during which Red Cloud was able to drive the Army out of Sioux territory and burn down the forts, if only for a few years. Red Cloud's War (1866–1868) had as its chief success the Fetterman Massacre, described here in detail. Chiaventone has thoroughly researched his characters, including Jim Bridger, Colonel Carrington, Captain Fetterman, Crazy Horse, Spotted Tail, and Jim Beckwourth among many others, and includes all the historical events including the building of Fort Phil Kearny. Red Cloud's motivation to drive the whites out of Sioux territory derived from a father who drank himself to death on white man's liquor, Red Cloud's rebuffed attempts as a youth to attain acceptance from whites, and his own pride and arrogance in wanting complete power over his people. The Cheyenne initially resist joining Red Cloud, not wanting to die to build up his reputation. The dialogue among those Cheyenne men as they discuss the campaign is often most amusing. Crazy Horse is the military master mind, but Red Cloud is the power that makes the other warriors obey the battle plans. Fetterman is a boastful incautious man, who brags at a party that he could whip the whole Sioux Nation with only eighty men. Ironically that is the number of men who die with him in the Massacre. Eventually Red Cloud's people called this the Fight of One Hundred Dead because they also lost many men to the Army guns. Years later Red Cloud turned away from fighting to try to cooperate and work with the government for peace. For this his people called him a traitor, but in truth he had learned the Sioux ultimately could not win. This is an excellent account of an event rarely written of in the literature on Native Americans.

Reviewed in: Publishers Weekly 4/4/02; Kirkus Reviews 2/1/02; Booklist 3/15/02.

46. Chiaventone, Frederick J. *A Road We Do Not Know: A Novel of Custer at the Little Bighorn.* NY: Simon & Schuster. 1996. 333 p.

Time: 1876
Tribe: Sioux, Cheyenne, Arapaho
Place: Montana

This is an excellent historical novel covering one day in the lives of the Sioux, Cheyenne and Arapaho camped along the Little Bighorn and the U.S. Army troops and scouts that arrive to attack them. Gall, Crow King, Sitting Bull, Crazy Horse, Two Moons and many other chiefs are there, along with over five thousand people gathered together for the summer Sun Dance and hunting. Custer's Crow and Arikara scouts try to tell him the encampment is too large to attack with his six hundred troops, but he won't listen. Reno's troops charge into a force they do not expect and are scattered. Custer takes the high ground, only to be totally wiped out. Benteen does rescue Reno's men, but later suffers official criticism for not arriving sooner. Gall's entire family is murdered by a revenge-filled scout, the half Sioux Bloody Knife, who was the butt of Gall's teasing as a child. This turns Gall into a madman, attacking and killing in a rage. Crazy Horse is oddly remote, not even wanting to continue the fighting after the initial encounters. The novel weaves back and forth between the Sioux and the U.S. Army, detailing the individual experiences of those involved in the battle. Based on Army records and extensive research, this novel rivals Skimin's *The River and the Horsemen* as one of the best books on the Battle of the Little Bighorn. Together they are a complete account of the events recounted in a calm and historically accurate manner. The personalities of the participants, from the two Sioux chiefs Gall and Crow King, jealous of Sitting Bull's power over the tribe, to the angry Bloody Knife, the hostile Benteen, the arrogant Custer, the brash Custer brothers, and the overwhelmed Reno are all well developed. One of Custer's scouts warns the soldiers that they will soon be traveling a "road they do not know" which is of course the way to their death. As the day unfolds, the dust swirls, the horses scream and die, the troopers try to crawl into hidden spots to escape the arrows and the reader begins to feel a part of the fear and confusion that ruled the battle. Arrows found targets in other warriors, bullets shot other soldiers, and finally the Sioux women came along to finish the killing. Only Crazy Horse tries to stop the battle, knowing that if the Army is pushed too far they will retaliate in a force greater than can later be met. This proves to be true, as crushing the northern plains tribes becomes the highest priority of the government after this devastating battle. A very effective novel, Chiaventone has turned one day into a lifetime for these participants.

Reviewed in: Kirkus Reviews 8/1/96; Publishers Weekly 7/22/96.

47. Christofferson, April. *Clinical Trial.* NY: Tom Doherty. 2000. 333 p.

Time: Contemporary
Tribe: Blackfeet
Place: Montana, Seattle

Isabel McLain is a young Seattle doctor working on the Blackfeet reservation, just as her father did many years ago. Isabel fled a terrible marriage to Alistair Bott, after turning him in for faking results of clinical drug trials. When an outbreak of Hanta virus kills several young people, Isabel agrees to do clinical trials on a vaccine, although she must overcome the reluctance of the Blackfeet who view her as an interfering white woman. Monty Four Bear is a lawyer and AIM activist living on the reservation who protests Isabel's trials and the possibility of opening up land for gold mining, another problem the Blackfeet are being confronted with. World Resources, Inc., an international mining company, needs the Blackfeet site to stave off financial disaster after terrible pollution accidents in other parts of the world. WRI acquires agreement from the Blackfeet to do exploration, which Monty and his band of activists protest until Monty's father is beaten and killed by goons hired by WRI. Monty is shot in a confrontation with them, and Isabel takes him in, hides him and they fall in love. Meanwhile the jealous Alistair has tracked her down and arranges for her Hanta vaccine to be corrupted by smallpox virus. Unaware, Isabel has taken the smallpox dose to prove its safety to the Blackfeet, and now fears she may die. An ancient Blackfeet woman tells Isabel she is one of them, and that she carries life. A vaccine is found for the smallpox and Isabel finds out the truth of her parentage. Cheyenne and Salish herself, and pregnant with Monty's child, she recovers from the virus and agrees to marry Monty and stay as the reservation doctor. A complex and gripping plot with excellent characters, this is a very good mystery and a good look at life on a very isolated and impoverished reservation in Montana.

Reviewed in: Library Journal 10/1/00; Publishers Weekly 9/15/00; Kirkus Reviews 9/15/00.

48. Climer, Steven Lee. *BearWalker.* Greenfield, IN: Indigo Publishing Paperbacks. 1999. 240 p.

Time: Contemporary
Tribe: Ojibwe
Place: Michigan

As a small boy David Walking Bear was recognized by members of his tribe as a Bear Walker, a being who could change without warning into a terrible bear which would kill anything in his way. Taken away from the reservation and dumped into the city's orphanage David grew into a man for whom only alcohol would tame the terrible rages which prompted the physical changes. Nurse Jeannette Towson has changed her identity several times for she is a Bloodstopper able to heal fatal injuries and to literally bring people back from the dead. It is obvious David and Jeannette are destined to meet and fall in love. They are also being stalked by tabloid reporter Paul Dillinger who senses the story of the century and by government agents who want to capture their powers for nefarious purposes. This book is extremely poorly written; the characters are flat, the dialogue is wooden, the plot doesn't grab the reader. It is also extremely poorly edited with numerous typos, misspellings, and poor grammar. While the legend of the BearWalker and the Bloodstopper may be authentic Ojibwe mythology, they are given very poor representation here.

49. Coel, Margaret. *The Eagle Catcher*. Niwot, CO: University Press of Colorado. 1995. 186 p.

Reviewed in: Publishers Weekly 4/3/95; Armchair Detective Fall/95; Kirkus Reviews 4/1/95.

The Ghost Walker. NY: Berkley. 1996. 243 p.

Reviewed in: Booklist 10/1/96; Kirkus Reviews 8/1/96; Publishers Weekly 8/19/96.

The Dream Stalker. NY: Berkley. 1997. 244 p.

Reviewed in: Library Journal 9/1/97; Kirkus Reviews 8/15/97; Booklist 8/1/97; Publishers Weekly 7/14/97.

The Storyteller. NY: Berkley. 1998. 214 p.

Reviewed in: Booklist 9/15/98; Library Journal 9/1/98.

The Lost Bird. NY: Berkley. 1999. 294 p.

Reviewed in: Publishers Weekly 10/4/99; Library Journal 10/1/99; Booklist 8/1/99.

The Spirit Woman. NY: Berkley. 2000. 258 p.

Reviewed in: Booklist 10/1/00; Library Journal 9/1/00; Publishers Weekly 8/25/00.

The Thunder Keeper. NY: Berkley. 2001. 245 p.

Reviewed in: Publishers Weekly 8/13/01.

The Shadow Dancer. NY: Berkley. 2002. 291 p.

Time: Contemporary
Tribe: Arapaho
Place: Wyoming

In her eight Wind River Reservation mysteries, Coel explores many similar themes. The old ways of the Arapahos are frequently juxtaposed against the new pressures of modern times such as jobs and economic stability. Environmental issues play a major role, and the relationship between Father John O'Malley and Arapaho attorney Vicky Holden deepens and grows. In *The Eagle Catcher* the issue is oil and in *The Ghost Walker* drug lords want to build a casino through which to launder the drug money. Tribal history is prominent in *The Lost Bird*, *The Spirit Woman*, *The Storyteller*, and *The Shadow Dancer*, while nuclear waste and diamonds are the themes of *The Dream Stalker* and *The Thunder Keeper.* As a contemporary woman attorney Vicky fights for her peoples' rights but is always haunted by her past; her abusive husband Ben and the two children whom she left to get her education. John O'Malley is a committed priest and a recovering alcoholic. He wants to stay at Wind River and to minister to the people, but must continue to fight against his feelings for Vicky. Each of them leave Wyoming at various times, but both are drawn back to the place where they feel at home and where they do their best work. While each mystery is easy to read and enjoyable on its own, taken together the eight novels present an excellent picture of contemporary Native American life, both on and off the reservation, and of the values and heritage of the Arapahos.

50. Cogan, Priscilla. *Compass of the Heart: A Novel of Discovery.* NY: Simon & Schuster. 1998. 351 p.

Time: Contemporary
Tribe: Sioux
Place: Michigan

In this sequel to *Winona's Web*, Meggie O'Conner continues to delve deeper into Lakota spirituality and practices. Winona has left Meggie the Lightning Pipe and the beginning of understanding, but she has also left her Hawk, who acts as medicine leader for his people. Meggie participates in the sweat lodge ceremonies and she and Hawk grow both physically and spiritually closer. When Hawk's ex-wife Rising Smoke arrives, Hawk is confused and feels he loves both women. He does not know of Meggie's pregnancy until she loses the baby and she is then unsure what brings him back to her. There are several other subplots in this novel as well: the injury to June Tubbs, the daughter of one of Meggie's friends, her troubled patient Andrea, the minister Karl who becomes involved with Meggie's partner Bev, her aging parents, and her dog Fritzie. In addition to Rising Smoke, Hawk must deal with his cousin Lucy and her children, his mentor Laughing Bear back at Pine

Ridge, and the increasing responsibilities of his position. Winona watches them all, but increasingly the bonds that bind her to earth are slipping and finally she is free to go. While the novel may not make sense in the retelling, this is a world the reader enjoys participating in when reading.

Reviewed in: Booklist 8/1/98; Publishers Weekly 7/13/98.

51. Cogan, Priscilla. *Crack at Dusk: Crook of Dawn, A Novel of Discovery.* Hopkinton, MA: Two Canoes Press. 2000. 345 p.

Time: Contemporary
Tribe: Sioux
Place: Michigan

In the third of the Winona trilogy, Meggie and Hawk are married in a Lakota ceremony and all seems well until Easter Week when young June Tubbs is kidnapped and then Hawk's nephew Adam is missing. Adam is found several days later, but his soul has been shattered and he will not speak. Worse, he has become violent towards his dog, his sister and himself. Treatment at a children's psychiatric hospital does not help him; Hawk wants to bring him home and use traditional Lakota ceremonies to heal the boy. Doubtful, Meggie reluctantly agrees, but also insists that Adam have a contemporary therapist. Through both techniques, Adam gradually is able to talk about what happened to him. He, June, and several other children and teenagers had been kidnapped by members of a Satanic cult, undergone physical and mental torture, and were forced to participate in their evil rituals. There is a great deal of discussion of religion, whether true evil exists, and how people can live in a world where it does. Although everything is wrapped up (perhaps too neatly), this novel is nevertheless a satisfying one to read.

Reviewed in: Publishers Weekly 1/14/02.

52. Cogan, Priscilla. *Winona's Web: A Novel of Discovery.* Mount Horeb, WI: Face to Face Books. 1996. 280 p.

Time: Contemporary
Tribe: Sioux
Place: Michigan

Winona Pathfinder is referred to psychotherapist Megan O'Connor because she has told her daughter Lucy she will die in two months. Since Winona appears healthy, Meggie at first tries conventional treatment, but gradually she begins to really listen to Winona and gradually Winona begins to teach Meggie the things she feels Meggie needs to know. Divorced, with strained relationships with her parents, her ex-husband and men in general, Meggie's life is out of balance. When Winona does indeed die because she is ready to go, she tells Meggie she will be all right for she has "learned how to pray." Both Meggie and Winona are well-developed characters and the novel portrays the importance of the "old ways" to contemporary life.

Reviewed in: Booklist 9/15/96; Publishers Weekly 8/19/96.

53. Coldsmith, Don. *The Long Journey Home.* NY: Tom Doherty. 2001. 400 p.

Time: 1890's–1930's
Tribe: Sioux
Place: Pennsylvania, Kansas, Oklahoma

Little Bull is a wonderful athlete, noticed by Senator Langtry on a visit to a Lakota mission school, and sent to the Carlisle Indian Industrial School to help build their athletic program. His name changed to John Buffalo, he excels in track, football and baseball. Unfortunately John attracts the attention of Jane Langtry and, appalled by idea of an "Indian" with his daughter, the Senator has Buffalo abruptly transferred to Haskill Indian School in Kansas. His athletic career ended, John Buffalo joins the 101 Ranch Wild West Show and lives happily there for years. Carlisle hires John back to train Jim Thorpe for the Olympics, where Thorpe competes successfully. John returns to the 101 and continues to tour with Tom Mix, Bill Pickett, Princess Wenona and the other notables of this famous company run by the Miller Brothers. Next John enlists in the Army, suffers through influenza, tries out acting and animal training in Hollywood, runs into old coaching friends, goes to the Berlin Olympics where Jesse Owens is highly successful, and sees the hatred for people of color among the powerful Nazis. John returns to his boyhood mission school to teach his tribes' children, only to joyfully discover Jane Langtry is teaching there already, hoping he would one day return. A detailed history of the Wild West Show culture and the changes which came to the American west between the time of the late 1800's and the early 1900's, Coldsmith knows his history and can share it in an engaging style. One has hopes John Buffalo's new teaching career back with his tribe and Jane will bring fulfillment to his life.

Reviewed in: Booklist 3/15/01; Publishers Weekly 12/11/00.

54. Coldsmith, Don. *Raven Mocker.* Norman: University of Oklahoma Press. 2001. 253 p.

Time: Early 1800's
Tribe: Cherokee
Place: Georgia and Arkansas

Snakewater is the conjure woman for Old Town, a traditional Cherokee town in Georgia. Rumors start about her being a raven mocker, a thief who steals the years from dying young people in order to extend their own life. Snakewater is very old and wonders herself if she is inadvertently a raven mocker, but is convinced by the Peace Chief Three Fingers, that she cannot be. If she did harm with her gifts, they would turn back on her and do her harm. Although a town council is called to settle the matter, it is too difficult for Snakewater and she leaves with another band of Cherokees for Arkansas. Too many White people are moving into their lands and some Cherokee decide to voluntarily move west over the Mississippi River to new lands. Kills Many accepts Snakewater into his band where she now becomes a storyteller. Many Cherokee legends are told and customs are portrayed in this short but excellent story. Although listed as a title in the Spanish Bit Saga, this novel stands alone as an example of Cherokee life and customs in the early 1800's.

Reviewed in: Booklist 3/1/01; Publishers Weekly 2/19/01.

55. Coldsmith, Don. *The Spanish Bit Saga.* Individual titles in chronological order are:

Quest for the White Bull. NY: Bantam. 1990. 209 p.
Return of the Spanish. NY: Doubleday. 1991. 179 p.

Reviewed in: Booklist 5/15/91.

Bride of the Morning Star. NY: Doubleday. 1991. 176 p.
Walks in the Sun. NY: Bantam. 1992. 240 p.
Thunderstick. NY: Doubleday. 1993. 182 p.

Reviewed in Publishers Weekly 5/10/98.

Track of the Bear. NY: Doubleday. 1994. 226 p.
Child of the Dead. NY: Doubleday. 1995. 245 p.

Reviewed in: Library Journal 2/1/95; Publishers Weekly 1/9/95; Kirkus Reviews 12/1/94.

Bearer of the Pipe. NY: Doubleday. 1995. 258 p.

Reviewed in: Booklist 9/1/95; Publishers Weekly 8/28/95.

Medicine Hat. Norman: University of Oklahoma Press. 1997. 266 p.

Reviewed in: Publishers Weekly 8/4/97.

The Lost Band. Norman: University of Oklahoma Press. 2000. 260 p.

Time: 1700's
Tribe: Composite Plains (Kiowa, Cheyenne, Arapahoe, Apache, Comanche, etc.)
Place: Great Plains

Coldsmith continues with his series of the People, a fictional Native American tribe of the Great Plains, based upon a buffalo hunting culture. He borrows from the Cheyenne, Sioux, Kiowa and Comanche traditions, and includes tribal councils, vision quests, and sun dances. The series continues to be well written, with gripping plots and well developed characters. The *Lost Band* reconnects the horse-influenced culture of the Plains with the original culture of the 1500's before the coming of the horse by a storyteller recounting history. Each title in the series is fairly short, but the writing continues to be excellent.

56. Coldsmith, Don. *Tallgrass.* NY: Bantam. 1997. 455 p.

Time: 1541–1840's
Tribe: Pueblo, Pawnee, Kansa (Caw), Comanche
Place: Kansas, Colorado

This novel contains short vignettes of the native peoples living on the central plains from first contact with the Spanish explorers to just before the Civil War and includes people from the Pueblo, Pawnee, Comanche and Kansa tribes. The Pawnee were comprised of four major groups, governing their nation in such an egalitarian way that the area between the Platte and the Kansas River became known as the Indian Republic. The Pueblo revolt led by Popé impacts Magpie, a peaceful man, who decides to move his family away to the central plains. The novel also follows the adventures of the French explorer Veniard, as he moves up the southern rivers. Members of the Kansa tribe intermarried with the French explorers, learned French and many became Catholic. Next came the early fur trappers along the Kansas River in the beginning of the 1800's, the opening of the Santa Fe Trail, and the encroachment of eastern tribes into this area in the mid-1800's. Liberty Franklin leads a fur trapping expedition into the central plains after returning from the Lewis and Clark Expedition and marries a Cheyenne woman. Easterner Jed Sterling, calling himself Long Walker, marries into the Pawnee tribe, while leading the Becknell expedition to Santa Fe and the Fremont Expedition with Kit Carson. When displaced Delawares attack the Pawnees' traditionally built half-timbered buried houses, burning out the people, his family is killed and he returns east. The Comanche welcome all the explorers and are responsible for the first resistance to White encroachment on their lands. The novel contains few hostile encounters, either between different tribes known to be each others' enemies, such as the Pawnee and the Comanche, or the tribes and the White explorers. This implies that the central plains were a more peaceful place of cooperation and harmony than was perhaps true. However, the historical details of the various stages of exploration, and the details on Pawnee culture especially, are accurate and add to our knowledge of these plains tribes.

Reviewed in: Library Journal 3/15/97; Publishers Weekly 3/3/97.

57. Cole, David. *Butterfly Lost.* NY: Harper Paperbacks. 2000. 373 p.

Time: Contemporary
Tribe: Hopi and Navajo
Place: Arizona

Laura Winslow is an assumed identity for a Hopi woman who no longer wishes to be associated with her tribe or her own personal history. Nonetheless she has returned to the Mesa where she grew up and now works for a bounty hunter tracking down missing persons. Laura's own daughter, Spider, was abducted by her abusive husband twenty years ago, never to be seen again. Elders from a neighboring small town come to ask for her assistance in locating several missing Hopi girls. Judy Pavatea's grandfather saw Laura in a vision, defeating a large black bird who was stealing the girls. Judy and her friend Mary have recently disappeared. None of the Hopi will talk to the Navajo Tribal Police or the Hopi Rangers, not trusting either. With the help of Kimo Biakeddy, an ex-con Navajo who remembers Laura from her youthful involvement in AIM, she tracks down and solves two mysteries. One mystery involves rodeo cowboys abusing young Native American girls, knowing contemporary society will let them get away with it, and explains the missing Hopi girls. The other mystery involves bounty hunters and stolen Hopi sacred objects, highly desired by wealthy white people. Well written, full of suspense and with a complex plot, this is an excellent first mystery from the author who established NativeWeb, an Internet corporation for Native Americans. Laura eventually confronts the reasons she is trying to escape her sad past and accepts that she is indeed Hopi by retaking her original name, *Kauwanyauma*, Butterfly Revealing Wings. She abandons her assumed identities and returns home to Kimo and to Mary, the missing Hopi girl she has rescued who now lives with her. Both are obvious replacements for her missing daughter and husband, but she is content with her new life. Further titles in the series are *The Killing Maze*, 2001, *Stalking Moon*, 2002, and *Scorpion Rain*, 2002, but Laura's Native American heritage plays no role in those novels and they are therefore not included here.

58. Cole, Judd. *Cheyenne Series.*
    Arrow Keeper
    Death Chant
    Renegade Justice
    Vision Quest
    Blood on the Plains
    Comanche Raid
    Comancheros
    War Party
    Pathfinder
    Buffalo Hiders
    Spirit Killer
    Mankiller
    Wendigo Mountain
    Death Camp
    Renegade Nation
    Orphan Train
    Vengence Quest
    Warrior Fury
    Bloody Bones Canyon
    Renegade Siege
    River of Death
    Desert Manhunt

NY: Dorchester. 1992 – 2000. Each title is approx. 175 p.

Time: 1840–1860's
Tribe: Cheyenne
Place: Colorado, Wyoming, Montana, Oklahoma, Texas

This series of western style novels all feature an orphaned Cheyenne boy raised as Matthew by the Hanchons in Wyoming until he turns sixteen and discovers he is not considered fit to be a White girl's husband. Matthew runs away and finds his Cheyenne people, is renamed Touch the Sky, and is trained to be a shaman by Arrow Keeper. Touch the Sky is also a fierce warrior, trying to win the approval of the other young "bucks" (as they call each other in these novels) and the heart of beautiful Honey Eater. His enemies are Black Elk, another warrior who wants Honey Eater, and Black Elk's band of friends, who all call Touch the Sky, "White Man Runs Him." These young men hate Whites, calling them *Mah-ish-ta-shi-da,* Yellow Eyes, because the first traders they met had jaundice. Touch the Sky proves he is worthy over and over again, saving enslaved women and children from the Comanches, fighting against the Pawnee, but also helping his White friends build the railroad and establish trading posts. Honey Eater is given in marriage by her father to Black Elk, who jealously watches her and her interactions with his hated enemy "White Man Runs Him." Touch the Sky is continually battling both the buffalo hunters and miners who invade their territory and kill their primary food supply, and also the treachery of Black Elk and his friends. Typical western fare, the stories are adequately written, the characters developed, and each title has another fresh challenge for Touch the Sky to surmount, which of course he always does.

59. Conley, Robert J. (Cherokee). *Captain Dutch.* NY: Pocket Books. 1995. 272 p.

Time: 1794–1848
Tribe: Cherokee
Place: Alabama, Texas, Oklahoma

In 1794, led by Chief Bowles, Tahchee moves west with his uncle and mother attempting to escape the encroaching White men. The Western Cherokee settled in Alabama Territory and immediately began a protracted war with the Osage already there. In an attempt at peace, Tahchee, called Dutch, marries an Osage woman and lives with her people. A year later peace ends and the Osage kill his wife as a traitor, turning Dutch into a vengeful man. Dutch joins the traditionalists under Degadoga, determined to fight the Osage and the White men rather than become assimilated. John Jolly leads the "britches Indians," the Western Cherokee who want to become educated and live like White people. Years of battles continue until finally Captain Dutch, promoted by Degadoga, leaves and moves his family to Texas. Disowned and called a renegade by Whites and Cherokee alike, he remains there until peace is finally established with the Osage and amnesty granted to all. Dutch becomes a leader of his people, a farmer, and rancher and a father. Not well known, this Western Cherokee worked hard for his people, both against the Osage and the Whites. When assimilation was inevitable, he gave in and worked in the new government in Oklahoma, after the Trail of Tears brought thousands more Cherokee out west. Conley's novel is full of historical figures and events which accurately portray this time period in Cherokee history. An excellent history, Conley has once again brought the culture and history of his people to readers in an entertaining novel. He concludes with an afterword explaining the background and future events in the lives of many of the historical figures from the book. In an interesting note he states is that Sequoyah did not invent the Cherokee alphabet, but rather resurrected an old form of writing the tribe had used in the past.

60. Conley, Robert J. (Cherokee). *Cherokee Dragon.* NY: St. Martin's. 2000. 289 p.

Time: 1737–1794
Tribe: Cherokee
Place: Tennessee, Virginia, North Carolina

Tsiyu Gansini, or Dragging Canoe, was a famous war leader of the Cherokee, son of the man known to the English as Captain Owen Nakan. Dragging Canoe's cousin was Nancy Ward, the Beloved Woman of the Cherokee. This family worked hard to maintain peace with the English, but encroachments upon their territory turned Dragging Canoe into a vengeful warrior against the settlers. The Cherokee took the side of the British during the American Revolution and consequently lost any bargaining power with the new nation's leaders. Driven from their ancestral lands, the Cherokee were harassed by the Army and formed a rebellious group known as the Chickamaugas, made up of Shawnee, Creeks, Cherokee and other disaffected tribes. Dragging Canoe became known as the Cherokee Dragon, feared and respected by his enemies. In 1791 Dragging Canoe died of a heart attack and John Watts assumed command. Watts was not an effective leader and ultimately the Cherokee lost their war against American settlers.

An excellent history of the time and of this little-known Cherokee leader, the novel contains many historical references and figures.

Reviewed in: Booklist 2/15/00; Publishers Weekly 2/14/00.

61. Conley, Robert J. (Cherokee). *Geronimo: An American Legend.* NY: Pocket Books. 1994. 218 p.

Time: 1886
Tribe: Apache
Place: Arizona

Written as a tie-in to the movie of the same name starring Cherokee actor Wes Studi, this novel covers the same ground with the same characters. Geronimo was born Gokhlaye to the Mescalero Apache, but later became associated with the Chiricahuas. It was the Mexicans who later referred to him as Geronimo, meaning Jerome. Conley quickly reviews the history of the battles of Cochise, the killing of Mangas Colorado and the Camp Grant massacre of peaceful Eskiminzin's band. Eventually the Army is able to turn some Apache against others and Chato, formerly a friend of Geronimo's, became an Army scout hunting him down. The main story plot concerns the friendship between Geronimo and Lt. Gatewood, the man who ultimately is responsible for Geronimo's surrender. The Army's killing of the Apache Dreamer at Cibecue drives Geronimo off the Turkey Creek reservation and the U.S. Army sends massive numbers of troops against the tiny band of thirty-some warriors. General Crook resigns and General Nelson Miles takes over. Geronimo, beaten and starving, surrenders, only to be sent to a Florida prison. All the Chiricahuas are sent with him, including the Army scouts. Chato learns how much he could really trust his new White masters as he rides the train to Florida with Geronimo. Geronimo never returned to Arizona.

62. Conley, Robert J. (Cherokee). *Medicine War.* NY: Signet. 2001. 298 p.

Time: 1880's
Tribe: Cherokee
Place: Cherokee Nation (Oklahoma)

George Panther is over fifty years old and concerned about who will take over his role as healer for the Cherokee people. His son Andy is good in school but is not interested in learning the healing songs and herbal remedies. His son Tom is a drunken brawling wastrel who ends up being shot by a cuckolded husband. George has a fast white stallion who wins all the horse races, which causes a stranger from the north, Big Forehead, a Shawnee, to become angry and jealous. Big Forehead decides to destroy George by pitting his bad medicine against George's good. First a White man is shot to death by George as the man attempts to steal the stallion. Then U.S. Marshals come to arrest George and take him back to jail at Ft. Smith. George knows he will go before the "Hanging Judge" and refuses to be arrested. Canoe and Beehunter, Cherokee friends, conduct repeated ambushes of the Marshals to keep them away. The U.S. Marshals have been told to bring George in, dead or alive. Finally Canoe hits upon a brilliant idea. The Marshals have never seen George, so when Bobby Stump, a Cherokee who resembles him, is killed in another ambush, Canoe and the high sheriff of the Cherokee Nation, Go-Ahead Rider, both adamantly insist to the remaining Marshals that the dead Cherokee is George Panther. Big Forehead's bad medicine cannot prevail against George's stronger good medicine. George also finally sees his successor in the form of his little niece, Annie, who has magical powers at a very young age. There is a bit too much crystal gazing by the medicine men in this novel, which gives one an impression of the witches in *The Wizard of Oz* instead of true native healing methods.

Conley, Robert J. (Cherokee).
The Real People Series.

While the entire series is set in historical times from the pre-1500's to 1650's, the following later novels in the series follow the adventures of Cherokee characters as they interact with the early Spanish explorers, later French traders and finally the first English settlers. In the interests of coherence, the titles in the series have been grouped together. Books one through three are included in the first bibliography and their titles are: *The Way of the Priests, The Dark Way,* and *The White Path.*

63. Conley, Robert J. (Cherokee). *The Real People Book Four. The Way South.* NY: Doubleday. 1994. 176 p.

Time: 1520
Tribe: Cherokee, Timucua, Calusa
Place: Florida and Southeastern United States

Carrier and his uncle Dancing Rabbit are traders, ready for a long trip to the south when Dancing Rabbit breaks his leg searching for ginseng. Carrier goes alone and encounters the hairy-faced White men riding their large dogs in the land of the Timucua. Fleeing them, he meets He-Fights-With-Alligators, a Calusa man captured by the Spanish who can now speak their language. The Timucua give refuge to the two men and Carrier falls in love with Potmaker. The Timucua fight the Spanish but lose and must flee. Potmaker is captured and raped by the soldiers. Carrier returns to the Calusa people and talks them into coming to help fight. He returns with many warriors and the combined Timucua and Calusa drive the Spanish off the land and back to their ships. The Spaniard, Francisco de Garay, gives up his plan to establish a colony on the northern coast of Florida. He-Fights-With-Alligators returns to his family in the Calusa tribe and Carrier brings Potmaker as his wife to the Cherokee. Potmaker is pregnant with a Spanish child but Carrier will accept any child of hers as his own. Dancing Rabbit is delighted to see Carrier again, as Carrier is the only person who he taught to keep the secret, written language of the Cherokee alive. Dancing Rabbit had been a priest, an *Ani-Kutani*, but had escaped when the Real People, the *Ani-yunwi-ya*, had risen up and slaughtered the priests, thereby also killing most all who knew the written Cherokee language.

64. Conley, Robert J. (Cherokee). *The Real People Book Five. The Long Way Home.* NY: Doubleday. 1994. 180 p.

Time: 1530's–1540's.
Tribe: Cherokee, Timucua, Choctaw, Apalachee
Place: Florida and Southeastern United States

When three Cherokee priests, or *Ani-Kutani*, are sent west to look for rain, they are captured by the Fierce People and enslaved. Sold to the Espanols, the *Ani-Asquani*, Deadwood Lighter's gift of languages makes him one of their translators. Taken by De Soto on an expedition across Florida and the southwest and renamed Juan Jose, the Cherokee man witnessed unbelieveable atrocities and cruelties by the Spanish to the native tribes. Years later Deadwood Lighter staggers home to his former Cherokee town, and relates the tale of Spanish exploration to the rest of the tribe. He hopes to prepare them for the coming of White men and the horrors of disease and massacres it will bring. De Soto's expedition is related in detail by Deadwood Lighter, and one of the listeners is 'Squani, a young Cherokee man whose mother was raped by the *Ani-Asquani* and who is the result of that union. He is repelled and yet fascinated by the kind of man his Spanish father must have been. A fascinating account of the De Soto expedition and this time period in early American history, contemporary readers will find the cruelty of the Spanish and the waste they left behind in diseased and murdered people appalling.

Reviewed in: Publishers Weekly 8/22/94.

65. Conley, Robert J. (Cherokee). *The Real People Book Six. The Dark Island.* NY: Doubleday. 1995. 181 p.

Time: 1540's
Tribe: Cherokee, Catawba
Place: Southeastern United States

Squani, the half Timucua, half Spanish member of the Cherokee band, has heard Deadwood Lighter's stories of the Spanish. Never having been adopted into any Cherokee clan, Squani feels an affinity for his father's Spanish people. He is a young man seeking his identity and goes south to see if he can find the Spanish, which he does on a small island off the coast. He is captured by soldiers and given to the priest, Father Tomas. A quick learner, Squani takes to the Spanish ways, language, reading and horseback riding. Taken along on an expedition, he sees the thoughtless cruelty of the Spaniards towards native peoples who only offer kindness. Squani meets Osa, a Catawba woman badly used by the soldiers. He rescues her, but incurs Father Tomas's wrath when the priest finds them together. Beaten, the young lovers run away and are chased by the soldiers and priest. Fortunately Squani encounters Cherokee friends and together with the help of some Frenchmen, they defeat the soldiers, kill the priest, and wipe out the settlement on the island. Squani is adopted into the Wolf Clan of the Cherokee and can marry Osa as a full-fledged member of the Cherokee tribe. A coming of age story, this novel reinforces the lessons taught about the Spanish cruelty in the previous book of the Real People.

Reviewed in: Roundup 8/96.

66. Conley, Robert J. (Cherokee). *The Real People Book Seven. The War Trail North.* NY: Doubleday. 1995. 183 p.

Time: 1540's–1550's
Tribe: Cherokee, Seneca.
Place: Southeastern United States

Young Puppy's older brother is killed by a Seneca and he sets out to find revenge, accompanied by Squani, now Asquani, a husband and soon to be a father. On their journey, Asquani teaches Young Puppy how to write the secret language of the Cherokee to keep the skill alive through the generations. They are successful in finding and killing Seneca and Young Puppy decides he is old enough now to marry Guwisti. The ancient shaman woman Uyona tells them they must wait a year; Young Puppy has to die and be reborn first, which confuses the young lovers. In frustration, Young Puppy sets off on another raid and during the fighting accidentally kills his friend and teacher, Asquani. The Wolf Clan is allowed revenge for Asquani's death by the hand of another Cherokee, but only if Young Puppy leaves the protection of Peace Town, Kituwah. He must stay there a year to be absolved of his crime, so he agrees to live in inactivity and isolation. The French traders led by Jacques Tournier are also in this story, attempting to bring peace between the Seneca and Cherokee in order to be allowed to trade freely with both tribes.

67. Conley, Robert J. (Cherokee). *The Real People Book Eight. The Peace Chief: A Novel of the Real People.* NY: St. Martin's. 1998. 339 p.

Time: 1540–1550's
Tribe: Cherokee, Shawnee, Seneca
Place: Southeastern United States

Young Puppy must spend a year in Kituwah to atone for his accidental killing of Asquani. To alleviate his boredom, Ahuli, who acts as the priest and leader of ceremonies for the Cherokee, decides to apprentice Young Puppy and teach him the ceremonies. Much of the novel describes the ceremonies of the year, such as *Ela talegi*, the Ceremony of the Bush, and *Nuwadi equa*, the Great Moon Ceremony. The Frenchman Jacques Tournier is studying the Cherokee and participates in the rituals, but his men are mutinous. Although Tournier is able to suppress the mutiny, he and his men are banished from the town and go to the Seneca to work out a peace settlement between the two tribes. Asquani's wife, Osa, gives birth to twins and Uyona the witch puts a spell on the daughter, Whirlwind, making her a demanding person. Eventually the year is over, Young Puppy is renamed Comes Back to Life, marries Guwisti and Osa and adopts the twins. After the tribe drives a forbidden town of Shawnee out of their land, part of the Cherokee move to New Town where Comes Back to Life becomes the Peace Chief and Oliga, a brave man, becomes the War Chief. The French succeed in creating a peace between the Cherokee and the Seneca and life appears good to all. Conley based his ceremonies on historical descriptions and one can trust their accuracy. He includes the usual glossary of Cherokee words as well.

Reviewed in: Booklist 11/15/98; Publishers Weekly 11/9/98; Kirkus Reviews 10/15/98.

68. Conley, Robert J. (Cherokee). *The Real People Book Nine. War Woman: A Novel of the Real People.* NY: St. Martin's. 1997. 354 p.

Time: 1580–1654
Tribe: Cherokee. Calusa, Timucca, Apalachee, Powhatans
Place: Southeastern United States

Osa's twins Whirlwind and Little Spaniard are now young adults eager for adventure. Together with handsome Daksi they set off to establish trade with the Spanish in Florida. Many adventures occur, Whirlwind and Daksi marry, trade is successful, but an infatuated Spanish Captain attempts to kill the young men to get Whirlwind and in the following battle she achieves her new name of War Woman. Years go by and the widowed War Woman marries a Spanish trader, Juan Morales. Together they organize gold mining on Cherokee land and make a fortune. War Woman realizes how much trade has changed the Cherokee, including her twin brother Little Spaniard who has become a worthless drunkard. When he kills the war leader Olig' and beats his own stepfather Comes Back to Life, Little Spaniard is condemned to death by the tribe. More years go by, and as an ancient and respected woman, War Woman is asked to help drive out the invasive Englishmen who have defeated the Powhatans. Together with Running Man, the Cherokee chief, they take a large contingent of Cherokee to Virginia and push the English settlers back to Jamestown. War Woman returns to New Town and dies satisfied with her long and fulfilling life.

Reviewed in: Publishers Weekly 8/25/97; Kirkus Reviews 9/1/97; School Library Journal 5/1/98.

69. Conley, Robert J. (Cherokee). *Sequoyah.* NY: St. Martin's. 2002. 213 p.

Time: 1826–1843
Tribe: Cherokee
Place: Tennessee, Arkansas, Oklahoma

Real facts about Sequoyah are hard to determine, but Conley has woven many of the common beliefs together in a fictionalized biography of the Cherokee man who created the written language, or syllabary, for the tribe. Some believe Sequoyah based his syllabary upon an ancient language of the Cherokee priests, all killed centuries ago. Whatever the source, Sequoyah's creation of an alphabet easily and quickly learned by the Cherokee was a tremendous asset to communication between the Eastern and Western Bands, living so far apart. The history of the move from the East to the Indian Territory is covered, as are the Ross and Ridge wars. Sequoyah is shown as a complex and imperfect man who loves his drink. When he joins a delegation of the tribe traveling to Washington D.C. to secure their property rights and this delegation instead gives away the Cherokee lands in Arkansas, Sequoyah's life is threatened. During the civil war between the Ross and Ridge factions, which included many assassinations, Sequoyah feels threatened again. Finally Sequoyah leaves the Indian Territory and goes to live the rest of his life in Mexico, where he dies. A very complex and rich depiction of a famous Cherokee man, Conley does justice to this amazing man's life and accomplishments.

Reviewed in: Publishers Weekly 5/20/02.

70. Conley, Robert J. (Cherokee). *Spanish Jack.* NY: St. Martin's. 2001. 210 p.

Time: 1841–1850's
Tribe: Cherokee
Place: Oklahoma

Conley once again takes an historical figure from Cherokee history and brings him to life. Jack Spaniard grew up in the early 1800's in Arkansas and Oklahoma with the Western Band of Cherokee. Pushed into Osage territory, Jack took an Osage wife and lived with her family until she was killed by her tribe for marrying a Cherokee. This is the same tale as Captain Dutch's life. Turning against the Osage, Spanish Jack kills all he finds until he and another severely wounded Osage man must live together to recuperate from broken bones. However, the Cherokee still consider Jack an outlaw, so he runs with the Starr Gang for a while, then goes to work for the Army rescuing horses from the Comanche. Finally he is pardoned by the Cherokee and allowed to return home.

Reviewed in: Publishers Weekly 7/30/01; Kirkus Reviews 7/1/01; Booklist 7/1/01.

71. Conley, Robert J. (Cherokee). *Zeke Proctor: Cherokee Outlaw.* NY: Pocket Books. 1994. 180 p.

Time: 1872–1874
Tribe: Cherokee
Place: Oklahoma (Indian Territory)

This slim novel concerns an accidental shooting and the blood feud it generated between the Proctors and the Becks. Zeke Proctor was a solid Cherokee farmer in Indian Territory, considered part of the Cherokee Nation, a sovereign nation within the boundaries of the U.S. When Zeke accidentally shoots a young Cherokee woman, Polly Beck, in an attempt to kill his sister's worthless White husband, Zeke surrenders himself and goes before a Cherokee court. Zeke is also charged with attempted murder by the neighboring state of Arkansas. The incident escalates when the young woman's family opens fire at Zeke's trial, killing many unarmed Cherokee. Since a Federal Marshall is killed in the crossfire, the U.S. Marshals come to arrest the Cherokee judge, jury, and several trial attendees. Many of the Cherokee, including Zeke, flee into the hills, hidden by the secret Keetoowah Society of full blooded Cherokee. The case goes all the way to President Grant, who rules that this was a Cherokee case, and although a Federal Marshall was killed, the Cherokee are not to be held accountable. Based on actual historical events and persons, the case pitted the Cherokee Nation against the United States, and proved the Cherokee had the right to try their own people without interference from the United States government.

72. Cook-Lynn, Elizabeth. (Sioux). *Aurelia: a Crow Creek Trilogy.* Boulder: University of Colorado Press. 1999. 416 p.

Time: 1960–1995
Tribe: Sioux
Place: South Dakota

These three novellas set on the Crow Creek reservation center around the life of Aurelia Blue, a Dakota Sioux woman. The first part, separately published earlier as *From the River's Edge* (1991) was reviewed in the first bibliography. Part Two, *Circle of Dancers,* and Part Three, *In the Presence of River Gods*, follow Aurelia's life after she leaves John Tatekeya and decides whether or not to marry Jason Big Pipe, the father of her children. Jason becomes more and more politicized as the sixties turn into the seventies, AIM influences are felt on the reservation, the water rights of the Sioux are infringed upon by desperate white ranchers in a time of severe drought, and the government pushes loans on the Sioux, then suddenly demands payment. Jason feels caught in forces he cannot control and turns away from Aurelia, living with her, but rarely sharing his thoughts and feelings. Aurelia was a "throw away child," abandoned by her parents when she was a baby and raised by her paternal grandparents. Aurelia loves her own children, Blue and Sarah, intensely and wants the best for them. As Jason's life deteriorates, she finally leaves him and moves to Eagle Butte where she meets Hermist, a widower with two sons. The political climate on the Cheyenne River Sioux reservation is just as intense and she becomes involved through members of her family. Injustices against the Sioux are exemplified by the disappearance of a young Sioux girl, found murdered, but with no guilty parties identified. Those guilty of injustices are never clearly identified, as the *Mni Sosa*, their Missouri River, is gradually damned and the water sold away. Many years later, the White men who brutally raped and murdered the young Sioux girl are found, tried, and convicted, and Aurelia is there to witness it. Excellent short novellas, these stories succinctly sum up the events of several decades in the lives of the Sioux on the reservations of South Dakota. Using Aurelia to tell the stories and her family members to participate in the events, makes the events more relevant and personal.

Reviewed in: *From the River's Edge*: Booklist 6/1/91; Publishers Weekly 5/17/91; Library Journal 5/15/91; Kirkus Reviews 5/1/91. *Aurelia*: wicazo sa review; a journal of native American studies 5/2/00.

73. Cramer, Roberta. *Mission to Sonora.* Sun Lakes, AZ: Book World. 1998. 297 p.

Time: Contemporary
Tribe: Tohono O'odham
Place: Arizona

Linda Bluenight's Cherokee ancestors left her her name and appearance, but Linda, a former police forensic anthropologist, is only remotely connected with her Cherokee heritage. Happily teaching school on the Tohono O'odham reservation and raising her teenage son Matty, Linda's serene world is shattered when Matty stumbles over the body of Benton Brody, a local real estate developer. The police quickly seize Ramon Morena as the killer, but after Linda is called in to help analyze the remains, she doesn't believe Ramon guilty. When Ramon is found dead in his jail cell as an apparent suicide, Linda knows she must use the skills from the world she thought she had left behind to solve this case. Many people wanted Brody dead, especially those who saw his real estate developments as rape of the land. Linda and Matty are subjected to increasingly violent threats until Linda almost loses her life in exposing the killer. The real hero of this novel is the Sonora Desert and Cramer's love for and knowledge of it shine through every page. Matty is a rather too-perfect teenager, but the mystery is good enough to keep the reader guessing.

74. Croswell, Lorraine. *White Wing, Princess of the Columbia Gorge.* Camas, WA: Columbia Litho. 1997. 145 p.

Time: 1835–1840's
Tribe: Cascade
Place: Oregon, Washington

The Hudson's Bay Company established trade at Fort Vancouver, with Dr. McLoughlin in charge during the mid-1800's. Richard Ough is a Royal Navy seaman working there when he meets White Wing (*Huchney*) a young daughter of Cascade Chief Schly-housh. Richard falls in love and finally is allowed to marry *Hucheny,* whom he calls Betsy. They live at the Fort but he is soon recalled to England. Betsy waits for several years for him to return, living with Dr. McLoughlin, learning his medicinal skills and how to read, cook and sew. She meets many historical persons, including naturalist Thomas Nuttall, Narcissa Whitman, Eliza Spaulding and preachers sent out by the Church of England. Finally Richard returns, they resume married life, and settle along the Columbia River, legally marrying and filing claims on property. A very simply told but true story of a Cascade woman who married one of the early English settlers of the Oregon Territory, there are many details of native life and customs of the times. Descendents of Richard and Betsy still live in the area today.

75. Crummey, Michael. *River Thieves.* Boston: Houghton Mifflin. 2002. 335 p.

Time: 1810–1820
Tribe: Beothuk
Place: Newfoundland

While Assiniwi's *The Beothuk Saga* is a strict historical account of the Beothuk in the 1700's and 1800's, this novel is a deeply moving, beautifully written, sympathetic account of the last of the tribe. The principal characters are the Peytons, John Senior and Junior, their housekeeper Cassie Jure, "Mary" the captured Beothuk woman, and the British Naval officer, David Buchan. The true history of the Peytons' interaction with the Beothuk is revealed slowly in stories told throughout the novel. It is a matter of historical record that a John Peyton Sr. did massacre a camp of Beothuk in 1781. Buchan wants to make peaceful contact with the Beothuk, but they have been too scarred by their treatment at the hands of the British invaders to trust anyone. The Buchan peaceful expedition up the Exploits River in 1811 ends in tragedy. While John Senior hates the Beothuk and only wishes to punish them for their thievery, his son is more sympathetic and willing to work with Buchan to make peaceful contact. John Peyton, the son, loves Cassie but believes she is committed to his irascible father. Cassie is her own person and committed to no one. Buchan is well-meaning, but ultimately exploits Cassie and the Beothuk woman the men are able to capture. "Mary" as the Beothuk is called, tells Buchan that her husband and brother were killed by the Peytons when she was captured. Buchan attempts to apply British justice to the case but lacks the courage to expose his own sins to do so. Mary sickens and dies of tuberculosis before she can be returned to her tribe. Buchan leads a party back to the site of the murders and her capture and buries the family together. A sad story of angry, misunderstood and misunderstanding characters, the text is so brilliantly written that one never wants it to end. The author is a poet and his literary style reflects that attention to detail in perfect word selection. If this novel and *The Beothuk Saga* are read in conjunction, the Beothuk people and history will come alive. A contender for the Canadian Giller Prize, this is an excellent book.

Reviewed in: Booklist 5/1/02; Library Journal 3/15/02; Kirkus Reviews 4/15/02; Publishers Weekly 5/27/02.

76. Davis, Kathryn Lynn. *Sing to Me of Dreams.* NY: Pocket Books. 1990. 549 p.

Time: 1860's–1880's
Tribe: Salish
Place: Vancouver Island, British Columbia

From the moment of her birth, Tanu was different. Daughter of a Salish mother and a French explorer, Tanu had the ability to put herself in others' dreams to heal both their physical and mental ailments. Tanu became She Who Is Blessed, the Queen of her tribe. She saw her best friend married but knew that even though she and Colchote' had strong feelings for each other, they could never marry, for the husband of a Queen would always be less than she was. When the Scarlet Sickness came, Tanu could not heal her people. Many died and they no longer believed in her powers. She was no longer She Who Is Blessed. Leaving her people, Tanu, now called Saylah, spent three years in a missionary school and was then sent to work on the Ivy Ranch. She knew immediately she had been sent to help Jamie Ivy, the father whose first wife, Simone, had left him. Jamie was distancing himself from his older son Julian, his second wife Flora and their son Theron. Jamie was also estranged from his best friend Edward Ashton and spent his days in a darkened room in a darkened house, waiting to die from a heart ailment. While Saylah cannot cure Jamie, she can bring help and comfort to the others. Gradually the stories of all these people merge into one of anger, naïve trust, betrayal and love. When she realizes her future lies with Julian and the White Strangers, Saylah makes one last pilgrimage to her people and sees that they have endured after the deaths of so many. Although Saylah is Salish and the first part of the novel is set among those people and their legends and customs, the second part of the novel, while intriguing, is less Native American. The character of Saylah could be any newly arrived "hired girl" who helps a family through troubled times.

Reviewed in: Library Journal 9/15/90; Publishers Weekly 9/28/90.

77. DeMoss, Robert W. *Exodus to Glory.* Tulsa, OK: Handi-Printing. 1991. 252 p.

Time: 1861
Tribe: Creek
Place: Arkansas, Oklahoma, Kansas

When the Civil War broke out, the Native American people of the southern and border states had to decide whether to join the Union or the Confederacy. The Cherokee supported the Confederacy under Stand Watie and John Ross, their principal leaders. The Creeks also owned slaves and could have supported the South. However, a large band of Creeks led by Opothle Yahola decided to flee the Indian Territory and go north to Kansas to support the Union. Chased by Colonel Cooper and his loyal Choctaws, the Creeks suffered terrible hardships in the winter of 1861 on their exodus to the North. This self-published novel is poorly written but historically accurate. While not a great literary work, it does provide details on an important incident in the history of the Creek Nation. Maps of the trek and battles with Cooper and Colonel MacIntosh are also included. The Creeks succeed in fleeing north with their goods and families, but Yahola, an elderly man, does not survive the experience.

78. Doane, Michael. *Bullet Heart.* NY: Knopf. 1994. 316 p.

Time: 1970's–1990's
Tribe: Sioux
Place: South Dakota

During the construction of a golf course, human remains are found, triggering the "Bones War." The bones of the White settlers are reinterred but those of a young Sioux girl are shipped to the state capital as "artifacts." Though the Sioux try to have her bones returned to them, the White politicians refuse. In the only option left, the bones are stolen, returned to Choteau and reburied with the proper ceremony. The FBI arrives and the White town of Wilma and the Red town of Choteau are fractured: Red against White, traditional against progressive, generation against generation. Told in alternating voices, Doane's powerful novel portrays the the tragedy of the past and the little hope for the future. While one understands his characters and their various motives, none of them are truly likeable. The American Indian Movement of the 1970's is an important part of Native American history and while this novel is perhaps brutally honest, the story of these times can still be told by a more compelling work.

Reviewed in: Library Journal 6/1/94; Booklist 6/1/94; Publishers Weekly 5/16/94; Kirkus Reviews 4/15/94.

79. Doss, James D. *The Shaman Sings.* NY: St. Martin's. 1994. 230 p.

Reviewed in: Armchair Detective Fall/94; Library Journal 2/1/94; NYTBR 3/20/94; Publishers Weekly 12/23/93.

The Shaman Laughs. NY: St. Martin's. 1995. 274 p.

Reviewed in: NYTBR 12/24/95; Publishers Weekly 10/23/95; Kirkus Reviews 10/15/95.

The Shaman's Bones. NY: Avon. 1997. 276 p.

Reviewed in: Library Journal 8/1/98; Booklist 8/1/98; Publishers Weekly 6/29/98.

The Shaman's Game. NY: Avon. 1998. 370 p.

Reviewed in: Library Journal 8/1/98; Booklist 8/1/98; Publishers Weekly 6/29/98; Kirkus Reviews 9/1/98.

The Night Visitor. NY: Avon. 1999. 392 p.

Reviewed in: Library Journal 9/1/99; Publishers Weekly 8/2/99; Booklist 8/1/99; NYTBR 10/3/99.

Grandmother Spider: A Charlie Moon Mystery. NY: William Morrow. 2001. 293 p.

Reviewed in: Booklist 1/15/01; Publishers Weekly 11/27/00; Mystery Review Winter/01.

White Shell Woman. A Charlie Moon Mystery. NY: HarperCollins. 2002. 293 p.

Reviewed in: Library Journal 1/1/02; Booklist 1/1/02; Publishers Weekly 12/3/01; Kirkus Reviews 11/15/01.

Time: Contemporary
Tribe: Ute and Navajo
Place: Southwest Colorado

The three main characters that appear in this mystery series are Daisy Perika, an ancient shaman who works with a *pitukupf*, a magical dwarf only she can see; her nephew Charlie Moon, a deputy sheriff who is a realist and does not believe in the old Ute ways; and his friend Chief of Police Scott Parris, who has a sense of mystical belief from his Celtic background. Often it is Parris and Daisy who communicate best with their belief in the supernatural, baffling the practical Charlie Moon. Each of the mysteries in the series builds on events from prior titles, carrying some characters, such as Sarah Frank, a Ute-Papago orphan girl that Daisy adopts and teaches, over to the next book. Charlie's career suffers setbacks due to tribal politics and he eventually leaves the police force to work his ranch, although still becoming involved in various investigations. Most events take place on or near the Ute Reservation in southwestern Colorado, with Doss creating a sense of place that transports the reader to this dry but beautiful land. Each mystery involves the supernatural, witches, potions and symbols, and myths from the Navajo and Ute cultures. The myth of Grandmother Spider, the Twin Monster Slayers, sons of White Shell Woman, the Moon who married the Sun, and others appear in the novels in detail. The Ute culture, its shamanistic background and its contemporary version, is thoroughly explored. Characters are believable and bad things can, and do, happen to very good people. Daisy is an irascible, stubborn old woman with a heart of gold. Her nephew Charlie is kind-hearted and long-suffering, caring deeply for his ancient aunt. The magic dwarf is a clever fellow and assists Daisy in unraveling many a mysterious event. Doss always leaves the reader with two possible versions of the outcome; one solved by the mystical shamanistic powers of Daisy, the other by the concrete evidence collected by the police. Oddly enough, both parties usually seem capable of responsibility for the crimes' solutions. This is an excellent mystery series, with well-drawn characters and complex plots. Few novels feature the Ute culture, therefore this mystery series is a great addition to the literature.

80. Dreamwalker, Richard. *Four Winds Returning.* Rapid City, SD: Sky & Sage Books. 1991. 204 p.

Time: 1990
Tribe: Sioux
Place: South Dakota

Mark Stanford, a White college graduate, environmentalist, pacifist, vegetarian and non-smoker, comes to the Pine Ridge reservation to learn the Native American ways of living with the land. A child of the 1960's, now his marriage has failed, his son is with his ex-wife, and Mark is looking for a purpose in life. He meets Ben and Jim Kills, brothers with very different views of life, in Water. Ben has been in the drug scene of Los Angeles and has returned to raise horses and live with the way of the Sacred Pipe. Jim has been a marine in Vietnam and is plagued with memories that make him a violent drunk. Their sister, Tela, has divorced her husband and is raising two small children alone. Mark and Tela are attracted to each other, which infuriates Jim. Jim and Mark are constantly battling with each other, sometimes to serious physical levels. Over the summer Mark helps Ben build a horse barn, goes through several sweat lodge ceremonies, helps out the people on the reservation, and finally finds his inner self. He also finds love with Tela and asks her to marry him. Jim finally goes on a vision quest and lays his Vietnamese ghosts to rest. They reconcile at the Fall Pow Wow. While this slim novel is probably self-published, and the author's name is perhaps a pseudonym, there are some honest truths in the text, and it is very believable in its simplicity. While there are many clichés in the White hippy looking for Native American spirituality to give life meaning, the terrible economic life of the Sioux on Pine Ridge is also shown to have a good side in the tight family structures and the sincere belief in a true and simple religion that honors the land. The novel reads as autobiographical and honest. At least Mark does not go through a vision quest to find himself, instead he does it through personal relationships.

81. Eagle, Kathleen. *Defender.* NY: Silhouette. 1994. 275 p.

Time: Contemporary
Tribe: Chippewa
Place: Minnesota

In the fifteen years since Gideon Defender first met Raina, he has grown up, gone through detox, and become tribal leader of the Pine Lake Band of Chippewa. Gideon has never lost his love for Raina, even though she married his brother Jared and they adopted a Chippewa baby, Peter. After Jared's death, Raina and Peter come to Pine Lake to expose Peter to the Chippewa culture, but his maternal grandfather, Arlen, petitions for custody under the Indian Child Adoption Act. Raina is willing to let Arlen into Peter's life, but she is not willing to relinquish her son. Knowing that only his biological father would have a better claim to the boy, Gideon tells the secret he has hidden for so long. The Pine Lake Band is also fighting for the fishing rights promised to them in numerous treaties which include the right to fish by their traditional means without regard to the white man's laws. Anger mounts on both sides and Gideon must try to strike a compromise while still trying to be a father to Peter. He also must convince Raina that while he loved her before, he was not ready for marriage and to demonstrate that he now is. One can see Eagle's development in the writing of this romance.

82. Eagle, Kathleen. *Diamond Willow.* NY: Silhouette. 1993. 250 p.

Time: Contemporary
Tribe: Sioux
Place: North Dakota

John Tiger is merely fighting for what is his when he barricades his land from those who would use it as access to the lake. They cut fences, leave trash, and let his cattle out. When old flame Teri Nordstrom returns to do a fashion shoot, John calls on her to help him get to Bismark to visit his mother in the hospital. John and Teri had been a couple eight years ago. Teri got pregnant and John joined the Army, and neither told the other. Since they certainly weren't ready for parenthood, Teri gave their daughter, Rachel, up for adoption to John's wrestling coach and his wife and went on to pursue her modeling career. When John learns of Rachel's existence, he starts to petition the court to have her returned to him under the Indian Child Adoption Act, but realizes she is best left where she is and that she can get to know his side of her heritage in other ways. While there are the Native American themes of child adoption and Indian land rights, the bulk of this book is merely a simple romance.

83. Eagle, Kathleen. *Reason to Believe.* NY: Avon. 1995. 375 p.

Time: Contemporary
Tribe: Sioux
Place: North and South Dakota

Although not divorced, Clara Pipestone certainly feels her marriage is over. Ben's drinking was bad enough, but when he was unfaithful to her, Clara kicked him out. Their teenager daughter Anna is in trouble, shoplifting and drinking, and Clara reluctantly allows Ben back in their lives. He has been sober for two years, but Clara will never trust him again. Ben's father Dewey is the current Keeper of the Pipe and wants Ben to take his place, but Ben doesn't believe he can be a spiritual leader for his people as he can hardly get through each day. Dewey wants Ben to participate in the Big Foot Memorial Ride held each December to commemorate Sitting Bull's death, the travels of Big Foot's band through the winter snows, and the Massacre at Wounded Knee. Anna is the only one who wants to go and as a means of keeping her out of trouble, the parents agree to accompany her on the two-week ride through the December cold. Clara and Ben both learn a great deal about each other, about what forgiveness and trust mean, and how being human means not being perfect. Although this is a rather simplistic story in that Anna quickly becomes a loving teenager with none of her earlier rebellion, the relationship between Clara and Ben is well portrayed and the history of the 1890 ride contrasted with the present day provides a solid background. The reader will painlessly learn some Sioux history and culture in this romance.

84. Eagle, Kathleen. *Sunrise Song.* NY: Avon. 1996. 366 p.

Time: 1930's and 1970's
Tribe: Sioux
Place: South Dakota

In the early part of the twentieth century, the Hiawatha Asylum for Insane Indians operated in Canton, South Dakota. The town's economy was heavily dependent upon it and its purpose was to attempt to "Americanize" the Indians: those who practiced the old ways were considered mentally ill and incarcerated. In 1930 nurse Rachel Trainor, whose brother is the Indian agent, begins work at the hospital. Among her patients is Martin Lone Bull, a young boy who has been diagnosed with tuberculosis but who shows no symptoms and who is not being treated for the disease. His brother Adam whom Rachel had met before she began work has been admitted for alcohol abuse. Rachel finds him chained to a bed in the cellar. In the 1970's Michelle Benedict inherits a house in Canton from her Aunt Cora, the wife of Dr. Tim, former head of the hospital. The hospital buildings have been torn down, but the Indian cemetery is still there and the house is full of records. Michelle starts to track down some of the relatives of the Indian patients and finds Zane Lone Bull. His brother Randy had been Michelle's contact, but Randy has been murdered—is there a connection between Randy's search for old land records and those of the Indian hospital? Eagle has woven two romances and a long-buried Indian policy into a fascinating story of betrayal, evil and redemption.

Reviewed in: Library Journal 2/15/96.

85. Eagle, Kathleen. *This Time Forever.* NY: Avon. 1992. 392 p.

Time: Contemporary
Tribe: Sioux
Place: North Dakota

Nurse Susan Ellison tries to do her best on the jury that is hearing the case of Cleve Black Horse, accused of murdering the man who picked him up after his truck broke down. Because he is Indian and assumed to have been drinking, the rest of the jury votes for "guilty" and Susan cannot stand up against them. Cleve is convicted and sent to prison. Shortly after his conviction, a Sioux woman, Darcy, is killed in a traffic accident and while her baby, Sam, survives, he is not expected to live or be normal. Susan finds herself spending more and more time with Sam and wants to adopt him. Darcy's sister Vera has too many children of her own and is more than willing to let Sam stay with Susan, but the judge feels Indian children should not be adopted by Whites. Before she was killed Darcy had told Vera the father of her child is Cleve Black Horse. Hoping that Cleve will acknowledge his connection to Sam, Susan starts visiting him in prison and they establish a relationship. When Cleve is released due to the actions of his new lawyer, he does claim Sam. However, Cleve thinks that Susan wants only Sam and not him. Susan has promised herself no more live-in boyfriends. Once the two of them acknowledge that marriage and Sam are what they both want, they can go on with their lives. This romance is an excellent portrayal of contemporary Indian life and the problems still encountered with prejudice.

86. Eagle, Kathleen. *What the Heart Knows.* NY: Avon. 1999. 375 p.

Time: Contemporary
Tribe: Sioux
Place: South Dakota

Helen Ketterling welcomed the chance to return to South Dakota as an undercover investigator for the BIA. As a blackjack dealer, her job was to report on any scams and irregularities in the casino operations, but she also hoped to meet up with Reese Blue Sky again. She hadn't seen Reese in twelve years, ever since he left to pursue a professional basketball career leaving her to raise the son he didn't know he had fathered. Helen and Reese found it easy to rekindle their love, but mysterious things are occurring around the gambling operation, including the hit and run death of Reese's father, Roy Blue Sky. He had suspected Ten Star, the corporation which managed the casino for the Bad River Tribe, was not returning the profits to the tribe. Reese assumed Roy's place on the tribal council and voiced the same concerns over the strong objections of his brother Carter, Indian manager of the casino for Ten Star. Complicating the situation is the arrival of Sidney, Helen's son, who had believed his father to be dead. Eagle has woven a contemporary romance with the unusual themes of the Indian Gaming Regulatory Act and the Indian Child Protection Act and has portrayed some of the issues concerning Native Americans today.

Reviewed in: Library Journal 8/1/99; Booklist 7/1/99; Publishers Weekly 5/31/99.

87. Eagle, Kathleen. *You Never Can Tell.* NY: HarperCollins. 2001. 306 p.

Time: Contemporary
Tribe: Sioux
Place: Minnesota and Western U.S.

Journalist Heather Reardon tracks down Kole Crow Killer to his remote Minnesota cabin where he's been hiding since he escaped from prison for a murder he didn't commit (think Leonard Pelletier). Heather wants to tell his story to the world, along with the current situation of American Indians and how they are portrayed in the media. Kole does not want to risk being recaptured, but soon his relationship with Heather is more than that of journalist and subject and they find themselves on an odyssey to Hollywood where their cause gathers in others and where the publicity will be greatest. Betrayal by Kole's old friend Barry Wilson who has sold out is also part of the plot of this novel, but it is badly overwritten and the characters are flat. The reader doesn't really care about Kole or Heather, let alone the cause they stand for. Eagle's previous romances are much better.

Reviewed in: Library Journal 5/15/01; Publishers Weekly 7/30/01; Booklist 7/01.

88. Earling, Debra Magpie. (Salish/Kootenai). *Perma Red.* NY: BlueHen Books. 2002. 288 p.

Time: 1940's
Tribe: Salish
Place: Montana

This brilliant first novel is set on the Flathead Indian Reservation near the towns of Dixon and Perma. St. Ignatius Mission, run by the Ursuline nuns, is a major influence on the lives of the young people, including Louise White Elk and Baptiste Yellow Knife. Louise is beautiful and wild and Baptiste loves her. Baptiste refuses to give in to the nuns, keeping the old ways and language. When Louise becomes a woman, she finds her power over men, hanging out in the bars and dancing with the handsome cowboy, Jules Bart, and wealthy real estate agent, Harvey Stoner. Charlie Kicking Woman is the tribal policeman, in love with Louise, trying to hide the fact from his wife, but lured by Louise's beauty into protecting her whenever he can. Baptiste finally casts his love medicine over Louise and she marries him, only to have the marriage run into problems within weeks. Baptiste's rebellion and constant drunkenness have angered everyone from the nuns to Charlie. When Baptiste beats up Louise in a drunken rage and then disappears, no one cares. But Baptiste cannot stay away from Louise and she cannot forget him. He returns and is nearly killed by Stoner and Bart, with the silent complicity of Charlie. Believing they have killed Baptiste, Stoner and Bart decide Louise must be murdered to keep her quiet. A terrible auto accident intervenes. Baptiste finally comes to his senses, stops drinking, and comes back for Louise. Beautifully written with characters full of pain and conflict, the language of the novel is on a par with much more published authors, reminiscent of Erdrich or Treuer, and we look forward to more from Earling. This novel was listed as one of the Top 10 First Novels of 2002 by Booklist, 11/15/02.

Reviewed in: Booklist 6/1/02, 6/15/02; Library Journal 5/1/02; Publishers Weekly 5/20/02.

89. Edson, J. T. *Texas Warrior*. Originally: *Is-A-Man.* NY: Dell. 1985. 230 p.

Time: 1860's–1870's
Tribe: Comanche
Place: Texas

Two stories in one, the first half of the book concerns Becky Ingraham, a Lady Wrestler in Texas, captured by the Comanche, and wife of Singing Bear. The second half of the western is about their daughter, Annie Singing Bear, who grows up determined to be a warrior. Called Should Be A Boy, the young woman proves her abilities as a hunter and as a fighter. Finally she exacts revenge on a band of Mexicans who raped and killed a young Comanche girl, earning her right to be called a *Tehnap*, a seasoned and fully trained warrior. Edson knows a great deal of Comanche words and customs, and the second half of the book is instructional, but overall this is a very poor quality western.

90. Egawa, Keith. (Lummi). *Madchild Running.* Santa Fe, NM: Red Crane Books. 1999. 222 p.

Time: Contemporary
Tribe: Lummi, Klallam, Flathead, Suquamish
Place: Washington State

Levi Shea has recently graduated from college and now works for the Urban Native Support Services in Seattle as a social worker. Levi has many issues from his own childhood he has never confronted, preferring to hide them under alcohol and drug abuse. Raised in an abusive household and abandoned by his father as a little boy, Levi has buried memories so deeply they only come late at night as flashbacks in dreams. Nicki is a twelve-year-old Suquamish girl with similar issues of abuse and abandonment, who also resorts to drugs and alcohol. The Urban Native Support Services have been assigned her case and Levi tries to help her, but his own problems constantly get in the way. As Nicki says, Levi has his own "Indian name" and that is Madchild Running, since he consistently flees from his own problems. When Nicki takes a drastic way out of her difficult life, Levi faces his own past. He returns to his great aunt on the Lummi Reservation and learns the old songs to sing his way back and heal himself. This novel is a realistic depiction of urban life for many Native Americans, dealing with unemployment, substance abuse, and difficult home situations. Levi's failure to help his clients because he has never helped himself is very realistically portrayed, not overly sympathetically.

Reviewed in: Library Journal 10/15/99; Publishers Weekly 9/27/99.

91. Ellington, Charlotte Jane. *Beloved Mother; the Story of Nancy Ward.* Johnson City, TN: Overmountain Press. 1994. 187 p.

Time: 1738–1822
Tribe: Cherokee
Place: Tennessee

This fictionalized biography of Nancy Ward is told through the eyes of her adopted daughter Dancing Leaf and tells of Ward's birth, childhood, marriages, and becoming an honored and respected Cherokee leader. Always her goal was peace, but in attempting to avoid war, the Cherokees sacrificed much of their land and, in trying to adopt the ways of the White man, left themselves vulnerable to exploitation and eventually to the terrible tragedy that was the Trail of Tears. There are few novels written about Nancy Ward so this is a welcome addition; however, it is very slight and the characters are flat. It will tell the reader the pertinent facts of Ward's life, but it does not get inside her and show the reader her motives, her thoughts and feelings. The definitive novel on this subject is yet to be written.

Reviewed in: Publishers Weekly 6/27/94.

92. Erdrich, Louise. (Chippewa). *The Antelope Wife.* NY: HarperCollins. 1998. 240 p.

Time: 1870 and Contemporary
Tribe: Ojibwe
Place: Minnesota

The novel takes place in two different time periods. The first is just after the Civil War when a troop of soldiers attack a band of Ojibwe and Trooper Scranton Roy deserts his company to rescue an infant tied to the back of a dog. Roy raises the girl, naming her Matilda. Later Blue Prairie Woman tracks Roy down and takes her little daughter back. When Blue Prairie Woman dies of fever, a herd of antelope find and save Matilda, raising her with along with their own. Generations later, Klaus Shawano sees an enchanting brown haired, brown eyed, brown skinned woman with her equally lovely daughters, drifting and floating through a powwow in Montana, and kidnaps her. Calling her Sweetheart Calico, he takes her back to live with him in Minnesota. Sweetheart Calico does not speak and others find her very mysterious, almost deer-like. The story centers now on Rozin Whiteheart Bead, her love for Klaus's brother Frank, her daughters Deanna and Callie, and her grandmothers, the sisters Zosie Shawano and Mary Roy, both of whom lived with and loved the same man, Augustus Roy, grandson of Scranton. The family connections are thoroughly interwoven, and as events occur, become even more so. Marriages fall apart, people turn to drink or love, new marriages happen, people die, and finally Sweetheart Calico speaks out and runs away, loping easily across the prairies back to her family of . . . perhaps antelope. This is a truly mesmerizing and intriguing novel, it has one asking questions and trying to untangle the networks that tie all the characters together. In the end it is clear that the lives of contemporary people are the result of actions taken by their relatives years ago.

Reviewed in: Boston Book Review 5/1/98; Booklist 3/1/98; Publishers Weekly 2/9/98; Kirkus Reviews 2/1/98; Library Journal 12/2/97.

93. Erdrich, Louise. (Chippewa). *The Last Report on the Miracles at Little No Horse.* NY: HarperCollins. 2001. 361 p.

Time: 1912–1996
Tribe: Ojibwe
Place: North Dakota

In 1966 Father Jude is sent by the Vatican to investigate the saintliness of Sister Leopolda, a nun raised on the Little No Horse reservation. He interviews Father Damien Modeste, a very old priest who arrived on the reservation eighty years ago. Father Damien recalls his life in flashbacks that start with his origins of being Agnes DeWitt, a very musical girl who enters the nunnery as Sister Cecilia, but ends up leaving and marrying a farmer, Berndt. This very complex story of Agnes, who becomes a priest when her husband dies and the real Father Damien is drowned in a flood, is full of characters from earlier Erdrich novels, especially *Tracks* (1988), centered on several Ojibwe families in North Dakota. Here are Nanapush and the Kashpaws, the Pillagers, the Lamartines and the Morrisseys, with complete family genealogies. Old Nanapush and Kashpaw are Father Damien's first friends at Little No Horse when he arrives. They help him become accepted by the *Anishinabeg*, the Spontaneous or Original People, and help him learn their language. They know he is a "man-acting woman" but keep it to themselves. When Agnes/Damien falls in love with a visiting priest, Gregory, and then sends him away, Nanapush restores Damien's will to live in a sweat lodge ceremony. Kashpaw's daughter Mary moves to the rectory to care for Agnes/Damien, also keeping the secret of his true nature. Sister Leopolda was a wicked and cruel woman, half Polish and part Ojibwe, who bears a child out of wedlock and abuses her (the Marie of *Love Medicine* [1984]).Father Jude finally discovers the true saint at

Little No Horse and after Father Damien's death, moves there to continue his research into the saintliness of Agnes/Damien. This novel is absolutely wonderful, with rich and complex characters, many Ojibwe stories, elaborate family histories, and the deeply troubled but religious Father Damien, devoted to helping his flock at Little No Horse.

Reviewed in: Library Journal 5/1/01; Publishers Weekly 7/2/01; Booklist 2/15/01; Kirkus Reviews 2/1/01; Christian Century 9/26/01; Virginia Quarterly Review 10/01/01; Multicultural Review 12/01.

For further criticism and interpretation of Erdrich's works, see: Chavkin, Allan. *The Chippewa Landscape of Louise Erdrich.* Tuscaloosa: University of Alabama Press. 1999; Jacobs, Connie A. *The Novels of Louise Erdrich: Stories of Her People.* NY: Peter Lang. 2001; Stookey, Lorena Laura. *Louise Erdrich: A Critical Companion.* Westport CT: Greennwood Press. 1999.

94. Evans, Max. *Bluefeather Fellini in the Sacred Realm.* Niwot: University Press of Colorado. 1994. 367 p.

Time: late 1950's
Tribe: Taos
Place: New Mexico

Home from World War II, geologist and miner Bluefeather Fellini is hired by wealthy Korbel to locate cases of Mouton Rothschild 1880 wines, buried somewhere in a cave or mine by another wealthy man, Tilton. With the help of his spirit guide, Dancing Bear, Bluefeather locates Dolby, a partner of Tilton's who might have some information on hiding places. Tilton also buried millions of dollars of gold bullion during the War. Marsha Korbel, an adopted daughter, is along to help or spy on Bluefeather. Dolby's assistant, Sherry, is an anthropologist, and she and Dolby let Bluefeather and Marsha in on a discovery. They have found a Cave of Marvels beneath the mountains which holds mysteries, rich minerals, strange creatures, monsters, and the gold bullion along with Tilton's severed head. Most of the novel concerns Bluefeather working his way through the dangers of the caves, seeing their wonders, and realizing everyone is double crossing him. Reminiscent of a Jules Verne novel, more science fiction than anything else, Bluefeather still remains a strong and sympathetic character, determined to do what is right. Korbel and Dolby come to their justified ends and Bluefeather gets at least some of the gold. The cave is sealed forever to protect the life forms within. The story ends with Bluefeather, now an old man, setting out to lie down in the desert and die. But once again fate intervenes; it is too noisy to die with jet airplanes and highway noises intruding on his solitary death, so Bluefeather gets up and goes home again.

Reviewed in: Publishers Weekly 8/15/94; Kirkus Reviews 7/1/94.

95. Fergus, Jim. *One Thousand White Women: The Journals of May Dodd.* NY: St. Martin's. 1998. 302 p.

Time: 1875–1876
Tribe: Cheyenne
Place: Western United States

Fact: In 1854 a Cheyenne chief proposed that one thousand White women be given to the Cheyenne. Since theirs was a matrilineal society, all children born would belong to their mothers' people and would therefore be a bridge between the white and Indian societies. This request was refused, but Fergus has taken it and fashioned a novel—what if the request had been granted? In 1875 the U.S. government is looking for women to become brides of the Cheyenne. They come from all walks of life, women from prisons and insane asylums, immigrants who haven't found the promised land, impoverished women jilted by their suitors, women for whom living among the "savages" is preferable to what they currently have. May Dodd was committed to an insane asylum by her wealthy Chicago family because she had two children out of wedlock by a man who was her social inferior. May is intelligent and outspoken, she is willing to take part in this "experiment" because it will release her from imprisonment and because she feels it her duty to help the Cheyenne learn the ways of the Whites. Mostly what they learn is the treachery of the White man's word, the duplicity of his religion, and the general unsavoriness of "civilization." May becomes friends with Capt. John Bourke and goes to her Cheyenne groom, the Sweet Medicine Chief Little Wolf, already pregnant with Bourke's child. Although she had persuaded Little Wolf's band to go to the reservation in the spring of 1876 once the snow would allow them to travel, the army does not wait; May and most of the village, including the newly-born children, are slaughtered in a Sand Creek-type massacre. May had kept voluminous journals which her heirs discover over one hundred years later. Although a fanciful novel, the depiction of the differences between the White and Cheyenne societies is very clear.

Reviewed in: Booklist 3/1/98.

96. Gangi, Rayna M. *Keepers of the Western Door.* Boston: Maple Street Press. 1992. 154 p.

Time: 1700's
Tribe: Seneca
Place: Western New York

This novel tells the story of Mary Jemison who was captured by the Seneca, adopted into their tribe, and who lived out her life with them, rejecting opportunities to return to White society. Mary sees her family killed; her defeated father has given up, her mother urges Mary not to run, to remember her name and the English language. Mary is adopted by two sisters who teach her their language and way of life. She has two Seneca husbands and bears several children, but her sons cannot live in either culture and end up killing each other. Mary receives land as payment for her goodness, but much of it is taken from her by trickery. While Mary is undoubtedly a fascinating woman whose story deserves to be told, this is such a flimsy novel that the reader is given little sense of time, place, or of Mary herself. A much better novel dealing with a "captivity narrative" is James Thom's *Red Heart* and the story of Mary Jemison is told far better in Larsen's historical novel, *The White.*

97. Gear, Kathleen O'Neal, and W. Michael Gear. *The Anasazi Mysteries Book One. The Visitant.* NY: Tom Doherty. 1999. 364 p.

Time: 1250–1300 and Contemporary
Tribe: Pueblo, Ancestral Pueblo, Seneca
Place: New Mexico

Skillfully woven between two very different time periods, the story of multiple murders of young Anasazi women by a Wolf Katsina is later discovered by anthropologists and archaeologists working in Chaco Canyon. In the 1990's archaeologist Dusty Stewart finds skeletons with their heads smashed and a limestone slab over them to trap their evil spirits. Maureen Cole, a Seneca physical anthropologist, comes to Chaco Canyon to help identify their ages and possible causes of death. Maureen notices they have been repeatedly struck on the speech centers of their brains for some time before being killed and that many were ill. Action jumps back to 1250 A.D. when Browser loses his wife, Ash Girl, and several other neighboring villages also lose young women to some mysterious killer. Browser and his friend Catkin ask Stone Ghost, a powerful shaman, for help in discovering the murderer. The contemporary site is being overseen by Hail Walking Hawk, the representative from the Keres Pueblo monitoring the site for NAGPRA, the Native American Graves Protection and Repatriation Act. An old woman close to death, Hail feels the bodies underground calling for discovery. She conducts cleansing ceremonies when corpse powder and evil amulets are found in graves. Eventually Browser is shown the truth behind his wife's angry and odd behavior. The identity of the ancient murderer is discovered, but the man behind the murders escapes to kill again. The depiction of the ancestral Pueblo in their struggles to survive during a time of drought and tuberculosis is excellent and the contemporary descriptions of archaeological digs are right on the mark. Of course since the authors are archaeologists, they have the backgrounds to provide the authentic details and history for this gripping mystery.

Reviewed in: Library Journal 8/1/99; Publishers Weekly 7/5/99; Booklist 7/1/99.

98. Gear, Kathleen O'Neal, and W. Michael Gear. *The Anasazi Mysteries Book Two. The Summoning God.* NY: Tom Doherty. 2000. 366 p.

Time: 1250–1300 and Contemporary
Tribe: Pueblo, Ancestral Pueblo, Seneca
Place: Four Corners (Colorado, New Mexico, Arizona, Utah)

In this continuation of the Anasazi mysteries, the tribe has moved to the Pueblo Animas, fleeing Two Hearts, the evil Wolf Katsina. Matron Flame Carrier leads them in their new religion, the Katsina People, who are pursued and massacred by the Flute Player Believers. Using the weaving of ancient ruins and skeletons being unearthed by contemporary archaeologists Stewart and Cole, history is written and given real context to assist in understanding the forces which eventually wiped out the Ancestral Pueblo peoples. Here the conflict between the Ancestral Puebloans is between what they believe are First People, arisen from an underworld, and Made People, created on this world from animals. A small core of First People still exist and are killing all who suspect their existence. The other conflict between Cole and Stewart is resolved as they realize and admit their attraction for one another. Well written and full of accurate historical details, this second mystery is as complex and gripping as the first. Two Hearts lives on and will no doubt continue to harass this beleaguered band of Anasazi.

Reviewed in: Publishers Weekly 6/26/00; Booklist 6/15/00.

99. Gear, Kathleen O'Neal, and W. Michael Gear. *The Anasazi Mysteries Book Three. Bone Walker.* NY: Tom Doherty. 2001. 445 p.

Time: 1300's and Contemporary
Tribe: Pueblo and Anasazi
Place: New Mexico

In the third of the Anasazi mysteries, the conflict between the First People and the Made People continues, as do the intense battles between the followers of the Flute Player and the believers in Katsinas. The evil Two Hearts still lives, with his twin daughters Shadow and Obsidian and granddaughter, Piper. Piper is found wandering by the wise, kind Stone Ghost, who gains her trust and calls her Bone Walker. With warriors Catkin and Browser they track down the kiva where Two Hearts is hiding and kill the evilness there. Centuries later archaeologists Ruth Stewart and Rupert Brown Horse open the kiva and release the evil. Dusty Stewart's mother Ruth and her colleague become infected with the evil of Shadow and Two Hearts. Decades later when their various children are grown and Rupert is dying of cancer, Rupert lures them all back to Chaco Canyon and begins exacting revenge. Dale Robertson, Stewart's father, mentor, and former rival with Rupert for Ruth's love, is killed first. Maureen Cole is there to help Stewart through the trauma, but it is Maggie Walking Hawk who listens to her dead aunt's mystical advice and finds a way to stop the reincarnation of Two Hearts in the form of Rupert. Many of the characters from the past have been introduced in the *People of the Silence* title from the First North Americans series by the Gears and it adds trememdously to have read that novel first. Another historically accurate, gripping mystery from the master Gears, both the contemporary story and the one set in the 1300's are excellent. Characters are fully developed, archaeological details are exact, and plots are very complex. The resolution of the mystery is complete and fulfilling.

Reviewed in: Publishers Weekly 12/3/01; Kirkus Reviews 11/15/01.

Gear, Kathleen O'Neal, and W. Michael Gear.
First North Americans Series. NY: Tom Doherty. 1991–1998. 400 p. to 608 p.

Time: 13,000 B.C. to 1300 A.D.
Tribes: Prehistoric undefined to Later Mississippian, Iroquoian, Anasazi.
Place: North America

The *People of the . . .* series of books by two experienced archaeologists are an excellent set of novels about the native peoples of North America. Many of the titles are set in remote prehistoric times and are outside the scope of this collection because the cultures depicted do not have a direct link to more contemporary tribes or Native American traditions. However, later volumes in the series do begin to reflect the more familiar cultures of the Mississippian Mound Builders, the Iroquoian and Algonquin Nations, and the Anasazi Chaco Canyon cliff dwellers. These will be reviewed below and are arranged in alphabetical order by title rather than as numbered in the series since characters and events are not related from book to book. All do share some common plot and character themes. Frequently there is a wise old shaman teaching a prepubescent youth the mysteries of their culture's religion. The powerful leaders of these often dying cultures are usually insane, but are followed in blind loyalty by their warriors. Strong women dominate most of the novels, often moving on to other places and ways of living to rescue the starving people. Most of the post-1000 A.D. titles do involve cultures in trouble due to famine or warfare. The novels from the series annotated below are all set in times after 1000 A.D. While the time period is pre-Columbian, they bear such close relationships to later Native American traditions and cultures as to be highly relevant to our current understanding of how these later tribal cultures and histories evolved. Each title in the series contains an extensive bibliography of sources for the content on the various different time periods and native cultures as well.

100. Gear, Kathleen O'Neal, and W. Michael Gear. *People of the Masks. First North Americans. Book 10.* NY: Tom Doherty. 1998. 414 p.

Time: 1000
Tribe: Iroquois Nation
Place: Upper New York State

Different bands within this related group of Native peoples have slightly different styles of living, raising or hunting for food, and worshiping. The Bear Nation lives in longhouses and are quite warlike. The Turtle Nation lives in conical lodges and tend to be more peaceful. Living in one of the Turtle villages is a young dwarf, Rumbler, who has special spiritual powers and is revered by both the Bear and Turtle people. Jumping Badger, a deranged war leader of the Bear, decides to kidnap Rumbler and bring his powers to their village. In the battle the Turtle war leader, Lamedeer, is killed, cursing Jumping Badger. The superstitious Jumping Badger carries Lamedeer's head around and talks to it, gradually becoming more and more insane. Little Wren, an orphan and friend of Rumbler, decides to save the dwarf. Her uncle Blue Raven also feels kindly towards the spiritual child. Little Wren and Blue Raven are determined to return Rumbler to his aunt and uncle, the shamans and healers Silver Sparrow and Dust Moon. Pursued by the evil Jumping Badger, the more intelligent Elk Ivory, a powerful warrior woman, and their Bear Nation warriors, most of the novel concerns this escape through the bitter winter of the northeast. Blue Raven had counseled a truce between the two nations to better work together against common enemies. This foretells the later Iroquois Nation of separate bands that formed centuries later. The culture of the Iroquoian people is carefully detailed, the characters are well defined, and the plot and action are excellent.

Reviewed in: Booklist 10/15/98; Library Journal 11/1/98; Publishers Weekly 11/2/98.

101. Gear, Kathleen O'Neal, and W. Michael Gear. *People of the Mist. First North Americans. Book 9.* NY: Tom Doherty. 1997. 432 p.

Time: 1300
Tribe: Algonquin Nation
Place: Chesapeake Bay, Delaware

In the villages around the Bay there is an intense power struggle between the small independent towns and Water Snake of the Mamanatowicks (Rappahannock) and Stone Frog of the Conoy people. Copper Thunder is a powerful man from the western Serpent People. Beautiful Red Knot is promised to Copper Thunder as wife to solidify the independent villages' power against Water Snake and Stone Frog. When Red Knot tries to run away with her lover High Fox, she is murdered. Believing High Fox is wrongly accused of murder, Sun Conch, who also loves him, goes to the old witch Panther, living on an island out in the bay, and asks for his help in identifying the murderer. The interrelationships between the villages, the personal histories of the individuals, and the past behaviors of some are all linked to the truth. Panther discovers the truth by examining the wounds and the possible weapons. He also learns of past events, adulteries, secret births and alliances that caused Red Knot's death. The authors include a great deal of detail about the funereal preparations of the Algonquin dead. Skinned, hides tanned, their bodies are stuffed with grass, then reassembled to live in the House of the Dead. The complex hierarchy of matrilineal inheritance and the struggle between the different village complexes is well documented. This is another excellent entry in the series on the native peoples in North America only a few hundred years before the arrival of Europeans.

Reviewed in: Library Journal 2/1/98; Booklist 2/1/98; Publishers Weekly 11/24/97.

102. Gear, Kathleen O'Neal, and W. Michael Gear. *People of the River. First North Americans. Book 4.* NY: Tom Doherty. 1992. 400 p.

Time: 1100–1300
Tribe: Mound Builders (Natchez)
Place: Illinois

The Mound Builders of Cahokia control trade along the major rivers and are sent harvest tribute by the other mound villages. When famine strikes the region, this tribute is resented by those who need the food themselves. The Sun Chief Tharon sends out his warleader Badgertail to attack and kill the resistors, even though many of these people are related to those in Cahokia. When Badgertail attacks River Mound he makes a serious enemy in Petaga, who then forms alliances with other towns to fight back. Twenty years ago, Badgertail had kidnapped Nightshade, a powerful Dreamer, from Talon Town, one of the southwestern pueblos. She is now the Priestess of Cahokia, determined to find out why First Woman has turned her back on the people, refusing to send rain. When a terrible case of incest is discovered and ended, the rains begin again. Petago defeats Cahokia and becomes the new Sun Chief, with little Locust, another Dreamer, taking over as Priestess. Nightshade is allowed to return home to Talon Town and brings with her the defeated Badgertail and the newly born, but hideously deformed Monster Twins, Born-0f-Water and Home-Going-Boy, integral in the Pueblo mythology. The novel contains excellent detail on the life and culture of the Mississippian Mound Builders, who also died out in the famines of the twelth to fourteenth centuries that so severely impacted the Anasazi.

103. Gear, Kathleen O'Neal and W. Michael Gear. *People of the Silence. First North Americans. Book 8.* NY: Tom Doherty. 1996. 488 p.

Time: 1100
Tribe: Anasazi (Pueblo)
Place: Arizona, New Mexico

The Anasazi culture is well depicted in the novel of the Chacoan people of the American Southwest in the time before the droughts which may have caused the end of this unique culture. As the Gears point out, the Anasazi did not really disappear, they became the Pueblo tribes of today, evolving from cliff dwellers in large communities to more sparsely settled villages spread out across the dry lands. The Chacoan First People, the upper class that rule over the Made People and the many slaves they hold, live in Talon Town, now known as the Pueblo Bonito. Chief Crow Beard, the Blessed Sun, is dying. His wife Night Sun, a healer, holds the power and wealth in this matrilineal society. Her wicked son Snake Head wants all the power and is determined to destroy her reputation and have her killed because of her affair years ago with the war leader Ironwood. That affair produced a secret child, the girl Cornsilk, raised by foster parents and unaware of her true inheritance. Cornsilk's friend is Poor Singer, a student of the old shaman, Dune. The training of Poor Singer is especially amusing and heart warming as his youthful pride is subjected to the harsh schooling of this ancient hermit. Dune is called to tend to Crow Beard's death and brings along the two young people. At Talon Town they find complex plots and schemes to allow the Mogollon chief Jay Bird to take over the town. Snake Head is killing his rival sisters and attempts to kill Cornsilk. Things come to a violent conclusion and the hastening of the demise of this cliff dwelling culture is furthered. The archaeological details are fascinating, the characters are very well defined, the plot and action are gripping. One can literally see the people, their clothing, their jewelry, their houses and tools and understand how elegant and complex a society this once was before the changing climate ended it.

Reviewed in: Booklist 1/15/97; Kirkus Reviews 11/15/96.

104. Giambastiani, Kurt R. A. *The Spirit of Thunder.* NY: ROC. 2002. 357 p.

Time: 1886–1887
Tribe: Cheyenne
Place: Northern Plains

In the sequel to *The Year the Cloud Fell*, One Who Flies, born George Custer Jr., continues in his battle to save his adopted people. The Cheyenne live in the Unorganized Territory, the Northern Plains, and are last to be conquered by President Custer in this alternative history. One Who Flies discovers gold in the Territory and with the help of a French prospector, collects enough to buy the tribe repeating rifles since they do not have any guns (in 1886?). The Cheyenne do have their dinosaur mounts, tamed *Parasaurolophus walkeri* and *Tyrannosaurus rex* monsters that amazingly still live in these lands, but the tribes need more of a weapons advantage against the Gatling guns of the U.S. Army. George Jr. travels back East with his gold, but is tricked and robbed by his French partner and left with nothing to buy guns. On his way home, George hears of a government trainload of guns and dynamite moving into the Territory to defend the construction of a huge bridge over the Missouri River. The plan is to build the bridge, protect it with a series of Army forts, and encourage White settlers to just take over the unclaimed farmland, used by the Cheyenne to graze and hunt. Robbing the train gives the Cheyenne repeating rifles, dynamite and Hotchkiss cannons. With these new weapons the Cheyenne wipe out the forts, kill the soldiers, and finally blow up the bridge. President Custer has once again been defeated by the Cheyenne Alliance, now led and trained in military skills by his own son. This is very entertaining fare, with accurate details of Cheyenne customs and a glossary of Cheyenne words to translate those used in the text. The *Parasaurolophus* "whistlers" sound like very nice pets to own and ride.

Reviewed in: Booklist 3/15/02.

105. Giambastiani, Kurt R.A. *The Year the Cloud Fell.* NY: ROC. 2001. 341 p.

Time: 1886
Tribe: Cheyenne
Place: Northern Plains

This is an alternative history account of the battle of the Cheyenne Alliance to keep settlers out of their Unorganized Territory, the last lands left unconquered by President George Armstrong Custer. President Custer sends his brilliant son, an engineer and military historian as well as an Army officer, to conquer the Cheyenne, but instead George Jr. is wounded in the crash of his dirigible and captured by Storm Arising, a powerful warrior. Speaks While Leaving, a healer and visionary, has seen young Custer falling from the sky in a dream years ago, and prophesies he will save them from the U.S. government. Renamed *Ame'haooestse*, One Who Flies, George Jr. initially resists becoming friends with the Cheyenne, but their honesty, kindness and obvious love of their homelands win him over. President Custer sends emissaries to talk peace with the chiefs, while secretly attacking a helpless village of women and children. Horrified by this dishonorable action, One Who Flies decides to fight for his new Cheyenne friends. The Cheyenne have a definite advantage in that they ride whistlers and walkers, otherwise known as giant lizards, and closely resembling *Parasaurolophus walkeri* and *Tyrannosaurus rex*. It seems dinosaurs live on in the Unorganized Territory, and scare horses to death when Cheyenne ride into battle on these ferocious beasts. The writing is excellent and the added advantage of owning a *T. rex* instead of a horse has the reader cheering for the warriors against the soldiers. One Who Flies leads a troop of dinosaur-riding Cheyenne all the way to the Capital Building in Washington D.C. and gets promises of a real treaty. His father is horrified when young Custer turns his back on his family and goes back with the Cheyenne. The Cheyenne culture is extremely well portrayed in these novels, and the author clearly is familiar with their language and customs. A glossary of Cheyenne words is included.

106. Gilchrist, Ellen. *Starcarbon: A Meditation on Love.* Boston: Little, Brown. 1994. 306 p.

Time: Contemporary
Tribe: Cherokee
Place: Charlotte, NC and Tahlequah, OK

Olivia de Haviland Hand is nineteen and failing in college. She decides to return to her grandparents Little Sun and Crow and her aunt Mary Lily in Tahlequah, the people who raised her after her mother died in childbirth. Olivia has deep intimacy issues, feels abandoned by her mother and does not trust herself to become involved with others. Bobby Tree, a Cherokee boy who also lost his mother, loves Olivia but realizes it will be hard to get her to commit to him. Olivia's father, Daniel, never knew of her existence until she showed up at his Charlotte farm when she was sixteen. Now he loves her dearly, but he has many problems of his own. Olivia returns to Oklahoma, renews her relationship with Bobby, sees an excellent therapist and gets good advice from a new friend. The novel contains many subplots involving other characters, but always returns to Olivia and Bobby. Finally they resolve to take some time off, get engaged, and go to work on a ranch in Montana. This novel is about Cherokee people living complex lives. While the grandparents are still tied to old ways, the young are not.

Reviewed in: Library Journal 3/1/94; Kirkus Reviews 2/15/94; Publishers Weekly 1/31/94.

107. Glancy, Diane. (Cherokee). *Designs of the Night Sky.* Lincoln: University of Nebraska Press. 2002. 157 p.

Time: Contemporary
Tribe: Cherokee
Place: Oklahoma

Native Storiers: A Series of American Narratives.

Ada Nonoter Ronner works as a librarian in the Manuscript and Rare Book Room at Northeastern State in Oklahoma, in charge of the historical record of the Cherokee housed there. She feels the books talking to her, trying to tell their stories of the Cherokee ancestors that came from the east to these lands on foot and on boats. The written word is a voice tamed, but also preserved. Her job is the quiet part of her life, as her three brothers fight constantly with each other, with their wives, and with their neighbors. Her sisters-in-law cast spells on each other and battle over girlfriends and religion. Her nieces and nephews are often dumped at her house for care and feeding. Ada's Bible study group, the Truthettes, is invaded by her sister-in-law Suba and the old Cherokee witches and spells. Her mother sickens and dies, her brother's divorced wife, Cora, moves in with Ada's father, Obed, who decides someone must care for Cora and her children. Through it all, her husband Ether (named for a chemistry experiment in high school) and her daughters Noel and Nolie are calm constants that keep her life on an even keel. A short book, nonetheless a whole family's structure and problems are contained in its pages.

Reviewed in: Library Journal 11/1/02; Kirkus Reviews 9/15/02.

108. Glancy, Diane. (Cherokee). *The Mask Maker.* Norman: University of Oklahoma Press. 2002. 139 p.

Time: Contemporary
Tribe: Pawnee
Place: Oklahoma

Recently divorced mixed-breed Edith Lewis travels to various schools in Oklahoma as an artist-in-residence, demonstrating and teaching the art of making masks. Edith has always used the masks both to hide her real feelings and to demonstrate them, but she has not yet come to terms with her failed marriage, her heritage, her craft, or much else about her life. Literature students may enjoy Glancy's mixing of narrative, poetry and inner thoughts on the same page, others may be confused and put off by the lack of a coherent story and in-depth characters. In her students' work, Edith sees them reveal facets of their personalities and experiences, but she cannot see the same thing in her own work. Perhaps the novel is not the vehicle for Glancy to express her own feelings about masks.

Reviewed in: Library Journal 3/1/02; Publishers Weekly 2/18/02; Kirkus Reviews 1/15/02.

109. Glancy, Diane. (Cherokee). *Pushing the Bear: A Novel of the Trail of Tears.* NY: Harcourt, Brace. 1996. 241 p.

Time: 1838–1839
Tribe: Cherokee
Place: North Carolina to Oklahoma

In alternating voices, Glancy tells the story of the Trail of Tears; the forced march of 13,000 Cherokee from their homes in Georgia, North Carolina and Tennessee to the new "Indian territory" in the winter of 1838–1839. The principal narrators are the fiercely independent Maritole, a young woman with a baby, and her proud and distant husband Knobowtee. Their marriage was not solid before the march, Maritole was his second wife and he primarily married her for the farm since Cherokee women owned the land. Maritole is briefly allowed to return to their cabin, already occupied by a White family, to retrieve some things. Knobowtee cannot forgive her for failing to get his musket and the seed corn, instead retrieving only blankets and a cooking pot she had to snatch from the fire. Maritole and Knobowtee each walk with their own families instead of with each other. There is also friction between the Cherokee on the march and their resentment of those who had gone ahead, particularly John Ross and Boudinot whom they see as traitors. The North Carolina Cherokee resent those from Georgia and Tennessee because they are left out of the councils. This is primarily a novel of the terrible conditions the Cherokee had to endure on the Trail of Tears, and how over three-quarters of them did manage to survive the 900 miles in the rain, snow and freezing cold. There are numerous novels of the Trail of Tears, but Glancy's, with its myriad voices, is one of the most powerful.

Reviewed in: Publishers Weekly 6/17/96; Kirkus Reviews 5/15/96; Booklist 8/1/96; Library Journal 7/1/96.

110. Glasco, Michael. *Angels in Tesuque.* Santa Fe: Sunstone Press. 1995. 157 p.

Time: Contemporary
Tribe: Tewa
Place: New Mexico

Ben Touchstone lives with his Anglo mother just outside the Tewa reservation in New Mexico. His father has abandoned his family for another woman and Ben is struggling to help his sick mother and his wild brother Henry. In the chapel on Christmas Eve, he sees an angel who tells him that love is the reason for existence. "Ben, you'll meet many people in your life. Some will be kind and thoughtful, but others will be dark, very dark, their souls filled with evil. You won't know the difference between them Ben, but they'll be there and so will I." Ben becomes a successful businessman working for an oil company that wants to exploit the mineral wealth belonging to the tribe. It takes Ben awhile, but he finally realizes that his loyalties lie with the tribe and in doing what is right for them and for the earth. This novel is very poorly written, the characters have no development and no motives for their actions. The reader will gain little knowledge of contemporary Tewa life.

Reviewed in: Publishers Weekly 9/18/95.

111. Goingback, Owl. (Choctaw-Cherokee). *Crota: A Novel.* NY: D.I. Fine Books/Dutton. 1996. 292 p.

Time: Contemporary
Tribe: Cherokee, Cheyenne, Sioux
Place: Missouri

When an earthquake shakes the New Madrid fault in Missouri, an ancient monster, the Crota, is released. In the early 1800's the famous earthquake in that region initially released this prehistoric monster, but the Creek led him to a deep cave and walled him in. Now the Crota is free again, to kill and mutilate deer, cows, and people in his bloodlust. Sheriff Skip Harding, and game warden Jay Little Hawk, a Cherokee, work together to defeat Crota. Jay goes to South Dakota and has the Yuwipi ceremony with George Stone Eagle, a Sioux medicine man who accompanies him back to Missouri. Finally it is Skip's Cheyenne medicine bundle with its sacred arrows, wielded by Little Hawk, that kill the Crota. Winner of the Bram Stoker award, the novel contains very little suspense, and a great deal of blood and gore. Jay Little Hawk is a very sympathetic character with an awareness of his heritage, but Skip only vaguely remembers he has a Cheyenne grandmother who gave him a hide-wrapped bundle of arrows.

Reviewed in: Publishers Weekly 2/19/96; Kirkus Reviews 2/3/96.

112. Goingback, Owl. (Choctaw-Cherokee). *Darker than Night.* NY: Signet. 1999. 342 p.

Time: Contemporary
Tribe: Hopi
Place: Missouri

Bram Stoker award winner Mike Anthony moves his family to his grandmother's old estate in Missouri after she dies and leaves him the house. His wife and children were not happy to leave New York City, and are even less happy when the local community turns against them because Mike is a horror fiction writer. They have the house renovated, but cracks appear in the walls and faces in the floor tiles. Shadows are seen flitting about the corners of the rooms and something kills and mutilates their pet cat. Only the old Hopi Sam Tochi believes Mike and Holly about the dark shadows. Mike's grandmother had a huge collection of kachina dolls and Cherokee masks which he leaves set out in the house. Sam explains they are to protect the family against the "boogers" or hobgoblins coming out of the underworld through the cracks in their house. Finally the only way to stop the attack of the boogers is to set the house on fire and return to New York. Let's hope Mike saved his precious Bram Stoker award before the fire. There is more suspense in this second novel, but less of an Indian influence.

113. Gray, Muriel. *The Trickster.* NY: Doubleday. 1994. 488 p.

Time: Contemporary and 1907
Tribe: Kinchuinick
Place: Alberta, Canadian Rockies

Sam Hunt is a snow groomer at a ski area in the Canadian Rockies where his tribe has lived for generations. At the turn of the century a train tunnel was blasted in Wolf Mountain, the work strongly opposed by the Kinchuinick people. Buried in the mountain was the Trickster, the spirit known as *Inktumi, Inktomi, Inktomni* and *Sitkonski.* Trickster was initially capable of good or bad, but has since turned against humans and wishes them gone from earth. The spirit exists in the rock and ice, but once released can take any animal form. The novel goes back and forth between events of 1907 and the current time. Sam is from the Hunting Wolf family of shamans and has denied his native beliefs for years. The Trickster uses animal forms to cause terrible murders while Sam is in an unconscious state. When Sam regains consciousness, he fears that he might be the Trickster murderer. Sam's neck amulet, *Isksaksin*, meaning boundary, will help him defeat the Trickster if he uses his teaching and knowledge to do so. Calvin Bitterhand, now an old drunk, but once Sam's Kinchuinick teacher, returns to awaken Sam to his native roots. Sam's wife Katie, son Billie who is to be the next shaman, and local policeman Craig McGee reenact the roles of the original Hunting Wolf, wife Singing Tree, son Walks Alone, and Reverend Henderson of the turn of the century when they defeated the Trickster and put him back in the mountain. The gripping novel rivals Stephen King for terror and gore. Sam's past history that forced him to deny his heritage is terrible, but his restoration of faith and belief in the old ways eventually saves him and the world from the Trickster.

Reviewed in Publishers Weekly 7/17/95; Kirkus Reviews 7/1/95; Library Journal 4/1/ 95.

114. Grove, Fred. (Osage). *The Years of Fear: A Western Story.* Waterville, Maine: Five Star. 2002. 240 p.

Time: 1920's
Tribe: Osage
Place: Oklahoma

When oil is discovered on the Osage Indians' lands, greedy Whites try to trick the people out of their property, often by marrying into an Osage family and becoming their inheritors. William Hale is a wealthy and well respected member of the community of Fairfax, befriending the Osage and ultimately placing them in his debt. He collects his debts by hiring hitmen to kill men and women so he can collect on insurance policies or on their estates. After twenty-four Osage people have died under mysterious circumstances, the U.S. Bureau of Investigation sends in agents Tom White and Frank Smith to identify the murderers. It soon becomes clear that Ernest Buckhart, Hale's weak nephew who has married into a wealthy Osage family, is part of the plot to kill rich Osage and collect their inheritances. White and Smith have severe difficulties getting anyone to implicate the powerful Hale until finally Buckhart confesses. The case comes to trial, has many setbacks, but ultimately Hale and Burkhart and their hired killer Ramsey are all sent to prison. Grove's novel is essentially a recitation of the historical events without a great deal of character development or plot. However, the fact that the Osage were so poorly treated, so many were murdered, and federal agents had to work so hard for justice, is worth knowing. Grove has done other books on this subject written entirely from the White perspective such as *Drums without Warriors.*

Reviewed in: Booklist 1/1/02.

115. Hackler, Micah S. *Coyote Returns.* NY: Dell. 1996. 326 p.

Time: Contemporary
Tribe: Navajo
Place: New Mexico

Whenever Man has forgotten his power and no longer follows the traditional ways, Coyote returns. It happened thirty years ago and it is happening again in San Phillipe County. Other things are happening as well. The body of a murdered man is found in the desert and the New Mexico state police seem very quick to conclude it was the result of a drug deal gone bad. New deputy Gabe Hanna realizes he needs to learn about his Navajo heritage. There is also conflict between the developers who want to harvest the timber and the ecologists who know what will be the outcome of barren land in this desert state. Sheriff Cliff Lansing has his own problems, his friend Marguerite lies in a coma after being shot while he was investigating a cave that Coyote lured him to. Gabe is attracted to Kim Tallmountain, daughter of the murdered man, and through her begins to learn about his background and what really happened to his father before Gabe was born. While this is a fairly simplistic mystery, the contrast between the White and Navajo cultures is well done, as is the dilemma the tribe finds itself in between wanting jobs for its people and wanting to preserve the land.

Reviewed in: Armchair Detective Fall/96.

116. Hackler, Micah S. *The Dark Canyon.* NY: Dell. 1997. 372 p.

Time: Contemporary
Tribe: Anasazi
Place: New Mexico

After his ranch house burns in the conclusion of *The Shadowcatcher*, Sheriff Cliff Lansing finds a hidden cache, left there by his great-grandfather Virgil Lansing. The cache contains Virgil's journal and a large green stone with strange carvings. Lansing sends both off to the University of New Mexico: the journal is heavily water damaged and needs expert attention.

As the restored pages are faxed to him, he becomes fascinated learning about Virgil's Army career, but that must take a back seat to what is happening in his county. Reports of vicious killings are coming in—first of livestock, then of sheepherders and of the hunters who are trying to capture whatever it is. The bodies are horribly mutilated; only a wild animal could do this damage, but the marks are not left by any normal bear or mountain lion. A graduate student on his own time has discovered a valley of graves marked by two stone lions, could this be an Anasazi burial place and the remains of Carleton's Lost Patrol? Gradually all the elements come together in a powerful conclusion in which Lansing, protected by a Mayan talisman, must kill the jaguar which the disturbance of the tombs has unleashed. The Anasazi theories are fascinating and the story is an intriguing one.

117. Hackler, Micah S. *Legend of the Dead.* NY: Dell. 1995. 244 p.

Time: Contemporary
Tribe: Anasazi/Zuni
Place: New Mexico

Sheriff Cliff Lansing doesn't know who or what killed pot-hunter Duke, but he's pretty sure it wasn't ghosts. Things get complicated when Senator Carter Williston comes to Mack McGarrity's ranch to negotiate for a piece of land called the Anasazi Strip. Why do the Zunis not want to trade 150,000 acres in New Mexico for the same amount of land in Arizona? The Senator is told he can only talk to "the Watcher" who doesn't exactly keep office hours. While the Senator is out in the desert learning more about Anasazi ritual and myth than he wanted to, Sheriff Lansing is busy trying to solve the murder. Both men are now targets of king-maker McGarrity who has discovered that the disputed land is a treasure trove of Anasazi materials. Helped by "the Watcher" and others from the past, Lansing and Williston do emerge triumphant and the evil McGarrity is vanquished. Although this has a Native American theme, none of the principal characters are Native American.

118. Hackler, Micah S. *The Shadowcatcher*. NY: Dell. 1997. 310 p.

Time: Contemporary
Tribe: Apache
Place: New Mexico

Sheriff Cliff Lansing has his hands full. Several murders in San Phillipe County and on the Apache reservation, each having an owl feather at the site, indicate that a serial killer may be on the loose. And is there a connection with the slaying of three Girl Scouts years ago which still haunts Lansing? He also has his twelve year old son, C.J., staying with him for the summer; he needs and wants to spend time with C.J., but how can he when the murders increase, drawing ever closer to home? When Lansing figures out that the source of the conflict lies in Apache tribal politics reaching back centuries, he is a little closer to the solution, but the killer has studied traditional Apache medicine ways, as well as those of other tribes, and seems to be able to become invisible. The mystery will keep the reader turning the pages and the theme of Apache medicine traditions will interest a wide audience.

119. Hager, Jean. (Cherokee). *The Fire Carrier.* NY: Mysterious. 1996. 245 p.

Time: Contemporary
Tribe: Cherokee
Place: Oklahoma

The seemingly sleepy town of Buckskin suddenly has several situations for Chief Mitch Bushyhead to be concerned about. An escaped convict may be heading home, the wife of the Job Corps Director is being battered but won't press charges, several large thefts of rodeo memorabilia and tack have been reported and The Fire Carrier, an evil Cherokee spirit, may have returned. To complicate his life, Mitch's previous relationship with Emily's teacher, Lisa, has not survived Lisa's move. When Tyler Hatch is found murdered after he tried to break into the Cherokee Medical Clinic, there is no lack of suspects since numerous people hated him including his battered wife, her brother the escaped convict, and those he worked with at the Center. While he is solving the crime, Mitch attends a stomp dance and begins to establish ties with his heritage. Hager presents a nice blend of mystery and Native American themes which makes for a pleasant read.

Reviewed in: Library Journal 5/1/96; Publishers Weekly 3/18/96; Kirkus Reviews 4/1/96.

120. Hager, Jean. (Cherokee). *Masked Dancers.* NY: Mysterious. 1998. 282 p.

Time: Contemporary
Tribe: Cherokee
Place: Oklahoma

When Chief Mitch Bushyhead's daughter Emily and her two friends discover a body in a cave during a rainstorm, Mitch's first concern is for the girls. Who would have bludgeoned the new game warden to death? Did the dead eagle Mitch discovered tie into the murder? High school principal Vian Brasfield is very interested in his Cherokee heritage and holds dances on his country property which infuriates his right-wing neighbor, fanatic Dane Kennedy. Although Brasfield is seen as one of the dancers on Friday night, Mitch cannot locate him until his pickup, and then his body, are found. How does the new murder tie in to the previous one? And do they both connect to what happened between the Brasfield and Kennedy families seventeen years ago? Mitch's relationship with Dr. Rhea Vann is improving as he solves the two murders and leaves the reader waiting for the next installment of Mitch's life.

Reviewed in: Kirkus Reviews 3/1/98.

121. Hager, Jean. (Cherokee). *The Redbird's Cry.* NY: Mysterious. 1994. 274 p.

Time: Contemporary
Tribe: Cherokee
Place: Oklahoma

During the week-long exhibition at the Cherokee National Museum, visitors expect to see both traditional and contemporary arts and crafts like Daye Hummingbird's paintings, Maud Wildcat's weavings, Regina Shell's baskets, and Wolf Kawaya's blow darts. They do not expect to witness the murder of Tom Battle, Cherokee story-teller and an attorney for the Cherokee Nation who had won recent court cases against the True Echota Band. Was Tom's killer Wolf, Daye's ex-husband, angry that Daye had taken up with Tom rather than come back to him? Maud's wild grandson Robert was the one who actually blew the poisoned dart that struck Tom, but did someone put him up to it? Is this a personal crime or a tribal one? Investigator Molly Bearpaw has her hands full as all signs seem to point to Wolf. She is also having trouble with sheriff's deputy D. J. Kennedy who has confessed his love for her, but Molly is not sure she is ready for a deeper relationship. Interspersed Cherokee legends add to the depth of this mystery.

Reviewed in: Booklist 4/1/94; Publishers Weekly 2/14/94.

122. Hager, Jean. (Cherokee). *Seven Black Stones.* NY: Mysterious. 1995. 294 p.

Time: Contemporary
Tribe: Cherokee
Place: Oklahoma

Zebediah Smoke is an old traditional Cherokee opposed to the building of a bingo hall next to his little shack. He knows the old medicines and rituals, so when a man is found dead of carbon monoxide poisoning, with seven black stones on his truck's seat, Zeb is suspected of being involved. Molly Bearpaw finds herself in the investigation after the murdered man's daughter begs her to help. The sheriff thinks it was suicide, Molly and the daughter think it was murder. But what was the motive? Another worker on the bingo hall is found murdered, with seven black stones next to his body. Suspicion naturally focuses on Zeb, but Molly is sure that someone else is behind the deaths. She finds the connection between the first man's death and the second worker's murder and discovers the culprit is a pillar of the community. During the course of the investigation, Molly helps the daughter deal with the possibility of her father's suicide and comes to terms with her own mother's suicide years earlier. This helps Molly in building her relationship with Deputy D. J. Kennedy, who has been trying to get closer to her for a long time. A complex mystery with lots of interest in finding the clues to situations which appear obvious but in fact are quite hidden.

Reviewed in: Booklist 4/15/95; Library Journal 3/1/95; Publishers Weekly 2/13/95.

123. Hager, Jean. (Cherokee). *The Spirit Caller.* NY: Mysterious. 1997. 257 p.

Time: Contemporary
Tribe: Cherokee
Place: Oklahoma

The Native American Research Library in Tahlequah has a ghost in it and spiritualist Talia Wind offers to settle its wandering with Cherokee rituals (heavily mixed with New Age). Talia herself has disturbed a few living spirits in the form of her ex-husband, Dell; her rival, the medicine man Agasuyed; and the wife of Josh, the church deacon who is having an affair with Talia. When Talia is found murdered and hanging outside the Library, Molly Bearpaw has too many suspects. Molly also has a recently returned father, whom she hasn't seen since she was four years old. Throw in her dying Honda Civic, and charming auto dealer Tim Dowell, along with a rash of stolen luxury cars, and Molly has her hands full. Molly must deal with the anger she feels towards a father who deserted her, but succeeds in doing so when she learns why he left. Solving the murder of Talia takes a little connecting of confusing events, then a dangerous confrontation. This is another excellent mystery putting the Cherokee people into a framework which shows them to be unique, but also similar to other people in the U.S.

Reviewed in: Library Journal 5/1/97; Publishers Weekly 3/17/97.

124. Haldeman, Jack C. II, and Jack Dann. *High Steel.* NY: Tom Doherty. 1993. 252 p.

Time: 2177
Tribe: Sioux, Navajo
Place: Space Station, Arizona, South Dakota

The world of the future is controlled by two large corporations that own the space satellites and stations, many of them heavily armed. John Stranger, a Sioux with training as a medicine man, has the intrinsic talents to supervise the building of a ship to explore alien worlds. Trans-United and Macro are the rival corporations vying to be first to contact alien intelligence. Meanwhile on earth, Anna Grass-Like-Water and Sam Woquini are assigned to recruit poor Navajo youth to join the space construction and repair crews. What they do not know is that the tribal youth are being used as test subjects for deep sleep experiments, needed for long-term space travel. Over all these actions and monitoring the participants is the consciousness of the old Sioux shaman, Broken-Finger, who recognizes Anna as Corn Woman, and Sam as Sandman, rivals to keep the earth in balance with their seasons of heat and cold. Trans-United and Macro rivalries turn deadly, top executives are killed, and in the space ship readied for exploration, John Stranger threatens the entire earth unless he, Anna and Sam are allowed to leave and find other intelligence. Something of a fractured novel with many plot lines, not all well developed, the story does incorporate Native American spirituality in a futuristic world.

Reviewed in: Booklist 7/1/93; Library Journal 6/15/93; Kirkus Reviews 5/15/93; Publishers Weekly 6/21/93.

125. Hansen, Karen. *Earth Walk* . Raleigh, NC: Pentland Press. 2001. 99 p.

Time: Contemporary
Tribe: Hopi
Place: Michigan and Arizona

At a private academy in Michigan Dr. Christine Bailey is contacted by the police. They are looking for a member of her faculty, the part Hopi woman Nancy Crane, who disappeared over the Christmas holidays. Nancy left a note for Christine asking her to feed her cat and pick up her mail, and in doing so, Christine discovers a very personal journal that leads her to believe Nancy has killed herself. Christine goes to Arizona to meet a Hopi man in Nancy's journal who seems to have had a deep effect on her life. There Christine discovers Timothy Proud, his wife Anna, oldest son Andrew and the ancient wise woman Marianne White Cloud. Gradually Nancy's sad life is revealed, one she has never told to anyone in Michigan. Obsessed with Timothy, Nancy has been trying for years to win his love and force him to leave his wife, eight children and five grandchildren. Timothy may have a large family, but he has not lost his sexual charm or attractiveness and Christine also falls under his seductive spell. The truth comes out about the real mother of Andrew and the affair Nancy has been having with Timothy for years. Nancy's body is found under the ice in a Michigan lake and is brought home to the Hopi reservation where she is buried with full Hopi ceremonies. Torn between her Hopi father and her Italian New York mother, Nancy has never been happy on her earth walk. Christine only hopes Nancy will be happier in her death and burial on the Hopi lands. A short novel, but quite effective in the portrayal of a half-Hopi girl and her difficulties in being accepted by her father's people.

Reviewed in: Publishers Weekly 3/19/01.

126. Hardy, Melissa. *Constant Fire.* Ottawa, Canada: Oberon Press. 1995. 149 p.

Time: 1960 to present
Tribe: Cherokee
Place: North Carolina

The Qualla Boundary is a reservation of the Eastern Band of Cherokee in North Carolina where there are reenactments for tourists every summer of the Trail of Tears. Living on the Qualla Boundary are many traditionalists who still practice the old medicine and tell the Cherokee legends to the young. Each chapter is a different person's personal tale, many of them full of tragedy. Coming Back Tuskateeskee is the conjurer whose spells sometimes cure, but sometimes kill. His sister Arminty suffers a stroke and her granddaughter is sent to live with her. Arminty teaches her how to make bean soup in the special bean pot before she dies, to pass on the treasured recipe. Peggie the dwarf is full of jokes, but when she loses her mother to a hit and run accident, and her brother becomes brain-dead from drinking Aqua Velva, Peggie uses a Cherokee myth of *Tsantawu* drowned by the Little People and drowns her evil father. Each story can stand on its own, but as a whole they involve many similar members of the Band. Written by someone who lived on the Boundary for years, they capture the spirit of the Cherokee legends and people.

127. Harper, Karen. *Black Orchid.* NY: Signet. 1996. 366 p.

Time: Contemporary
Tribe: Seminole
Place: Florida

Orchid grower Jordan Quinn has tried to put her teenaged romance and brief marriage with Seth Cypress behind her and move on to a new life as a businesswoman. She has a new marriage with Lawrence Quinn, a brilliant researcher who is investigating the endangered Florida panther as a possible link to a cure for AIDS. Son of his band's shaman, Seth is now an attorney and Seminole tribal chairman himself and has tried to make a new life without Jordan. Several of the Florida panther team are shot with tranquilizing darts, Lawrence goes missing and later is found dead. Jordan feels there is no one else she can trust and turns to Seth for help. Complicating the situation is retired movie director Winston Rey whose movie *Everglades Victory* was responsible for so much of the bad blood that exists between the Seminoles and their white neighbors. While this is primarily a romance and a mystery involving Jordan's parentage, there is enough of the contemporary Native American theme to make this novel worth reading.

128. Harrigan, Lana M. *Acoma: A Novel of Conquest.* NY: Forge. 1997. 383 p.

Time: 1598–early 1600's
Tribe: Pueblo
Place: New Mexico

Based upon the diaries of the Spanish explorer, Juan de Onate, the Governor of New Mexico, this historical romance tells the story of the conquest of the native peoples of the Southwest by Spanish explorers in the sixteenth century. The events are familiar, with cruel overbearing soldiers demanding corn and food from pueblos barely able to support themselves in the harsh semi-arid land. The town of Aco, high on a mesa, attracts the attention of Captain Vizcarra, and in 1599 he leads troops to massacre the people, dragging off the survivors to be slaves for the Spanish settlers. Rohona, a young man of Aco, has his right foot severed at the instep to prevent escape, as did all the men from Aco. Rohona then becomes a slave to the Zaldivar family, tending their garden and acting as chaperone to the wife on her daily rides. Vicente Zaldivar is a rude and abusive husband, intent upon finding gold and becoming wealthy. His neglected wife Maria Angelica falls in love with Rohona. Their love lasts for years and produces a son, who is not told about his parentage. Maria also has a daughter by her husband. The two children grow up together, fall in love, marry and move back to Aco. Finally they are told of their incestuous relationship, the daughter dies in childbirth and the son falls to his death off Aco mesa. The child is reared by his grandfather, Rohona. The novel is a very accurate historical account of the conquest of the new lands by the Spanish and their submission of the local peoples. The romance assumes prominence but is well written. Unfortunately more time is spent on the Spanish than the Aco people, but little is written about this era and these events, so this book is a welcome addition.

129. Harrigan, Lana M. *K'atsina: A Novel of Rebellion.* NY: Tom Doherty. 1998. 350 p.

Time: 1629–1679
Tribe: Pueblo
Place: New Mexico, Mexico

Rohona's grandson Mastya meets the new Franciscan friar who has come to convert the Acoma. Father Juan Ramirez is determined to win over the Aco people by building a church and slowly gaining their trust. He succeeds initially only with the little boy. When Ramirez realizes how intelligent this half-Spanish child is, he asks Rohona to allow him to send the boy to Mexico City for schooling. There Mastya becomes Augustin, dedicated to becoming a Jesuit priest. Augustin is a tutor to a wealthy Creole family for many years, watching a very bright little girl, Antonia, grow up. When she becomes an adult, they admit their love, and flee back to his pueblo on Aco and his family there. A son, Mokaitsh, is born, also known as Aurelio. Augustin dies protecting a child from rattlesnakes and his wife Antonia continues to live in Aco. She learns their ways and Mokaitsh eventually is inducted into the *k'atsina* society of religious dancers. Father Ramirez has finally succeeded in building a flock of believers but also allows them their own religious practices. This ends when two new fathers come to take over after his death, but they are driven away and replaced by Fray Lucas, a more tolerant man. The Pueblo peoples are sick of Spanish rule and oppression. All the pueblos in the region finally rise up in revolt, in the uprising of 1679 under the charismatic leader, Popé. Aco also participates in the revolt, led locally by Diego, a half-Apache man who lives in Aco. They throw Fray Lucas off the mesa to die on the rocks below. Mokaitsh secretly buries Lucas, but decides his place is with the Acoma, marries and continues the line of Rohona. A decade later, Diego de Vargas returns to conquer the Pueblo peoples once again and the revolt is over. Very well written and historically accurate, this sequel to *Acoma* continues to recount the early period of conquest and revolt in the history of the Pueblo peoples of the southwest.

Reviewed in: Library Journal 9/1/98; Booklist 8/1/98; Publishers Weekly 7/20/98.

130. Harris, Christie. *Raven's Cry.* Vancouver, Canada: Douglas & McIntyre. 1996. 194 p. Originally published: NY: Atheneum. 1966. 194 p.

Time: 1775–1948
Tribe: Haida
Place: Queen Charlotte Islands, British Columbia

In the 1770s British traders found Haida Gwaii, the large islands off the coast of British Columbia while they were searching for a source of sea otter pelts. Offering the Haida Indians metal chisels for hides, they were able to buy pelts inexpensively and sell them for a fortune to the Chinese. Yankee traders followed and initially trade was positive on both sides. When the Haida demanded cloth and clothing instead of chisels, tempers flared. Captain Kendrick in 1791 massacred a Haida village, enraging Chief Koyah who swore vengeance. Koyah captured two ships and beheaded their crews. The British and Yankees had guns and used them to demand the pelts and frighten the Haida. Chief 7idansuu realized that the power of the Haida had been compromised. He knew they must change to live with the White men and encourages his nephew Da.axiigang to carve the black slate, argillite, found only on the newly named Queen Charlotte Islands. Da.axiigang becomes a reknown carver, his work in demand all over the world. Christian missionaries arrive to convert the Haida and give them English names. Chief 7idansuu becomes Edenshaw. Lineage is traced down through the mother's line and nephews are heirs to their maternal uncles, not their fathers, whose heirs are their sister's sons. Royal first cousins were expected to marry and uncles often married their nieces. Da.aziigang becomes Charles Edenshaw, carving for the American Museum of Natural History in the late 1800's and finally dying in 1920 of consumption. During his long lifetime he saw the 1857 gold rush bring whiskey traders and disease. In 1862 small pox wiped out all but two Haida villages, reducing their numbers to only one thousand people from an original count of nearly ten thousand when traders first arrived seventy years before. In 1884 laws were passed forbidding potlatches and totem poles were cut down for firewood as they represented pagan gods. In 1948 a great nephew felt the urge to carve and began making jewelry. He found Charles Edenshaw's pieces in museums and began to rework the designs. The nephew, Bill Reid, illustrator of this historical novel, has since also had his work purchased and displayed in many museums. This is a complete history of the Haida people from first white contact to the present, succinctly but clearly written, with full character development and many cultural details.

Reviewed in: Voice of Youth Advocates 8/1/93.

131. Harris, Julie. *The Longest Winter.* NY: St. Martin's. 1995. 306 p.

Time: 1926–1950
Tribe: Aleutians
Place: Alaska, South Carolina

In 1926, John Robert Shaw was attempting to set a distance record in a biplane when it went down in the Aleutian Islands off Alaska. Shaw is rescued by the native peoples from the uncharted island of Kulowyl, who are unaware of western civilization. Badly injured, he is nursed back to health by the medicine man Asuluk and his daughter Kioki. Eventually Shaw marries Kioki and her sister Tooksooks and has two children, Billy and Lily. This novel, based on fact, is structured around Shaw's journal and his memories of life as a pilot in the South. He dreams frequently of his best friends and family there, hoping someday to go back. In 1943 during World War II, these islands are evacuated by the U.S. Army and Shaw is sent home. His native family is relocated to Saint Lawrence Island off the coast of Alaska. Shaw returns home to find his sister married and a mother, his own mother dead, and his teacher, Billy Taylor, still alive and well. But Alaska pulls him back and he returns to Kioki and his children. Most of the story involves Shaw's life with the Aleutians and their difficult lives on an icy, freezing island in the middle of the Bering Sea. One is constantly amazed that humans are able to live in such a cold and barren land, still building their societies, forming families, living by rules and codes of behavior which put the community first, the rugged individual last. A fascinating and heart-warming story of one man's true experience living a stone age life in the twentieth century.

132. Harrison, Sue. *Mother Earth, Father Sky.* NY: Doubleday. 1990. 313 p.

Reviewed in: Publishers Weekly 4/20/90; Library Journal 5/1/90.

My Sister the Moon. NY: Doubleday. 1992. 449 p.

Reviewed in: School Library Journal 10/92; Publishers Weekly 1/13/92.

Brother Wind. NY: Morrow. 1994. 494 p.
Song of the River. Book One of The Storyteller Trilogy. NY: Avon. 1997. 484 p.

Reviewed in: Booklist 11/1/97; Publishers Weekly 9/29/97.

The Cry of the Wind. Book Two of the Storyteller Trilogy. NY: Avon. 1998. 464 p.

Reviewed in: Publishers Weekly 11/23/98; Booklist 11/15/98.

Call Down The Stars. Book Three of the Storyteller Trilogy. NY: Morrow. 2001. 464 p.

Reviewed in: Publisher's Weekly 10/22/01; Booklist 10/1/01.

Time: 7056 B.C. – 6460 B.C.
Tribe: Aleuts
Place: Alaska, Aleutian Islands

Well written and full of historical details about prehistoric times in the Aleutian Islands, Harrison develops extensive family histories full of colorful characters in her two series. Harrison based her research on the historic myths and legends of numerous American Indian tribes including the Cree, Athabascan, Aleut, Denali, Tlingit, Haida, Nootka, and Yup'ik. She skillfully applies the more contemporary stories and fables to the life and circumstances of the Aleuts in the harsh islands of the Bering Sea in more ancient times. Some reviewers liken her books more to fantasy literature than historical fiction because of the placement in prehistoric times for which there is no real written record. However, since these novels are set in the concrete reality of hunting and gathering in a frozen environment, her fiction works well as a portrayal of what life could have been like in those times. The elaborate family conflicts and relationships with extensive lists of participants are too complex to cover in detail here. The tribe in the early series calls itself First Men and begins with the young girl Chagak and her husband Kayugh and their families. The First Men are followed throughout the series as they migrate from the Aleutians to finally settle in northern Michigan. The people in the second Storyteller series are from the Near River, Cousin River and Sea Hunters tribes in the Aleutian Islands, long at war with each other. Here a powerful healing woman, K'os, her adopted son, the storyteller Chakliax, and beautiful witty Qumalix are central characters in the plot which is full of drama, tale-telling, violence, romance and treachery. Both series are set in similar times and places. Harrison includes glossaries of Aleut and Athabascan words in her books, which she also uses liberally throughout the text to add authenticity and atmosphere to her stories. Romantic, complex, and long, the books in this series definitely contribute to our knowledge about the seal hunters of the Aleutian Islands in early times, many details of which are no doubt are similar to the lives of individuals today.

133. Haseloff, Cynthia. *The Chains of Sarai Stone: A Western Story.* Thorndike, ME: Five Star Western. 1995. 218 p.

Time: 1836–1861
Tribe: Comanche
Place: Texas

When Sarai Stone is ten, she and her brothers are captured by the Comanches and adopted into the tribe. Jacob Logan and Hugh Kane were hired by Silas Stone to find his grandchildren, but they only found the boys, who refused to return. Sarai is later married to Nobah and has three children. When Kane and dragoons hit a Comanche camp, wounding Nobah, they capture Sarai and her daughter Summer. They take her back to Silas and his fanatically religious son, Ben. Silas loves Sarai and she him, but when Silas is accidentally killed, Ben takes over. Ben hates the wicked, despoiled pagan hostiles and Sarai is included in his hatred. But Sarai is strong and resourceful, racing her small Indian pony against White men's bigger horses, gambling her silver jewelry against land deeds, and winning. She sets up freed slaves, Jack and Delia, on her land. Meanwhile Logan has been captured by Nobah, holding him hostage for Sarai. Kane is told to bring her back to save Logan, his best friend. When Sarai discovers some White men have killed her oldest son for his pinto, she exacts revenge and goes back to Nobah herself. A fairly standard western, similar to the Cynthia Ann Parker story, but with a very different woman in the role, one who survives and returns to the Comanches.

134. Haseloff, Cynthia. *The Kiowa Verdict.* Unity, ME: Five Star. 1997. 258 p.

Time: 1871
Tribe: Kiowa
Place: Oklahoma, Texas

Satank, Satanta, and Adoltay (Big Tree) are three Kiowa leaders responsible for the Warren Wagon Train Massacre, involving over one hundred Kiowa and Comanche men. Seven civilians were killed in the raid and forty-one mules were stolen by the Kiowa. Satanta brags to Indian Agent Lawrie Tatum about the raid, resulting in the arrest of the three men and the determination they should stand trial. Satank attacks a guard and is shot. Kicking Bear, another Kiowa chief, tries to return the mules, but their new Kiowa owners won't give them up. Joseph Woolfolk and Thomas Ball are assigned to defend the remaining two Kiowa before Judge Charles Soward in Jacksboro, Texas. The argument that the attack was an act of war between the Kiowa and the United States doesn't hold up because of the robbery of the mules. The mutilation of the civilians' bodies and the burning alive of one of the teamsters also inflames the jury, who bring back a guilty verdict. The Kiowas' sentences are commuted to life imprisonment instead of hanging after Agent Tatum, a Quaker, and Adrienne Chastain, a White woman and former captive of Satanta, plead for their lives. Haseloff does an excellent job of showing the conflict that the lawyers and judges feel in prosecuting and defending the Kiowa, whose lands have been stolen, and who are fighting a war with white people. Eventually the two men were freed from prison two years later, only to have Satanta returned to prison again, where he eventually died.

Reviewed in: Publishers Weekly 10/20/97.

135. Haseloff, Cynthia. *Man Without Medicine: A Western Story.* Unity, ME: Five Star. 1996. 236 p.

Time: 1890's
Tribe: Kiowa
Place: Oklahoma

Daha-hen, the "man without medicine" who rejected the power of the owl medicine of the Kiowa, lives on the reservation in Oklahoma, and is a law-abiding rancher. When White men steal his horses and those of his neighbors, he receives permission to go off the reservation to retrieve them. Daha-hen takes with him young Thomas Young Man, a *dapom*, or "throw-away" Kiowa boy, abandoned by his family. Thomas's mother was once young, beautiful and deeply loved by Daha-hen when he was known as Big Bow, before he was disgraced by her rejection. As the two follow the trail of the horse thieves, Daha-hen tells Thomas the history of the Kiowa in their wars to resist takeover by the Whites. He tells of the great chiefs, Satanta and Kicking Bird. He tells of how he himself became a "pipe carrier" and led war parties at only seventeen. And finally he tells of his involvement in bringing in the last of the Kiowa resisting life on the reservation. When all the warriors and chiefs were brought to Kicking Bird, some were chosen to be sent off to prison. For his assistance to Kicking Bird, Daha-hen was spared. Since then some have called him a traitor, but he only wanted the best for his tribe. Eventually the horse thieves are encountered and defeated. Daha-hen and Thomas return everyone's horses and Thomas's place is restored in the tribe. An excellent account of the last days of freedom for the Kiowa, Haseloff definitely knows the details of their tragic history.

Reviewed in: Booklist 11/15/96; Publishers Weekly 10/28/96; Roundup 12/96.

136. Haseloff, Cynthia. *Satanta's Woman: A Western Story.* Unity, ME: Five Star. 1998. 284 p.

Time: 1864–1878
Tribe: Kiowa
Place: Texas

The Kiowa and Comanche raid Texas farms and ranches, running off cattle and horses and stealing hostages. Adrienne Chastain and her two little granddaughters, Millie and Lottie, are captured by Satanta. Her son Joe Carter is also captured, a weak and spoiled thirteen-year-old. Satanta is disgusted by Joe and kills him on the trip home. Millie disappears to another band, but Lottie and Adrienne are kept by Satanta. Lottie quickly adapts to being a member of the tribe and Adrienne works so hard that she becomes a respected member of Satanta's household. The specific descriptions of the daily activities of the Kiowa women in butchering buffalo, tanning the hides, sewing the tents and making clothes, are all excellent and enlightening. Life was very hard for these people. Satanta wants Adrienne as a wife and gradually she agrees. She is happier than she has ever been until she learns Lottie has disappeared during the Sand Creek Massacre. Later Adrienne hears Lottie was taken to Council Grove and is determined to go also. Soldiers rescue Adrienne and a young German boy and take them away from the Kiowa. Although Adrienne returns to her life on her Texas ranch, she never forgets her life with Satanta and the Kiowa. Haseloff's book *The Kiowa Verdict* continues the story of Satanta and Adrienne.

Reviewed: Booklist 8/1/98.

137. Henry, Gordon Jr. (Chippewa). *The Light People: A Novel.* Norman: University of Oklahoma Press. 1994. 226 p.

Time: 1960's to 1980's
Tribe: Ojibwe
Place: Minnesota

American Indian and Literature Critical Studies Series, v. 7

This novel is a series of interconnected stories, each told by a different member of what is a closely related set of people on the reservations of northern Minnesota. Each story brings the reader deeper into the world of the Anishinabe. Beginning and ending with Oshinaway as a young boy and later a grown man, the middle tales are about Jake Seed the tribal healer; his artist daughter Rose; Oshawa, a little boy at the mission school and his uncle Oshawanung; Elijah Cold Crow who lost his voice at mission school and now can only speak and write in haiku poetry; and finally Bombarto Rose, a scholar who collects Cold Crow's poems. As the stories cycle in towards the middle, they also cycle out in the same teller's order. The effect must be read to be fully experienced and shows the influence of Gerald Vizenour, the editor of the series. An example is the tale of old Four Bears who loses his leg in an accident, wraps it in ceremonial leggings and asks Oshawanung to bury it, only to have it drift downstream. Later the wrapped leg is found by a visiting anthropologist, taken to a museum in Minneapolis and discovered there by Oshawa on a school trip, then fought over in court to have it returned. This is typical of the tales in this novel and shows the warmth, humor, and interconnectivity of all the people of the tribe.

Reviewed in: Booklist 2/15/94; Publishers Weekly 1/10/94; Library Journal 2/1/94; Choice 7/1/94; Kirkus Reviews 1/1/94; NYTBR 7/3/94.

138. Hillerman, Tony. *The Fallen Man.* NY: HarperCollins. 1996. 294 p.

Reviewed in: NYTBR 12/8/96; Booklist 11/1/96; Library Journal 10/15/96; Atlantic Monthly 1/97.

The First Eagle. NY: HarperCollins. 1998. 278 p.

Reviewed in: Library Journal 7/1/98; Publishers Weekly 7/13/98; Booklist 7/1/98.

Hunting Badger. NY: HarperCollins. 1999. 275 p.

Reviewed in: Publishers Weekly 10/18/99; Library Journal 11/15/99; Booklist 10/15/99.

The Wailing Wind. NY: HarperCollins. 2002. 232 p.

Reviewed in: Library Journal 3/15/02.

Time: Contemporary
Tribe: Navajo
Place: Arizona, New Mexico, Colorado

Retired Lieutenant Joe Leaphorn has a hard time staying retired in these four mysteries, becoming involved in several cases with Jim Chee and the new police officer, Bernadette Manuelito. In *The Fallen Man*, a rock climber is found dead of thirst high on *Tse' Bit'ai*, or Shiprock but one day after his birthday when he inherited a ranch full of mineral reserves. In *The First Eagle*, Chee and Leaphorn face a drug resistant strain of plague, which is killing the researchers working on it. Chee must capture a wild eagle in the traditional way to prove a young Hopi man's innocence. *Hunting Badger* is based loosely upon the true story of the paramilitary men who hid for months in the Four Corners area deserts, tracked by the Navajo. *The Wailing Wind* revisits an old criminal case of Leaphorn's and finds out the long-sought truth of several murders. During the course of solving mysterious crimes, Chee breaks off his relationship with Janet Pete, the public defender, and begins to have feelings for Bernie Manuelito. Leaphorn meanwhile is involved with Professor Louisa Bouirebonette, who is collecting and translating old Ute, Pueblo and Navajo myths and stories told by the old people in the area. The southwestern setting, the perspective of the Navajo people as it opposes the white point of view, and the friendship between Chee and Leaphorn are still extremely well done by a master story teller.

For further criticism and interpretation of Hillerman's works, see: Reilly, John M. *Tony Hillerman: A Critical Companion.* Westport, CT: Greenwood Press. 1996.

139. Highway, Tomson. (Cree). *Kiss of the Fur Queen.* Norman: University of Oklahoma Press. 1998. 310 p.

Time: 1951–1987
Tribe: Cree, Ojibwe
Place: Manitoba, Canada

American Indian Literature and Critical Studies Series, v. 34

The Okimasis family live on a Reserve where life is primitive and few children survive. The Cree are a Catholic tribe, so the brothers Jeremiah and Gabriel are sent to the Birch Lake Indian School, a boarding school run by priests. Jeremiah is musically inclined and loves to play the accordion or piano and sing. His younger brother Gabriel is a beautiful boy and a gifted dancer. Gabriel attracts the attention of a homosexual priest who molests him. The brothers keep the abuse from their parents and internalize it to the point it eventually destroys their lives. When they graduate from the boarding school they go on to high school in Winnipeg. Gabriel, now a homosexual himself, secretly takes ballet lessons and after school leads a very private life in the gay bars. Jeremiah takes piano lessons and even wins coveted prizes. Amanda Clear Sky is an Ojibwe at the high school and tries to open the brothers up to their own traditions, but initially fails. Gabriel joins a dance troupe and leaves Canada for San Francisco. Jeremiah, shocked at discovering his brother's homosexuality, abandons the piano and becomes a social worker among the Indians of the back alleys of Winnipeg. Years go by, Gabriel is too old to dance, Jeremiah encounters Amanda again working as an actress and the three team up to produce theatrical productions based upon Cree legends and songs. Reconciled, Jeremiah discovers his brother Gabriel is dying of AIDS. The themes are ones heard and read of before, from punishments for speaking Cree in school, to abuse from priests, to censure of homosexuality. Highway provides an excellent account of how personal these experiences can be and how lasting the after-effects can be on the individual. His inclusion of Cree songs and legends and his glossary at the end of Cree terms used in the text definitely enhance the novel.

Reviewed in: Choice 11/1/00.

140. Hirsh, M. E. *Dreaming Back.* NY: St. Martin's. 1993. 257 p.

Time: Contemporary
Tribe: Hopi
Place: New Mexico and Arizona

When Leni Haring is murdered in Chama, her sister Leigh flies in from Boston to deal with the paperwork and to find out what was going on in her sister's life that made her a target. Leni had just been let go from her college teaching job where her specialty was exposing subliminal advertising. She had also done research on mind-altering drugs and their uses in various cultures through the centuries. Leni's Hopi lover Ben seems an obvious suspect since they had been working together on a secret project, on which Leni was about to ask her ex-MIT professor father's help. Ben has seen Army helicopters land on the Hopi reservation and dig up a mysterious crystal-like substance. When Ben gives Leigh a fragment and she takes it back to Boston for analysis, her life is also in danger. Subplots of Hopi legends which might be linked to previous alien encounters and the death of Leni and Leigh's mother while on LSD as an experimental patient years ago, pull the story together and make it more than an average murder mystery.

Reviewed in: Booklist 9/1/93; Library Journal 9/15/93; Publishers Weekly 8/16/93.

141. Hobbs, Will. *Beardance.* NY: Atheneum. 1993. 197 p.

Time: Contemporary
Tribe: Ute and Tlingit
Place: Southern Colorado

A sequel to Hobbs's *Bearstone*, the novel features Cloyd Atcitty and Walter Landis, the young Ute boy and the old rancher/miner. Cloyd lives with Landis, helping him out on the ranch and accompanying him to the high mountains of the Weminuche Wilderness Area. Landis is looking for a fabled cache of Spanish gold and Cloyd is looking for the last remaining grizzly bears, his totem animal. In May, Cloyd danced in the Spring Ute bear dance and became one with the spirit of the bear. In the mountains they meet Ursa, a Tlingit woman researcher from the University of Montana, looking for evidence of grizzlies. If she can prove one remains, the Fish and Wildlife Service will bring in more. Cloyd and Ursa share their cultures' stories of the bear and how important it is in their separate tribal lore. Ursa tells Cloyd the story of the Woman Who Married a Bear. Cloyd shows her how to attract bears with growler sticks. They end up attracting a sow and her three cubs. When the sow and one cub are killed by a rock fall, Cloyd decides to stay up high with the surviving cubs until winter comes even though an Outfitter seems to be hunting them down. The saga of Cloyd finding food for the cubs, making warm clothes out of mountain goat fur, catching fish by hand, etc. seems a bit far-fetched, especially to anyone who knows how harsh life is at high altitudes in Colorado. Nonetheless, he dens the cubs, returns to Landis, and discovers the Outfitter has secretly reintroduced a young male grizzly to the Weminuche as forgiveness for killing another grizzly previously. Good tales of the bear in Ute and Tlingit culture redeem the novel.

Reviewed in: Horn Book 3/1/94; School Library Journal 12/1/93; Voice of Youth Advocates 12/1/93.

142. Hobson, Geary. (Cherokee-Quapaw/Chickasaw). *The Last of the Ofos.* Tucson: University of Arizona Press. 2000. 114 p.

Time: twentieth century
Tribe: Ofo (Mosopelea)
Place: Louisiana

An American Indian Literary Series. Sun Tracks, v. 39.

Thomas Darko is the last of the Ofos, a small Southern Indian tribe related to the Tunica and the Choctaws. Through his story, Hobson also tells the story of the twentieth century, the Depression, bootlegging and gangsters, World War II, Hollywood, and—coming full circle—Native Americans being treated as museum specimens. Darko is a likable character and the reader is able to easily identify with him. One by one his family is killed off or dies, until he is the only person left who speaks Ofo and realizes he will never again hear it spoken to him. Although short, this little gem of a novel sums up the Native American experience and is not to be missed.

Reviewed in: Booklist 1/1/00; Kirkus Reviews 12/15/99; Multicultural Review 12/00.

143. Hockenberry, John. *A River Out of Eden.* NY: Doubleday. 2001. 364 p.

Time: Contemporary
Tribe: Chinook
Place: Oregon and Washington

When Grand Coulee Dam was built on the Columbia River, the thunderous Celilo Falls were silenced and the salmon runs could no longer be fished by the local tribes. Charlie Shen-oh-way follows the prophet Smoholla and believes that he can assist Coyote in bringing the salmon back to the river. Although in love with Mary Hale, daughter of Frank Hale, builder of the Columbia River dams, Charlie abandons her during her pregnancy and disappears for years. Their daughter Francine Smoholla grows up to be a fish hatchery worker, trying to preserve the salmon populations. Her truck drivers are found killed by handmade Chinook harpoons before they can deliver their salmon smolt to the river. Eventually she discovers her father Charlie is back. Joe Moses, Charlie's brother, runs a giant casino for the Chinook tribe near the river. Gambling draws a diverse population, including white supremacists and disgruntled Hanford Atomic Works employees with plutonium bombs. A dangerous mix, together these societal outcasts conspire to blow up the dams and thereby release the salmon. Oddly enough, this fulfills the ancient prophecy and Coyote can once again lead the salmon back up the unimpeded Columbia River. Beautifully written with complex and involving characters and plot, this novel leads to a conclusion that some might wish would come true someday.

Reviewed in: Publishers Weekly 3/19/01; Library Journal 6/1/01; Booklist 3/15/01; Kirkus Reviews 2/15/01.

144. Hogan, Linda. (Chickasaw). *Power.* NY: Norton. 1998. 235 p.

Time: Contemporary
Tribe: Taiga (Calusa)
Place: Florida

Omishto, a sixteen-year-old girl whose name means "Watcher," lives in southern Florida, one of the final thirty members of a little-known swamp tribe, the Taiga, related to the Calusas. Janie Soto and Annie Hide are the elderly matriarchs of the Taiga, hoping that Ama Eaton, an independent woman in her thirties, will soon take over their role. Omishto and Ama are very good friends, in spite of their age difference. Omishto's mother has denied her roots, become a fundamentalist Christian, and married a man who is always after Omishto. A terrible hurricane strikes southern Florida, causing wide spread devastation in a fragile land already negatively impacted by civilization. Omishto follows Ama when the woman goes into the forest, hunting one of the last panthers, which Ama finds and kills. The authorities arrest Ama, although they cannot find the panther's hide or her gun, and put her on trial. They try to make it sound as though Ama has killed the cat to eat it and acquire its power for herself, a distortion of her religion. Called to testify, Omishto realizes Ama has performed a sacred ritual, the duty of the Taiga to kill a panther to save the world from sickness and disharmony. The panther is a sacrificial victim. Ama is released by White authorities but is then brought to tribal court, convicted, and banished for four years. Her real crime was not delivering the dead panther to the matriarchs as she should have. Osmishto knows it is because Ama wanted to spare the old women from seeing how sick and diseased the animal had become. Hogan writes beautifully and her descriptions of the Florida swamps and the few Taiga left, trying to hang onto their old culture, is very moving. Although the Taiga are not a known tribe, their similarities to other Florida tribes, such as the Calusas and the Tequestas, is often commented upon in the story. Ama is a strong and sacred woman and one hopes that she will return to lead the tribe when her banishment is over.

Reviewed in: Boston Book Review 7/1/98; Kirkus Reviews 5/1/98; Publishers Weekly 4/20/98.

145. Hogan, Linda. (Chickasaw). *Solar Storms.* NY: Scribner. 1995. 351 p.

Time: 1970's
Tribe: Cree, Chickasaw, Ojibwe
Place: Boundary waters of Northern Minnesota

Foster child Angel Wing comes back to her birthplace of Adam's Rib in northern Minnesota to find her mother Hannah. Moving in with her grandmother Agnes and great grandmother Dora-Rouge, Angel tries to find the true story of her youth. Bush, a strong independent Chickasaw woman living on her own, has Angel eventually move in with her. The women grow comfortable with each other, but they have unresolved desires. Dora-Rouge wants to go north to die, Agnes to find medicinal roots, and Angel to find her mother. Bush organizes the canoe trip for the old women, with herself and Angel as the strong ones to make it possible. The trip north is complicated by rising waters from dams which the native peoples are trying to prevent. This is a time of radical movements and the Indians of this area have a cause to fight for in saving their ancestral lands from flooding. Events do not go as expected, Dora-Rouge is not the one to die, and Angel finds another relative besides her mother. The local native peoples protest the dam and suffer the retributions. Angel returns to Adam's Rib and life with a young man there, her search for the truth having been satisfied in unforeseen ways. The language in this novel is beautiful, the scenes of water and forest and islands are mystical, and the characters are strong women whom elicit respect. Winner of the Colorado Book Award for Fiction, Hogan could not have deserved it more.

Reviewed in: Booklist 9/15/95; Publishers Weekly 8/28/95; NYTBR 11/26/95; Choice 2/96.

146. House, Silas. *A Parchment of Leaves: A Novel.* Chapel Hill NC: Algonquin Books of Chapel Hill. 2002. 275 p.

Time: 1913–1920
Tribe: Cherokee
Place: Kentucky

Vine is a beautiful Cherokee girl who is suspected of having the power to bewitch. Saul Sullivan falls in love with her and they marry. His brother Aaron also falls in love with Vine and makes her life miserable pestering her. Vine tells Saul over and over, but he won't believe her or defend her. When the Great War breaks out, Saul goes to work in a distance logging camp, leaving Vine to Aaron's unwanted attentions. She drives him away and he marries a *Melungeon*, a half-Cherokee woman who looks exactly like Vine. Although Aidia is pregnant, Aaron physically abuses her. Esme, Saul and Aaron's mother, refuses to intervene between Aaron and the two women. Only the midwife, Serena, takes their side. One night a drunken Aaron rapes Vine and goes after her frail daughter, Birdie. Vine defends her child and murders Aaron, burying him on a remote mountain side. She never reveals to Esme, Aidia or Saul what happened, and the guilt is overwhelming: "guilt is the worst, smallest kind of jail. I was trapped inside myself from now on." Aidia leaves the community, Esme dies of old age and grief for the missing Aaron whom she loved, and Saul turns cold and hostile. Finally Vine tells him the truth and he storms off, never sympathizing with her reasons. Vine decides to go back to her Cherokee family and rides off to find them in North Carolina. Saul realizes if she reaches her family, he will lose her forever. This is a wonderful, eerie, beautifully written novel that evokes the life of those in Kentucky, Tennessee and North Carolina during World War I.

Reviewed in: Library Journal 9/15/02; Publishers Weekly 8/5/02; Kirkus Reviews 8/1/02; Booklist 8/1/02.

147. Howe, LeAnne. (Choctaw). *Shell Shaker.* San Francisco: Aunt Lute Books. 2001. 222 p.

> **Time**: Contemporary and 1750's
> **Tribe**: Choctaw
> **Place**: Lower Mississippi Valley and Oklahoma

Howe has woven two stories together; the contemporary one concerns the murder of Choctaw Chief Redford McAlester supposedly by Auda Billy; the previous one concerns the murder of Red Shoes by his own people. Howe attempts to draw parallels between these two events, tracing the lineage of the women involved and the willingness of mothers to confess and die for their daughters' crimes, but the attempt is not always successful. Auda and Redford had been lovers, she was his Assistant Chief and saw great things in him. That was until he began using the earnings from the casino for his own ends, laundering the money through the Mafia to finance IRA activities against the still hated English. Red Shoes' story is very convoluted and confusing; it is hard to keep the names of the characters straight, and the time periods skip back and forth. Howe is a good writer with excellent descriptive abilities; it is hoped that future novels will be clearer to understand.

Reviewed in: Multicultural Review 6/02.

148. Hoyt, Richard. *Whoo?* NY: Tom Doherty. 1991. 214 p.
Bigfoot. A John Denson Mystery. NY: Tom Doherty. 1993. 224 p.

Reviewed in: Booklist 1/1/92; Publishers Weekly 11/16/92; Kirkus Reviews 11/15/92.

Snake Eyes. A John Denson Mystery. NY: Tom Doherty. 1995. 255 p.

Reviewed in: Booklist 12/1/95; Publishers Weekly 11/13/95; Kirkus Reviews 11/1/95.

Time: Contemporary
Tribe: Cowlitz, Umatilla
Place: Oregon, Washington State

Private investigator John Denson and his Cowlitz partner Willie Prettybird get themselves involved in cases with typically Pacific Northwestern issues: Sasquatch, spotted owls, logging, cattle poisonings and murder. Willie is the personification of Coyote, a deputy of the Spirit Animals, and believes in the Great Hoop of Life that rules every individual's behavior. Willie's world of peyote visions and animal people is not John Denson's world of logic, but together they are perfect partners and discover the answers to many mysteries. *Whoo*, set in the logging town of Sixkiller, shows both sides of the spotted owl controversy, with the loggers feeling their livelihoods are just as endangered as the owls. A lightweight set of mysteries, those who love this part of the country will enjoy the scenes and characters.

149. Hudson, Joyce Rockwood. *Apalachee.* Athens: University of Georgia Press. 2000. 400 p.

Time: 1704–1716
Tribe: Apalachee
Place: Florida

The Appalachian Mountains are named for this tribe, once a large and flourishing Florida people wiped out by disease, slavery and warfare. This well written novel follows the story of Lucia and Carlos, Apalachees converted to Christianity by the Spanish. Lucia is also the White Sun Woman, who must greet the sun each morning to insure the health of the tribe. Carlos is fervent in his Catholicism and initially critical of her, but eventually falls in love and marries her, abandoning his Christian beliefs. When the English attack the missions in Florida and defeat the Spanish, the Apalachees are sold into slavery for the colonial estates in Carolina. Lucia is caught, branded and made a housemaid on the English estate of a cruel owner. Carlos escapes to become King Carlos, a leader of his people against the Cherokee, the Creeks and the English. Lucia spends many years with the African slaves in the Carolinas. Finally in 1715–1716 the tribes of the southeastern colonies rise up against the English in the Yamassee rebellion, killing settlers and burning homes and estates. Carlos and his men are part of the rebellion and he finds Lucia again. Secret treaties between the English and the Cherokee to trick these tribes and the Creeks lead to his assassination. Lucia is caught again and sold to the estates in the Caribbean, a sad fate for Indian people unable to cope with the heat and intense labor demanded of them. This part of Native American history has not been extensively covered in fictional literature. The Apalachee peoples were a mound-building tribe so diminished now that their history is not well known. The slavery encouraged by the English that turned tribe against tribe for the profits in human trade to establish the colonial estates has also not been well documented in the fiction about the native peoples. *Apalachee* provides extensive details on these little-known facts in the history of southeastern United States and is an important contribution to Native American literature.

Reviewed in: Booklist 4/1/00; Publishers Weekly 3/27/00.

150. Hudson, Janis Reams. *Winter's Touch.* NY: Zebra. 1999. 350 p.

Time: 1800's
Tribe: Arapaho
Place: Colorado

Winter Fawn, a half-Arapaho and half-Scottish young woman, is old enough to marry but rejects her suitor, Crooked Oak. He's had a vision that the two must marry for him to be the great leader of the Arapaho against the hated White man. Crooked Oak almost kills Carson Dulaney, a young man returning to his family ranch outside of Pueblo after the Civil War. Carson is dragged back to the Arapaho camp as a hostage, under the protection of Winter Fawn's Scottish father, Innes MacDougall. Crooked Oak tries again to kill Carson, who flees with Winter Fawn. Eventually the MacDougall family of father, daughter and son Hunter go to live on Carson's ranch. Carson doesn't want to love Winter Fawn, who loves him, but he succumbs and they agree to marry. Carson's sister Bess wants to marry Hunter and Innes falls in love with Carson's aunt Gussie. Crooked Oak appears once more to try to take Winter Fawn back. He is defeated and this mixed family all ends up happily together. Good character development but the pairing off of all participants is a bit contrived, as is the thick Scottish accent the two Arapaho children have learned from Innes.

151. Hunt, Angela Elwell. *Rehoboth.* Wheaton, IL: Tyndale House. 1997. 356 p. (*Keepers of the Ring, 4*)

Time: 1650's
Tribe: Wampanoag
Place: Massachusetts

Half-breed brother and sister Mojag and Aiyana Bailie are "praying Indians," Christians all their lives who want to spread God's word to others. Raised as Whites they are not accepted by either side of their family, and not always by the church either. Leaving their home on Martha's Vineyard, they journey with their father to Rehoboth, where Aiyana becomes a servant to a wealthy merchant and falls in love with his son, Forest. Mojag goes to the camp of Metacomet (King Philip) to convert him, but is converted himself in every way but spiritually to the ways of the Wampanoags. Chief Metacomet attempts to unite the various local tribes to drive out the English once and for all. Although the united tribes achieve many victories, they are eventually defeated. The superior numbers of their English enemies, and treachery on the part of those who might have been expected to support the Native peoples' cause, cannot be overcome. Aiyana and Forest go through many trials, including Forest's capture, before they can be married. Mojag's Wampanoag wife sacrifices herself for him and he vows to continue to work with his people. This might have been an exciting novel, but it reads more like a Christian text. Similar books on this time period with the Christian perspective are the Cross and the Tomahawk Series by Mark Ammerman.

152. Hunt, Bonnie Jo (Hunkpapa Lakota), and Lawrence J. Hunt. *The Lone Wolf Clan Series.*

The Lone Wolf Clan.
Raven Wing.
The Last Rendezvous.
Cayuse Country.
Land without a Country.
Death on the Umatilla.
The Mounted Riflemen.

Albuquerque: Mad Bear Press. 1998–2002.

Time: 1820's–1840's
Tribe: Nez Perce
Place: Western United States

In these seven volumes the Hunts have undertaken a labor of love: that of telling the history of the Nez Perce tribe. They have chosen a broad palette, but their skills as novelists are not equal to the task. The Lone Wolf Clan is headed by Lone Wolf, a proud if not always wise man, and his three children: Many Horses, Vision Seeker and Raven Wing. Many Horses is killed, Vision Seeker spends a snowbound winter with white trappers, and Raven

Wing marries one of them, Little Ned. She bears his son Buffalo Boy whose white name is Michael. Raven Wing runs off with the evil French trapper Francois, and Little Ned abandons both his Indian family and his White family in the East for a life of trapping. His white son, Joe Jennings, comes West to find his father and finds his half-brother Michael Two Feathers. Many of the middle books in this series describe the coming of the missionaries, the Spauldings and the Whitmans. Michael spends time at the Whitman Mission and while he admires them, he fears for their safety as the Cayuse become increasingly hostile. Neither Joe nor Michael are present at the Whitman Massacre, but both participate in the inept Army effort to capture those responsible. When that fails, they join the Regiment of Mounted Riflemen, the first large military force to make the two thousand mile journey from St. Louis to the Pacific Northwest. The Hunts get further and further away from the story of the Lone Wolf Clan and focus many of the stories on White characters such as Colonel Gilliam, the Whitmans, and Major Cross of the Mounted Riflemen. While these incidental bits of American Western history are interesting, they do not add to the reader's knowledge of the Nez Perce. The characters of both Indian and Whites are one-dimensional, much of the action takes place off-stage, and each novel ends without resolution.

153. Jekel, Pamela. *River Without End: A Novel of the Suwanee.* NY: Kensington. 1997. 436 p.

Time: 1790–1920's
Tribe: Seminole
Place: Florida

The subtitle says it all, this really is a novel of the Suwanee. But it is also primarily the story of the Seminoles, how they first tried to keep their land under the leadership of Osceola, how they withdrew deeper into the wilderness of Florida, and how parts of their culture merged with the whites. After Osceola's death, the narrative shifts to his granddaughter, Not Black, who falls in love with a White man. Despite her parent's protests and objections, Not Black marries Tom Craven according to the ways of her people. Tom's father also objects strongly and refuses to recognize the union, but the Civil War begins and both Cravens enlist. Not Black bears his son and for four years manages their small land holding, always waiting for Tom to return. When the war is over, Tom does return, with a White wife and no use for Not Black. He does want their son, however, and reluctantly Not Black lets Small Warrior go, knowing that as a half-breed, he would have no place with her people. Thirty years later Sam Craven is married with three children of his own and only a dim recollection of his mother, her stories, and her people. When Captain Harry Jackson undertakes the huge project of draining the swamps, Sam signs on as a day laborer, leaving his family in charge of his wife and their eldest son Gaddy. Gaddy manages the farm all right, but he yearns to be free and when he is sixteen, he steals a horse and heads for the lumber camps up north where they are clear cutting all the cypress. Marrying and becoming a father himself, Gaddy tries to ally himself with the new Florida, but he cannot help but see and deplore what the massive logging effort is doing to the land. When his father and brother ask him to come home to work the farm again, Gaddy agrees and concurs with his father that the "Indian blood" is stronger than they knew. Jekel also includes numerous stories of the creatures of the swamp, the birds, animals, insects, and fish. Through the stories of Osceola, Not Black, Sam, and Gaddy, the reader gains a vivid picture of Florida's history and of the Suwanee.

Reviewed in: Publishers Weekly 5/19/97.

154. Jekel, Pamela. *She Who Hears the Sun: A Novel of the Navajo.* NY: Kensington. 1999. 351 p.

Time: mid-1800's
Tribe: Navajo
Place: Arizona/New Mexico

Granddaughter of Narbona, born of Manuelito, Pahe's early life is one of happiness. Her grandparents and parents are leaders of their bands, they have many sheep and goats, slaves to do the hard work, and time for their ceremonies and weaving. But when the Whites come to Dine'tah, The Land of the People, all is changed forever. Pahe's grandfather, father, and her husband try to deal with the Whites, both by raiding and killing, and by trying to make peace and save something of their land and their way of life. The Whites are relentless, they want the land and they want to subdue, if not eliminate, the Navajo. Pahe's husband is killed in one of the white raids on their encampments and she, her two children, and her mother follow Manuelito as he desperately tries to save his people, retreating further and further away from their homeland. When the people are starving, their numbers severely reduced, their flocks almost gone, most of them surrender and are forced to Bosque Redondo where others of the Navajo have been kept for several years after The Long Walk. Manuelito remains free and when the White government finally realizes the terrible conditions that exist at Bosque, it is Manuelito who negotiates for the Navajo to return to their ancestral lands. Jekel has written a rich novel portraying the Navajo culture and people at various times in their history. Pahe grows from a bold, impetuous girl to a wise, serious woman who takes her place in the councils of her people.

155. Johnson, Wayne. *Don't Think Twice.* NY: Harmony Books. 1999. 291 p.

Time: Contemporary
Tribe: Chippewa
Place: Northern Minnesota

Paul Two Persons and his wife Gwen own a lakefront summer resort on thousands of acres of land in northwest Minnesota. They lost their young son in a suspicious hunting accident a year ago and their marriage is now suffering, as is their resort which needs repairs and funding to continue. Clark is Paul's best friend, a wealthy lawyer who offers to help but is rejected by a suspicious Paul since he believes Clark and Gwen are having an affair. Paul has always been disliked by Tribal Officer Parker, who resents the Two Persons' entire family tradition of opposing development on Indian land. Paul's grandfather died under suspicious circumstances, and an opposition group Paul's father started also lost members under mysterious circumstances. Accidents befall the resort all summer; cabins are burned and boats are blown up which cost Paul dearly. Another friend is found dead with tribal burial markings on his body, but done incorrectly. Obviously this was a murder because this man also opposed gambling interests moving onto Chippewa land. Paul and the local sheriff Charlie start to work on who is behind all the accidents and suspicious deaths. The final night of the summer season Paul's resort is sabotaged, Clark is killed, Gwen is threatened, and Paul takes drastic action to stop the men involved. This novel is a well-written, gripping story of today's conflict between Native Americans eager to cash in on gambling profits versus those who wish to keep the reservation lands pristine and natural.

Reviewed in: Publishers Weekly 5/31/99; Library Journal 4/1/99.

156. Johnson, Wayne. *Six Crooked Highways.* NY: Harmony Books. 2000. 302 p.

Time: Contemporary
Tribe: Chippewa
Place: Northern Minnesota

Developers are threatening the pristine beauty of the Minnesota lakeland region, trying to build roads and secretly mine reservation land. Paul Two Persons owns and runs a resort on land in the heart of the proposed development and refuses to consider selling. His wife Gwen and daughter Claire are threatened, his young Chippewa resort workers seem to be involved, and then bodies start showing up. One is Eugene, a traditionalist strongly opposed to development, who was one of Paul's young workers. Paul finds a core sample sheet listing all the metals in the soil under the proposed highway which indicate a fortune will be made by someone. It is up to Paul and his now-discredited friend, Sheriff Charlie, to clear up the confusion. Paul has an ugly secret in his past which he does not want revealed to anyone. Members of the tribal council have knowledge and proof of his youthful crime and he fears they will use it against him to push the highway onto his land. Finally Paul discovers BIA agent Michaels is behind the plot and exposes the murders. An extremely tense well-written mystery with excellent tribal characters, Johnson includes sage wise men and crooked tribal elders equally, making clear that the Chippewa tribe has as many different facets of human character as any other society.

Reviewed in: Publishers Weekly 7/11/00; Booklist 6/15/00.

157. Johnston, Terry C. *The Plainsmen Books.*

Time: 1870's
Tribe: Sioux, Cheyenne, and Nez Perce
Place: Western United States

Johnston continues his planned twenty-two volume series with these six titles, all well researched, well written, and full of historical events and personages. Army scout Seamus Donegan leads us through the series of events, although distracted by thoughts of his wife, Samantha, back at Fort Laramie. Each one of the volumes is a major work, between four hundred and six hundred pages long, including photographs, forewords and afterwords, and long lists of characters involved in every battle or campaign. Johnston promises historical accuracy and we have no reason to doubt him after finishing his series. Once again each campaign and battle has been thoroughly researched, both sides of the conflict are portrayed in a fair and honest manner, white and Native American, and all the characters are so well drawn that we are fully engaged in the conflicts. Although Donegan/Johnston is clearly sympathetic to the plight of the Sioux and Cheyenne, his role is as a scout in the U.S. Army and he fulfills it. An excellent continuation of a popular historical approach to the Indian Wars of the 1870's, Johnston includes all of the most renown battles, such as the Dull Knife Battle and the Nez Perce War. These volumes also include the long bitter campaigns which brought an end to the Cheyenne, Sioux and Nez Perce presence on the Northern Plains, and the defeat of Dull Knife, Chief Joseph, Crazy Horse and Sitting Bull. Highly recommended, this set of historical fiction focusing on the Indian Wars of the last half of the nineteenth century in the Northern Plains is an accessible way to learn honest and accurate facts about a shameful time in the United States' government dealings with our nation's original peoples. Each title includes a list of fictional and historical personages and many historical photos.

Book 10. *Trumpet on the Land.* NY: Bantam. 1995. 639 p. The Aftermath of the Custer Massacre, The Sibley Scout, the Skirmish at Warbonnet Creek, the Battle of Slim Buttes and Crook's "Horse-Meat March."

Reviewed in: Roundup 3/95.

Book 11. *A Cold Day In Hell.* NY: Bantam. 1996. 480 p. The Spring Creek Encounters, the Cedar Creek Fight with Sitting Bull's Sioux, and the Dull Knife Battle, November 25, 1876.

Reviewed in: Roundup 2/96.

Book 12. *Wolf Mountain Moon.* NY: Bantam. 1997. 424 p. The Fort Peck Expedition, the Fight at Ash Creek, and the Battle of the Butte, January 8, 1877.

Reviewed in: Roundup 2/97.

Book 13. *Ashes of Heaven.* NY: St. Martin's. 1998. 398 p. The Lame Deer Fight, May 7, 1877, and the end of the Great Sioux War.

Book 14. *Cries from the Earth.* NY: St. Martin's. 1999. 458 p. The Outbreak of the Nez Perce War and the Battle of White Bird Canyon, June 17, 1877.

Book 15. *Lay the Mountains Low.* NY: St. Martin's. 2000. 495 p. The Flight of the Nez Perce from Idaho and the Battle of the Big Hole, August 9–10, 1877.

Reviewed in: Library Journal 9/15/00; Publishers Weekly 5/15/00.

Book 16. *Turn the Stars Upside Down: The Last Days and Tragic Death of Crazy Horse.* NY: St. Martin's. 2001. 384 p. Crazy Horse's surrender to the U.S. Army at Fort Robinson, Nebraska.

Reviewed in: Kirkus Reviews 6/1/01; Publishers Weekly 7/30/01.

In this last volume of the series, the extensive coverage of the events leading up to the murder of Crazy Horse is so movingly written that one cannot fail to understand the fear and awe this charismatic leader of the Sioux warriors elicited in others. The scheming of Red Cloud to undermine Crazy Horse's credibility with General Crook is infuriating. The duplicity of Woman's Dress, No Water, interpreter Grouard and even Crazy Horse's uncle Spotted Tail, is overwhelming. In the end Crazy Horse was defeated by the disloyalty of those he once called friends and relatives. The accuracy of the events is without question and Johnston adds both a forward and an afterword to his text with more details. Johnston makes a point of Crazy Horse's mysticism, his humbleness, and his devotion to the warrior life of the Sioux. Sadly, this novel on the death of one of history's most renowned Native Americans was also Terry C. Johnston's last. Johnston died in Montana in March of 2001 and will be remembered as one of the best writers on these years and events in the history of the American West during the Indian Wars.

158. Jones, Stan. *White Sky, Black Ice.* NY: Soho Press. 1999. 264 p.

Time: Contemporary
Tribe: Inupiat
Place: Alaska

State Trooper Nathan Active straddles both worlds of White and Native People. Born to an unwed fifteen-year-old Inupiat girl, he was given up for adoption and raised by White parents in Anchorage. Now he is back in the village of Chukchi, hoping to be transferred to Anchorage as quickly as possible. When there are two apparent suicides in two days, both victims shot through the Adam's apple, Nathan wonders if there is more to the story. Each man worked at the Gray Wolf copper mine which has brought economic prosperity to the region. Does the fact that fish are dying in the river have a link to the mine and therefore to the deaths? Before his investigation is through, Nathan has uncovered a complex scheme involving the local Inupiat promoter Tom

Werner, the management of the mine and its international owners GeoNord. Contemporary Inupiat life is well described and Jones gives the reader a good picture of the complexities facing these people.

Reviewed in: Library Journal 5/1/99; Booklist 4/15/99; Publishers Weekly 4/5/99; NYTBR 6/13/99.

159. Jones, Stephen Graham. (Blackfeet). *The Fast Red Road: A Plainsong.* Normal/Tallahasssee: FC2. 2000. 326 p.

Time: Contemporary
Tribe: Piegan, Navajo
Place: New Mexico

Pidgin returns home from Utah for the final burial of his father Cline's body, used for nine years as a research cadaver due to its reverse organs. Pidgin's uncle Birdfinger had thrown Pidgin out several years before, taking over Cline's trailer as his own. Many years ago, Pidgin's mother, Marina Trigo, Cline, Birdfinger, and a few others had been members of the Goliard cult, devoted to robbing mail trucks. Living off the money they find, Cline, a disturbed Vietnam veteran, believed there was a government conspiracy being run through the U.S. postal system. Birdfinger was in love with Marina, who loved Cline. Pregnant Marina was put into a coma from a truck accident, gave birth to Pidgin eight months later, then died. Birdfinger searched for her in young women forever, sure she is still alive somewhere. Pidgin discovers Cline's body being stolen by the Mexican Paiute, another Goliardian. Pidgin spends the rest of his time seeking his father's body. A strange, disjointed, rambling piece of fiction full of hurting characters, nothing much is ever really resolved or understood by any of these people. Birdfinger finds yet another Marina-substitute who lures him into a robbery where he is killed and the story ends. Pidgin finds the Mexican Paiute and is finally resolved about his father's death. Similar to Gerald Vizenor's fiction, Jones's novel will challenge the reader to follow and understand the characters and their motivations.

Reviewed in: Choice 6/1/01.

160. Joynes, Monty (St. Leger M. Joynes). *Lost in Las Vegas.* Charlottesville, VA: Hampton Roads. 1998. 300 p.

Time: Contemporary
Tribe: Hopi
Place: New Mexico, Nevada

Booker Jones has exchanged his fast paced life on the east coast for a contemplative life of sharing and giving in a Hopi pueblo in New Mexico. When the tribal elders ask him to go to Las Vegas and retrieve one of their promising young men, lost to the glitter and money of that gambling town, he agrees. On the reservation, Booker is known as Anglo and he is sent to find Ramon Ortiz, White Wing, "the Dancer," who is a prize-winning Fancy Dancer now performing in a Tropicana show every evening. Dancer is handsome and has become friends with two showgirls who dress him and introduce him to wealthy lonely women for evening accompaniment. Dancer is wealthy in money, but poor in spirit. By tribal custom, Dancer must offer Anglo hospitality and allows Anglo live with him. Gradually Anglo gains Dancer's trust and respect. Anglo asks Dancer to be his Helper on Anglo's vision quest in the Valley of Fire National Park. Dancer agrees, helps build the sacred circle and sweat lodge and then realizes he is the one to go on the quest. Dancer spends days in the desert and has a fantastic vision telling him to return to walk in harmony, to learn the Thunder Dance and bring rain to feed his people on the pueblo. Dancer's vision quest ends in a terrible rainstorm and flash flood which almost kills Anglo. Found by the two showgirls, Debbie and Sue, Dancer and Anglo are taken to a hospital to recover and then return home to New Mexico. The author knows much about Native American music and ceremonies and sincerely conveys the sense of needing a true purpose to one's life to feel fulfilled. One part of a series featuring Booker Jones, this is the only volume which concentrates on the Hopi ways.

161. Kemprecos, Paul. *The Mayflower Murder: an Aristotle Socarides mystery.* NY: St. Martin's. 1996. 292 p.

Time: Contemporary
Tribe: Wampanoag, Narragansett, Mohawk
Place: Massachusetts

Soc is a Greek fisherman, a Vietnam veteran, and a private investigator when he gets cases. He is asked by a friend to look into the charges of murder against Joe Quint, a Native American lawyer and vocal activist and finds himself embroiled in controversies around sales of Wounded Knee artifacts, murders, gambling and the mob, destruction of historical sites, and state politics. Joe Quint is a difficult person to like, but his viewpoints on the treatment of the New England tribes have a lot of truth to them. Soc goes to work for an archaeologist on an ancient site and discovers illegal trade in artifacts. He also looks into Indian gaming resorts and finds the fingers of the mob are intruding. Behind and under it all are the tribal conflicts which have plagued Native Americans forever. Joe Quint is actually being stalked by the Warriors of the Mohawks, set up by his own friends. Eventually everything is resolved, charges are dropped, Soc saves the *Mayflower* ship from being bombed, but Plymouth Rock barely escapes. Amusing characters in this novel help the reader realize that injustices against native tribes began many centuries earlier than when we usually realize.

Reviewed in: Booklist 5/15/96; Kirkus Reviews 5/1/96; Publishers Weekly 5/20/96.

162. King, Thomas. (Cherokee). *Truth and Bright Water.* NY: Atlantic Monthly Press. 1999. 266 p.

Time: Contemporary
Tribe: Ojibwe, Cree
Place: Montana/Canada

Tecumseh narrates this coming of age, magical realism story, set on the Bright Water Reserve and in the town of Truth, just across the Shields River and the Montana-Canada border from each other. Tecumseh's parents are separated, so he spends most of his time with his Boxer dog, Soldier, and his cousin Lum. Soldier is one of the best characters in the story with great loyalty and strength. Lum is the saddest. He is a long distance runner, who refuses to believe his mother is dead, killed in a car accident by his abusive father, Franklin. Franklin is the head man of the band, full of misguided money making schemes. Tribal member Monroe Swimmer, a famous artist and gifted restorer of old paintings, returns to the reservation, as does Aunt Cassie, Tecumseh's mother's sister, who has a deeply buried secret. Monroe has been fired from museums all over the world. Hired to restore their paintings, he has been stealing back the bones of Native American children he finds in their archives. Monroe makes a ceremony of throwing the repatriated bones into the Shields River. He also paints away the old Methodist Church, blending it back into the landscape, and plants wire frame buffalo all over the prairie to lure back a live herd. When the annual Indian Days begin, the foreign tourists pour in to buy "genuine" trinkets and watch the foot races, in which Lum is favored by everyone to win. Severely beaten by his father a few days before and thrown out of the house, Lum is unable to compete. Discouraged and depressed, Lum takes Soldier and goes for a long run. Tecumseh watches Lum and the loyal, supportive Soldier run off the bridge over the Shields, into the deep and swiftly flowing water. The pain of these two young boys is poignant, the loyalty of Soldier is deeply moving, and the confusion of the adults is frustrating. Only Monroe Swimmer with his magical skills to change buildings into landscape and return children to their homeland is uplifting. This is a wonderful, mystical novel, very moving, beautifully written and guaranteed to affect the reader.

Reviewed in: Library Journal 9/15/00; Publishers Weekly 8/11/00; Booklist 8/10/00; Kirkus Reviews 8/1/00; Quill & Quire 9/1/99; NYTBR 12/31/00.

163. Kirkpatrick, Jane. *Love to Water my Soul.* Sisters, OR: Multnomah Press. 1996. 368 p.

Time: 1860–1880's
Tribe: Modoc, Wadaduka Band of Northern Paiute
Place: Oregon, Washington

In the 1860's, a little girl is left behind by her wagon train and found by the Modoc. Called Asiam, she is tattooed on her chin, marked as a slave. Initially taken in by Wuzzie, the old man shaman, she is treated harshly. Later she is adopted by Lukwsh, mother of Shard, Wren and Stink Bug. Although Asiam is still basically a slave, she has a better life with this family. Grey Doe, the grandmother, dislikes Asiam intensely, but takes her through the ceremonies necessary when Asiam becomes a woman and is renamed Shell Flower. Shell Flower and Shard fall in love with each other. Times become very difficult and the tribe suffers at the hands of White men. Shaman Wuzzie blames the outsider, Shell Flower, and she is selected for sacrifice. Shard tells her to run away. Found next by kindly White people, the Sherars who run a toll bridge on the Deschutes River, Asiam becomes Alice M. Here she grows up, marries a doctor, works with the mentally ill, and finds old Wuzzie in the asylum in Portland. Wuzzie is a woman, a shock to Alice. Through Wuzzie's stories, Alice traces back what happened to the Paiutes and finds Lukwsh and Shard. After her doctor husband dies of a stroke, Alice marries her true love, Shard, with whom she has several children. This is the true story of the author's husband's great grandmother. An excellent account of the history of the Paiute tribe and their battles with the Army, their persecution, their imprisonment, and later their settling on the Warm Springs reservation in Oregon, the novel adds to the literature on a tribe not often encountered in fiction.

164. Kosser, Michael. *Autumn Thunder.* NY: St. Martin's. 1997. 333p.

Time: 1870's
Tribe: Kiowa
Place: Oklahoma

When Autumn Thunder comes of age, the Kiowa are still a free people, hunting buffalo, raiding into Texas, living as they always have. Autumn Thunder cannot believe that this will ever end, that the buffalo will be exterminated, or that the whites will punish them for the Texas raids. He does not believe that the proud Kiowa warriors will be lumped into "Indians" like the weak Caddoes and the agricultural Wichitas. Autumn Thunder participates in the Warren Wagon Train Raid and sees the Kiowa leaders imprisoned and killed. He has the opportunity to kill a cavalryman, Sweeney, but spares his life and gives him to Gathers the Grass as a present. Gathers the Grass nurses Sweeney back to life and when Sweeney returns to the Army he becomes the one person who can deal with both the Kiowa and the Whites. Autumn Thunder doesn't really trust Sweeney, but as more and more constraints are put on the Kiowa, he turns to him for assistance. To save their people, most of the Kiowa go to live on the reservation, but Autumn Thunder has one last kill to make—that of the buffalo hunter Tuck who not only slaughtered the once vast herds, but also killed Autumn Thunder's best friend for no reason. This is a powerful story of the end of the free Kiowa.

165. Kosser, Michael. *Walks on the Wind.* NY: St. Martin's. 1998. 347 p.

Time: 1800's
Tribe: Arapaho
Place: Colorado

In the early 1800's the Southern Arapaho band of Left Hand (Niwot) camped along the South Platte and Cherry Creek and hunted buffalo freely. The Colorado gold rush of 1859 brought settlers and cities to this area, called Denver by the White men, and drove out the Cheyenne and Arapaho. Walks on the Wind is a member of Niwot's band, trying to maintain peace with Whites. After their women are raped and beaten by a mob of drunken Whites while the Arapaho are out fighting Utes, the situation worsens. Personal confrontations and a decision by some to join more warring tribes, like the Sioux, split up the Southern Arapaho band. The Civil War brings Colonel Chivington and his Colorado troops, used by Governor Evans to clear out the Cheyenne and Arapaho at Sand Creek and to also gain title to the land Denver is built upon. This well-written novel portrays the Arapaho in a realistic light, even to the eventual drunkenness of the formerly proud Niwot. The White men, Evans and Chivington, are painted rather blackly, but no more than what they deserved. A side of Colorado history not too often told in such a sympathetic light, the novel depicts the Native American lifestyle well and how history negatively impacted it.

166. Kosser, Michael. *Warriors' Honor.* NY: St. Martins. 1999. 263 p.

Time: 1860–1870's
Tribe: Crow
Place: Western United States

Young Buffalo is a Crow warrior whose life revolves around his people and their enemy, the Sioux. The Crow have allied themselves with the White man against the Sioux, believing they are just another tribe, not realizing their enormous power and that the defeat of the Sioux will be the defeat of all the tribes. Wayne Braddock was on the losing side of the Civil War, and with his family and land gone, has joined the Western Army. He makes friends with Young Buffalo and eventually joins with the tribe, marrying, fathering children, and serving as one of the "wolves" for the white army. After the Battle of the Little Bighorn, Braddock and Young Buffalo both see that their way of life is over. Braddock takes his wife and children home to Tennessee to try and make a life there while Young Buffalo will try to preserve what there is left for the future. "So it is for the children of the long-beaked bird. We are an old people. Our force has been spent in many battles with those who would wipe us from the face of the earth. But we have survived and we are free. It is up to us to preserve what we have so our children will have their land to make them strong again, some day." This well-written novel is unusual in presenting the Crow point of view as they are usually portrayed as traitors, working as Army scouts against the Sioux. The characters are well developed with all the human strengths and weaknesses and while the plot is familiar, Kossner makes it appear fresh. This is definitely worth seeking out.

167. Krueger, William Kent. *Boundary Waters.* NY: Pocket Books. 1999. 325 p.

Time: Contemporary
Tribe: Ojibwe
Place: Northern Minnesota

Shiloh is a successful young country singer spending the summer in the remote boundary waters of Minnesota where she has been guided by a member of the Wolf Clan, Wendell Two Knives, an *aadizookewinini,* a storyteller. As winter approaches she realizes Wendell is not coming to lead her home to Aurora, Minnesota. Starting out on her own, a large wolf assists her in her journey. Cork O'Connor is asked by Arkansas Willie Raye, Shiloh's stepfather and manager of her recording company, to find her. Several purported FBI agents also show up looking for her and they all start off together, led by Stormy and Louis Two Knives, Wendell's relatives. Louis is only ten, but he has learned the way through the waters from Wendell's Anishinabe tales of the rivers and lakes. Two other men, *majimanidoo*, or evil spirits, are following the group, killing them one by one. The motives appear to lie in the long-ago murder of Shiloh's mother, Marais Grand. Several men come to Aurora claiming to be Shiloh's father to further complicate the story. Finally in a heroic marathon run through the forest, Cork manages to rescue Shiloh. The truly evil man is revealed, although Shiloh's father is not. A gripping mystery interspersed with wonderful Anishinabe tales, the story ends with young Louis creating a new legend and story based on his dead uncle Wendell.

Reviewed in: Publishers Weekly 4/5/99.

168. Krueger, William Kent. *Iron Lake.* NY: Pocket Books. 1998. 330 p.

Time: Contemporary
Tribe: Ojibwe
Place: Northern Minnesota

Cork O'Connor, sheriff of Aurora, Minnesota, until a recall election removed him from his office, runs a small burger shop left to him by an Anishinabe, or " Shinnob, " friend, Sam Winter Moon. Cork's mother was half Ojibwe and he grew up listening to Henry Meloux, an Ojibwe *midewiwin*, a medicine man, relating the legends. One legend Cork especially remembers is of Windigo, the cannibal giant with the heart of ice who calls your name on the wind when he plans on coming for you. Windigo calls the name of several people in this small town, starting with conservative Judge Parrant and moving on to right-wing militant Harlan Lytton and Russell Blackwater, the head of the Chippewa Grand Casino. Cork discovers the judge was blackmailing townspeople with compromising photographs taken by Lytton and using the money to fund the Minnesota Civilian Brigade, an anti-government paramilitary group. Judge Parrant's son Sandy is a newly elected liberal Senator, involved with Cork's estranged wife, Jo, an attorney for the Anishinabe in Aurora. Cork is seeing Mandy, a young waitress, but really wants to go home to Jo and his three children. Events escalate, secrets are revealed, Sandy turns out to be completely involved in the murders and attempts to kill Jo and Cork. They are saved by the Anishinabe *midewiwin* Henry. Krueger includes legends and history of the Ojibwe in this fascinating and well-written mystery. He also provides the fact that the Iroquois were responsible for pushing the Anishinabe, originally an Atlantic coastal tribe, far west to the Great Lakes, and that Ojibwe means "roast until puckered," a fate suffered at the hands of their Iroquois enemies.

Reviewed in: Library Journal 3/15/99; Booklist 6/15/98; Publishers Weekly 5/26/98.

169. Krueger, William Kent. *Purgatory Ridge.* NY: Pocket Books. 2001. 352 p.

Time: Contemporary
Tribe: Ojibwe
Place: Northern Minnesota

John LePere, half Cree, mourns his brother, lost to the waters of Lake Superior, *Kitchigami*, when a Fitzgerald shipping company ore boat sank in a storm. When Fitzgerald's daughter, Grace, and grandson, Scott, move next door to him on Iron Lake, he is open to the idea of kidnapping them for ransom. Encouraged by an ex-Navy SEAL, Bridger, John not only grabs Grace and Scott, but Cork O'Connor's wife and son too. Jo O'Connor had been discussing divorce with Grace, who no longer loves her husband, Lindstrom, the owner of the town lumber mill. Anishinabe and White activists are working against the lumber company to prevent their logging old growth timber. Cork has been removed as sheriff but the townspeople want him to run again. He works on the case, assuming the eco-terrorists have kidnapped the women and children. John LePere's heart is not in this crime, so when a forest fire threatens the victims' safety, he rescues them. Everyone finally discovers who actually is behind the demand for a two million dollar ransom, which the kind-hearted Anishinabe tribe offers from gaming revenue. A final battle onboard a sinking vessel on Lake Superior leaves the women and children free, Cork wounded, and the men responsible for the crimes drown. Another excellent mystery full of native traditions, a feel for the preservation of the earth and the old growth timber, and a complex plot.

The characters are all fully drawn and one can even feel sympathy for those responsible for the kidnapping.

Reviewed in: Publishers Weekly 1/8/01; Kirkus Reviews 1/1/01; Booklist 12/15/00.

170. Lackey, Mercedes. *Sacred Ground.* NY: Tor. 1994. 381 p.

Time: Contemporary
Tribe: Osage
Place: Oklahoma

Jennifer Littledeer is a private investigator in Oklahoma, doing mostly divorce and abuse cases. She jumps at the chance to investigate possible insurance fraud: Indian bones have been discovered at a development project headed by slimy Rod Calligan. The presence of the relics as well as numerous accidents may cause the project to shut down. As Jennifer investigates, she realizes that the bones were planted there, but why? Where had they originally been buried? And did their removal release evil forces into the world; forces which Jennie and her Osage grandfather cannot overcome? With the help of David Spotted Horse, Jennie's former lover and native rights activist, who is now willing to trust his heritage, the mysterious happenings are explained and the forces of evil routed, at least temporarily. Although this was reviewed as science fiction, it all seems perfectly plausible contemporary fiction. Jennifer Littledeer and her grandfather are believable, likable characters.

Reviewed in: Booklist 2/15/94; Library Journal 2/15/94.

171. La Duke, Winona. (Ojibwe). *Last Standing Woman.* Stillwater, MN: Voyageur Press. 1997. 303 p.

Time: 1800–2001
Tribe: Ojibwe
Place: Minnesota

In 1800 the Ojibwe first encountered Christian missionaries and killed them. Jumping ahead to 1862 and the Sioux involvement in the Spirit Lake Massacres, an Ojibwe brother and sister rescue one of the Dakota Sioux women injured in the Army's roundup of the tribe. They bring her back to the White Earth Reservation, where she introduces them to the drum and drum songs.

In the 1910's white retaliation against Ojibwe means loss of lands and loss of lives, without any justice. The drums are passed down until finally the missionaries forbid them, and they are hidden in the rafters of the Episcopalian church for safety. In the 1960's pride returns to the people with the Civil Rights movement. In the 1980's the courts recognize that their lands were indeed stolen through illegal transactions and start returning them to the reservation. In the 1990's corrupt tribal government is resisted by the Protect Our Land militants, who occupy tribal headquarters and achieve a national forum for their grievances. Throughout the generations there has always been one woman designated the Last Standing Woman, a woman of courage who works for her tribe. Initially it was Ishkweniibawiikwe, the woman who brings the Dakota woman and the drum ceremonies to the Anishinabe. In the contemporary years it is Lucy St. Clair, a strong and independent leader of the Protect Our Land group, later mother to six sons and a daughter. The final chapters in the novel concern individual events: the Women's Warrior Society publicly humiliating a tribal leader who abuses his young daughter; a winner of the lottery who uses the funds to repurchase tribal lands; and Moose who brings back the bones of ancestors from the Smithsonian, with the unusual assistance of an aging Dead Head and a young State Trooper. Very reminiscent of the Louise Erdrich novels, especially her recent *The Last Report on the Miracles at Little No Horse*, there are many similarities between Lucy St. Clair and Lulu Nanapush. Harvard-educated La Duke is a Native American activist and has written an excellent warm, caring and fascinating history of her people on the White Earth Reservation in Minnesota. Includes a glossary of Anishinabe words.

Reviewed in: Library Journal 11/15/97; Booklist 11/1/97; Publishers Weekly 10/20/97.

172. LaFavor, Carole. (Ojibwe). *Along the Journey River.* Ithaca, NY: Firebrand Books. 1996. 184 p.

Time: Contemporary
Tribe: Ojibwe
Place: Minnesota

Renee LaRoche grew up on the Red Earth Reservation in northern Minnesota and was active in the Indian Rights Movement all over the country for years. Now she is older and has returned to Red Earth with her daughter Jennifer, J. J., to teach and sell her prize-winning beadwork. Her lover, Samantha, is a White Woman's Studies professor from the East doing research on the reservation. Renee loves to help out the Tribal Police by assisting in solving crimes. She is from the Coon family, members of the Bear Clan, the peace-keepers of the tribe. When sacred ceremonial items loaned to the high school are stolen, Renee links it to other thefts. Artifacts from the Zuni Tribe and from the Browns Valley Man, an eight-thousand-year-old skeleton, have also been stolen. A cave full of three-thousand-year-old Ojibwe skeletons is on Coon land and someone is robbing that too. The dishonest tribal Chairman, Jed, is found murdered and a search of his property reveals his connection to the thefts. The leaders of the whole criminal ring are "chimook" (White) disaffected professors at Stanford and Columbia Universities, although that aspect is not well explained. The book's strength lies in its clear portrayal of the importance of family connections and tribal responsibilities to the individual, and vice versa. Many Ojibwe words and traditional stories are woven into the plot, as smoothly as Renee does her beadwork.

Reviewed in: Booklist 5/1/96.

173. LaFavor, Carole. (Ojibwe). *Evil Dead Center.* Ithaca, NY: Firebrand Books. 1997. 221 p.

Time: Contemporary
Tribe: Ojibwe
Place: Minnesota

Caroline Beltrain, an activist and former lover of Renee LaRoche, asks for Renee's help in solving the murder of a young Cree woman. Renee and Chief Hobey Bulieau of the Ojibwe tribal police on the Red Earth reservation discover a pornographic ring involving several Ojibwe men, very young boys in foster care, and Floyd Neuterbide, a White college professor and pillar of the local community. The tribal social services people place Ojibwe children in White families and Floyd has taken in young boys for years. He has also been making them "star" in pedophile videos. When the ring is exposed, more people are murdered. Floyd escapes into the boundary waters, but Renee and Caroline go after him, tracking him down and bringing him back to justice. Renee's current lover, Samantha, is much calmer and more understanding of Renee's need to help the police. These mysteries are excellent not only in their plots and action, but also in portraying the fact that Native American women are also sometimes well-adjusted lesbians with solid family relationships. Called "Two-Spirits" because of their homosexuality, they are fully accepted as part of the tribal social structure. The Red Earth Reservation is shown in a realistic but honest light as it tries to cope with the struggles of the people who live there.

Reviewed in: Kirkus Reviews 2/15/97; Publishers Weekly 3/3/97.

174. Laird, Brian Andrew. *To Bury the Dead.* NY: St. Martin's. 1997. 179 p.

Time: Contemporary
Tribe: Tohono O'odham
Place: Arizona

Gray Napoleon is bringing his old friend Ryder Joaquin home to the Tohono O'odham to be buried. Ryder was working for an arts dealer before he was gunned down in Los Angeles for mysterious reasons and the mystery deepens when his casket is stolen from Gray's truck in Why, Arizona. Gray is a botanist for the Desert Museum, but he has also been an eco-terrorist and a prisoner of war in Vietnam, so is used to hard times and hard people. The desert and the O'odham have calmed him, as has his Apache girlfriend, lawyer Marie Kazhe. Gray's calm is disturbed by hired goons who are trying to track down Las Estrellas for their rich boss, Torrance Power. Power wants the five mythical gemstones theoretically given by the Queen of Spain to the missionaries to build a church in Arizona for the Indians. They disappeared years ago but the art dealers found them and set up a deal between Ryder's French girlfriend and Power. Ryder got caught in the middle and now Gray finds himself there. By the time Gray sorts all this out, Power has lost his fortune, the French girl and her brother have lost their lives, and Las Estrellas are lost in the desert. Fortunately Ryder's body is found and Gray returns him to be buried by his Tohono O'odham relatives. This is an ordinary mystery but features a tribe not often encountered in fiction.

Reviewed in: Kirkus Reviews 2/15/97; Publishers Weekly 3/3/97.

175. Lambert, Page. *Shifting Stars: A Novel of the West.* NY: Tom Doherty. 1997. 352 p.

Time: 1816–1855
Tribe: Sioux
Place: Wyoming

Turtle Woman is married to Sunstone, and their daughter Breathcatcher is married to fur trapper MacDonald, a hearty Scot, envied by Caws Like

Magpie, who wanted Breathcatcher himself. Breathcatcher has a daughter Skye, who was a little girl when her mother is killed by a cougar, and she is raised alone by her father MacDonald. As Skye approaches womanhood, MacDonald takes her back to her grandmother, Turtle Woman, to learn the ways of the Sioux and of being a woman. At first Skye is not accepted, nor willing to stay, but she gradually learns to love her grandmother, learns the ways of the Sioux, makes friends, and even falls in love with Mahto, a young scout. Caws Like Magpie is still full of anger and envy and makes life miserable for MacDonald and for Skye. When he tries to rape Skye, Sunstone fights him, but is killed. Banished by the tribe, Caws Like Magpie attacks MacDonald and kills him too. Now Turtle Woman and Skye are alone and set out on a pilgrimage to the sacred Medicine Wheel in the Shining Mountains. Followed by Caws Like Magpie and also by the protective Mahto, eventually evil Magpie is killed. Turtle Woman's quest has ended and soon her life ends as well. Skye becomes a woman of the tribe, marrying Mahto. The novel is full of Sioux traditions and practices of daily life. Many details, from the scrapers used by the women, to the quilling, to the cooking and water-carrying, are all described in detail. However, there are also some ceremonies, such as the Bite the Knife, Bite the Snake ceremony of the virtue gathering, which may not be historically true. The tradition of banishing someone who has murdered another member of the tribe and the behavior of a *witko,* or crazy person tolerated by the tribe, is authentic. The family interactions are excellent, as is the character development, although Caws Like Magpie is overly repugnant, even to his own mother.

Reviewed in: Library Journal 8/1/97; Booklist 6/15/97; Publishers Weekly 5/27/97.

176. Lane, Christopher. *Elements of a Kill.* NY: Avon. 1998. 340 p.
Season of Death. NY: Avon. 1999. 338 p.
A Shroud of Midnight Sun. NY: Avon. 2000. 342 p.
Silent as the Hunter. NY: Avon. 2001. 342 p.
A Deadly Quiet: An Inupiat Eskimo Mystery. NY: Avon. 2001. 337 p.

Time: Contemporary
Tribe: Inupiat
Place: Alaska

Police officer Ray Attla was raised by his grandfather and taught the native skills necessary for survival in a harsh environment, as well as the native stories and spiritual beliefs. Education at the University of Alaska has caused

Ray to dismiss the spiritual side of his Inupiat culture, even though he frequently has complex dreams built from native stories that metaphorically explain difficult criminal situations. Ray has excellent survival skills and these mysteries make it clear to readers in warmer climes just how dangerous the dark and cold of Alaskan winters can be, where a dead battery may mean a dead motorist. Ray also has a Texan partner, Deputy Billie Bob Cleaver, clueless on how to dress or live in the cold Alaskan winter. The crimes Ray deals with are murders used to cover up drug dealing, illegal mining or oil drilling, or to influence tribal politics. How crimes are worked and solved in the frozen north is very different from urban scenes. Ray often is assisted by either the visions of his grandfather in warnings that come from afar, or from the powerful spirituality of his own daughter, Keera. While Ray constantly dismisses their validity, in truth he also recognizes their power. A nice balance of an "educated" Inupiat trying to put his culture's mysticism aside, while at the same time having his own dream-visions, and listening to the spiritual advice from his near relatives. Inupiat, Inuit and Yup'ik stories and legends are incorporated into all the mysteries. Traditional religious dances and festivals are always attended and honored. Inupiat culture consists of traditional ways mixed with modern conveniences and Ray incorporates both in his own life. At one point, an Inupiat visionary sees Ray as a Lightwalker, capable of overcoming *Nahani*, the dark evil. His daughter Keera is recognized as an *angulcaq*, a person who can see into the night. This is an excellent mystery series, with engaging characters, a great sense of humor, and the ability to impart a strong feeling for the darkness, cold, superstition and danger of Alaskan life. The author contributes a great deal to opening our awareness to the depth of Inupiat culture and spiritual life.

177. Larsen, Deborah. *The White.* NY: Knopf. 2002. 219 p.

Time: 1758–1800
Tribe: Seneca, Delaware
Place: Pennsylvania, Ohio

This is a lyrical novel based upon the history of Mary Jemison, captured at sixteen by Shawnee who killed the rest of her Irish farming family. Adopted by the Seneca sisters Branch and Slight-Wind to replace their dead brother, she is treated kindly and encouraged to join in tribal life. At first mute and withdrawn, eventually Mary, now called Two-Falling-Voices, learns to speak Seneca, as Slight-Wind learns some English. Slight-Wind teaches the Engish to a young handsome Delaware, Sheninjee, who wins Two's heart and hand. Two bears him a son, named Thomas after her dead Irish father. After Sheninjee dies of sickness, Two marries an older Seneca man, Hiokatoo. Hiokatoo was a strong and fierce warrior in his past and is a good father to their five children. They all live in the Genesee Valley with the Seneca, where Mary acquires ten thousand prime acres of land. Mary's sons eventually become drunkards and kill each other, but these events are only lines in the text, there is no emotion involved in their telling. She becomes a legend, the White Woman of Genesee, and tells her story to Dr. James Seaver. Mary never leaves her Seneca people, dying in her nineties on the Buffalo Creek Reservation. The novel is short, poetic, and a joy to read. Perhaps because Larsen is a poet, the novel is more of a long poem than a full exploration of character. At the end of the novel, Mary is still a legend, not a real person.

Reviewed in: Library Journal 6/15/02; NYTBR 8/4/02; Publishers Weekly 6/3/02.

178. Lassiter, Karl. *The Battle of Lost River.* NY: Kensington. 2001. 346 p.

Time: 1869–1873
Tribe: Modoc
Place: Northern California, Southern Oregon

An excellent account of the Modoc War and all of its participants, the novel follows the events on nearly a daily basis from the initial conflicts to the ultimate resolution. One of the most expensive wars in U.S. history, with a large Army force constantly turned back by only a handful of Modocs, and the only killing of a general in any Indian conflict, this is a story of incredible courage. Kintpuash, known to whites as Captain Jack, witnesses the deliberate poisoning of over forty Modocs by white settlers when he is a child. Forever distrusting them, he nonetheless realizes he must come to some terms with the white settlers, as *tyee*, or leader of his tribe. The Modoc are sent to the Klamath reservation, their traditional enemies, and refuse to stay there. They want their own reservation on Lost River, their own homelands, but the U.S. government refuses. All the historical figures, General Canby, Meacham, Frank and Tobey Riddle, Boston Charley, Reverend Thomas, Schonchin John, Shacknasty Jim, and Curly Headed Doctor, the shaman who believes in the power of the Ghost Dance medicine, are fully developed characters. Captain Jack is forced into actions just to preserve his leadership from rivals. Hiding in the maze of the lava beds by Tule Lake, the Modoc are finally forced to surrender when the Army cuts off their water supply. Several Modoc leaders are hanged, including Captain Jack, but the fiercest warriors are saved because they had betrayed Jack and worked with the Army to track him down. A grim endnote adds that the heads of the hung Modoc were removed and sent East for phrenological examination. Historically accurate and well written, this might be the definitive fictional work on the Modoc War.

179. Lassiter, Karl. *The Long Walk.* NY: Kensington. 1996. 415 p.

Time: 1860–1894
Tribe: Navajo
Place: New Mexico

Manuelito was one of the Navajo headmen who opposed being sent to Bosque Redondo in Apache territory when the U.S. Army tried to force the Navajo onto a reservation. The novel follows Manuelito's long battle against Kit Carson and General Carleton, resisting all efforts to be sent away from the Navajo traditional lands. Between 1863 and 1866 Manuelito hid in *Tseyi'*, called Canyon de Chelly by White men. Carson burned their crops, confiscated their sheep and goats, destroyed their hogans and endlessly harassed the people until they were starving and homeless. In 1866 Manuelito finally surrendered and was sent to a horrible existence at Bosque Redondo with the Mescalero Apaches. Dr. Steck argues incessantly with General Carleton to let the Navajo return home, to no avail. Finally in 1868 General Sherman inspected the reservation, found it appalling, and allowed the Navajo to return to New Mexico. The actual Long Walk of the Navajo only fills one chapter in the novel, but the historical figures, events and situations are well portrayed. Kit Carson is portrayed sympathetically, not as an Indian fighter, but as a man following orders to bring in the Navajo. This he tried to do not by killing them, but by destroying their ability to live how and where they wished. A very good introduction to this troubled early chapter in Navajo history, the novel is also a biography of Manuelito but avoids the sad last chapters of his alcoholic life.

180. Lassiter, Karl. *The Warrior's Path.* NY: Kensington. 1998. 350 p.

Time: late 1800's
Tribe: Apache
Place: Southwestern United States

This novel clearly depicts the Apache Wars through the eyes of Victorio and his sister Lozen and through the fictional character of Captain Lester Boynton. Boynton's family was killed by Victorio's warriors and he has vowed revenge, frequently letting that motive overpower his Army training. His men and other Army commands are killed because of Boynton's ineptness, until he learns Victorio's tricks and how to outwit him. Victorio and his people fight bravely, but they cannot prevail against the U.S. Army and after years of fighting, he is finally killed. The novel reads more like an account of the various battles, with little character development on either side. It also depicts Victorio and Geronimo as fighting each other. Other books on the Apache Wars, such as Simmons' *Brothers of the Pine,* are better novels.

181. Lawrence, Martha C. *Pisces Rising.* NY: St. Martin's. 2000. 254 p.

Time: Contemporary
Tribe: Luiseno
Place: Southern California

Psychic investigator Elizabeth Chase is still reeling from the death of her lover Tom McGowan, but is ready to go to work on a new case, that of the murder and scalping of casino manager Dan Aquillo. As manager, Aquillo had worked hard to make the Mystic Mesa Casino an economic success for the Luiseno people, but someone had wanted him dead. Was it the habitual gambler Bill Hurston, found unconscious in the murder room? Or Aquillo's teenaged nephew, convinced his uncle had sold out the tribe? Were the anti-gambling forces truly against gambling or was Las Vegas money fueling their cause? In the course of her investigation Elizabeth meets Sequoia Wilson, a healer of both physical and emotional wounds. The mystery keeps the reader guessing until the end and the Native American themes of the contemporary gambling business and the traditional rituals play nicely against each other.

Reviewed in: Publishers Weekly 2/28/00; Booklist 2/15/00; Kirkus Reviews 2/15/00.

182. Leffers, Laura Lynn. *Dance on the Water.* Sun Lakes, AZ: Blue Star Productions. 1996. 266 p.

Time: Contemporary
Tribe: Miami
Place: Indiana

When Belle MacKay accepts the terms of her grandfather's will to live in his home on an island in Lake Papakeechie and to conduct genealogical research on her paternal blood line, she gets more than she bargained for. Belle never knew her grandfather, Reason MacKay, who was killed in Vietnam. Belle's mother ran off, leaving Belle with her grandmother. She only knows Reason was the great-grandson of Chief Papakeechie, Flat Belly of the Miami. Reason has left Belle bags of receipts, papers, diaries, and clues which gradually enable Belle to piece together the story of the Miami and her family's part in their history. She also stops being a victim, giving up her egotistical lover and boss, and becoming her own woman as she befriends a troubled boy, David, who appears to have also been sent by Reason. While little of the plot is overtly Native American, the Miami history and rituals permeate the novel. The author has provided an extensive bibliography and Belle's story is enjoyable to read.

183. Legg, John. *Cheyenne Lance.* NY: Dorchester. 1984. 240 p.

Time: Early 1800's
Tribe: Cheyenne
Place: Western United States

Zack Dobson is a fur trapper in the Rocky Mountains in the early 1800's who came from Virginia to make his living. His best friend is Mose and they spend summers in Sante Fe together. The rest of the year Zack spends with the Cheyenne along the Arkansas River and trapping in the mountains with his Cheyenne wife, Wind in the Morning. Zack fights the Blackfeet with Mose and fights the Kiowa with the Cheyenne. Zack becomes a Cheyenne Dog Soldier and goes through the sun dance ritual. The Comanche strike, killing many Cheyenne including Zack's family. After a year of mourning, Zack retaliates, killing many Comanche. Taking Wind in the Morning's sister as his wife, he heads back up into the mountains. Good for the portrayal of a fur trapper's life in Colorado long before mining or ranching, but a simply told story nonetheless.

184. Legg, John. *War at Bent's Fort.* NY: St. Martin's. 1993. 370 p.

Time: 1830's
Tribe: Cheyenne
Place: Colorado

The Bent brothers, Charles and William, built an adobe fort on the Arkansas River in the early 1830's. Charles and their partner Cervan St. Vrain focused their trading in Sante Fe and Taos, under Mexican rule, while William stayed in the Colorado area. William befriended the Cheyenne and Arapaho tribes, marrying a Cheyenne woman. He even brokered a peace with these tribes and the Comanches and Kiowas, which lasted for a few years. Legg's novel dramatizes historical facts, embroidering upon small battles to give more importance to the Bents, but not enough to distort history. Many other famous mountain men play roles in the tale, including Kit Carson. Several other Bent brothers come out to join William at the Fort, but die from disease and at the hands of Comanches. In 1849 the partnership with St. Vrain dissolved, Charles was killed by a mob in Taos, and the Southern Cheyenne tribe was devastated by disease. William gave up the Fort and moved to another location, where he built a small trading place. The Bent brothers were instrumental in bringing trade goods to the tribes of southern Colorado and northern New Mexico. Legg's historical fiction brings their personalities and contributions to life in a well-researched and well-written novel.

Reviewed in: Roundup 5/94.

185. Lesley, Craig. *Storm Riders.* NY: Picador. 2000. 339 p.

Time: 1977–1987
Tribe: Tlingit
Place: Oregon, Massachussetts, Alaska

Clark Woods is raising Wade, his foster Tlingit son, who has fetal alcohol syndrome and is very difficult to teach or control. Wade is Clark's wife Payette's cousin and was the victim of severe abuse. Clark worries that Wade is secretly more violent than he appears. When a little Japanese girl drowns in Amherst where Clark and Payette are going to graduate school, Wade is implicated. Nothing can be proven, but Payette, spoiled and selfish, has had enough and leaves Clark. He remains committed to the child and tries different schools, psychologists, medications and treatments, to no avail. Clark moves back to Oregon, marries Natalie, and they try hard to succeed with Wade. When Wade becomes a teenager, stealing cars and ending up in jail repeatedly, they are forced to give up. Wade is sent back to Angoon in southeast Alaska to live with his Uncle Sampson, a totem carver. There Wade does well, on a tiny island with no cars to steal and plenty of physical exercise. Clark goes to visit after several years and sees that Wade belongs with his Tlingit relatives in Angoon. He also hears the story of how the U.S. Navy massacred the village and stole all its religious artifacts a hundred years ago, refusing to ever apologize to the Tlingit. A beautiful and painful story of trying to cope with a severly handicapped child, finally accepting failure, and allowing the boy to return where he always belonged, to his own tribal culture and people.

Reviewed in: Kirkus Reviews 12/15/99; Library Journal 12/1/99; Publishers Weekly 11/8/99.

186. Lewis, Janet. *The Invasion. A Narrative of Events Concerning the Johnston Family of St. Mary's.* East Lansing: Michigan University Press. 2000. 248 p.

Time: 1791–1928
Tribe: Ojibwe
Place: Upper Michigan

Although written as a novel, this story is of the family that includes Henry Rowe Schoolcraft, one of the early Indian agents in the upper mid-west. In 1791–1792, the Irish trader John Johnston, working for the Northwest Company, meets the family of Waub-Ojeeg, White Fisher, chief of the Ojibwe. Johnston marries the daughter, Woman of the Glade, and they produce a large family that intermarries with whites and other Ojibwe, all living in the Upper Michigan Penninsula. Daughters Jane and Anna Marie marry the Schoolcraft brothers, Henry and James. The history of the Ojibwe is traced over the years, with the attempts by Henry Schoolcraft as the official Indian Agent to the Ojibwe to keep these people on their Great Lakes hunting grounds. Although they lose many acres, the Ojibwe are not relocated to another part of the U.S. Henry Schoolcraft collected the Ojibwe tales in his *Algic Researches*, used as a source for Longfellow's Song of Hiawatha. Henry is largly responsible for the retention of these tales and for the Ojibwe being able to stay on their traditional lands. The novel is not easy to read, written in an awkward and stilted style, but it is full of accurate historical detail. Obviously based upon family histories, it also includes photos of the descendents of Johnston and Neengay, Woman of the Glade.

187. Littell, Robert. *Walking Back the Cat.* Woodstock, NY: Overlook Press. 1996. 220 p.

Time: Contemporary
Tribe: Apache
Place: New Mexico

Ex-Gulf War soldier Finn, escaping from the Seattle police, flies his hot air balloon to the Suma Apache Reservation in New Mexico, where he is greeted warmly by Eskeltsetle, the headman. The Apache are running a casino, but are being blackmailed into laundering money for persons unknown, perhaps the Mafia, perhaps the Russians. Eskeltsetle believes Finn, part Navajo himself, can help. All the Apache people who have tried going to the authorities or police have died very suspicious deaths before contacting anyone. Finn is confronted by a Russian hit man, Parsifal, sent to murder him as he has murdered the Apache. Between the two of them, they "walk back the cat" and figure out that the Russians and the Apache are all being used by ex-CIA agents who are determined to keep the Cold War alive. Parsifal completes his final mission, taking out the head of the ex-CIA agents' cell. Eskeltsetle is killed trying to rescue his young son Doubting Thomas from the evil ex-CIA agents, who are then attacked and killed by Apache warriors. Finn ends up with Eskeltsetle's widow, Sonseeahray, the Morning Star. The novel uses the Apache people, their sense of justice, and their desire to improve their economic lives, even if it means running a casino for White gamblers, as a vehicle for a well written spy thriller with an intricate plot and excellent characters.

Reviewed in: Booklist 5/15/97; Publishers Weekly 5/12/97; Library Journal 5/1/97; Kirkus Reviews 5/1/97; Times Literary Supplement 3/8/96.

188. London, David. *Sun Dancer.* NY: Simon and Schuster. 1996. 318 p.

Time: 1990–1996
Tribe: Sioux
Place: South Dakota

Clem and Joey are brothers on the Pine Ridge Reservation and are as poor and discouraged as most of the other men there. Joey is involved with a White rancher's daughter, while Clem has a good wife and several children, as well as a drinking problem. Clem begins to believe in the old religion, Joey is asked to join the newly revived Tokalas society and everyone focuses on attracting public attention to the plight of the Sioux. The Tokalas plan on taking Mount Rushmore hostage, staking themselves on top of the carved heads and telling the news reporters about the broken treaties and stolen lands of the native peoples. The government is stronger and far more resourceful than they could have imagined. Fake reporters are sent in, real ones kept out due to a "toxic railroad spill" caused by drunken Indians. Military troops land and squash the rebellion, all participants are hauled off to jail, and the movement is crushed. Clem is killed and Joey sent to jail. The development of Clem's salvation, his sun dance, his belief in following the old ways is well drawn. A de-frocked Jesuit priest is the center of the rebellion, chased by the demons following him from Central America. Other Sioux men are totally believable characters, many left over from the Wounded Knee stand in the 1970's The role of all of the various churches and religions on the reservations in the exploitation of the Sioux is also addressed. This is a wonderful novel which brings the sun dance principles, the struggle for public awareness of the plight of the Sioux, and the need to rectify the injustices of the land grabs in South Dakota to the reader's attention.

Reviewed in: Booklist 7/96; Library Journal 3/15/96; NYTBR 11/24/96; Publishers Weekly 7/3/96.

189. Louis, Adrian C. (Paiute). *Skins.* NY: Crown. 1995. 296 p.

Time: Contemporary
Tribe: Sioux
Place: South Dakota

Rudy and Mogie Yellow Shirt are Oglala Sioux brothers on the Pine Ridge Reservation but have followed very different paths. Rudy is a policeman, spending his weekends locking up drunks. Unfortunately Mogie often is one of these people. He has returned from Vietnam a damaged soul and has been drinking himself to death ever since. Rudy reminisces about their childhood, their abusive parents, their good times together, and their bad times. Rudy himself is going through a divorce and is looking for a new wife. Rudy feels sometimes like "*Iktomi*," the Trickster, has taken control of his soul, causing him to perform illegal (but morally justified) acts against liquor stores and young thugs. Eventually Mogie dies of liver disease and Rudy carries out his final promise to Mogie, which again exhibits some "*Itktomi*" traits. A warm, funny, contemporary, but ultimately sad novel about conditions on the South Dakota reservation, written by a professor at Oglala Lakota College at Pine Ridge. Nothing is glossed over here and the real life of unemployed Sioux who turn too easily to alcohol is fully exposed for the destructive behavior that it is. In 2002 the novel was made into a film starring Graham Greene and Eric Schweig, directed by Chris Eyre.

Reviewed in: Booklist 7/95; Choice 12/95; Library Journal 6/1/95; Publishers Weekly 5/29/95.

190. Louis, Adrian C. (Paiute). *Wild Indians & Other Creatures.* Reno: University of Nevada Press. 1996. 185 p.

Time: Contemporary
Tribe: Sioux
Place: South Dakota

These twenty-five pieces weave together the people of the Pine Ridge Reservation with Coyote, Raven (a gourmet cook), and Old Bear. Marianna Two Knives is a pretty girl who gradually falls into heavy drinking and prostitution to support her alcoholism. Teddy Two Bears is a decorated Gulf War veteran with a deep secret; he is gay on a reservation with little tolerance for homosexuals. When his friends hire Marianna to initiate him to sex and she discovers the truth, she threatens blackmail. In a panic Teddy accidentally kills her and hides her body. Hearing of Marianna's death, Verdell Ten Bears, one of her old boyfriends, decides to track down her killer. Teddy is wracked with guilt and hangs himself from a cottonwood tree. Luckily Old Bear has just awakened from hibernation and is in the trees relieving himself when he looks up and sees Teddy hanging dead. Old Bear cuts Teddy down and prays over him, asking the Great Spirit, the Great Bear and Jesus to bring the boy back to life. When Teddy wakes up, Old Bear asks why humans commit suicide and why they name themselves after animals. "What is all this Bear naming crap with you Indians, anyways? Us bears don't go around naming our kids Jimmy Nine Indians . . ." As this indicates, Louis blurs the line between man and creature and finds humor in the saddest times. These pieces show many Sioux at their lowest; drunk, abusive, homophobic and cruel. However, his Raven, Coyote and Old Bear pick up one's spirits when necessary and help everyone move on.

Reviewed in: Publishers Weekly 3/18/96.

191. Lucero, Evelina Zuni. (Isleta Pueblo). *Night Sky, Morning Star.* Tucson: University of Arizona Press. 2000. 228 p.

Time: Contemporary
Tribe: Pueblo, Apache
Place: New Mexico, Nevada

Julian Morning Star, a member of AIM who has been in prison for over twenty years, has led the fight for recognition of Native American rights and religious practices. Attacked and almost killed by another prisoner, Julian is transferred to a hospital, where he meets a kindly nurse and begins to write down his tragic story. Cecelia Bluespruce was his high school sweetheart who Julian left pregnant and abandoned years ago. She has made a life for herself as an artist, raising their son Jude, who is ignorant of the identity of his father. Jude demands to know the truth, Cecelia has disturbing dreams about Julian, and both the dreams and Jude's demands result in her tracing backwards through old friends to find Julian. Cecelia's friend Marli, ineffectually working on her Ph.D., is most effectual in tracking down Julian through his parents, encouraging Cecelia to tell Jude the truth and to meet with Julian. The story is told in chapters from different characters' perspectives, with each chapter's character given a unique identifiable voice and personality. The individual characters' vocabularies reflect their pasts, education, current ages and living conditions, so Julian sounds like a prisoner, Jude a young man, Marli a frustrated academic and Cecelia a mystical artist. The meeting between the estranged family members of Julian, Jude and Cecelia is moving, but encouraging for all. Everyone's personal conflicts and problems will not be solved, but the truth will help them all deal better with reality.

Reviewed in: Library Journal 11/1/00.

192. Lucas, Janice. *The Long Sun.* NY: Soho Press. 1994. 266 p.

Time: early 1700's
Tribe: Tuscarora
Place: Pennsylvania

John Billips, his wife Lydia and their children are trying to wrest a living from a small land-holding in western Pennsylvania when they are befriended by the young Indian Lame Crow. He learns some of their language and ways and they learn his, so that when a warring tribe threatens the area, Lame Crow persuades the Billips' to come with him to his village. They voluntarily follow him, are adopted into the tribe, and give up most of their White ways. Their son Takime becomes a warrior, their daughter Sassy marries Runs with the Wind, and John and Lydia are respected people of the Tuscarora. When many of the tribes decide to fight the British in hopes of driving them out once and for all, John and Takime join the warriors. Left alone, Sassy is kidnapped by two White men and taken to their mother's home. Sassy is attracted to Paul and might have been willing to stay there, but his mother does not like her and Sassy starts off to find her husband's people. Although her father has been killed in battle, Sassy finds Takime and Runs with the Wind and they make plans to move their people further west. This is a very simplistic story; there is always enough to eat, cloth and hides for clothing are available, all the killing is done off stage.

Reviewed in: Kirkus Reviews 6/1/94; Publishers Weekly 6/13/94.

193. MacDonald, Elisabeth. *Voices on the Wind.* NY: Avon. 1994. 342 p.

Time: 1870's
Tribe: Navajo
Place: New Mexico

Although The Long Walk of the Navajo and its aftermath do not seem to be a subject on which to base a romance novel, MacDonald has done a creditable job. Sialea is eight when her world is shattered by seeing her father murdered by the bluecoats. She, her mother and young brother Ashki make The Long Walk and endure the four horrible years at Bosque Redondo until the Navajo are allowed to return home. Lea's friend Nathan saves her from being raped by two soldiers but is severely beaten by them and loses his manhood. Lea had always wanted to marry Nathan and even though he shares his terrible secret with her, Lea feels they can have a happy marriage. She had not counted on meeting Rafe Douglas, son of the Indian trader Ian Douglas. Though they dislike each other at first, they are drawn together. Rafe hates the idea of slavery and is appalled to learn that Navajo women and children are still being stolen and sold as slaves. When this happens to Lea, he rescues her and they consummate their love for each other. Lea bears a child whom Nathan grudgingly accepts, but Nathan is fighting his own demons in the form of Navajo witches. Lea has dreams of Changing Woman who tells her she can never leave Dinetah, but that love and respect can overcome all barriers. The story is woven with Navajo legends and ceremonies and the plight of these people at the hands of the military, the Indian agents, and the missionaries is well done.

194. Madison, Guy M. (Tulalip). *The Res: An American Novel.* Marysville, WA: M2 Publishers. 1998. 371 p.

Time: 1959–1970's
Tribe: Snohomish (Tulalip Tribe)
Place: Washington State, Oklahoma

The Esque family lives on the Tulalip Reservation, just outside Marysville in western Washington State. Their father, Franc, has a serious drinking problem and their mother, Lois, a Swedish woman, tries to protect and feed their many children. Older brother Cajun is athletic and charming, but younger brother Jonny has a serious speech defect which keeps him shy and withdrawn. In 1959 when Nicki-D, a Chinese-American girl, moves to the reservation because her father runs the bank there, she and Jonny become close friends. The novel follows the lives of these three children as they grow up. Caj goes to Vietnam, Jonny is sent to an Indian boarding school in Oklahoma after his mother's nervous breakdown, and Nicki-D goes off to college. Caj returns a broken man, drunk and cold after his experiences in Vietnam. Nicki-D falls in love with a man who is killed in Vietnam, and returns to the "Res." in a deep depression. Jonny suffers severely at boarding school, finds his totem animal in a wolf pup, and learns an inner strength and personal conviction which makes him a leader of his tribe when he returns. Nicki-D's mother, Ginny, a strong Chinese woman, works with Jonny to help the tribe financially and the Esque family personally. After Lois dies a premature death and Jonny gives a moving and deeply felt speech at her funeral, members of the family realize they have an amazing younger brother. Jonny realizes he and Nicki-D belong together as more than friends. A very personal novel, the travails of a child rejected by his father and his peers due to a speech defect which has nothing to do with his intelligence, are well presented in the character of Jonny. The novel is part of a proposed trilogy following other members of the Esque family and would be very suitable for young adults.

195. Maracle, Lee. (Metis). *Ravensong.* Vancouver, Canada: Press Gang Publishers. 1993. 199 p.

Time: 1954 to 1980
Tribe: Salish
Place: British Columbia

Stacey and Celia are sisters living in a small town near Vancouver when the Hong Kong flu strikes in 1954. Stacey is seventeen and an excellent student, but stays home to nurse the sick people of her tribe. The town's White doctors refuse to treat the Indians and many people die, including the disheartened village shaman and Stacey's own father. Momma (the only name Stacey's mother ever had) is very depressed without her husband and Young Jim, the son, has to take over many family responsibilities. Stacey befriends Rena, a member of the tribe, and her partner, German Judy. Lesbians, they are included in the tribal activities to some degree, but Stacey forces more acceptance of the women. Ned, her father's charming twin brother, shows up to court a most willing Momma. Stacey is furious when she discovers Ned is far more closely related than merely being her uncle. The older women of the tribe, especially her grandmother, show Stacey how to accept human nature and not to condemn what is not harmful. Meanwhile Celia, a very young girl, watches all these events, communicating with Raven and Cedar, who have planned all the plagues and epidemics as a way of bringing the white and native peoples together. Stacey graduates, is accepted at the University of British Columbia, and leaves to become a teacher. The language in this short novel is lyrical and sweeps the reader into another dimension of understanding. Maracle is a very talented novelist with a real gift for mystical language which is rooted in the earth and nature.

196. Maracle, Lee. (Metis). *Sundogs: A Novel.* Penticton, Canada: Theytus Books. 1992. 214 p.

Time: Contemporary
Tribe: Salish
Place: British Columbia

In 1991 Marianne is working hard to succeed in college, living at home and surrounded by an extended family with many needs. She feels endless demands to assist in the care of the numerous children and take sides in their domestic disputes. Her mother is a highly political woman and is very vocal in her anger against the current government policies regarding Native Rights. Her sister Rita divorces her abusive husband and comes home with four children, followed closely by her brother Rudy's wife and their children after Rudy beats them. Older brother Joseph says everyone must pool their funds and buy a house to hold this new large family. Marianne resists, angry that this is being asked of her. Gradually she comes to see that as the youngest she has been protected from reality, never taught the indigenous language, called "Baby" by her siblings and treated as one. She begins to take responsibility for others and enters a deep relationship with a Native activist, Mark, rejecting a White boy, James. The culmination of events comes when Marianne joins the Peace Run across Canada in support of the Mohawks resisting at Oka, Quebec, where White men are trying to build a golf course on Native graves. During the run Marianne comes to realize how her mother's political nature is also how Natives will succeed in Canadian society, resisting oppression and standing up for their rights. Marianne finally takes her adult place in her family.

Reviewed in: Publishers Weekly 10/18/99.

197. Marshall, Joseph III. (Sioux). *Winter of the Holy Iron.* Santa Fe, NM: Red Crane Books. 1994. 294 p.

Time: 1740's
Tribe: Sioux
Place: South Dakota

When the Lakota Sioux first encounter white trappers' guns, they name their flintlocks *maza wakan,* meaning mysterious, or holy iron. War leader Whirlwind takes a gun away from a trapper who tries to shoot him and hides it from the tribe. He fears the power of the holy iron. "Did he shoot at me because he knew he could kill easily? Did he shoot at me because he felt his weapon gave him the right to kill?" Whirlwind's long time rival Bear Heart knows of the gun and wants to include it with their weaponry against other tribes. The Sioux had already been driven from their former homes around the Great Lakes by the Ojibwe who have guns. Whirlwind finds another White man, Gaston De la Verendrye, shot by Bruneaux, an evil Frenchman, and Whirlwind brings Gaston back to camp to heal. Bruneaux comes after Gaston, kills an elderly grandmother, kidnaps the young girl betrothed to Whirlwind's son, and flees. Whirlwind goes after him. Suffering endless hardships, having his horse shot out from under him, losing all his weapons and having to make new ones, wrenching his knee so he has to walk with a cane, Whirlwind is then attacked by Pawnee. He kills the two enemies, takes their horse, and keeps up the pursuit of Bruneaux. Finally deep snows slow the Frenchman down. Meanwhile Whirlwind's son, Walks High, Bear Heart and Gaston are following to aid the war leader in his pursuit. Gaston has been loaned the hidden gun by Whirlwind's wife and Bear Heart tries to take it away. When he fails, Bear Heart goes back to camp, takes his band of followers and breaks away from the larger band of Lakota. With Gaston's help the Sioux overpower Bruneaux and rescue the young girl. In the end Whirlwind knows that next summer his people will be eager to go to the large trading event on the Missouri and start acquiring the White men's tools and weapons. He realizes change is inevitable and he must learn to cope with it. This is an excellent novel with a strong intelligent central character in Whirlwind. The Native American spirituality is clearly explained, as is their philosophy of life, which are intertwined. This is a very genuine story of a time when the effect of white men upon the Sioux was just beginning to be felt.

Reviewed in: Publishers Weekly 7/11/94; Bloomsbury Review 11/94; Western American Literature Falll/95.

198. Martin, Larry Jay. *Sounding Drum.* NY: Kensington. 1999. 345 p.

Time: Contemporary
Tribe: Salish
Place: New York City

When you think you can't take one more book on the Trail of Tears or the Long Walk of the Navajo, try *Sounding Drum.* The good guys win! Steven Drum is a consultant for Indian gaming operations, what contemporary Indians call "the return of the buffalo." An anthropologist friend of Steve's finds an historic document deep under Manhattan—a signed treaty returning the island to those who sold it. Steve instantly realizes not only what this means in the short term, but what it could mean in the future. Native people would own part of the richest real estate on earth and they could open a casino that was close to the population base instead of at hard-to-get-to reservations. Through clever financial and political maneuvering, Steve and his associates manage to acquire Rockefeller Center and will use the money from the gaming tables that will pour in to help peoples of all tribes. Although far-fetched, this is a fun and amusing thriller.

Reviewed in: Publishers Weekly 5/31/99; Kirkus Reviews 3/1/99.

199. Martin, Marianne K. *Never Ending.* Tallahassee, FL: Naiad Press. 1999. 202 p.

Time: Contemporary
Tribe: Seneca
Place: Eastern United States

Sage Bristo is the last of her family's female line, the Clan of the Doe. Without a daughter to carry on, the tradition will die. Sage is a lesbian, with no desire for children. She could donate her eggs to her sister Cimmie, who has been unable to conceive, and perpetuate the line that way. Sage was abused as a child by both her mother and stepfather. Her mother did nothing to stop the abuse and her stepfather hated first Sage's rebellious ways and then her sexuality. When Sage decides to have a child (before the egg donation decision is made) she does so without telling her long-time lover Deanne who naturally feels hurt and left out. Both Sage and Deanne must come to terms with their decisions and the other's place in their lives. When the baby is born, Sage's stepfather tries to harm the infant, only to be shot by their mother who has finally asserted herself in her love for her children. This is much less a Native American novel than it is a lesbian novel; the two themes do not tie together; the characters are weak and one-dimensional, and the plot flimsy.

200. Masterson, Graham. *The Manitou.* Chicago: Olmstead Press. 2001. 174 p.

Time: Contemporary
Tribe: Sioux and Manhattan
Place: New York City

Harry Erskine is a quasi-mystic, preying on gullible old women, when he is visited by a beautiful young woman named Karen who consults him about strange dreams she has had since a mysterious growth began on the back of her neck. The growth is a tumor, but her physician, Dr. Hughes, discovers it contains a human fetus. Inside is the evil shaman Misquamacus, who has reincarnated himself from the time of the Dutch invasion of the island 350 years ago. Erskine and Hughes watch as the tumor quickly grows huge, realize its danger and call in a Sioux medicine man, Standing Rock, to confront it at its birth. Karen dies when giving birth to a fully developed shaman man. The confrontation between the two shamans is extremely violent as they compete using all their spiritual powers. Several attempts are made to destroy Misquamacus but he is supernatural. Finally the concept of pitting the ancient shaman's native powers against new technological powers using the *Manitou* or spirit of the supercomputer Unitrak is seized upon by the desperate men. Erskine, as a White man, must call up Unitrak's spirit to confront Misquamacus and his ancient demons. The computer wins. Made into a movie, this horror tale did not translate well, according to reviews. However as horror fiction, employing the concept of all beings having a *Manitou,* and using Native American spiritual beliefs, it is quite effective.

201. Masterson, Graham. *Tooth and Claw.* NY: Severn House. 1997. 234 p.

Time: Contemporary
Tribe: Navajo
Place: Los Angeles and Arizona

Jim Rook is a special education teacher at California's West Grove Community College working with disadvantaged students. Catherine White

Bird has recently moved from Window Rock, Arizona, with her father and very protective older brothers. Henry Black Eagle, Catherine's father, tells Jim of Catherine's betrothal to Dog Brother, a powerful medicine man on the Navajo reservation, who might have killed Martin, Catherine's boyfriend. Henry begs Jim to take Catherine back to Arizona and free her by offering Dog Brother money. Jim takes his girlfriend Susan along as a chaperone and is assisted by John Three Names. Three Names tells Jim of the myth of Changing Bear Woman, a reluctant Navajo woman loved by Coyote whom he transformed into a bear. Coyote needs to marry a Navajo woman and produce his next incarnation every generation. Gradually Jim realizes that Dog Brother is the present incarnation of Coyote and Catherine is his Changing Bear Woman. In violent confrontations, Susan and John Three Names are killed, but Jim escapes and returns to Los Angeles followed by Dog Brother and Catherine. Catherine as Changing Bear Woman kills Dog Brother, but Jim restores him to life with the promise that Martin, Susan and Three Names may also be restored. The Coyote and Changing Bear Woman stories are good and the plot is full of suspense and surprise. As horror fiction this is quite entertaining and gripping. The complaints of the Navajo that Coyote is only doing to Martin and Susan what Army soldiers did to their families creates a sense of justice.

202. Matheson, David. (Coeur d'Alene). *Red Thunder*. Portland, OR: Media Weavers. 2001. 316 p.

Time: early 1700's
Tribe: Coeur d'Alene
Place: Northern Idaho, Eastern Washington, Western Montana

This is the story of Sun Bear and his sister Rainbow Girl, children of Black Hawk and Basket Weaver, as they grow up and become adults and parents in a time before any Coeur d'Alene contact with White men. Rainbow Girl loves Deer Hooves, but he is killed in a horse raid. She becomes severely depressed and finally her *Peepa* and her *Noona*, her father and mother, arrange a marriage for her with One Star, a widower with children. Because of her loss of Deer Hooves, Rainbow Girl is overly protective of her husband and children, which causes a strain in the marriage. Sun Bear marries Yellow Flower Girl, who is his supportive and traditional wife. Their older sister, Berry Woman, is beaten by her husband and Black Hawk asserts his grandfather's rights to bring her and her children back home. The husband, Mountain-side, must prove his love and worth again before he is allowed to move back into Berry Woman's family. The novel covers many of the ceremonies and traditional rituals of the Coeur d'Alene people, including the marriage and birth ceremonies and the relay horse races. This is the time period when their famous chief, Circling Raven, leads the *Schee-tsu-umsh*, the Coeur d'Alene. When their enemies, the Chop Faces, attack the tribe and steal Rainbow Girl's young son, a band including Sun Bear, One Star and Black Hawk go after them. Rainbow Girl secretly follows and saves her father from certain death at the hands of the Chop Faces. Sun Bear saves his nephew and all flee the larger enemy force. A mysterious and magical red thunder and snow storm cover their retreat to safety. The nephew is renamed Red Thunder in honor of the event. The novel is somewhat idyllic in tone, with little real hardship afflicting these people. Perhaps this was in fact the case for this tribe, but life does seem too perfect to be true.

Reviewed in: Publishers Weekly 2/11/02.

203. Mayhar, Ardath. *Island in the Lake.* NY: Diamond. 1993. 260 p.

Time: circa 1000
Tribe: Prehistoric Caddo
Place: East Texas

Since the Mound Builders left no written history, only their artifacts and the mounds themselves, Mayhar has fashioned a story of how life might have been. Talicha is the Turtle Woman of the Nadicha, wise in the ways of plants and herbs, but she senses a danger to her people, especially to the children. Ootenec, Alligator Man, was kidnapped from his home as a boy, taken on a forced march to the Azteca people where he watched his brother sacrificed to appease their gods. Helped to escape, Ootenec is still haunted by these experiences. He lives alone in the swamp, has terrible nightmares, and kills alligators to satisfy the thirst for blood and violence. He is not a part of the Nadicha village, but brings them meat and hides and takes four young children to instruct in the ways of the swamp. When the bloodlust comes upon him, he nearly kills a young girl, but Talicha senses the danger, swims the lake, killing an alligator herself, saves the child and saves Ootenec from himself by the use of burning herbs which drive out the bad dreams. The depiction of the swamp and the life that flourishes there is good, but the story itself is rather flat.

204. Mayhar, Ardath. *People of the Mesa.* NY: Diamond Books. 1992. 297 p.

Time: 1200's
Tribe: Anasazi
Place: Southwestern U.S.

After visiting Mesa Verde, Mayhar became fascinated by the Anasazi, by what little is known of their culture and by the various theories on what happened to them. From this fascination she has fashioned a novel which tells the story of Uhtatse, the One Who Smells the Wind, and warns his people of danger. She depicts Uhtatse's boyhood and the learning of his skill, his marriage to his beloved wife Ihyannah, and the tragic loss of their only child. Enemies come to the people, some can be driven off, others must be hidden from. It is Uhtatse who builds the first cliff dwelling and then finally persuades his people to abandon their pit houses and pueblos built on top of the mesa. What Mayhar depicts may be accurate, but the story is flat, the characters one-dimensional, and it is hard to care about them, their culture or their history.

205. McCarthy, Gary. *Mesa Verde*. NY: Kensington. 1997. 382 p.

Time: 1888 and 1200's
Tribe: Anasazi
Place: Mesa Verde, Colorado

Set in 1888 with extensive excursions back in time to developmental periods of Anasazi history, this novel depicts the discovery, exploitation, and protection of the Mesa Verde historical site. Found by the Wetherill ranching family on their land, these incredible early settlements were an attraction for archaeologists and collectors. Lisa and Andrew Cannaday are on a archaeological expedition for the Smithsonian and find artifacts and skeletons being sold off by the Wetherills. After Andrew's accidental death Dr. Michael Turner follows and spends years collecting specimens for the museum. Lisa falls in love with Turner and devotes her life to supporting his research, only to discover he is already married and involved in selling Mesa Verde artificacts on the black market. Eventually President Roosevelt signs a bill designating Mesa Verde as a national treasure. Interspersed throughout this plot are tales of the ancient peoples. When and how the desert dwellers moved to the mesa top, how they farmed and hunted, and finally what drove them off the mesas and out of their cliff dwellings are all depicted in detail. All the Old Ones are well developed characters, better than the more contemporary Lisa and Turner. A wonderful historical account of Mesa Verde, the novel is an excellent source for learning about this unique and amazing archaeological site.

Reviewed in: Library Journal 9/15/98.

206. McCreede, Jess. *Blue Sky, Night Thunder.* Encampment, WY: Affiliated Writers of America. 1993. 401 p.

Time: 1870's
Tribe: Ute
Place: Colorado

In the late 1870's the Ute Indians had reached agreements with the U.S. government and lived in peace. When the Utes' allotments were held onto by the Union Pacific Railroad for failure of the government to pay shipping charges and the Utes suffered starvation, this fragile peace suffered as well. The White River Utes disagreed with Chief Ouray's policy of signing away the lands and mountains of Colorado and resisted efforts to turn them into farmers. Nathan Meeker, fresh from his failure in Greeley, was given the White River Agency to run to help pay off his debts. Meeker did not make any attempt to understand the Utes' culture and quickly antagonized them. McCreede brings each character in the drama of the Meeker Massacre to life, from the guide Joe Rankin to Major Tip Thornton. He also presents the Ute perspective through the eyes of Quinkent, known as Douglas, and his rival Nicaagat, whom the Whites called "Captain Jack." Miscommunication, hostility, and a clash of different cultures all contributed to the massacre. Well-intentioned persons on both sides tried to prevent the tragedy, but ambitious and ignorant Army leaders did not listen. The Utes, furious at the loss of their lands and Meeker's insistence on agricultural labor, plowing the land and digging irrigation ditches, were ignited by the Army's marching onto their reservation after promising not to do so. Following the massacre and the kidnapping of the Agency White women, the parties worked together to resolve the conflict. McCreede uses historical documents to tell this story and has written an excellent account of all that led up to this event in Colorado history.

207. Medawar, Mardi Oakley. (Cherokee). *Death at Rainy Mountain.* NY: St. Martin's. 1996. 262 p.

Reviewed in: Armchair Detective Fall/ 96; Booklist 7/96; Publishers Weekly 7/1/96.

Witch of the Palo Duro. A Tay-bodal Mystery. NY: St. Martin's. 1997. 224 p.

Reviewed in: Booklist 9/15/97; Library Journal 11/1/97; Publishers Weekly 9/22/97.

Murder at Medicine Lodge. A Tay-bodal Mystery. NY: St. Martin's. 1999. 262 p.

Reviewed in: Library Journal 3/1/99; Publishers Weekly 2/22/99; Booklist 2/1/99.

The Fort Larned Incident. NY: St. Martin's Minotaur. 2000. 270 p.

Reviewed in: Booklist 7/10/00; Kirkus Reviews 8/9/00; Publishers Weekly 6/26/00.

Time: 1866–1868, 1920
Tribe: Kiowa
Place: Texas, Oklahoma, Kansas

The Tay-bodal mysteries feature a Kiowa medicine man with a very scientific mind who lives outside the strict classes, casts and societies of the Kiowa. Tay-bodal believes in the healing arts based upon scientific method and is a very analytical and thorough person. Not belonging to either the spiritual Owl Doctors or the medical Buffalo bleeders, but married to Crying Wind, a member of the *Ondes,* the highest Kiowa class, he is both free from traditions and powerful in status. Tay-bodal lives with White Bear/Satanta's band in the last days of the Kiowa freedom before they are consigned to a reservation. He is a healer, having learned medical arts at Fort Bent and from his friend Harrison, a U. S. Army doctor. He also has a close friend in Skywalker, an Owl Doctor with mind-reading powers. Tay-bodal is often called in by the tribal chiefs to settle disputes involving murder or bewitching, because of his logical mental processes. Not belonging to any caste or society, he is free to question all involved freely without giving offense. These mysteries include many details of Kiowa societal structure, hierarchy and rules. Medawar is thoroughly versed in the class structure and how one gains or loses status in the tribe. The plots are complex, the characters are well-defined, the text is often humorous and contains illustrative depictions of life among the Kiowa in the mid-1800's.

The Kiowa chiefs, Satanta and Kicking Bird, and the Welsh journalist Henry Stanley, are true historical figures, as are some events, such as the treaty at Medicine Lodge, Kansas, as well. Tay-bodal is an excellent character with humor and insight. His highest priority is always maintaining peace in the tribe, as well as dealing with everyone involved in the murder or other crime completely fairly. The final mystery is not thoroughly solved to Tay-bodal's satisfaction until 1920, when the participants are elderly members on the Kiowa reservation.

208. Medawar, Mardi Oakley. (Cherokee). *Misty Hills of Home.* NY: Penguin. 1998. 394 p.

Time: 1920–1950's
Tribe: Osage
Place: Oklahoma

This family chronology of the Rainwater/Fallen Hawks is an historical romance with very slight reference to the culture or history of the Osage. Claude Rainwater marries May Rose Fallen Hawk and they have a number of sons, some good, some better, some evil. Later on a daughter is added to the family. The family goes through the Depression, the dust bowl, the rise and fall of the petroleum industry, and the personal travails of courtship and marriage. They might as well be of German or Italian descent, for all their Osage heritage figures into any of their personal lives.

209. Medawar, Mardi Oakley. (Cherokee). *Murder on the Red Cliff Rez.* NY: St. Martin's Minotaur. 2002. 207 p.

Time: Contemporary
Tribe: Ojibwe
Place: Wisconsin

Medawar starts a new contemporary mystery series with Karen "Tracker" Charboneau and Chief of Police David Lameraux on the Red Cliff Ojibwe reservation of Wisconsin. Several years ago Karen and David were lovers, but a bitter quarrel has separated them, and both are too subborn to apologize. Karen is a very successful potter, selling her highly artistic work to galleries. She is also the tribe's best tracker and is often called upon by the police department. When Judah Boiseneau, the tribal attorney who abuses his wife Imogen, is found brutally murdered, Karen is called in to track down her dear friend Benny Peliquin, Imogen's lover. Meanwhile Karen's old Uncle Bert has disappeared and all his pet dogs have been shot. Forced to work with Chief David on the case, eventually the two discover a plot to secretly log the reservation's old growth timber. The tone of this mystery is very humorous, sometimes overly cute, but the characters are very likeable. The closeness and responsibility that members of the tribe feel for each other clearly comes through.

Reviewed in: Publishers Weekly 5/20/02.

210. Medawar, Mardi Oakley. (Cherokee). *People of the Whistling Waters.* Encampment, WY: Affiliated Writers of America. 1993. 442 p.

Time: 1854–1886
Tribe: Crow
Place: Montana

French Canadian Renee DeGeer moves to Montana and marries Tall Willow of the Whistling Waters band of Crow. They adopt an orphan boy from the Crow agency and name him Nicholas, raising him with their son Jacques and daughter Marie. Nicholas is White, but dark-haired and most believe he is another Crow. Together the family goes through good times and bad, with Renee attempting to assist the various Army leaders at the Agency manage the tribe in a fair manner. The novel tracks the events in the DeGeer family, including Marie's kidnapping and marriage into the Lakota band, Jacques's marriage to a White girl who is soon killed by the Cheyenne, and Nicholas's marriage to Eyes that Shine, a Crow. Years go by, the brothers are involved in the Battle of Rosebud, where Jacques is killed and Nicholas wounded, ending his warring days. Nicholas manages the family farm, land Renee has wisely set aside for his family. Finally Tall Willow and Renee die and Nicholas finds he must go back to his White name, Egbert Higgins, to hold the land. Although the novel is a family saga rather than a history of the Crow, the characters and story are nonetheless engaging.

Reviewed in: Publishers Weekly 7/5/93.

211. Medawar, Mardi Oakley. (Cherokee). *Remembering the Osage Kid.* NY: Bantam Books. 1997. 373 p.

Time: 1876–1965
Tribe: Osage
Place: Oklahoma

The story opens during the last days of C. R. Jones's life recounted in the journal passed on to his enemy Everett Jakomin. Charlie Richard Bear Chief Jones was raised in Oklahoma in a traditional Osage family. His father was brutally murdered by cowboys stealing their cattle when Charlie was only ten years old. Charlie witnessed the murder and set out to exact revenge, joining an outlaw troupe and hunting down the cowboys responsible. The outlaws, Belle and Sam Starr, are Cherokees who keep Charlie with them, calling him the Osage Kid, and taking him on their robberies. Eventually Charlie is arrested but a kindly priest rescues him and takes him home. Charlie concentrates on learning White men's ways, uses the oil found on his family's farm to build the Red Bird Oil company, but cannot win the hand of Cassie DePree, the love of his life. Married to an evil man, Cassie lives in misery, giving birth to Everett Jakomin, and eventually dying. Charlie never forgets her. Everett believes Charlie is his enemy, but discovers after Charlie's death that the man has watched over him, as Cassie's son, his whole life. Mostly a family chronicle, there is a great deal of early Oklahoma history involving the Cherokee and Osage, and the difference in status between French Osage and darker skinned pure Osage. Long chapters devoted to Charlie's sons are the least interesting from a Native American perspective, but overall the novel is entertaining.

212. Metcalf, John. *Kayhut; a Warrior's Odyssey.* Minneapolis: Four Directions. 1988. 242 p.

Time: 1400's
Tribe: Tlinkit (Chilkat)
Place: Alaska

The tribes of Alaska, the Pacific Northwest Coast, and Puget Sound fell into several major linguistic groups, but had many separate tribal identities. Metcalf spent many years in Puget Sound learning these tribes' customs and tales and has written a simple, but involving story. A young Thlinkit [sic] boy, Kayhut, wanders his way from tribe to tribe, living sometimes as a respected member and sometimes as a beaten slave, but always learning what the tribe had to teach. Born in Klukwos in Alaska, Kayhut flees when he fears retaliation for the drowning deaths of his uncle and brother. Crippled and mauled by a bear, Kayhut is found by Klaquet (Salish) people and nursed back to health. Kayhut recovers to become a fierce, one-eyed warrior, winning the heart of the chief's daughter, Nanitsa, but hated by a rival, Doonah. Kayhut kills Doonah in a confrontation and is sold to the Kwakuital as a slave. Gambled away to the Tsimeans, Kayhut's life worsens and he finally escapes to return to the Klaquet and warns them of an attack coming to their village. They ignore his warning and head off to join the Cowichans in attacking the Klallams and Skagits on Puget Sound. Kayhut goes along, fighting so fiercely that he enters the Klallam legends as the One Eyed Monster. Returning to the Klaquet villages, the men find them devastated by the Tsimeans and Haidas, the women and children stolen. Kayhut leads the warriors to fight for and retrieve their families and is finally given Nanitsa's hand in marriage. Many happy years later, visiting his son's family to hand down a special ivory bear carving amulet to his grandson Walmish, the family group is attacked by Klallums and Kayhut is killed. They have found and vanquished the One Eyed Monster. Walmish and his sister Neeota are sold into slavery and the cycle continues. Full of information about rituals, customs, legends and these tribes, the novel may not be a literary masterpiece, but it is extremely informative about these little-known tribes.

213. Meyers, Harold Burton. *Reservations.* Niwot: University Press of Colorado. 1999. 287 p.

Time: 1928–1944
Tribe: Navajo
Place: New Mexico

Will Parker and his wife are Indian Service teachers on the Navajo reservations during the Depression. Their son Davey grows up on these reservations, going to school with the Navajo, but always aware he is not one of them. Will and Davey take turns telling the story of these years and the changes in policy which John Collier, the head of the Indian Service in Washington D.C., enacts. Will is not a strong man, but he is determined to teach native children in a more humane way than has been traditional in the Indian Service. He brings bus service to the reservation to encourage attendance at school by providing transportation. The mechanic, Garlen, is a vicious abusive man whom Will is powerless and reluctant to control and the tribe must deal with Garlen instead. As Principal, Will transfers teachers who mistreat the students, but never confronts them directly. The novel includes a great deal of Navajo history and culture, especially in how Whites have treated the tribe and they how have responded. Without Hosteen Franklin Begay, the school policeman and Will's tribal assistant, the school would never have been as effective, nor reached as many children, as it did. Without Franklin's intervention in matters of shoes for the walking children, or bus service for all, or large festivals to bring in the parents, or free government food distribution in the depth of the Depression, the Navajo would not have survived and been educated as they were. Beautifully written with characters who clearly know their limitations and their strengths, this is a wonderful novel about a time period and a cultural process, the Indian Service and its reservation teachers, about which little has been written in fiction.

Reviewed in: Booklist 5/15/99; Publishers Weekly 4/19/99.

214. Mihesuah, Devon Abbott. (Choctaw). *The Roads of My Relations.* Tucson: University of Arizona Press. 2000. 235 p.

Time: 1820's–2000
Tribe: Choctaw
Place: Mississippi, Oklahoma

Sun Tracks, v.44. An American Indian Literary Series.

Billie McKenney and her sister Survella take turns narrating this chronicle of a Choctaw family's history from their farm in Mississippi, through their Trail of Tears journey to Oklahoma and beyond the Civil War into the twentieth century. Their descendents finish the tale. Throughout this family's history lurk the Crow family, evil Choctaws who are *opa-men,* owl witches no one can kill except someone who tried and failed to kill, still bearing a mark of the attempt. Billie relates the horrors of the family's forced move to Oklahoma, losing many members of her family along the way. She describes Choctaw life, the *ishtaboli* game of lacrosse, the bone pickers who clean skeletons for burial, and the class structure in the mission schools based upon skin tones, lightest being highest among the mixed-bloods. She and her sister grow, marry, have children and grandchildren, and some are murdered by the Crow owl witches. Even after these evil men are shot and burned, heavy stones cannot keep them from flying out of their graves. Finally in the year 2000, two cousins, with the help of an ancient Choctaw relative, bring back the one who can kill the *opa-men* and the witches are vanquished. An excellent account of Choctaw life over the generations and all the travails which afflicted them, the accounts of life in the missionary schools of Oklahoma are especially revealing in their prejudices.

215. Mitchell, Kirk. *Ancient Ones.* NY: Bantam. 2001. 326 p.

Time: Contemporary
Tribe: Sahaptin, Wasco, Northern Paiute
Place: Oregon

A fossil hunter finds a skeleton along the John Day River near the Warm Springs Reservation and then is found tortured to death. Anthropologist Dr. Rankin states the skeleton is over 14,000 years old and has Caucasoid features. The Wasco, Paiutes and Sahaptins want the skeleton back, using the NAGPRA, the Native American Graves Protection and Repatriation Act to enforce their case. Rankin finds evidence of cannibalism on the skeleton, insists it means Caucasians preceded Amerinds in the New World, have prior claim to the land, and that cannibalism was widespread. Into this controversy come Comanche BIA Agent Emmett Parker and Modoc FBI Agent Anna Turnipseed, working together on this case and on their difficult personal relationship. The John Day Man is put under government protection, but shortly thereafter Willow Creek Woman is found with the same Caucasoid features and leg scrapes indicating cannibalism. Parker and Turnipseed suspect a hoax is being played by Rankin to further his personal theories. A Norse Pagan conference further complicates the case while bombings, murders and disappearances proliferate. Another complex and very involving plot featuring two Native American agents, the mystery has fascinating characters and unique circumstances. Learning Rankin is suffering from kuru after eating Fore brains in Papua New Guinea is just one instance of the unusual content. Turnipseed and Parker do make some progress in their troubled relationship, but further work will need to be done to overcome Anna's memories of childhood abuse.

Reviewed in: Library Journal 4/15/01; Publishers Weekly 3/5/01; Booklist 5/1/01; Kirkus Reviews 3/1/01.

216. Mitchell, Kirk. *Cry Dance*. NY: Bantam. 1999. 354 p,

Time: Contemporary
Tribe: Havasupai
Place: Arizona

Emmett Parker, a Comanche, is a special investigator for the BIA sent to the Havasupai reservation when a White real estate agent is found dead in a cave. Her face has been torn off and her fingers amputated to hide her identity. Anna Turnipseed, a Modoc rookie FBI agent, is assigned to the case with Parker, who feels both protective and resentful of her. The murder seems tied into land swaps and the Indian gambling casino on the reservation, run by Cyrus Fourkiller, a Lakota. Shoshone and Pai work in the casino, but many on the reservation resent its presence. Anna goes undercover there as a blackjack dealer, winning the attention of Fourkiller, whom she suspects is the murderer. Parker believes the murderer is another Lakota he knew from Wounded Knee many years ago. Behind the casino are corrupt influences from Jamaica, using it to launder drug money. Parker and Turnipseed expose the killer and his accomplices and are nearly killed themselves. An excellent mystery full of complex plotting and well developed characters, the book presents both sides of the Indian gaming issue, its advantages and disadvantages to the operations and the survival of a tribe in the southwestern United States.

Reviewed in: Publishers Weekly 5/29/00; Library Journal 5/15/00; Booklist 5/1/00.

217. Mitchell, Kirk. *Spirit Sickness.* NY: Bantam. 2000. 354 p.

Time: Contemporary
Tribe: Modoc, Comanche, Navajo
Place: Arizona and New Mexico

BIA Agent Emmett Quanah Parker and FBI Special Agent Anna Turnipseed are working together on the case of a murdered Navajo policeman. Burt Knoki and his wife Aurelia were found burned in their truck on the reservation outside Gallup, New Mexico. John Tallsalt, a Navajo Lieutenant in the Criminal Investigative Services and an old friend of Parker's, is also on the case. During the course of the investigation, Parker and Turnipseed find ties to Navajo youth gangs, drug production, and Gila Monsters. These reptiles have been stolen from a scientific study, starved, and set as traps for the Agents, including Turnipseed who suffers a serious bite. Tattoos representing the Gila Monster are found on gang members and the image is painted on buildings. Eventually Parker and Turnipseed find the murderer, who imagines himself as a Gila Monster and Avenger of the Moth People. An adopted child, this young Navajo man is the product of incest and is determined to kill his offending parents. The Knokis had originally adopted him but his epilepsy caused them to give him up to a fringe Mormon family, which instilled in the man a belief in the Moth People (incestuous siblings) and the need for revenge. The novel is extremely suspenseful with an intricate plot and excellent characters. The violent and confrontational resolution is unexpected and effective. Contemporary problems with young people on the Navajo reservations are well portrayed, including the urban gang influences which negatively impact even these isolated tribal groups.

Parker and Turnipseed come closer to admitting their deep feelings and attraction for each other.

Reviewed in: Publishers Weekly 5/29/00; Library Journal 5/15/00; Booklist 5/1/00.

218. Moore, Christopher. *Coyote Blue*. NY: Simon & Schuster. 1994. 303 p.

Time: Contemporary
Tribe: Crow
Place: California

Sam Hunter is a wealthy, successful California insurance agent, but twenty years ago he was Samson Hunts Alone, a Crow Indian who fled Montana after he accidentally killed a policeman. Sam thinks he has left his past behind, until a Native American in black buckskins appears and starts to work his magic tricks upon Sam. Coyote the Trickster has come to torment Sam and quickly disrupts his pleasant California life. In Montana, Sam's uncle Pokey, an unrecognized medicine man, is having visions of death surrounding Sam. During a series of rapid events Sam falls in love with beautiful Calliope, her son Grubb is kidnapped by evil motorcyclists, Coyote and Sam join her in pursuit, Pokey nearly dies during his visions, and the Underworld sends a savior in the form of a seven-foot-tall African American named Minty Fresh (M. F. to those who are not his friends). There are deaths, near-deaths, rescues, and the creation of new Coyote tricksters. Moore's style is very similar to Sherman Alexie's and Thomas King's with a little bit of David Seal's thrown in. Humorous, interspersed with Coyote Tales, incorporating the supernatural as a natural part of life, this novel is full of warmth, life, and people caring for others as "family" whether they are strictly speaking or not.

Reviewed in: Publishers Weekly 1/17/94; NYTBR 5/15/94; Booklist 1/15/94; Library Journal 1/94.

219. Morgan, Speer. *The Freshour Cylinders.* Denver: MacMurray & Beck. 1998. 345 p.

Time: 1930's
Tribe: Unknown
Place: Arkansas, Oklahoma

In the 1960's attorney Tom Freshour recorded the events which took place in the 1930's. The cylinders lay undisturbed until the 1990's when historian Carl Penfield managed to locate a machine on which to hear them. The cylinders contained information about murders, about Indian artifacts from the Spiro mound, and about the greed and corruption present in Depression-era Arkansas and Oklahoma. Although a half-breed, Tom doesn't even know which tribe he belongs to; he was raised in an orphanage and then sent to law school. His current position as county prosecutor brings him in contact with most of the criminal element of the area. When Lee Guessner, an avid collector of Indian artifacts, is murdered and his friend Judge Stone asks Tom to investigate, he never imagined that the trail would lead to Rainy Davis, daughter of Tom's first love Samantha King. Rainy, an archeologist, has been willed Guessner's collection, but there is a problem—it has been stolen. Rainy and Tom find the men who are literally mining the Spiro mound, selling everything they bring out. There are rumors of people living far back in the hills. Are they descendents of the Spiro people, bands of Indians split off from their tribes and trying to survive? The place is spooky, full of fires, horrendous smells, and death. Before Tom and Rainy arrive at the solution, they uncover a crooked sheriff, a homosexual judge, and the graft and corruption that pervade the guardianship system for the Indians who inherited the oil-rich Oklahoma lands. A sequel to *The Whipping Boy*, *The Freshour Cylinders* present a gritty, realistic picture of life in this part of the country in the 1930's.

Reviewed in: Booklist 10/15/98; Kirkus Reviews 9/1/98; Publisher's Weekly 8/24/98.

220. Morgan, Speer. *The Whipping Boy.* Boston: Houghton Mifflin. 1994. 326 p.

Time: 1890's
Tribe: Unknown
Place: Oklahoma

In 1894 half-breed orphan Tom Freshour is allowed to journey to Fort Smith with several of his classmates to see a young murderer hanged. This event changes Tom's life forever as he becomes a courier for Dekker Hardware, taking the money and land deeds collected from the store's debtors back to Fort Smith. Times are tough, the country is in an economic slump and the Indian lands are about to be released from the reservation system to become available on the open market. Something strange is also going on at the store since Ralph Dekker's son Ernest took over the management. There is little stock coming in, all the effort seems to be concentrated on getting these land deeds. Tom has known nothing but the orphanage and its cruel master the Reverend, but he begins to learn the ways of the world through his friendships with the salesman Jake Jaycox and the beautiful Samantha King who teaches him the fascinating relationship between men and women. Tom finds Ralph Dekker murdered and a photograph album which surely has a picture of Samantha as a child. Then he and a classmate finally confront the Reverend and mete out their own form of justice. Tom realizes there is nothing left for him in Fort Smith. The Reverend's records indicate he might be an Apache, given up at Big Tree, and Tom starts off to find out who he really is. Morgan has written a very realistic novel about men and women, good and evil, greed and corruption.

Reviewed in: Library Journal 4/15/94; Publishers Weekly 3/21/94; Kirkus Reviews 3/1/94.

221. Morris, Irvin. (Navajo). *From the Glittering World; a Navajo Story.* Norman: University of Oklahoma Press. 1997. 257 p.

Time: Contemporary
Tribe: Navajo
Place: Arizona and New Mexico

American Indian Literature and Critical Studies Series, v. 22.

A combination of personal memoir and Navajo history, traditional stories, and what appear to be a few short stories included at the end, this book begins with the complete creation story of the Navajo. We are now in the fifth world, the glittering world, after earlier peoples went through the first four, driven ever upwards. Irvin accounts his own trials of growth, as he enrolls in schools, drops out, becomes a street person, cleans up, and starts the whole circle over again. Since he is now a teacher at SUNY, Buffalo, eventually he was able to succeed. He describes some *Dine* ceremonies in detail, such as the Enemyway ceremony, and recounts the Long Walk of the Navajo story several times. His descriptions of the sordid life of Gallup, New Mexico would keep anyone away. The whole tale is a web and he weaves it well.

Reviewed in: Choice, 8/1/97; Publishers Weekly 1/6/97.

222. Mosionier, Beatrice Culleton. (Metis). *In the Shadow of Evil.* Penticton, Canada: Theytus Books. 2000. 316 p.

Time: Contemporary
Tribe: Cree, Metis
Place: Ontario, British Columbia

Christine and Leona Pelletier are Metis girls raised in foster homes and sent to Catholic schools. Leona is beautiful and outgoing, but Christine is dark-skinned and shy. Christine is the victim of molestation by foster parents and priests but no one believes her. One particular man, Dr. Coran, was sexually molesting his daughters and, when Christine exposed him, apparently died in a car accident with them. Eventually Chrisine falls in love with Nick, who cheats on her with Leona. Christine cuts off all communication with her sister and moves to Vancouver. Years later Leona contacts Christine, telling her she has a son named Michael—Nick's son although they never married. Christine has a son Toby with her mystery-writing husband Peter. Peter and Toby disappear, apparent victims of a car accident, although no bodies are found. Leona is in prison and Social Services asks Christine to take Michael. Christine lives in a remote rural area of British Columbia, her closest neighbors the Cree couple Kit and Mona. Her other close neighbor is the wolf Wapan, caring for two orphan wolf pups. The local people think Christine is somehow responsible for Peter and Toby's deaths. Her cabin is burnt down and Wapan is shot, but Christine and Michael refuse to leave. A strange man, Howard, attempts to befriend Christine, but she is suspicious. In the final confrontation Christine discovers Howard is really Dr. Coran and he has kidnapped Peter and Toby. Christine, with the help of Kit, Leona, and the local police, rescues her husband and son and apprehends Coran and his thugs. She also discovers Wapan is still alive, another wolf had been killed instead. An odd contrived ending to an otherwise suspenseful story, the trials of Native children in foster homes is the principle theme and is done well.

223. Muller, Marcia. *Listen to the Silence.* NY: Mysterious. 2000. 289 p.

Time: Contemporary
Tribe: Shoshone, Modoc
Place: Montana, California

PI Sharon McCone is well known in Muller's series, but in this entry discovers she does not know her own past. Going through her father's legal documents after his death, she discovers her adoption papers. Sharon knew she had a Shoshone great-grandmother, the cause of her dark hair and skin. Now she discovers her Shoshone ancestry is a lot more recent; her real birth mother. Tracing Saskia Hunter's journey from a poor reservation in Montana to the Arapahoe/Shoshone reservation in Wyoming to finally becoming Indian activist Saskia Blackhawk in northern California, Sharon also traces a history of crime. Sharon meets the Tendoy families, her real family, and hears much family history from Elwood Farmer, a wise and kind Shoshone man. Sharon finds her mother Saskia and new siblings in California, but when Saskia is hospitalized from a hit and run murder attempt, Sharon sets out to discover why someone tried to kill her. The Modoc tribal lands are being threatened by developers and Saskia was trying to prevent it. Sharon solves the mystery of Saskia's attempted murder and finally discovers who her real father is. Sharon McCone is not merely one-eighth Shoshone, she is a Full Blood. Well written, full of suspense from a master at the trade, the mystery contains much information on the history of the Modoc, and the policies of termination during the 1950's, when the federal government abruptly ceased support for many Native American tribes.

Reviewed in: Publishers Weekly 6/12/00; Library Journal 6/1/00; Booklist 5/1/00.

224. Munn, Vella. *Blackfeet Season.* NY: Forge. 1999. 376 p.

Time: early 1800's
Tribe: Blackfeet
Place: Northern Plains

Raven's Cry and Night Thunder are both sons of the shaman Bunch of Lodges, but their problems are very different. Raven's Cry was raised to be a warrior. Now that his older brother Red Mountain has been killed by a Cree, his father expects him to become a shaman. Raven's Cry has very few dreams and worries that his visions may not be good enough to help his people. Night Thunder has been barely acknowledged by his father and whatever he does, whether counting coup, killing buffalo, or striking down the Cree warrior who killed Red Mountain, it is never enough. From the time she was a small girl White Calf has had visions, visions of her people starving in the snow, and of pale-skinned peoples from the East. When she marries Raven's Cry, it is hoped that their combined medicine will show the people where to go to find buffalo. Raven's Cry must learn he is just a man with a man's strengths and weaknesses; it is White Calf with her woman's wisdom who will be of spiritual help to the people. Night Thunder takes Little Rain, the Cree wife of the warrior he killed, as prisoner, but he cannot kill her. Gradually the two learn to respect each other and to blend their two tribal beliefs. Munn has great character development and the book is intriguing because the conflicts are between tribal members, not between the Blackfeet and the Whites.

Reviewed in: Booklist 2/15/99; Publishers Weekly 2/8/99.

225. Munn, Vella. *Cheyenne Summer.* NY: Forge. 2001. 366 p.

Time: early 1800's
Tribe: Cheyenne
Place: Western United States

It is a summer of terrible drought, the buffalo and other game have vanished, and the Cheyenne are starving. What have they done wrong to offend the spirits and what can they do to make the rain and the buffalo return? Nightelk feels it is entirely his fault since he accidentally killed a white buffalo calf, but he tells no one of his misdeed. Grey Bear, the warrior, feels that the Cheyenne must avenge the death of Porcupine, killed by the Pawnee. Lone Hawk wonders if the Pawnee are not in just as dire straits as the Cheyenne; what honor can there be in killing an already beaten enemy? The women, too, have their own problems. Touches the Wind, the daughter of poor and complaining parents, wonders if any man, especially Lone Hawk, would be interested in her. Seeks Fire is attracted to Grey Bear, but does not realize the violence that is in him. Walking Rabbit mourns the death of her husband Porcupine and when her small daughter Follower is apparently lost in a prairie fire, the tribe fears for Walking Rabbit as well. Again, Munn has written a novel where the struggles of the tribe are internal and against the elements, not against the Whites. In spite of the numerous typographical errors especially with the names, this is an enjoyable book with an excellent portrayal of a people struggling to survive.

Reviewed in: Publishers Weekly 7/16/00.

226. Munn, Vella. *Daughter of the Forest.* NY: Forge. 1995. 410 p.

Time: late 1700's
Tribe: Nisqually and Tillamook
Place: Pacific Northwest

When Twana, a Nisqually, is captured by the Tillamook Madsaw, she almost doesn't care. Being held hostage for ransom to avenge the killing of Madsaw's father by her stepfather Tatooktche might be preferable to being given in marriage to an old man with rotten teeth. Twana has never known who her real father was and is still mourning her mother who has mysteriously disappeared. Twana has the same gift as her mother, the ability to seek out animals in their natural habitat, especially the fierce grizzly bear One Ear. One Ear is angry with man because of the death of his mother, but Twana can seek him in her mind and know where he is. Madsaw believes her when she shares this information with him, but the shaman of his tribe fears her power and proclaims her a witch. Without Madsaw's knowledge the shaman sells her to the White sea-trader Conrad who identifies her as his daughter by the gold necklace he had given her mother. Wanting to use her gift of knowing where the animals are, Conrad holds her prisoner. Twana summons One Ear who kills Conrad, but spares both Twana and Madsaw. This is a very simple love story, but the setting of the Pacific Northwest tribes is a change from the typical Indian romance set in the Great Plains.

227. Munn, Vella. *The River's Daughter.* NY: Tor. 1993. 412 p.

Time: 1850's
Tribe: Rogue
Place: Oregon

Dark Water feels her life is shattered when her husband Running Wolf is killed by the pale skins. When she sets out to find his body, she goes into premature labor and would have died along with her stillborn son if Barr Conner had not helped her. Barr speaks Rogue since he was captured as a boy and made a slave, but now he is a miner, hoping the rivers of Oregon will be as fruitful as those of California. Conflicts between the Rogues and the pale skins increase with deaths of innocent people on both sides. Owl Calling, Dark Waters' brother-in-law, decides someone of their tribe must learn English and since Dark Waters already has a relationship with Barr, she is chosen. In addition to learning English, in the improbable time of one month, Dark Waters falls in love with Barr, but they realize their worlds are incompatible. She would die in "civilization" and he would be killed if he tried to live with her people. Together they travel to the territorial governor to try and arrange a treaty, but neither the pale skins nor the Rogues are willing to compromise and war seems inevitable. Aware of the stronger power of the pale skins, Barr gives up mining to become an Indian Agent in hopes of lessening the coming disaster.

228. Munn, Vella. *Seminole Song*. NY: Forge. 1997. 315 p.

Time: 1830's
Tribe: Seminole
Place: Florida

Calida is a slave to Reddin Croon, a cruel master who repeatedly rapes her. After Calida frees the Seminole warrior Panther and witnesses Croon kill his wife, she flees into the Everglades in search of the Seminoles. Her mother has told her to "follow the river" and after several days and near death, Calida is taken in. The Egret clan is a mixture of Indian and Black, escaped slaves whom the Whites still consider their property. Osceola, the Seminole chief, is very ill and cannot lead his people. Each clan is left to either make peace and agree to move to Oklahoma or to flee deeper into the swamp. It is the question of the former slaves which becomes the turning point; sometimes the Whites say they are the property of the Seminoles and will be moved with them, other times they vow to return them to their former owners. With no time to plant and harvest crops, always on the run, more and more bands give up. Panther and Gaitor, his Black friend, vow to never surrender, especially since Croon has joined the army and is determined to get Calida back and to kill Panther. While there is a love story between Panther and Calida, the novel is best read for its depiction of the Second Seminole War and the relationship between the Seminoles and the Blacks.

Reviewed in: Publishers Weekly 3/17/97.

229. Munn, Vella. *Soul of the Sacred Earth.* NY: Forge. 2000. 350 p.

Time: 1599–1628
Tribe: Hopi and Navajo
Place: New Mexico

Morning Butterfly does not understand why the Spanish will not leave her Hopi people alone. They interupt the rhythm of life, desecrate sacred places and are convinced their beliefs are the only correct ones. Cougar, the Navajo, wants the Spaniards' horses for his people and is willing to steal and fight for them. Although they are of different beliefs themselves, both Morning Butterfly and Cougar respect each other's ways—something the Spanish will never do. Cougar tricks them by showing them "emeralds" which he claims can be found in the great canyon and the soldiers eagerly ride off in search of wealth, leaving Fray Angelico at the "mission" trying to raise a church. While the novel is based on the premise that Cougar can speak Hopi and Morning Butterfly Spanish, it does provide a good contrast between the arrogant ways of the Spanish church and military and the more tolerant ways of both tribes. Novels depicting the first encounters between the Spanish and the Southwestern Indians are rare, and Munn always tells a good story.

Reviewed in: Booklist 5/1/00

230. Munn, Vella. *Spirit of the Eagle.* NY: Forge. 1996. 352 p.

Time: 1860's
Tribe: Modoc
Place: California

Luash is a young Modoc woman who has an eagle as her spirit guide. Leaving her father who forced her mother and then tried to force her to sell themselves to the Whites for bullets, Luash runs away to her uncle Kientpoos, called Captain Jack by the soldiers. She feels a strange attraction to Jed Britton, survivor of the Fetterman Massacre, and he is drawn to her as well (conveniently Luash has been taught English by a settler's wife). Nothing can stop the inevitable war between the U.S. Army, who want to remove the Modoc to a reservation shared with their hated enemy the Klamash and the Modoc, who want only the land that has always been theirs. In the end, of course, the Army wins, Captain Jack is hanged for the murder of General Canby, Jed gives up his military career to become an Indian agent with Luash as his wife. The only victory the Modocs gained was that they would all go together to the reservation and would not be split up. This is one of Munn's earlier works and is not as good as her later books.

Reviewed in: Publishers Weekly 11/27/95.

231. Munn, Vella. *Wind Warrior.* NY: Forge. 1998. 350 p.

Time: 1809
Tribe: Chumash
Place: Alta California

Black Wolf is a Chumash warrior, imprisoned as a child at the mission *La Purisima*, now free with his people in the hills, but still powerless to stop the invasion of the Spanish military and the Spanish church. Lucita Rodriguez accompanies her parents as her father takes over command of the small garrison and is fascinated by the country and repelled by the conditions she finds at the mission. The Spanish have enslaved the Chumash, forcing them to work to produce the hides, tallow and wine demanded by the Crown, robbing them of their language, culture and religion, and beating them to death. Black Wolf sees Lucita as she arrives at the mission and is drawn to her, risking his life again and again to talk with her. Lucita also risks her father's wrath as she ventures outside the mission to meet Black Wolf and struggles to understand what it means to be a Chumash. Although a wealthy merchant whom she likes offers for her hand in marriage, Lucita feels the call of Black Wolf and his people and casts her lot with them. This is a cut above the typical romance as Munn has included an abundance of knowledge of the Chumash and of life in a Spanish outpost mission.

Reviewed in: Publishers Weekly 12/15/97.

232. Murphy, Garth. *The Indian Lover.* NY: Simon & Schuster. 2002. 439 p.

Time: 1845–1850
Tribe: Pauma, Cupeno, Cahuilla (Luisenos)
Place: Southern California

Pablo Verdi, High Cloud Comes of the Pauma tribe, befriends Bill Marshall and takes him to California to make his fortune. Pablo has been educated by the missionaries and is an Indian of culture. California in 1845 is ruled by Mexico, which has successfully broken away from Spain. The missions have been closed and pillaged, the local tribes allowed to live in peace. The *Luisenos*, the tribes located around the mission of San Luis Rey, are the Pauma, the Cupa, the Ipai and the Cahuilla. In San Diego, Bill falls in love with Lugarda, a *Californio*, as the Mexian residents of California are known. She is rich and promised to another, so Bill takes his broken heart and joins the Cupa Indians, and finds a wife there in Falling Star. Falling Star is the daughter of No'ka, chief of the Cupas, and together they have several children. Bill is very happy living with the Cupa and he considers himself a member of the tribe. When gold is discovered in California the idyll is over. America goes to war with Mexico and wins California. The various California tribes are caught in the middle, attacked by both sides. When the gold seekers come pouring in, everything gets worse. Although the U.S. government says the Indian tribes are a soverign nation, and Indians not U.S.

citizens, any tribal member who converted to Christianity is considered a citizen and heavily taxed. The Cupa and Pauma rebel, killing both Mexicans and Americans. Bill and Pablo are arrested as traitors to their government. This is an excellent novel, full of cultural and historical details about little-known California tribes, and covering a time period of immense change in California. The characters are all well developed, with understandable flaws and motivations for their actions. Not everyone behaves in an exemplary way, all have deep flaws that make them more realistic as true characters.

Reviewed in: Library Journal 11/1/02; Kirkus Reviews 10/15/02; Booklist 11/15/02.

233. Murray, Earl. *Spirit of the Moon.* NY: Forge. 1996. 304 p.

Time: early 1840's
Tribe: Nez Perce
Place: Intermountain West

In 1841 a young girl, daughter of a Nez Perce woman and a French fur trader, made a journey with her father on a beaver trapping expedition through the intermountain west from Wyoming to the Gulf of Cortez. Her story was found in a ledger of the Hudson's Bay Company, written by her husband, who was the chief trader for the company. Murray has based his novel on this story, but what should have been an exciting, entertaining tale is flat and pallid. Spirit of the Moon is to marry James Condon, son of an influential British military man and part owner of the Hudson's Bay Company, which has employed her father. Since the beaver have been depleted in the upper Rocky Mountains, the plan is to travel south through the desert of Coyotero to the waters of the Colorado and the Gila which still are plentiful with beaver. Spirit finds she does not like James Condon—he is a weak man who is terrified of the wilderness. Her heart is taken by Baker McLeod, a daring White trapper who signs on with the expedition. Most of the novel tells of the hazardous journey the brigade makes south, the Mojaves, Apaches, and Spanish they encounter, and their run-ins with LeGrange, who is determined to steal their pelts and kill them all. Neither Spirit nor any of the other characters come alive and the reader is just as relieved as they are when the long trek is over.

Reviewed in: Booklist 10/1/96; Publishers Weekly 9/9/96; Roundup 10/96.

234. Murray, Earl. *Whisper on the Water.* NY: Forge. 1982. 309 p.

Time: 1830's
Tribe: Salish
Place: Western United States

Whisper on the Water sees her people killed by the hated Siksika and vows revenge, especially against their leader Walking Head. She kills several warriors while escaping and attaches herself to a pair of White beaver trappers. She loves Jim, one of the trappers, and carries his child, but still wants to avenge the deaths of her family. When she and Jim are attacked and she loses the baby, Whisper becomes very depressed and goes on a vision quest. Her vision tells her she is Spirit Woman, warrior of her people, but that she must not plan revenge, it will come to her. A small band of Salish warriors want her to join them as they too want Walking Head's death, but Whisper is captured and spares the war party in exchange for going with Walking Head. He thinks he can convince her to adopt the ways of the Siksika but Whisper remains true to her people and to Jim. Walking Head finally acknowledges this and sets her free, just in time for her to save his life against a Cree war party. This whole novel is very contrived, full of every cliché imaginable, and little of it rings true.

235. Mustain, Gordon, and Stoney Livingston. *Apache Tears.* Sun Lakes, AZ: Blue Star Productions. 1996. 352 p.

Time: Contemporary
Tribe: Apache
Place: Arizona

As a boy Clay Price became a blood brother to Apache youths Billy, Oscar and Elmer. In Vietnam, he was unable to save Billy's life, but was himself saved by Billy's cousin, Frank Redhawk. Years later he returns to the Apache reservation and he and Frank witness the rape and shooting of Angela Stillwater by two White men. One is a U.S. Senator's son and when both are released without trial, Frank knows that the Apache must declare their independence from the United States as the sovereign nation of Chiricahua, even though they may all die in the attempt. With the help of their spirit world, and the remembered old ways and arms purchased in Mexico, the Apache prepare to fight off the U.S. military. They are successful in the short term but know they cannot hold out indefinitely; their only hope is that American public opinion has changed and will come down on their side. With the help of Navajo television reporter Teresa who films the action and the meetings and feeds it live to the networks and with augmentation of their forces by military personnel from other tribes, the Apaches do win. The United States is willing to negotiate through the State Department, not the BIA, and they have an opportunity to preserve the land of Cochise, Nana, and Juh. Although this may seem to be a fantasy novel, it is solidly grounded in history and tradition. For a first novel, it reads very well; even the battle scenes with their military terminology hold the reader's attention.

236. Newcomb, Kerry. *The Arrow Keeper's Song.* NY: Bantam. 1995. 402 p.

Time: 1890's
Tribe: Southern Cheyenne
Place: Oklahoma Territory and Cuba

Tom Sandcrane feels that the future of his people lies in adopting the ways of the Whites. Although he is the son of the Keeper of the Sacred Arrows, Tom refuses to accept the responsibility for them, he wants nothing to do with the old ways. He favors the breakup of the reservation system since it will mean his people can file on the land, especially the oil-rich tracts. Half in love with the Indian Agent's daughter, Tom does not realize until it is too late that the Whites have filed ahead of time on the land, there is nothing left for the Cheyenne. In anger and self-disgust, Tom joins up with the Indian Brigade and is sent to Cuba where he encounters a woman doctor, Joanna Cooper. Joanna enlists Tom's help in rescuing a Cuban rebel leader, but he is gravely wounded in the attempt and leaves Cuba immediately. Two years later he returns to Oklahoma to find Joanna practicing medicine, the Cheyenne poorer than they were before and the old ways nearly lost. Tom's experiences in Cuba have made him realize that without their heritage, the Cheyenne are lost. He must fight one of his own for the power of the Arrow Keeper, for Jerel Tall Bull wishes to use that power for evil, not to restore the harmony of the Cheyenne. Although the interlude in Cuba is perhaps overlong, this is nevertheless an intriguing story of what happened when the reservation system was abolished and of one man's struggle to come to terms with his past.

Reviewed in: Kliatt 9/95.

237. Niswander, Adam. *The Charm: An Integra Southwestern Supernatural Thriller.* Phoenix: Integra Press. 1993. 280 p.

Time: 1991
Tribe: Pima, Hopi, Navajo, Apache, Yaqui, Havasupai, Tohono O'odham, Mohave, Zuni and Maricopa
Place: Arizona

When two White archaeologists pry open an ancient kiva, they release a dust devil of epic proportions. Consuming people for power and strength, this demon from five hundred years ago becomes ever larger and more dangerous. Archaeologist Jack Foreman finds a beautiful old charm in the kiva and keeps it. Tom Bear, the Pima witch, feels the need to gather the surrounding tribes' elderly shamans for consultation. As the shamans begin to come together in Phoenix, they bring old stories of their ancestors collecting at the kiva site in the first Great Gathering to wall away a demon hundreds of years ago. The demon appears and speaks to the Peace Man of the Hopi, Harold Laloma, asking him to protect his people by allowing the demon to kill all the Navajo. Harold refuses, but the demon destroys the Navajo at Chaco Canyon, including the old shaman singer, Archie. Fortunately Navajo singer Gordon Smythe has been trained in the Gathering Song and is saved. The shamans all collect into the Second Great Gathering, after suffering broken legs and heart attacks. They each offer the charm some strength, perform sacred rituals, and together with Jack and his ancient charm are able to defeat the dust demon for the final time. Jack sacrifices himself to do so and the shamans promise to gather every year to remember him. Although this is supposed to be a supernatural thriller, the solid down-to-earth personalities of the old shamans are calming and comforting.

Reviewed in: Library Journal 9/15/93; Publishers Weekly 9/20/93.

238. Niswander, Adam. *The Hound Hunters: A Novel in the Shaman Cycle. An Integra Southwestern Supernatural Thriller.* Phoenix: Integra Press. 1995. 310 p.

Time: 1993
Tribe: Pima, Hopi, Zuni, Navajo, Apache, Yaqui, Havasupai, Tohono O'odham, Mohave, Maricopa, Cocopah
Place: Arizona

The time for the twelve shamans to gather comes again and another supernatural threat must be confronted by their combined powers. Garfield Laurent, half French and half New Guinea Fore, runs a huge drug operation distributing the chaos drug, Tohu-Bohu, to young people in Arizona. The drug enforcement police are unable to locate his headquarters, but he is able to find and kill two dozen of the DEA. Garfield uses their brains in his religious ceremonies and in his drug, as the Fore ate the brains of their dead. Tohu-Bohu is supposed to take the user into another dimension and allow him to communicate with the Hounds. The Hounds are trapped in the between worlds and want to come here for food: humans to eat. If this sounds silly, it is. However, the communication between the old shamans and their honest desire to work together to overcome this evil is still very moving. The characters of the shamans develop more with each novel in the series. One begins to really care about the Havasupai Rattle and his Deer Spirit, George/Geronimo the Apache, Juan Mapoli the Yaqui and Tom Bear the Pima witch. This time the White man who makes the crucial thirteenth shaman is Police Chief Greg Johnson. Together they all take the drugs, fly into the outer dimension with their protective spirits, and send the Hounds back to their original home.

239. Niswander, Adam. *The Serpent Slayers: An Integra Southwestern Supernatural Thriller.* Phoenix: Integra Press. 1994. 308 p.

Time: 1992
Tribe: Pima, Hopi, Navajo, Apache, Yaqui, Havasupai, Tohono O'odham, Mohave, Zuni, and Maricopa
Place: Arizona

Rattlesnakes begin acting oddly in Arizona, aggressively attacking in coordinated groups and biting with much stronger venom. Herpetologist Jeremy Myers studies the snakes and wonders why. The southwestern tribes' shamans are gathering for their annual ceremony (see *The Charm*) and also notice the snakes' behavior. The Hopi, handlers of snakes, are having difficulty controlling them for their annual snake dance. Then the Scaled One, the Father of Snakes, visits Rattle, the Havasupai Deer Man shaman, and tells him that people must stop killing his children, the snakes. Meanwhile over at Casa Malpais, the Mollogon archaeological site inhabited from 1200 to 1400 A.D., a lower chamber is discovered. In that chamber lurks a giant serpent, asleep for 25,000 years. This serpent can use telepathy to control snakes and people, luring them towards her to be eaten. The shamans gather and decide that with the help of Myers as their token White man, they must defeat this evil, murdering serpent. The Scaled One comes to them and says the ancient serpent is his daughter and must not be killed. Myers arranges for curare and liquid nitrogen to paralyze and freeze the huge serpent back into her underground chamber beneath Casa Malpais. The Father of the Snakes is appeased. The aggressive snake behavior ends. The characters of the shamans are not as well developed in this second in the series, obviously because the author expected us to all know them from *The Charm*. The sudden ability of Myers to acquire twenty-four syringes of curare and tanks of liquid nitrogen overnight from the government is contrived. It is interesting that the Scaled One, a Native American god, continues to reign over his snake children unopposed by the shamans. There are apparently good gods and evil gods and the shamans know the difference.

Reviewed in: Publishers Weekly 2/7/94.

240. O'Brien, Dan. *The Contract Surgeon.* NY: Lyons Press, 1999. 316 p.

Time: 1876–1877
Tribe: Sioux, Cheyenne
Place: Fort Robinson, Nebraska

A heartbreaking novel of the death of Crazy Horse in September, 1877, the story is told by Dr. Valentine McGillycuddy, the Army surgeon contracted by General Crook to tend to the soldiers on the Yellowstone Campaign. Crazy Horse is accused of planning to kill Crook, a rumor begun by the jealous Red Cloud, and is arrested and brought to Fort Robinson. General Crook, Red Cloud and Lt. Philo Clark plot to have Crazy Horse killed while in custody, but then reconsider. Nevertheless, during a struggle Crazy Horse is stabbed in the back and then tended by Dr. Mac, as he is known, until the Sioux warrior dies. While Crazy Horse lingers near death, attended by his brother-friend, the Minniconjou warrior Touch the Clouds, Dr. Mac reminisces about his first meeting years ago with Crazy Horse in a swimming hole on the Knife River. Dr. Mac remembers his later presence at battles between the Army and the Sioux, and his care of Black Shawl, Crazy Horse's wife, sick with consumption. Dr. Mac and Crazy Horse had become very close friends during Black Shawl's illness and Dr. Mac decides to try a revolutionary surgery, taking out the damaged kidney to save Crazy Horse's life. Fanny, Dr. Mac's wife, also deeply cares for Crazy Horse. They discover that if Crazy Horse recovers, Lt. Clark has arranged for the powerful warrior to be sent to Florida to serve a life sentence in prison. Clark does not want Crazy Horse to die a martyr to the Sioux cause, but instead wants him to waste away in prison, forgotten by all. Knowing what the future holds for Crazy Horse, Fanny and Dr. McGillycuddy decide to fulfill the vision of Crazy Horse's dream, the dream of dying with his arms held by his friends.

Reviewed in: School Library Journal 5/1/00; Booklist 10/15/99; Kirkus Reviews 10/1/99; Publishers Weekly 9/27/99.

241. Owens, Louis. (Choctaw/Cherokee). *Bone Game.* Norman: University of Oklahoma Press. 1994. 243 p.

Time: Contemporary
Tribe: Choctaw, Navajo
Place: California

In this sequel to *The Sharpest Sight,* Cole McCurtain is a Choctaw/Cherokee mixed blood visiting professor at University of California, Santa Cruz, troubled by his failed marriage, the death of his brother, his Choctaw heritage and horrible dreams at night. Robert Malin is his teaching assistant and Paul Kantner is an older student in one of his classes, both in need of his attention. Cole's attention is diverted by dreams of Padre Quintana, a sadistic missionary friar from California's past, and Venancio Asisara, the Indian who murdered Quintana long ago. Cole is also seeing visions of the bone gambler, whose body is painted half black and half white. Added to all these problems is the presence of a serial killer in Santa Cruz. When Cole's daughter Abby arrives unexpectedly to live with him, he fears for her safety. Back east, Cole's grandparents, Luther and Onatima, feel his troubled mind and decide to come to California to help him, also arriving unexpectedly. Events come to a head, a resourceful Abby defeats the murderers and Cole confronts his demons, including the memory of his dead brother Attis. Owens includes a wonderful cross-dressing Navajo man, Alex Yazzie, a fellow faculty member who decides to become Cole's friend, buys him a bull mastiff on drugs to protect the family, asks Abby for advice on his makeup and outfits and helps her capture the killers. Abby and Alex fall in love, which all fits somehow. This is a very complex and troubled novel about a man dealing with the long ago past of White and Native American interactions, the recent past of his failed life, and the present of his intrusive but supportive family and friends.

Reviewed in: Booklist 10/1/94; Library Journal 9/1/94; NYTBR 10/23/94.

242. Owens, Louis. (Choctaw/Cherokee). *Dark River.* Norman: University of Oklahoma Press. 1999. 286 p.

Time: Contemporary
Tribe: Choctaw, Apache
Place: Arizona

Jacob Nashoba, a Choctaw Vietnam veteran, married into the Black Mountain Apache tribe and became the game warden on the reservation. His wife, Tali, has set him aside because of his violent nightmares, but she still loves him. Jake spends most of his days fishing in the Dark River canyon. When the tribal leader Two Bears orders Jake to stay out, he goes down anyway, looking for his granddaughter on her vision quest. Jake finds a group of anti-government paramilitaries have kidnapped her and a French woman and killed Jessie, the young Apache man who led the vision quests. Jessie returns to the captured women as a ghost, changing shape from himself to a wolf to help them escape. The paramilitaries capture Jake, disarm him and send him off into the woods to be hunted down as prey. Some old men in the tribe, including the anthropologist-turned-Apache, Avrum Goldberg who dresses only in "traditional" clothing, sense the danger and come down to assist the victims. On the way down the Apache explain to Avrum that there is no such thing as "traditional" because the Apache were always changing and adapting to new ways. His idea is a static one. Between the efforts of wolf-ghost-Jessie, the old Apaches, and Avrum, the paramilitaries are killed, but not before shooting and mortally wounding Jake. He sees his vision and returns in his dreams to the land of his Choctaw fathers. There is a great deal of humor inserted in this violent story and some truths about how Whites see American Indian culture as a defined, static ideal. The use of ghosts as real people and an ending which goes through various permutations until all the victims are happy with the results, has a sort of magical realism which adds another dimension.

243. Owens, Louis. (Choctaw/Cherokee). *Nightland.* NY: Penguin Books. 1996. 217 p.

Time: Contemporary
Tribe: Cherokee, Pueblo, Apache
Place: New Mexico

Two longtime friends, Will Striker and Billy Keene, are out hunting when a man falls out of the sky, impales himself on a tree, and dies. A suitcase full of money follows him down. Will and Billy retrieve the money and are instantly attacked by a helicopter, which they shoot down in self-defense, killing those on board. Assuming this is a drug deal gone bad, they go back to their ranches and hide the money. Grandpa Siquani, so old he must have been on the Trail of Tears, hears evil is coming in the talk of the crows on the barn. A row of buzzards sits on Will's fences, killing his chickens. Two men drive up to kill Will, but he shoots and buries them both. Will and Billy are half Cherokee who moved with their families from Oklahoma to ranch in New Mexico, but the streams and wells have dried up and their ranches are dying. The money will help dig deeper wells to start raising cattle again. Billy buys a truck and meets a beautiful Apache woman, Odessa. She moves in, but Siquani hates her, as do Will's dog and pet pig. Siquani starts playing checkers with Arturo Cruz, the Pueblo man who fell on the tree, now a restless ghost. Arturo teaches Siquani how to drive a car, run a chain saw, and retrieve Arturo's rotting body out of the tree. Siquani buries Arturo at the site of the dried up spring which used to feed the streams and wells on the ranches. Arturo's uncle Paco comes to find the money, drug proceeds from selling destructive illegal substances to Whites to achieve retribution for wrongs done to the Pueblos in the past. Odessa kills them all: Paco her former lover, Billy her current lover, and the thugs brought along for muscle. She tries to kill Will but the dog and pig alert him and he kills her. She had double-crossed Paco as an Apache seeking retribution for wrongs done to her peoples. The money is all gone, lost in the battles, but the water has returned to the streams and wells. Will and Siquani know this is the real treasure. This novel sounds more violent than it is and in fact it is Siquani who is at the core of the story.

Reviewed in: Library Journal 7/96; Booklist 8/96; Publishers Weekly 6/24/96.

For further criticism and interpretation of Louis Owens' works, see: LaLonde, Chris. *Grave Concerns, Trickster Turns: The Novels of Louis Owens.* Norman: University of Oklahoma Press. 2002.

244. Padgett, Abigail. *Moonbird Boy.* NY: Mysterious. 1996. 259 p.

Time: Contemporary
Tribe: Kumeyaay
Place: Southern California

Today there are numerous bands of the Kumeyaay people on reservations in San Diego County, one of the little known tribes nearly eradicated by contact with Whites. Iroquois psychologist Eva Blindhawk Broussard has sent her patient, child investigator Bo Bradley, to the Ghost Flower Lodge, run by Zach Crooked Owl. The Lodge is located in the dessert and offers traditional Kumeyaay methods of restoring mental health to those troubled with depression or other disorders. Bo's fox terrier Mildred has died, throwing Bo into a deep depression, which comedian Mort Wagman, recovering from a schizophrenic episode, helps cheer her out of. Zach conducts a *Kurok*, a grieving ceremony for Mildred and Bo finally feels better, but after the ceremony Mort is found shot to death. Bo takes the case and discovers that the Ghost Flower Lodge is in serious financial trouble, about to be taken over by a crooked medical management corporation. Bo investigates Mort's personal life, necessary because he has left a six-year-old son, Bird, who suffers from ADHD, and who has no apparent living relatives to contact. Bo discovers the secret of Mort's true identity and the person behind the murder of a wealthy woman, Hopper Mead, benefactor of the Ghost Flower Lodge, girlfriend of Mort, and chief stockholder of the medical management company. Needless to say the mystery is very complex. Zach performs a ceremonial dance and finds the casing of the bullet that killed Mort, his mother finds the murderer, and Bo ties it all together, also coming up with a concerned grandmother for little Bird.

245. Padgett, Abigail. *Strawgirl.* NY: Mysterious. 1994. 245 p.

Time: Contemporary
Tribe: Iroquois
Place: San Diego, New York State

When a three-year-old girl is found dead from sexual assault, child abuse investigator Bo Bradley is brought into the case. The mother's boyfriend, Paul Massieu, is the prime suspect, mostly because he is a member of the Shadow Mountain Seekers, believers in extraterrestrial encounters. The small upper New York sect is headed by Eva Blindhawk Broussard, an Iroquois Onondaga, member of the Heron Clan and a psychiatrist. The little girl's mother commits suicide and Paul takes the older sister Hannah and flees to Eva for protection. Bo follows them to the lodge at the base of Shadow Mountain and meets Eva. Bo realizes Eva is really Hannah's salvation and allows Eva to adopt her into the Heron Clan as her granddaughter. Eva gives Hannah three Iroquois straw grieving beads to wear, explaining there is a bead to see, to hear, and to speak for Hannah during her grief over her mother and sister's death. Under Eva's care and protection, Hannah opens up and tells Bo about "Goody," the man who hurt her little sister. Bo shares her life experiences of losing her own sister to suicide and Hannah shares her Iroquois beads with Bo, since they are both *Otadenon*, the Last Ones Left.

246. Page, Jake. *Apacheria.* NY: Del Rey. 1998. 342 p.

Time: 1884–1921
Tribe: Apache
Place: Arizona and New Mexico

A novel of alternative history, here the Apache win the battle for control of their lands in 1885. All the historical figures are represented, with Juh and Victorio the master planners of the Apache wars against Generals Crook and Miles. On a trip out West, President-elect Cleveland is rescued from bandits by Geronimo. The two become close friends when Geronimo is appointed the ambassador from the new country of Apacheria, located in the southern parts of Arizona and New Mexico. Juh, Victorio, and ten other chiefs share responsibility for the tribe, which continues its traditional lifestyle while acquiring income from mining leases sold to Whites. Juh's son Little Spring introduces Teddy Roosevelt to the wilds of Apacheria, instilling a love of wilderness which later President Roosevelt turns into the concept of national wilderness areas. Little Spring attends Princeton and marries a wealthy White woman, Muriel Freeman, whose father runs brothels in Chicago. Little Spring comes back to Apacheria to assume leadership of the tribe when battles with White miners and a false Comanche prophet endanger their welfare. After Juh's death, Little Spring becomes known as Juh and works with J. Edgar Hoover to foil the attempts of Al Capone and his mob to create a huge crime syndicate. Obviously requiring some stretches of the imagination, this version of history is quite entertaining. The portrayal of the historical personalities is accurate and the Apache wars are well described.

247. Page, Jake. *The Knotted Strings.* NY: Ballantine Books. 1995. 247 p.

Time: Contemporary
Tribe: Hopi
Place: New Mexico

Page writes mysteries featuring Mo Bowdrie, a blind sculptor, and his woman friend Connie Barnes, a Hopi of the Eagle clan. This mystery also involves the Pueblo of Santo Esteban, where director Andrew Pindaric is trying to film *The Knotted Strings*, a movie based upon the Pueblo Rebellion of 1680 when the followers of Po'pay drove out the Spanish. Luis Rodriguez, the Pueblo Governor, dies of an apparent heart attack and the symbol of his power, a cane with a silver head given to the tribe by President Lincoln, disappears. His son Martin takes over but is opposed by the traditionalists in the Red Ant moiety, led by Tupatu, who do not want a film production in their pueblo or White people anywhere nearby. The Hispanic actors begin to be murdered, the set is cursed by a witch, and Pindaric's car is bombed. Mo and his friends in law enforcement step in to solve the mystery behind these events, committed by two separate groups. One group is the Red Ants, but another seems to be working against the Pueblo legal case to get disputed lands back from the government. This group is led by the elegant but treacherous lawyer Templeton. Mo discovers the truth, using the heightened powers that his loss of sight have given him to untie the knotted strings of this complicated case.

Reviewed in: Armchair Detective Winter/95; Library Journal 2/1/95; Publishers Weekly 1/16/95.

248. Palmer, Diana. (copyright held by Susan Kyle) *The Savage Heart.* Rockland, MA: Wheeler. 1997. 281 p.

Time: 1903
Tribe: Sioux
Place: Chicago

When Tess Meredith is fourteen years old, she says goodbye to her best friend Raven Following as he leaves Montana after the Wounded Knee Massacre to begin a new life in Chicago. Ten years later, after her physician father has died, Tess comes to Chicago to be with Raven, now called Matt Davis, the owner of a successful detective agency. Declaring themselves "cousins," Tess takes a room in Matt's boarding house, finds work as a nurse and becomes active in the Women's Suffrage Movement. She befriends Nan Collier, a young woman who denies her injuries are the result of her husband's beatings, but there is little Tess can do since Nan won't admit she needs help. Besides, most of Tess's time is consumed with Matt who has vowed he doesn't believe in mixed marriages. Tess decides she will stay single but when their passion overwhelms them, even Matt feels that marriage and children with Tess might not be so bad after all. Although this romance has interesting sub-themes of battered women and the Right to Vote Crusade, there is not enough of that to make up for the flat characters and the unrealistic plot developments.

249. Parks, Mary Armstrong. *The Circle Leads Home.* Niwot: University Press of Colorado. 1998. 259 p.

Time: Contemporary
Tribe: Lushootseed
Place: Washington State

Katherine Jack flees the big city of Seattle after her thirteen-year-old son spends the night in a crack house. Going home to "the rez" may be safer, but it has its own problems, namely re-establishing her relationship with her mother Ada from whom Katherine has been estranged since she married a Black man fifteen years earlier. It is obvious that Ada favors Katherine's younger son Tony who looks like Katherine's father and can barely tolerate Victor who looks like his Black father Larry. Katherine brings her mother-in-law from Louisiana for an extended visit, finds a job with the tribal council and tries to make a life for herself and her sons. Only thirty-two, Katherine must also come to terms with her own sexuality, why she invariably falls for the wrong man, and what family secrets her mother has hidden all these years. In dealing with these issues, Katherine also comes up against tribal politics. It appears that the old growth forest is to be sold for far less than it is worth and Katherine must decide if she's on the side of her lover Mark or on that of the tribal council members. Although her problems seem easily resolved, this is a very good book about a young woman finally learning who she is, where she belongs, and what's important to her.

Reviewed in: Library Journal 5/1/98.

250. Penn, William S. (Nez Perce/Osage). *The Absence of Angels.* Tucson: University of Arizona Press. 1994. 274 p.

Time: 1950's–1970's
Tribe: Nez Perce, Hopi, Navajo
Place: California, Arizona

American Indian Literature and Critical Studies Series, v. 14.

When Albert Hummingbird is born, he is rescued from hovering Death by his Grandfather, who drives all the way from Chosposi Mesa in Arizona to Los Angeles, grabs Death and takes Him back to the Rez. Albert, called Alley, grows up with two sisters, an absent father and a crazy mother who talks to toasters and undergoes electroshock therapy. Alley therefore spends a lot of time at Chosposi with his Grandfather and a reservation activist named Rachel. Alley meets smooth-talking Sanchez on a bus and brings him to Chosposi, where he sets up a lucrative trading post and marries Rachel. When Alley goes off to school at Clearmont Men's College in California, he meets Sara Baites and Proctor and Mrs. Tompson. They become his family, Sara his girlfriend, and all are concerned with Alley's heavy use of amphetamines to block his serious headaches. Finally they urge him into treatment and doctors discover a large brain tumor. After a successful operation, his bedside attended by all his relatives and friends, Alley recovers and learns that Grandfather's time is up. Death has come for him. Written in a magical-realism style with a great deal of wry humor, the novel seems as though it could be autobiographical. The contributions of the elders to the young, in the form of Grandfather to Alley are well portrayed, although the text does not always flow smoothly.

Reviewed in: Library Journal 1/94; Publishers Weekly 1/10/94; Kirkus Reviews 12/15/93.

251. Penn, William S. (Nez Perce/Osage). *Killing Time with Strangers.* Tucson: University of Arizona Press. 2000. 282 p.

Time: early 1970's
Tribe: Nez Perce, Osage
Place: California

Sun Tracks, v. 45. An American Indian Literary Series.

Mary Blue's grandfather was Chief Joseph and she has his patience. She also has the power to call *weyekin,* spirit guides to help her son Palimony through difficult times in his life. Mary and her husband, La Vent Larue, an Osage, intended to name their son Palomino, but the records clerk renamed the infant on the birth certificate. La Vent works as a city planner for Gilroy, soon to be swallowed up by Silicon Valley. He compromises his ethics and sells his soul for the mayor until he is driven mad and shoots the mayor, wounding him. When released from prison, La Vent becomes a born-again Christian. Pal grows up confused and compliant with few friends. Mary calls Chingaro, a *weyekin*, to leave his spirit world and his other *weyekin* friends to become Pal's friend. Chingaro gets Pal into and out of a great deal of trouble and difficult situations. The story is mostly told through Chingaro's eyes and is extremely humorous. As a young man, Pal gets involved with preachers' daughters, bar waitresses and spoiled rich girls, always dreaming of his future wife, Amanda. Finally he meets her and his life is complete. Written in the relaxed, humorous style of a few other contemporary Native American authors such as Sherman Alexie, the spirit world is incorporated naturally into the physical world and both benefit from it.

Reviewed in: Booklist 10/15/00; Publishers Weekly 9/15/00; Library Journal 9/1/00.

252. Perry, Thomas. *Blood Money.* NY: Random House. 1999. 351 p.

Time: Contemporary
Tribe: Seneca
Place: United States

Jane Whitefield, the Seneca woman who helps people disappear and make new lives, is married and retired. Rita Shelford comes to her, afraid for her life. Rita had been an old man's companion until he was murdered. When Jane discovers the man is Bernie Lupus, the Mob's money handler, she knows she must help Rita and the suddenly very-much-alive Bernie. Bernie holds all the accounts for five families in his head and he agrees to donate billions of dollars to charities, foundations, and scholarships in return for Jane's help. Together with another accountant from the west coast, they succeed in setting up false short-lived foundations to distribute the funds without the mob families being able to trace it. The five families are furious and send out hit men to pursue Jane as she drives across the U.S. with Bernie and Rita, mailing thousands of envelopes at hundreds of post offices. They track the route and nearly catch her, but she and her charges elude capture using many false identities. Finally the money is gone and the five families all begin to blame each other for its loss. They erupt into warfare, killing each other off to gain control of territory and power. Jane and Rita are forgotten, Bernie is still assumed dead. There are frequent references to the Seneca twins Hawenneyu, the good right-hand twin and Hanegoategeh, the evil left-hand twin. They are the powers of good and evil in the world, always trying to find a balance between their individual powers. Bernie did a great deal of evil in his life, but now as an old man he is balancing it with the ability to do good.

Reviewed in: Publishers Weekly 10/18/99; Library Journal 10/1/99; Booklist 9/1/99.

253. Perry, Thomas. *Dance for the Dead.* NY: Random House. 1996. 324 p.

Time: Contemporary
Tribe: Seneca
Place: Upstate New York and elsewhere

Jane Whitefield is a Seneca woman who makes a profession of helping people disappear into new lives. When a little boy's life is threatened by those wishing to steal his trust fund and his parents, foster parents and guardians are all killed, Jane helps to hide and protect Timmy. Weary and going home, she meets Mary Perkins, fleeing the people out to track down the millions she stole from savings and loan banks. Jane tries to help Mary start over in a new life, but someone is too good at finding the people Jane hides. Finally Jane makes the connection between a large private security firm and the men tracking both Mary and Timmy, the little boy. Jane frequently uses dreams involving Seneca rituals, past lives, and ceremonies which help her deal with the present situations she finds herself in. Her Seneca past holds her sanity together and her Seneca people are ultimately the saviors of both Mary and Timmy. Mary's involvement with savings and loan scandals is described in detail, for those who might want to learn how those financial dealings were conducted.

Reviewed in: Booklist 2/15/96; Library Journal 3/1/96; NYTBR 5/5/96; Publishers Weekly 2/19/96.

254. Perry, Thomas. *The Face-Changers.* NY: Random House. 1998. 372 p.

Time: Contemporary
Tribe: Seneca
Place: Upstate New York and other US cities

Jane Whitefield thinks she has retired from the business of helping people disappear. Now married to surgeon Carey McKinnon, she no longer gets desperate phone calls in the middle of the night. When Richard Dahlman, Carey's former teacher and mentor, is accused of murdering his research partner and arrives in the hospital, wounded and seeking Jane's help, she cannot refuse. Using her old skills, Jane manages to get Dahlman out of the hospital, out of New York, and into a new identity. The police are still watching Carey, hoping he will lead them to Dahlman, and Jane realizes that in helping one man, she has condemned herself and Carey to a life of suspicion; Carey could lose his license and his career if he is convicted of obstructing justice. There are other suspicious things happening and Jane must unravel the entire plot before she and Carey, let alone Dahlman, will be free. While this story is not on the surface a Native American novel, Jane's Seneca heritage is a factor and the theme of the Seneca Right-Handed Twin and Left-Handed Twin, the Creator and the Destroyer, nicely reminds the reader that things are not always what they seem.

Reviewed in: Library Journal 5/15/98; Publishers Weekly 4/13/98.

255. Perry, Thomas. *Shadow Woman.* NY: Random House. 1997. 350 p.

Time: Contemporary
Tribe: Seneca
Place: Nevada, Montana, Massachusetts

Pete Hatcher needs to hide from Pleasure, Inc., a gambling company he works for in Las Vegas. He knows things about their plans to expand into eastern Indian reservations which the FBI would be very interested in learning, as would members of the Mafia. Jane agrees to help him as her last job before her marriage. Things go wrong and Pete is found by two professional killers, Earl and Linda. Jane is forced into helping Pete again, against her husband Carey's wishes. Fleeing across the west, Jane and Pete are barely able to stay ahead of Earl and his Rottweilers. Fed information by Linda who has moved in on Carey in Jane's absence, Earl is closing in on Pete. Finally on a high peak in Glacier National Park, Jane is able to defeat Earl and his dogs, using an old *Nundawaono* decoy trick on *Nyakwai*, the grizzly bear. This mystery contains information about the history of the Seneca, and some of their beliefs, as in the *Jo-Ge-Oh*, whom Jane honors and respects, the Little People who take and hide those in fear and needing concealment. These mysteries are very well written and full of suspense until the very end.

Reviewed in: Booklist 5/1/97; Library Journal 5/1/97; Publishers Weekly 4/21/97.

256. Perry, Thomas. *Vanishing Act.* NY: Random House. 1995. 289 p.

Time: Contemporary
Tribe: Seneca
Place: New York State, Vancouver, Canada.

When John Felker comes to Jane for help in disappearing from men intent upon killing him, Jane not only agrees to help, but falls in love with him. Jane is filling the ancient role of Jigonsasee, the woman who helped warriors along the warpaths, then later with Hiawatha and Deganawida founded the basis for the Iroquois League. Jane and John begin an intense affair, she believing that John is an ex-policeman turned accountant now being framed for embezzlement. John believes his helping an old friend, Harry, escape from the Mob now has him targeted as their victim instead. Jane explains how she hid Harry five years earlier, takes John to Canada for a new identity, then bravely turns him free with no commitments. Returning home she discovers Harry has been murdered, her Canadian contacts have been murdered, and John is not in the Oregon town she sent him to. Jane learns she has been a fool and John has used her to find Harry to kill him. Jane goes after John, finding him in the North Woods, fully equipped to hide out in them for some time. She pursues him relentlessly, losing her gear, her weapons and her food in the process. Falling back upon her Seneca heritage and remembering the stories of her youth, Jane fashions clothing and weapons from the woods around her, making a bow and arrows, a war club, and a pit trap. She lures John to his death at her hands then hides all evidence of his existence. Returning home, she finds another pair of frightened people, seeking her help. The process of Jane's utilizing the resources of the North Woods to exact her revenge is fascinating, as are the characters and plot development in this excellent mystery.

Reviewed in: Booklist 12/15/94; Library Journal 12/94; NYTBR 2/5/95; Publishers Weekly 12/5/94.

257. Peyton, John L. *Faces in the Firelight.* Blacksburg, VA: McDonald and Woodward. 1992. 267 p.

Time: 1850's–1950's
Tribe: Ojibwe
Place: Lake Superior

Now and then a book comes along that captures the essence of a lost way of living. Peyton spent time with the Ojibwe at the turn of the century and this novel reflects stories and practices he must have heard or witnessed. The time covered in the stories is a year in the life of a small family band of Anishinabe on the Canadian Shield above Lake Superior. Exact details are given on moose hunting, fur trading, traveling long distances over snow and ice, berry picking and drying, dangerous fish harvesting in turbulent *'Tschgumi* (Lake Superior), the gathering of widespread families for summer games, and finally dealing with White traders. The family is headed by Iron Feather and Otter Woman with several children, grandchildren, and adopted children. Dawn Sailing is the healer, formerly a Sioux captive, now an old woman. The stories are all told to a young White boy in the early 1900's by He-Rises, an elderly Anishinabe guide, and are of his family in the mid-1800's and includes how He-Rises acquired terrible scars of his own. Peyton truly captures how times changed the people, once struggling to get through one entire winter without starving or losing members. Later in the 1950's, when the young boy returns as a grown man to see He-Rises, he learns of tribal politics, polluted rivers, and leaders selling out their people to put dams on the streams.

258. Pfaff, Eugene E. Jr., and Michael Causey. *Uwharrie.* Greensboro, NC: Tudor. 1993. 243 p.

Time: Contemporary
Tribe: Uwharrie (Mythical tribe)
Place: North Carolina

The Uwharrie are an extinct tribe, no trace of them apparently remains in the mountains of North Carolina. Or does it? Librarian David Hale is bored with his job and with the town of Clearview and agrees to help his old professor Arthur Walters with an archeological dig. Walters hopes to find evidence of the Lost Colony; Hale is primarily interested in Walters' dauighter Diana, now an anthropologist. Strange things are happening in the town and at the dig. Men who have never been violent become so, strange fires are seen at night, and people begin dying. Try as they might to pass the deaths off as accidents, it is obvious that evil spirits are at work. When the Uwharrie were massacred, one woman and her infant son escaped, it is from this lineage that the massacre must be avenged against those who slaughtered them. While there are several interesting premises in this novel, the language is stilted, the characters flat, and what might have been terrifying is merely boring.

Reviewed in: Publishers Weekly 7/19/93; Library Journal 8/93.

259. Plumlee, Harry James. *Shadow of the World: an Apache Tale.* Norman: University of Oklahoma Press. 1997. 206 p.

Time: 1870's–1881
Tribe: Apache
Place: Arizona

Nakaidoklinni is the White wolf shaman of the mountain Coyoteros Apaches, a visionary who is the tribes' healer of soul and body. The Apache have always raided Mexico for food and horses, but the U.S. Army puts a stop to this warrior tradition. The Apache are sent to Camp Grant and Fort Apache to live off White men's beef and rations. When the warriors break out they are hunted down and Mangos Colorado and Eskiminzin are killed. Although General Howard truly wants to help the Apache, General Crook only wants to conquer them. The peaceful Coyoteros are used as scouts by the Army to hunt down the renegade Apaches and Nakaidoklinni becomes a scout. When all the renegades are rounded up or killed, the Army moves the mountain tribes down to the hot desert of San Carlos where they are miserable. Finally allowed to return home, the Coyoteros return to the Cibique and Nakaidoklinni creates a dance of peace and prayer ceremony. Similar to the Ghost Dance which was so threatening to the Army in the north, the dance of the white wolf shaman finally causes the Army to send tribal police to bring in Nakaidoklinni, but he refuses to come. The Army returns with the scouts and the battle of Cibique Creek in August, 1881, results in the death of the shaman and his family. Nakaikoklinni was an actual historical figure, described as a dreamer or medicine man, who created a religious dance of peace which threatened the Army in Arizona. The massacre at Cibique did occur and the Apache scouts in fact turned on their Army leaders during the battle, trying to protect the shaman. The scouts, Sergeants Dead Shot, Dandy Jim and Skippy, and two privates were later tried and hung by the Army for their "traitorous" behavior. The sad similarity to the later Ghost Dance massacre at Wounded Knee is obvious. The novel contains many Apache ceremonies and tribal customs in detail and although fairly short, is full of cultural and historical information about the mountain Apache.

Reviewed in: Kirkus Reviews 1/1/97; Library Journal 1/97; Publishers Weekly 1/27/97.

260. Power, Susan. (Sioux). *The Grass Dancer.* NY: Putnam. 1994. 300p.

Time: 1860's–1980's
Tribe: Sioux
Place: North Dakota

While this is a deceptively easy book to read, it is a difficult book to describe. Each chapter can stand alone, but read together they go further and further back into the past, like peeling the layers of an onion. Harley Wind Soldier is a young Lakota man whose mother has not spoken since his father and brother were killed by a drunk driver before Harley was born. He meets the grass dancer, Pumpkin, at a pow-wow and is entranced by her, but his attraction is noted by Charlene Thunder who thinks of Harley as hers. Charlene is the granddaughter of Anna Thunder who knows how to make bad medicine and who has no compunction about doing so. When Pumpkin is killed in a car crash, Charlene fears that either she, inadvertently, or her grandmother, deliberately, caused her death. The Thunder women are linked to their ancestor Red Dress while Harley's lineage goes back to Ghost Warrior; these two were linked in the Old Times and the lives of their descendants continue to be interwoven. This novel can be read on many levels and should be savored again and again.

Reviewed in: Booklist 8/1/94; Publishers Weekly 6/6/94; Library Journal 10/1/94; Kirkus Reviews 6/1/94.

261. Proctor, George W. *Blood of My Blood.* NY: Bantam. 1996. 307 p.

Time: 1836–1911
Tribe: Comanche
Place: Oklahoma, Texas

John Teller and Cynthia Ann Parker are captured as children by the *Nermernuh,* the Comanche, and although John escapes, Cynthia Ann becomes Naduah, wife of Peta Nocona and mother of Quanah Parker. Quanah is only fourteen when his mother is taken back by the Texas Rangers and his father is killed by a fall from his horse. Not accepted by the Comanche for his White blood, Quanah must prove himself a hunter and a warrior. Eventually he becomes the war leader, fighting against Colonel Mackenzie. When Quanah finally surrenders in 1875, he has the respect of Mackenzie and is granted privileges others do not receive. Quanah learns English and learns to deal, working out leasing arrangements for reservation grazing land to local ranchers. He establishes an Indian Court to handle the small infractions on the reservation and serves as a judge. Quanah also believes strongly in the visions induced by peyote and establishes a whole religion around use of the cactus. He fights the Dawes Act that will break up the Comanche Kiowa reservation into tiny farms and let much of the land fall into White hands. The Dawes Act and the land grab of Indian Territory happened in spite of his efforts. Over the years Quanah loses his fortunes and standing as Principal Chief of the Comanches, in part because he refuses to give up his eight wives. A thorough account of an amazing man's life, the obvious intellect and ability to change in changing circumstances were Quanah's strengths.

Reviewed in: Kliatt 9/96; Roundup 10/96.

262. Prowell, Sandra West. *The Killing of Monday Brown: A Phoebe Siegel Mystery.* NY: Walker. 1994. 255 p.

Time: Contemporary
Tribe: Crow
Place: Montana

Phoebe Siegel, a private investigator, is asked by the Wolf Family to help prove their son Matthew innocent of murder charges. Monday Brown, a White man married to a Crow woman, has been robbing graves and selling Native American artifacts to a German, Jurgen Mueller, for collectors overseas. Now Monday has disappeared along with a large collection of artifacts, after several young Native American men were seen fighting with him. Next a young Crow and then a young Cheyenne man are found murdered, both involved in the fight with Monday. Kyle Old Wolf, a policeman and friend of Phoebe's, takes her to meet Genevieve Cramer, a Native American psychologist who was adopted by Whites, but now has returned to the Crow people in Montana. Genevieve and Phoebe become friends. Phoebe has a sweat lodge ceremony and wins the confidence of the Crow on the reservation to help her clear Matthew. Depictions of the close family ties on the reservation and the hostility with which the Crow people initially confront Phoebe are excellent. The offensiveness of selling precious possessions from plundered Native American graves to wealthy Europeans, an escalating problem, is also clearly described. At one point Genevieve asks Phoebe how she would feel if her father's grave were opened, his uniform and police medals removed from his body and sold to art collectors. The murderer of the young men is revealed but has diplomatic immunity. Phoebe is visited by an ancient Crow woman, Anna, in disturbing dreams and shown how Monday was murdered. Phoebe finds the responsible person, who commits suicide, but who first confides to Phoebe the hidden location of the plundered artifacts, now hidden forever from collectors.

Reviewed in: Booklist 5/15/94; Publishers Weekly 4/18/94; Library Journal 4/1/94; Kirkus Reviews 3/15/94.

263. Querry, Ron. (Choctaw). *Bad Medicine.* NY: Bantam. 1998. 315 p.

Time: Contemporary
Tribe: Navajo, Hopi, Choctaw
Place: Arizona

Doctor Pushmataha Foster, a Choctaw from Oklahoma, arrives on the Navajo reservation in 1993 just as the first cases of a mysterious respiratory disease are killing the people. His Navajo friend Dr. Sonny Brokeshoulder is there and they try to determine the cause or source of the disease. All the dead are Navajo, so the state government doesn't seem to care. Foster contacts the CDC, which collects samples from the dead peoples' homes and determines it is a form of Hanta virus, first identified in Korea in the early 1950's. But identifying a disease and convincing the Navajo and Hopi of its source in rodent droppings are two different things. The reservation Navajo healers come for a large gathering, with representatives from the Hopi Mesa in attendance. Clifford, *kikmongwi*, or leader, of Hopi Mesa, believes a Navajo shaman, Slow Talker, is responsible for the evil. Slow Talker has given an ancient sacred Hopi tablet to White archaeologists to sell, disrupting the harmony of the two tribes. Foster and Clifford find one of the archaeologists dead of the virus in her tent and are chased down the highway in their truck by a shape shifter, a skinwalker, who is Slow Talker. Foster discovers complexities of traditional beliefs he had never suspected to be true. Throughout the epidemic, the specter of Tall Warrior Woman appears to Foster and to others. Killed in an Army massacre of Navajo women and children two hundred years ago, she has been brought back by the desecration of the site by the archaeologists. Tall Warrior Woman breaks all the pots dug up from the site and kills Slow Talker as he tries to kill Clifford on the same cliff as the original massacre of her tribe. The epidemic settles down as the people learn how to handle deer mice on advice from their doctors. The friendship between the traditional Navajo Sonny and his more acculturated Choctaw friend Foster is very well done, full of humor, and a slow realization by Foster of how integral the traditional beliefs of the Navajo are to their lives. The Navajo and Hopi are accurately portrayed, as are their tribal conflicts, and their deep beliefs in witchery and traditional medicine. Not a medical thriller on the discovery of the Hanta virus, this is more of an introduction to how the Navajo *ndilniihii,* hand tremblers, and *hataalii*, the singers, work within their tribal belief systems.

Reviewed in: Library Journal 2/15/98; Publishers Weekly 2/9/98.

264. Rainey, Clarice Hove. *Mountain of Death.* n.p. [Rainey]. 1995. 231 p.

Time: 1980
Tribe: Yakama
Place: Mt. St. Helen's, Washington State

The old Indian Skamoot knows something is coming since all the signs and his dreams point to a terrible catastrophe. What he does not know is when this will happen. Is the calamity far off in the future or will it happen soon? Scientists studying the nearby volcano do not know either. All their studies and instruments tell them that something may happen, but then again it may not. Maude Cloud, owner of the Chinook Lodge on Spirit Lake, doesn't believe either the scientists or the shaman of her husband's people. Maude is only concerned with keeping the lodge running, denying her heart condition, and worrying about the future of her nephew Sam Cloud, a pre-law student at the University who seems to have fallen in love with the wrong girl. Rainey has numerous characters in this community including an out of work logger and his pregnant wife, a rich controlling bitch, her ineffectual husband and his ex-prostitute girlfriend and the couple who own the local grocery store. None of these people believe that the mountain could erupt but many of them Rainey manages to have conveniently absent when it does. Only Maude Cloud, her handyman Bert and Skamoot are killed in the eruption. There is a great deal of Yakama lore and legal battles over fishing rights and treaty violations included in this novel and while Rainey is not a polished writer, the reader is presented with a snapshot of life on Mt. St. Helen's in the spring of 1980.

265. Red Corn, Charles H. (Osage). *A Pipe for February: A Novel.* Norman: University of Oklahoma Press. 2002. 269 p.

Time: 1924
Tribe: Osage
Place: Oklahoma

American Indian Literature and Critical Studies Series, v. 44

When the Osage lands in Oklahoma are found to have wealthy resources of petroleum in the early 1900's, riches came to the individual tribal members, administered by government bureaucrats and agencies. White men deliberately married into the tribe to inherit their spouses's wealth and unscrupulous Whites cheated and murdered the Osage for their money. John Grayeagle has been raised by his traditional grandfather after his parents were killed in a mysterious car accident. His cousin Mollie's parents were also killed that way. John has artistic talent but no vision or personal drive to succeed. The money comes too easily to such a wealthy Osage. His lawyer, Sanders, tries to talk Mollie, John and another friend, Ted, into a joint beneficiary will. John suspects Sanders' motivations when the elders of the tribe warn the young people of too many dangers, too many murders, too many accidents happening to their tribal members. John and his family friend Tom, a World War I veteran, track down the culprits, expose the crooked lawyer, and drive him out. Very poorly written in a flat emotionless style that never develops any of the characters, this first novel nonetheless is very important. One does not often hear the voice of a young Osage of the 1920's living in the midst of the Osages' murders by Whites jealous of the oil money. When John finds his calling in painting the traditional stories and ways of his people, his literary voice finally awakens too, and the ending is quite moving.

Reviewed in: Kirkus Reviews 9/1/02; Publishers Weekly 11/4/02.

266. Reynolds, Father Brad, S.J. *A Ritual Death.* NY: Avon. 1997. 242 p.

Time: Contemporary
Tribe: Swinomish
Place: Pacific Northwest

Father Mark Townsend has come to LaConner to take his grandparents to see the tulips in the Skagit Valley, but ends up becoming involved in a murder. The body of Dutch Olsen, his grandfather's best friend, is found washed up on the beach, deep cuts across his back, his right hand missing, and a bullet hole in his side. It is well known that both GrandSam and Dutch were opposed to the Indian Fishing Rights ruling and Dutch had a run-in with Indian fisherman, Greg Patsy, the day before he was killed. When Greg is taken to jail, Mark's grandmother persuades him to try and help Greg's wife Linda and daughter Jesse prove Greg's innocence. Although this is outside the scope of his priestly duties, Mark does do some investigating and turns up tales of old treasures, sale of Native American artifacts, and smuggling, both old and new. While the main characters of this novel are White, the setting and themes are Native American, and provide an intriguing glimpse into two cultures forced to co-exist with each other.

267. Riddle, Paxton. (Cherokee). *The Education of Ruby Loonfoot.* Waterville, ME: Five Star. 2002. 349 p.

Time: 1957
Tribe: Ojibwe
Place: Wisconsin

Ruby Loonfoot is thirteen and rebellious, always finding herself in trouble with the nuns at St. Nicholas, the Catholic girls boarding school she attends all winter long. Sister Margaret and Father Slater are especially hard on the girls, but Father Potts, an ex-Army chaplain, is positively cruel. Ruby befriends pretty eight-year-old Kathy, a happy orphan girl. Kathy has no one else to turn to when she finds herself being molested and then raped, by Father Slater. Only Sister Steph will listen to Ruby and Kathy and writes a letter to the Bishop about the evils of St. Nicholas. Unfortunately the Bishop is Father Slater's uncle, so the letter is ignored and Sister Steph is transferred. The girls at the school are always hungry, homesick, and cold. When two run away and die in a blizzard, Father Potts takes steps to be sure none run away again, building an electric chair in the furnace room to torture the troublemakers. Over the summer Ruby goes home and spends time with her grandmother Cecelia, a wise traditionalist. She tells Cecelia of the evils of the school and her grandmother and the tribal chairman, Luther White Bear from the Loon Lake Reservation, go to speak to the BIA Agent and the Bishop. Both reject their request for a school on the reservation, run by the Ojibwe themselves. Ruby becomes a woman over the summer and has the Coming of Age ceremony of the traditional Ojibwe. Riddle uses the puberty ceremony described by Black Elk rather than offend the Ojibwe by describing theirs in detail. Back at school in the fall, Ruby discovers nothing has changed. After being tortured on the electric chair, Ruby leads a student revolt against the nuns and priests, calling the fire department and police. The evils of the school are exposed. The Ojibwe tribe finds the money to start their own school and Sister Steph, now no longer a nun, is the new Principal. The novel is quite effective in portraying the faults of boarding schools run by people who look down upon their charges. The final revolt and exposure are simplistic, with a fatherly policeman believing Ruby and arresting everyone else. The best character is Grandmother Cecelia, determined to affect change for her tribe even at a very advanced age.

Reviewed in: Booklist 11/15/02; Kirkus Reviews 9/1/02.

268. Riddle, Paxton. (Cherokee). *Lost River.* NY: Berkley. 1999. 449 p.

Time: 1860's–1870's
Tribe: Modoc
Place: Southern Oregon, Northern California

Winema is the cousin of Kentapoos (Captain Jack) and lives traditionally with her Modoc people, trying to accommodate the ever-increasing Whites, their demands and their treachery. When she marries miner Frank Riddle they settle on their own ranch, but become increasingly involved in trying to arrive at peaceful solutions for both the Modocs and the Whites. As with all tribes, this is impossible. There is murder and bloodshed on both sides as unruly Army officers and civilians alike slaughter Modoc women and children, while the Modocs retaliate with raids on White settlers. Kentapoos attempts to bargain for a Modoc reservation of their own, for the Modoc cannot share one with their traditional enemies, the Klamath, but his efforts are in vain. Pushed by the Hot Creek members of his Modoc tribe, Kentapoos murders General Canby at a peace conference and is hung for his "crime." Based upon the life of Riddle's cousin by marriage, Tobey Winema Riddle, a Modoc woman who was the liaison between the U.S. Army and Captain Jack, Riddle does a good job of portraying the incidents and events of the Modoc War and is obviously very sympathetic towards the Modocs and the injustices done to them. He appears, however, to have borrowed several traditions from other tribes. Did the Modocs play the ball game as did the Cherokee? Were their children captured and sold into slavery as happened to the Navajo? Did they use peyote in religious ceremonies like the Southwestern tribes? The Modoc War is a strong enough subject without these extraneous additions.

269. Riefe, Barbara. *The Woman Who Fell from the Sky.* NY: Forge. 1994. 332 p.

Time: 1750's–1760's
Tribe: Oneida
Place: New England

Coming to the New World to meet her French husband whom she has married by proxy, Margaret Addison's party is attacked by Mohawks. The sole survivor, Margaret is rescued by a band of Oneidas, led by the attractive and powerful Two Eagles. Through a perilous journey back to their camp, Margaret, at first repelled by her captors, gradually begins to learn their point of view and falls in love with Two Eagles. Though the author has included an enormous amount of Oneida lore and though her sympathy in this clash of cultures clearly lies with the Indians, the characters are flat and the story implausible.

Reviewed in: Booklist 7/1/94; Library Journal 6/15/94; Kirkus Reviews 5/15/94.

270. Riefe, Barbara. *For Love of Two Eagles.* NY: Forge. 1995. 394 p.

Time: 1750's–1760's
Tribe: Oneida
Place: New England

In this sequel to *The Woman who Fell from the Sky*, Margaret Addison and Two Eagles now have a son and Margaret has a firm place in the tribe as Two Eagles' wife. Not all accept her, however, and a plot is underway to kidnap her son. Her father in England has sent Seth Wilson to find Margaret and return her to her home. True love triumphs in the end, of course, but not before the reader has waded through vivid descriptions of torture and rape and has become hopelessly bogged down in the numerous Oneida and Mohawk words and phrases. Both Margaret and Two Eagles are too good to be believed; it is hard to imagine this novel holding anyone's interest either as a romance or as historical fiction.

Reviewed in: School Library Journal 9/1/95; Booklist 2/15/95; Publishers Weekly 2/13/95.

271. Riefe, Barbara. *Mohawk Woman.* NY: Forge. 1996. 378 p.

Time: Early 1700's
Tribe: Mohawk
Place: New England

Singing Brook and Sky Toucher marry for love, against their tribe's tradition of arranged marriages. When Sky Toucher becomes a scout for the English against the French and is captured, Singing Brook undertakes a perilous winter rescue mission. In addition to flat characters and large doses of Mohawk words, Riefe seems to have imposed twentieth-century feminist values on an eighteenth-century Mohawk couple. While there is a great deal of Mohawk custom and lore, surely the reader could better obtain that elsewhere.

Reviewed in: Library Journal 12/1/95; Publishers Weekly 11/27/95; Kirkus Reviews 11/15/95.

272. Rishell, Lyle. *Where the Wind Blows Free: A Story of the Cherokee Indians.* Fairfax, VA: George Mason University Press. 1994. 258 p.

Time: 1780's to early 1800's
Tribe: Cherokee
Place: North Carolina

Snow Deer, daughter of Chief Oconostata of the Cherokee, is rescued from attacking Creeks by trapper Nathanial Tennyson. Na-tan, as the tribe calls him, is accepted into the Cherokee community and is eventually allowed to marry Snow Deer. He learns the ways of the Cherokee through elaborate lessons taught him, and the reader, by Bear Claw, who acts as Na-tan's uncle. Na-tan learns to play the stick game, to make and shoot a bow and to use the blow gun and darts. He learns the matriarchal structure of the tribe, the annual festivals, the rituals of marriage and child rearing, and finally becomes a valuable warrior against the Creeks. Na-tan feels he is no longer a White man, but a Cherokee. When White settlers and the Army intrude, Na-tan leads the tribe to Grandmother Mountain in western North Carolina, and they build a fort on top. When the Army attacks, the Cherokee defend their homes, but many are killed, including Na-tan. Snow Deer and their son Little Eagle survive and continue hiding. The book then goes on to explain the history that follows, the Cherokee and Creek confederacy against

Colonel Sevier, Dragging Canoe's valiant efforts, and the eventual collapse of Cherokee resistance. The story is full of cultural and historical details which are accurate and informative. Unfortunately the characters are one-dimensional and uninteresting.

273. Roberts, Mark K. *Prairie Fire.* NY: Zebra Books. 1993. 285 p.

Time: 1854
Tribe: Cherokee, Choctaw, Chickasaw
Place: Cherokee Nation (Oklahoma)

In this volume of his series on the Cherokee Lighthorse, Texans are frightened of the raiding Comanche and turn on their peaceful neighbors, the Cherokee, as a scapegoat. Colonel Britton Ashley, head of a large family, decides to build a vigilante movement against the Cherokee, run them out of the Red River Valley, and then move into the Cherokee Nation to kill even more. He is up against the Cherokee Lighthorse, the tribal militia and police, led by Chad Shining Bear Conroy. When kindly George Fox is hanged and Analocee Ross, sent to spy on the Ashleys, is caught and hung, the Lighthorse must act. As the vigilantes cross the Arkansas River they are attacked by a band of Lighthorse with their Choctaw and Chickasaw allies. But Ashley's cannon wins the day. A large force of Cherokee men join the Lighthorse and they beat back the Texans, with a one-on-one battle between Chad and Britton. Britton is killed, but not before he cuts off Chad's lower left arm. Saved by a White doctor, Chad returns to his farm and the White doctor is adopted by the tribe and allowed to farm a homestead. The emphasis of these novels is to stress the civilized nature of the Cherokee. It is frequently pointed out that they can read and write, speak their own language as well as English, and are far more cultured than the Whites who look down on them. In return the Cherokee tend to look down upon their less civilized brothers, the Choctaw and Chickasaw, whom they view as savages.

274. Roberts, Mark K. *Thunder Hooves.* NY: Zebra Books. 1993. 254 p.

Time: 1846
Tribe: Cherokee
Place: Cherokee Nation (Oklahoma)

The first volume in a series on the Cherokee Lighthorse, this classic western is quite a good account of early Cherokee life in the Cherokee Nation in the 1840's when they were trying to achieve recognition for their sovereignty as a nation separate from the United States. The U.S. Army under Colonel Kearny is marching through the Nation with impunity, on their way to war with Mexico. The Cherokee Lighthorse, the Nation's mounted police, are sent by the First Woman to ask them to take another route. Followers of John Ridge, Stand Watie and Elias Boudinot, the Cherokee Lighthorse, led by Gavin Hood, are opposed by the followers of John Ross, led by Rafe Terrant, an albino, part-White Cherokee. Terrant's followers number in the hundreds, while the Lighthorse are only a few dozen men. In the Army troops are two very different men: Lt. Colonel Brady, a real Indian-hater, and Captain Pruitt, an honorable and decent man. Roaming the Nation also is a band of White bootleggers and ruffians, who rob and murder people on the farms and stage coaches. Hood and his men clean up this mess, talk the U.S. Army into rerouting their path to Mexico, and Hood takes on Terrant one-on-one in a battle to the death. Standard western fare, but well written.

275. Roberts, Mark K. *War Drums.* NY: Zebra Books. 1993. 256 p.

Time: 1861
Tribe: Cherokee
Place: Cherokee Nation (Oklahoma)

The Cherokee support the Confederacy during the Civil War, with most of the men in the Army of Tennessee under Stand Watie. Lt. Segeeyah Oaks leads the few remaining Lighthorse in the Cherokee Nation, mostly young boys and older men. When Colonel Augustus Moritus arrives in the Cherokee Nation with his band of Leatherlegs, robbing and murdering innocent people, it is Oaks' job to stop him. The Union soldiers at Fort Gibson, just outside the Nation, are searching for deserters who have also joined the Leatherlegs. The Lighthorse join up with the Union Army to hunt down the renegades. Meanwhile Kiowa and Creeks are banding together to attack the Army for past injustices. The Lighthorse and Army are successful in defeating and killing Moritus and his band. They next take on the Kiowa and defeat them. Considering the hostility between the Cherokee and the White men up until this time, it is very odd to have the Cherokee turn on their own Native American brothers, the Kiowa. Perhaps the Cherokee had assimilated to the point of no longer identifying with their own people.

276. Roberts, Mark K. *Warrior Outlaws.* NY: Zebra Books. 1993. 255 p.

Time: 1875
Tribe: Cherokee
Place: Cherokee Nation (Oklahoma) and Arkansas

The final volume on the Cherokee Lighthorse features Sargeant Elias Hand of the Lighthorse and U.S. Marshall Heck Nelson from Arkansas. Relations have been very bad between the two police forces since the Going Snake Massacre of 1871, precipitated by U.S. Marshalls intruding upon a peaceful Cherokee court session which caused the deaths of men on both sides. However, the gang of renegade Cherokee, Osage, Delaware and Kiowa bandits led by the psychopath Wili "Little Bill" Dill requires they work together. The Dill gang is running whiskey from Arkansas to road ranches (illegal saloons) in the Indian Territory. Little Bill is quick to murder any resistance. Having robbed banks in Arkansas and killed innocent White people, he is wanted by the U.S. Marshalls. Running whiskey and cold-bloodedly killing a young Lighthorse spy, means he is wanted by the Lighthorse. Together the two police forces hunt down the gang in their secret cave. Elias must fight and kill Little Bill in a hand-to-hand knife battle. U.S. Marshall Nelson takes control of the prisoners since the cave is in Arkansas. Elias, in an attempt at reconciliation, allows this without objection. This volume is the most superficial of the series and the same elements that appear in the others are here again, including the final battle confrontation between good and evil. Wisely it is Robert's final volume.

277. Robson, Lucia St. Clair. *Ghost Warrior.* NY: Forge. 2002. 496 p.

Time: 1850's–1890's
Tribe: Apache
Place: Arizona, New Mexico, Mexico

Lozen was Victorio's sister, one of the leaders of the Apaches as they fought against the Mexicans and the Americans, trying desperately to hang on to their way of life in the face of insurmountable odds. Robson tells the story of the last years of the Apache Wars partly through Lozen's eyes and partly through those of Rafe Collins, a teamster who seems to have been everywhere. All the important elements are here: the death by trickery of Mangas Colorados; the nobility of Cochise and the hanging of his relatives;

Geronimo's battles and the dislike of other Apaches toward him; the massacre at Camp Grant; the last desperate flight of a people without food or shelter relentlessly pursued by the Army. But somehow neither Lozen nor her people ever really come alive. The skill that Robson used so well in *Ride the Wind* which made Cynthia Ann Parker and the Comanche so vivid to the reader seems to be lacking here. Lozen and her people remain ghosts.

Reviewed in: Publishers Weekly 4/1/02; Kirkus Reviews 3/1/02.

278. Rogers, Samuel W. Jr. *In My Father's House: The Life and Times of Chief John Logan (A Biographical Novel).* Logan, WV: Radarta Book. 1990. 284 p.

Time: 1689–1780
Tribe: Cayuga (Mingo), Shawnee
Place: Pennsylvania, Ohio

Jean Paul LePare II was captured by the Oneida in 1689 and became Chief Shikelimo of the Cayuga Nation, fathering Tahgahjute, later named James Logan after William Penn's secretary. Tahgahjute/James Logan became a military leader of the Ohio Mingo, friendly to the English. When White settlers killed Tahgahjute's family at Yellow Creek, Ohio, in 1774, he retaliated by killing families of Whites. In Lord Dunmore's War, one of the precursors of the Revolutionary War, Logan allied himself with the Shawnee Chief, Cornsilk. The Virginia militia defeated the joined tribes of Mingo, Shawnee, Cayuga, etc. at the Battle of Point Pleasant in 1774 and Logan's spirit was broken. In 1780, a sad alcoholic, Logan was murdered, probably by a relative. Rogers' biographical novel is well researched, but poorly written. Full of more historical detail than necessary, the characters are one dimensional. Badly in need of an editor, the novel nevertheless does bring to our attention a notable American Indian whose speech to Lord Dunmore, Governor of Virginia, was highly praised by Thomas Jefferson as equivalent in eloquence to Cicero.

279. Ruvinsky, Morrie. *Dream Keeper: A Novel of Myth and Destiny in the Pacific Northwest.* Seattle: Sasquatch Press. 2000. 271 p.

Time: 1800's and Contemporary
Tribe: Kwakiutl
Place: Pacific Northwest Coast

Jason Ondine arrives on the northwest coast with a band of settlers in the early 1800's and lives with a tribe headed by Dzarilaw. Jason is held in awe by the other Kwakiutl's and is believed to have supernatural powers. When he falls overboard on a hunt, the three Sisters of Creation rescue him, giving him the form of a sea lion and eternal life. The Sisters, Sedna, Adee and Gyhldeptis watch over Jason for centuries and are with him when he is hauled to shore in a fisherman's net two hundred years later. Hospitalized, subjected to medical experiments and falsely accused of murder, Jason escapes and finds a woman he had fallen in love with twenty-five years earlier on a brief visit to shore as a human. Unbeknownst to them, their son happens to be the detective assigned to recapture Jason. Legend has it Jason can only be killed by his son. The novel is full of detail about Adee, Ruler of the Sky, Gyhldeptis, the raven called Hanging Hair, and Sedna the Orca, Mother of the Sea as well as other details about northwest coastal myths and beliefs. Before Jason is captured he is able to restore life to Dzarilaw's destroyed village Eulakon. He rescues Dzarilaw's bones from a museum, collects various members of coastal tribes, and dances and sings their lost songs and legends to them. After a prolonged chase, Jason is hunted to the edge of a sea cliff and dies protecting his son, the detective. Even though Jason is dead, his former adopted tribe, their myths, legends, songs and dances live on.

Reviewed in: Booklist 3/1/00; Publishers Weekly 2/28/00.

280. Sabbeleu. (copyright held by Trula Johnson) *Witch or Prophet? A Medicine Woman's True Tale of Kidnap and Murder.* Newalla, OK: Arcada Classics Publications. 1994. 166 p.

Time: Late 1800's
Tribe: Delaware (Lenape)
Place: Missouri and Indian Territory

Born with a veil over her face, Josie has had visions and unusual healing abilities since she was a child. She herself can't decide if she is to be a witch or a prophet; to use her skills for good or evil. Learning about natural foods and herbs from her mother, Josie also becomes a medicine woman, in demand by both Indians and Whites. For some people her remedies are not successful and her life is threatened. At the age of seventeen, Josie is kidnapped by White rancher Jim Turney and carried off to his large ranch in Indian Territory. At first Josie wants to go back to Missouri, but gradually decides she loves Jim and wants to marry him. His "family" of Sarah, the housekeeper who raised him, Chinese Charlie who became his surrogate father, and Rosa the young Mexican girl, hate Josie and her Indian ways and want her out of Jim's life. Only when they are all killed in a fire intended to kill Josie can Josie and Jim begin to see a future for themselves. This novel is apparently based on the author's grandmother's life. It is very poorly written and has numerous typos and anachronisms and is not recommended.

281. Salter, Robert B. *Chamisa Dreams.* Santa Fe, NM: Sunstone Press. 1994. 128 p.

Time: 1980's
Tribe: Navajo
Place: New Mexico

Jed Flyway is a contract archaeologist in New Mexico disturbed by the negative health effects the uranium mines have on the Navajo people who work or live near them, because the drinking water has been contaminated. The Laguna people worked many years in the mines, which have now fallen on hard times. There is little to no action taken by the government to clean up the mining sites or water supply of the Navajo. Jed and his Navajo girlfriend Lucy Begay decide to do something about the situation themselves. El Malpais is the name given the lava flow from Mount Taylor which covered the area 2,000 years ago. Jed decides to call upon the ancient caciques, the powerful medicine men, to create another Mt. Taylor eruption. Pajarito, a ghost cacique, comes to put Jed through some difficult tests and trials to discover if his intentions are true. He teaches Jed the strength to go through with the magic needed to cause the mountain, known to the Navajo as Tsoodzix, to erupt. Jed spends much of the preparatory time under the influence of drugs and alcohol, partaking of peyote rituals in the Native American Church ceremonies. One gets the impression the author is either reliving his wild youth or going through a midlife crisis through Jed. Lucy does not join in Jed's plot and seems only to exist to satisfy his sexual needs, which are prodigious. In the end Jed does not have the power to cause Tsoodzix to erupt, only to cause some earth tremors. The novel had great promise in confronting the issue of uranium mine poisoning of the Navajo, but ends up in silly drunken eco-terrorist behavior.

282. Sanders, William. *Blood Autumn: A Taggart Roper Mystery.* NY: St. Martin's. 1995. 272 p.

Time: Contemporary
Tribe: Cherokee
Place: Oklahoma

When Rita Ninekiller, Tag Roper's lover, asks him to look into the circumstances surrounding the jailing of her cousin Chris Badwater, who is accused of murdering the Sheriff of Sizemore County with a tomahawk, Tag thinks this will only take a few days. Arriving in Redbud, he finds a young man who will not defend himself, a very corrupt and brutal law enforcement system, a nuclear power plant and Indian protesters, and the wheelchair-bound widow of the late Sheriff who is not what she seems. The more Tag tries to find out what really happened, the more the townspeople clam up and the more he is harassed and attacked by various officers and deputies. While neither Roper nor the victim are Native American, the plot revolves around Native American themes and there is a strong feeling for contemporary Cherokee life.

Reviewed in: Booklist 4/1/95; Kirkus Reviews 3/1/95; Publishers Weekly 2/27/95.

283. Sarris, Greg. (Miwok). *Grand Avenue: A Novel in Stories.* NY: Hyperion. 1994. 229 p.

Time: Contemporary
Tribe: Pomo
Place: California

The Pomo Indians have moved to the town of Santa Rosa, named after one of the last surviving Pomo women, who generations ago single-handedly revived the tribe. These tribal people do not have any reservation lands and many live along Grand Avenue in the city, mostly in abject poverty. While this is a novel of stories, all the characters are related and appear in all the stories. Nellie Copaz weaves beautiful baskets and knows the secret songs and medicine of the tribe. She sees Old Uncle in an odd-toed frog that is always her companion. The Pomo had once lived on Old Man Benedict's rancheria, but when his son falls in love with Nellie's mother, the tribe is banished. Sam Toms is notorious for his liaisons and has many children by many women. Zelda Toms, his daughter, also has six daughters by six fathers. One of them, Pauline, has a child by Steven Pen, her half-brother, and raises the boy as Tony Ramirez. When Steven finds out, he changes his whole life to follow his son. Anna, a cousin, is married to Albert, and their daughter Jeanne is dying of cancer. All these stories weave in and out amongst the characters whose blood and life experiences are all related. This novel is an excellent addition to the literature of Native Americans by Sarris, himself a Miwok and chairman of the Coastal Miwok Tribe. In 1996 Home Box Office (HBO) made a special based upon these stories, with a screen play written by Sarris. Although it achieved critical acclaim, it is rarely rebroadcast, and has never come out on video.

Reviewed in: Booklist 9/1/94; Library Journal 9/1/94; Publishers Weekly 8/8/94; Kirkus Reviews 7/194.

284. Sarris, Greg. (Miwok). *Watermelon Nights.* NY: Hyperion Press. 1998. 425 p.

Time: 1929–Present
Tribe: Pomo
Place: Northern California

Sarris returns to the Pomo families of *Grand Avenue* to further expand upon their shared history. There are three principal story tellers; Johnny Severe, his grandmother Elba, and his mother Iris. Johnny lives with Elba in Santa Rosa, selling used clothing and working at the local dairy for Del, an elderly Filipino man who once loved Elba. When handsome and charismatic Felix, another Pomo, comes to the neighborhood, the equilibrium is seriously disturbed. Not until the truth of Felix's troubled past is revealed is the tribe able to deal with his evil. Johnny is deeply hurt by his friendship with Felix, but in the end his relationships with his people are restored. Elba tells the story of her upbringing on the Benedict Rancheria where all the tribe lived and worked for generations. When Benedict's young son impregnates the beautiful Pomo woman Chum, who hangs herself in their barn, the tribe is sent away. Elba lives with aged relatives and plays with Nellie and Zelda. Nellie ends up marrying another young Benedict while Elba and Zelda become prostitutes. One night Elba is gang raped by White men and later gives birth to Iris, but changes her lifestyle to become a quiet and hard-working woman. When Iris has Johnny, the grandson and grandmother bond instantly and he only wants to live with her. Iris's story is last and the most troubled. Elba and Johnny believe in the tribe and Johnny is even working to get federal recognition for them. Iris wants to live another life, working as a clerk in a department store and wearing nice clothes. Not until Johnny has his terrible trouble with Felix can Iris come home to admit her love for him and who he is. This is an excellent novel that develops complex characters and family relationships. We see little Zelda grow up from a sneaky child to an ugly unloved adult, selling herself to any buyer. Nellie grows from an introspective child to a medicine woman of the tribe. Reminiscent of Erdrich's novels, the characters from *Grand Avenue* all reappear here, with their complete stories told. The deprivation and hardships suffered by these Pomo is often shocking, but their resilience is admirable.

Reviewed in: Booklist 9/1/98; Kirkus Reviews 8/1/98; Publishers Weekly 7/31/98.

285. Scarborough, Elizabeth Ann. *The Godmother's Web.* NY: Ace Books. 1998. 308 p.

Time: Contemporary
Tribe: Hopi and Navajo
Place: Arizona

Cindy Ellis is riding her horse Chaco cross-country when she picks up an old woman near the Hopi-Navajo reservation. Grandmother Webster seems to be everyone's relative, both Hopi and Navajo. Years ago the Hopi people had taken in the Navajo after they returned from Bosque Redondo, but now the Hopi feel they want their lands back. The federal courts have approved and the Hopi Rangers are moving the Navajo off, taking their horses and sheep away. The Navajo who have lived there for generations are angry and unwilling to give up their homesteads. Grandmother Webster visits with families on both sides of the conflict, telling all the Creation myths which are common to both. Michael Blackgoat, a Navajo, tries to steal back his appropriated horses and gets Chaco by mistake. Other characters include Doctor Marie Chee, a Navajo recently arrived to help her people, Carl Loloma, a substance abuse counselor, his niece Sela and Sela's boyfriend, an orphan called Wiley who discovers he is a Coyote. The lines between reality and fantasy are blurred but completely natural. Grandmother is, of course, Spiderwoman, or *Kokyanwuhti*, the Hopi woman who taught the Navajo to weave. She weaves her spell here, knitting together Navajo and Hopi again to recognize both have claims to these desert lands. They learn to share when they must face outside enemies and drug dealers who are much more worth fighting than is fighting among themselves. This is an entertaining and nicely written story with a gentle and strong central character in the shape-changing and well-intentioned Spiderwoman. A glossary of very useful terms is included at the end.

Reviewed in: Booklist 2/15/98.

286. Schlesier, Karl H. *Josanie's War: A Chiricahua Apache Novel.* Norman: University of Oklahoma Press. 1998. 290 p.

Time: 1885–1886
Tribe: Apache
Place: Arizona, New Mexico, Mexico

American Indian Literature and Critical Studies Series, v. 27.

An excellent account of the culture of the Chiricahua Apache in Arizona and New Mexico, this novel covers the year of freedom several bands enjoyed when they broke free of Fort Apache. In May, 1885, five bands leave the reservation, led by Geronimo, Naiche, Nana, Mangus and Chihuahua, and head either north back to their mountain homes or south to hide in the mountains of Mexico. Troops immediately follow them, harassing them, capturing their women and children, killing some, but not harming the actual fighting men themselves. Chihuahua and his brother and war chief, Josanie, take their band of Chiricahua Apaches north first, but are attacked in the Mogollon mountains. They flee to Mexico and are safe long enough to provide a young girl, Ramona, her coming-of-age ceremony, the *gotal*, danced by the mountain spirit dancers, the *gahe*, who represent the Blue, Yellow, White and Black mountains. The full ceremony is described in detail and the beautiful and poetic songs, which have since been recorded for history, are included throughout the text. During the *gotal*, the girl portrays White Painted Woman, the sacred being responsible for restoring new life to the tribe. Finally, tracked down by their own White Mountain Apache people serving as scouts for the Army, the bands are surrounded. They promise to talk peace with General Crook if he will come alone. Bravely, he does and the tribes agree to come in with the promise they will only have to go off to prison in Florida for two years. President Cleveland overrules Crook and commands the Apache to prison in Florida for life. General Crook, his word to the Apache broken, resigns from the Army, an ethical General in an Army that lacked any ethics when dealing with the native tribes. The accounts of the Apache songs, dances, and ceremonies are excellent, written by an author who is an authority on American Indians.

287. Schonberg, Leonard. *Deadly Indian Summer.* Santa Fe, NM: Sunstone Press. 1997. 182 p.

Time: Contemporary
Tribe: Navajo
Place: New Mexico

One his way back from a funeral, Secretary of State Sam Spencer picks up a sick Navajo boy and takes him to the Indian Health Service hospital in Gallup. There the boy is treated by Dr. John Hartman, who cannot diagnose his severe illness. The boy is rapidly declining even with aggressive treatment. The boy's grandmother comes to the hospital and takes the sick child away for traditional treatment. Taking him to a hand trembler for diagnosis and to a singer for the appropriate chant is what she believes will cure him. The lab discovers the boy is carrying pneumonic plague, caught from flea bites off a wild rodent. The plague spreads, infecting and killing hospital employees. The town fathers in Gallup try to shut the city down, keeping all Navajo on the reservation. Hartman tries desperately to find the grandmother, the boy, and all the attendees at the Sing, now exposed to the plague. The depiction of the hand trembler's diagnostic procedures and the intricate steps and elaborate procedures involved in a four day Sing of the Windways Chant, are the best found so far in Native American fictional literature. Finally Hartman wins the support of Sam Begay, the Singer, who urges the wary Navajo to go to the hospital for vaccinations. The boy is healed, whether by his initial medical treatment or the Sing is left unclear. The point is made that healing is a complex affair, using both traditional and modern methods.

Reviewed in: Library Journal 10/1/97; Booklist 10/1/97; Publishers Weekly 9/29/97.

288. Seals, David. (Huron). *Thunder Nation.* Sturgis, SD: Sky & Sage Books. 1996. 750 p.

Time: Contemporary
Tribe: Hopi, Ottawa
Place: Los Angeles and South Dakota

This long novel is a rambling journey through the life and actions of failed actor Michael Hankins, half-Hopi and half-Ottawa, who moves back to South Dakota to start up a movie company. He sets up an armed movie studio called Medicine Wheel, not far from Mount Rushmore, and becomes a thorn in everyone's side. Endless numbers of characters and events appear, happen, and disappear. Dialogue resembles conversations around the table after dinner. Originally published by the author under the name Davydd Ap Saille, David Seals' original Welsh name, the novel was initially four volumes and 1,752 pages in length. It is more readable in the newer edited edition.

289. Shuler, Linda Lay. *Let the Drum Speak: A Novel of Ancient America.* NY: Morrow. 1994. 446 p.

Time: 1293–1297
Tribe: Pueblo and Caddo
Place: Oklahoma

Chomoc, the son of Kokopelli, and his wife and child, Antelope and Skyfeather, travel east from their home in New Mexico to trade. They encounter the Caddoan culture of the City of the Great Sun on the Arkansas River and decide to stay awhile. Antelope is the current incarnation of She Who Remembers, the teacher of womanly secrets to young girls. In Caddoan culture, however, her teachings are not welcome. The Great Sun is an arrogant man who desires Antelope. Queen Tima-cha of the City of the North (Cahokia) comes to visit and takes Chomoc home with her, a more than willing captive. Antelope and Skyfeather are taken in by kindly people and Far Healer, the tribal medicinal person, falls in love with Antelope. Events unfold, the Great Sun is killed in a giant storm which puts out the Sacred Fire on top of the city's tallest Mound and it is revealed that Far Healer is the true Great Sun, switched at birth. He marries Antelope, which angers his ambitious half-sister who wanted to be Great Sun. She tries to turn the people against Antelope. Chomoc escapes and returns with stolen fire from Queen Tima-cha, who sends warriors after him. To preserve peace Far Healer agrees to return the stolen fire to the queen, a journey that takes quite a long time. In the meantime Antelope is elected the temporary Great Sun. Unhappy, Antelope wants to be She Who Remembers, the teacher of young girls, not the Great Sun. When Far Healer returns, he allows her to return to her Pueblo people and take Skyfeather with her to be the next She Who Remembers. The novel includes many details of early Caddoan,

Cherokee and Creek cultures and the practices of the Mound Builders of the lower Mississippi. Shuler has researched these cultures well and she includes an extensive list of references. It is very important to remember that Native American cultures existed in highly evolved and very sophisticated states long before the arrival of the Spaniards. After the 1500's these Mound cultures disappeared from the Mississippi and Arkansas valleys. The City of the Great Sun is based upon the archaeological discoveries of Spiro Mounds on the Arkansas River and the City of the North is based upon the even taller mounds across the river from St. Louis at the site of the Cherokee town of Cahokia.

Reviewed in: Booklist 5/15/96; Kirkus Reviews 3/15/96; Library Journal 3/15/96; Publishers Weekly 6/3/96; Roundup 4/97.

290. Silko, Leslie Marmon. (Laguna Pueblo). *Gardens in the Dunes.* NY: Simon and Schuster. 1999. 479 p.

Time: 1890's
Tribe: Sand Lizard People (similar to Mojave)
Place: California border, Arizona

Indigo and Sister Salt live in the desert dunes with Grandma Fleet, raising food in the sand and hiding from the Indian Police who want to take the girls to school. Their mother has disappeared with the Messiah Dancers and they never see her again. When Grandma Fleet dies, the police come and send Indigo to a boarding school in California, keeping the older Sister Salt at the Parker Reservation, working in the laundry. Indigo runs away from school and is taken in by a wealthy, educated Victorian couple, Hattie, a disappointed Harvard scholar, and her older botanist husband, Edward Palmer. They take Indigo on their travels throughout the world. Meanwhile Sister Salt has become Big Candy's lover, the Black cook for the Parker Canyon Dam construction crew. She also does laundry and is a prostitute for the crew. Candy gets into running gambling games and trying to make money off the construction workers. A gypsy woman steals his money and he goes after her into the desert, nearly losing his life. Indigo returns from her travels and finds her Sister Salt. They decide to hold a messiah dance to bring back their mother, but it fails. Eventually the girls return with Salt's infant, called Little Grandfather, to the gardens in the dunes and move back into Grandma Fleet's house. The girls have traveled far geographically and in their experiences, but tending gardens and being part of the sand dunes is where they belong. The novel is complex and the extensive passages on Hattie's poor choices and disappointed life take up too much of the text. However, the story is rescued by the love the two sisters have for each other and their neverending desire to rebuild a family.

Reviewed in: NYTBR 5/21/00; Chicago Tribune 8/8/99; American Indian Quarterly Spring/99; The Progressive 2/00.

For further criticism and interpretation of Silko's works, see: Barnett, Louise K. and James L. Thorson. *Leslie Marmon Silko: A Collection of Critical Essays.* Albuquerque: University of New Mexico Press. 1999. Jaskoski, Helen. *Leslie Marmon Silko: A Study of the Short Fiction.* NY: Twayne. 1998. Salyer, Gregory. *Leslie Marmon Silko.* NY: Twayne. 1997.

291. Silver, Alfred. *Keepers of the Dawn.* NY: Ballantine. 1995. 468 p.

Time: 1740's–1780's
Tribe: Mohawk
Place: New York State

This is the fascinating story of Molly Brant, her brother Joseph, and the powerful Englishman William Johnson in the years before and during the American Revolution. Molly and Joseph's father was a powerful warrior, their mother a respected woman of the tribe. After the death of her father, Molly is sent to learn the White man's language and customs, the better to represent the interests of her people in dealings with the Whites. She attracts the eye of William Johnson, "Gets Business Done," marries him and bears numerous children. After defeating the French for the control of the North American colonies, the English and their various Indian neighbors live in relative peace. The ever-increasing White population creates a demand for land—land which the Indians feel is theirs and which has been designated as such by numerous treaties. When the war against the English King breaks out, the Mohawk and other tribes side with the English and attempt to put down the rebellion. Only when it is too late do the Mohawk realize they have sealed their own fate. Nothing could have stopped the inevitable destruction of the Indian way of life and the ability of the two peoples to live in harmony. Although little is known about Molly Brant, Silver has created a picture of a talented, strong-willed woman caught up in circumstances beyond what she could control.

Reviewed in: Publishers Weekly 1/16/95.

292. Simmons, Tim. *Brothers of the Pine.* Sun Lakes, AZ: Blue Star Productions. 1995. 338 p.

Time: 1850's–1886
Tribe: Apache
Place: Arizona, New Mexico, Northern Mexico

Far and away the best history of the entire war between the Chiricahua Apache and the U. S. Army, this novel covers every battle, every raid, and includes every historical figure involved in the struggle. The brothers are Gadoa and Nah kah yen, born under the same pine tree to the same parents. They share a blood bond, but live very different lives. Gadoa is a man of peace, who wants to settle on a reservation, farm, work for a White rancher, and raise his children. Nah kah yen follows the renegade Apache chiefs, running and hiding from the Mexican and U.S. soldiers trying to kill them. All the great names are here, from Mangas Colorado to Nana, to the Dreamer Nochay del klinne and his cult followers massacred at Cibique, to Geronimo, the unscrupulous leader who will abandon women and children to save himself. By the repeated accounts of attacks, the effect of the Army's harassment of the Apache people is conveyed, with the killing of women and children forcing the men to start over again and again building new families. The White Mountain Apaches turn against their Chiricahua brothers, becoming scouts for the Army and helping defeat the wild ones. Finally all the Chiricahua come in to the reservation, expecting to settle somewhere in Arizona. Instead they are put on trains and sent to Florida to die in the humid heat. This novel with a bit of editing should be republished for a wider distribution because it is excellent. Included is a glossary of terms and the text includes many Apache rituals such as the Sunrise Ceremony of White Painted Woman, Child of the Waters warrior training, the Mountain Spirits dancers, and others. Obviously well researched, the history is accurate and complete.

293. Simon, Lorne. (Micmac) *Stones and Switches.* Penticton, Canada: Theytus Books. 1994. 146 p.

Time: 1930's
Tribe: Micmac
Place: Eastern Canada

Megwadesk is confused. He doesn't understand why his nets are empty while those of his friend Skoltch teem with bass every night. He doesn't understand why his lover Mimi wants to convert to the Protestant religion if the Catholic priest won't marry them before her baby is born. He doesn't understand the place the old legends and stories of his people have in his life; surely ghosts and witches and spells don't exist in the twentieth century. Gradually Megwadesk begins to learn that all men are caught between good and evil and that they can make a choice in the way they live their lives and respond to events around them. Simon has written a deceptively simple story which gives the reader much to ponder. He was a writer with a promising future ahead of him who was sadly killed in an automobile accident just after this book was accepted for publication.

294. Simpson, Marcia. *Crow in Stolen Colors.* NY: Berkley. 2000. 304 p.

Time: Contemporary
Tribe: Tlingit
Place: Southeast Alaska

As the owner of a boat running freight service between the islands of Southeast Alaska, Liza Romero is unprepared when she rescues a young boy from the frigid waters. Terrified, the boy will tell her only his first name, James, but not where he's from, or what happened to him. She is also unprepared for the feelings of protectiveness she develops towards James and the feelings developing between her and police Lieutenant Paul Howard. Howard is receiving reports of missing Indian artifacts and James seems to know more than he's telling. Mysterious accidents happen to both Liza and her boat until she finally realizes that someone is willing to kill her to get to James and the secret he knows. Liza and Howard also have Native American issues to deal with since Liza is half Lummi, but by her own acknowledgement knows nothing of its culture. Howard, also Native American, is trying to come to terms with the loss of his son, taken by his ex-wife back to the "Lower 48." Throughout the story runs the character of Crow, who used to look at the old pictures in the library. James knows of Crow but does not like him. Crow finally risks everything to assuage the shame he has brought to his village. This well-constructed mystery/romance has an intriguing plot with well-rounded characters.

Reviewed in: Library Journal 5/1/00; Publishers Weekly 4/17/00; Kirkus Reviews 3/15/00.

295. Simpson, Marcia. *Sound Tracks.* Scottsdale AZ: Poisoned Pen Press. 2001. 244 p.

Time: Contemporary
Tribe: Tlingit
Place: Southeast Alaska

While this is a fascinating mystery involving the whales in the bays of southeastern Alaska, it is not really a novel with a Native American theme. Policeman Paul Howard is Tlingit, but the only reference to his heritage is his size. Mink, a friend of Liza Romero's, is also a native, but no tribal affiliation is ever given. The mystery of why whales are running aground and not hearing ships' engines is solved when Liza and Paul discover a ship using seismic airguns to locate heavy minerals on the ocean floor, specifically gold. The feel for Alaska, and the life of living and working on boats is excellent. Perhaps this is a time when the ethnic background of the characters should be just part of the whole and not necessarily the focus of the plot.

Reviewed in: Publishers Weekly 4/30/01; Booklist 6/15/01.

296. Skimin, Robert with William E. Moody. *Custer's Luck.* NY: Herodias. 2000. 297 p.

Time: 1876–1882
Tribe: Sioux
Place: Montana, Washington, D.C.

This is revisionist history, giving Custer the victory at Little Bighorn and handing the defeat to the Sioux instead. Red Elk, a character from *The River and the Horsemen,* sees his pregnant wife Late Star killed by the soldiers and vows revenge on Long Hair Custer. Custer goes on to glory; backed by Bennett, owner of the New York Herald, he is elected President of the United States and begins empire-building by planning a war with Spain to gain possession of her New World territories. Red Elk learns some English from scout Frank Grouard, the Polynesian translator adopted by Sitting Bull who later is so instrumental in Crazy Horse's downfall. Red Elk decides to take his mission east after Custer is elected and attends the Carlisle Indian School to learn more about the White ways. He is often near Custer, but never has a chance to kill him. Finally changing his name to James Elkins, and claiming to be from Ceylon, a member of the Royal Indian Hussars, he joins the U.S. Army as one of Custer's guards. A sharpshooter, Elk/Elkins tries again and again to get Custer. Finally in a scene deliberately reminiscent of Kennedy in Dallas, while in a parade down the streets of San Antonio, Custer is shot with a high powered rifle from the rooftops by Red Elk in full war paint. Tom Custer brings Red Elk down, in the midst of his victory dance. Sitting Bull had seen Red Elk during his Wild West Show travels and told the young Sioux warrior there was nothing left to return home to on the Sioux reservation but poverty and despair. Red Elk finishes his task and his life. Custer's ego is well portrayed and he rubs shoulders (and more) with many notable men and women of the time period. Well researched and intriguing, this novel is an entertaining version of how different history might have been.

Reviewed in: Booklist 10/15/00; Publishers Weekly 9/8/00.

297. Skimin, Robert. *The River and the Horsemen: A Novel of the Little Bighorn.* NY: Herodias. 1999. 364 p.

Time: 1876
Tribe: Sioux, Cheyenne
Place: Chicago, Montana, North Dakota, South Dakota

This is an excellent and thorough account of the events leading up to the Battle of the Little Bighorn. Skimin provides complete historical backgrounds on all the people involved on both sides of the war. He also includes a great deal of cultural detail about the Sioux way of life, such as the beading and quilling societies of the women. Custer's family and personality are elaborately described, his role in the Civil War, his friendships with unscrupulous men, his loss of fortunes, and his machinations in Washington, D.C. portray a man with a less than exemplary character. The historical detail is overwhelming, but Skimin is such an expert author that the reader is intrigued and fascinated with the multitude of details. He describes the rivalry between the Army scout Bloody Knife and the Sioux chief, Gall, the love Captain Tom Weir has for Libbie Custer, and other rivalries among the enlisted men. Skimin provides the history and causes for the envy, resentment and even hatred that Benteen and Reno have for Custer, which adds to the disaster of that summer day. The complete battle is described, event by event, suspense building as the day progresses. Other lesser characters also have their dramas included and, although they are fictional, they are no less gripping. This is a highly recommended book, well researched, well written, and showing the parallels between Sioux society and their politics, and White society and its politics. There probably is no better fictional source on General Custer and the Battle of the Little Bighorn than this novel. Even the fact that the message from Custer to Benteen to come to his assistance was delivered by an Italian who spoke poor English, resulting in a complete misunderstanding on Benteen's part, is depicted in detail. History books should be written so well. See also Chiaventone's *A Road We Do Not Know: A Novel of Custer at Little Big Horn* for another excellent historical account of this fateful day.

Reviewed in: Library Journal 8/1/99.

298. Slater, Susan. *The Pumpkin Seed Massacre.* Philadelphia: Intrigue Press. 1999. 234 p.

Time: Contemporary
Tribe: Tewa
Place: New Mexico

Ben Pecos has returned to the Tewa Pueblo outside Albuquerque to become reacquainted with his Native American heritage. When several elderly people, including Ben's grandmother, die suddenly, the Indian Health Service thinks that they are just old. When a three-year-old White girl is stricken, but recovers, the IHS begins to wonder. Samples are sent to CDC and the result is terrifying; it is a new strain of hanta virus which attacks the lungs. The old governor of the pueblo is among the victims, did his opposition to a new casino on the reservation have any connection with his death? Julie Conlin, a novice reporter from an Albuquerque television station, is assigned to the story and uncovers more than she bargained for, including a connection with her boss. The mystery is catching, but both Julie and Ben seem rather flat characters and much of the action takes place off-stage. Since this is the "first Ben Pecos mystery," Slater might work on her character development.

Reviewed in: Publishers Weekly 9/27/99; Library Journal 9/1/99; Booklist 9/1/99.

299. Slater, Susan. *Thunderbird.* Philadelphia: Intrigue Press. 2002. 280 p.

Time: Contemporary
Tribe: Navajo
Place: New Mexico

Brenda Begay is on her way home from night school when she sees what is apparently a plane crash. In trying to help, Brenda is tackled by a man who is the father of her child, supposedly stationed in Germany. Amos Manygoats sees the same plane crash, but he thinks the Thunderbird has come, especially since one of his goats has been mutilated. Park Ranger Edwina Rosenberg hopes the handsome young man who comes to the Information Center is a character out of one of her romance novels, but when she is killed, her death becomes another piece of the puzzle. Officer Tommy Spottedhorse must try and figure out what really happened, where Brenda is, and who killed Edwina, not an easy task when the military are involved. Did the plane crash, or was it deliberately landed so its state-of-the-art computer systems could be stolen? As Tommy's friend and Brenda's teacher, Ben Pecos also becomes involved and is there at the end when the villain's plans unravel and he tries to get Brenda to kill her ex-lover. While there are some Native American aspects to this story, it is basically a murder mystery, and not a particularly good one.

Reviewed in: Library Journal 1/02; Booklist 1/02.

300. Slater, Susan. *Yellow Lies.* Philadelphia: Intrigue Press. 2000. 297 p.

Time: Contemporary
Tribe: Tewa
Place: New Mexico

Four years after *The Pumpkin Seed Massacre*, Ben Pecos has accepted a position as the first psychologist with the Indian Health Service for the Hawikuh tribe in northern New Mexico. Before his first day on the job, Ben finds strange things happening at the boarding house where he lodges. The handyman and master carver Sal Zuni discovers the murdered body of the trader Ahmed, his landlady Hannah Rawlings can't wait to get out of New Mexico, and her large retarded son, named .22, sees things that no one else does. He also appears to have a large collection of frogs in his bedroom. Ben is hoping to renew his relationship with Julie Conlin, now working for *Good Morning America* and in New Mexico to film a segment on Native Americans. Sal's carvings are done in amber and sell back east for large sums, but Sal has a secret that is beginning to weigh on him. The amber he uses is not natural; Sal has discovered the formula for making perfect, but artificial, amber and now feels he should stop. Hannah, the mastermind behind this scheme, attempts to get Sal's notebook and when that fails, locks him underground. Ben and Julie's relationship flowers, but there is growing suspicion that .22 may not be retarded and may be in cahoots with Hannah to claim .22's inheritance. While the amber aspect is unique, the characters still don't come alive and the novel doesn't grab the reader.

Reviewed in: Booklist 8/10/00.

301. Slipperjack, Ruby. (Ojibwe) *Weesquachak and the Lost Ones.* Penticton, Canada: Theytus Books. 2000. 203 p.

Time: Contemporary
Tribe: Ojibwe
Place: Ontario, Canada

As a child, Janine was promised by her father to marry Fred, a local traditionalist Ojibwe trapper. When she turns nineteen, Janine leaves her rural community of Nakina to live in Thunder Bay and escape the Ojibwe life. There she finds loneliness and prejudice against Indians. Returning home for a visit she falls under Fred's spell and marries him. They move out to his remote cabin where he traps, hunts and guides tourists over the summer while Janine keeps house. Janine is under the watchful eye of the *Weesquachak*, the Trickster who takes the form of a raven, a dog, a wolf, or even a handsome Ojibwe man named Nisha. He causes Janine endless grief, inciting Fred to jealous outbursts during which he beats Janine. Janine has become friends with Fred's aunt, *Gookom,* or grandmother, who warns Janine to leave Fred if he begins to kill her spirit. When Janine's baby is born dead after a harrowing trip to the hospital, she and Fred separate. Their failure was a lack of communication. Finally they try again, this time with Janine living with Fred as an equal, not a wife. They speak only Ojibwe and she hunts and traps with Fred, instead of cleaning and cooking like a White wife. But *Weesquachak* is not done with the couple, and comes back as Ron, an old friend of Janine's, who tries to lure her away from Fred. She sees the Trickster in Ron's eyes and realizes what is happening. Ron is driven away and she and Fred are once again man and wife. The trapping life in remote Ontario is beautifully described and Janine's fight for equality in the eyes of a traditionalist husband is a hard won battle.

302. Smyth, Dan, and Junice Smyth Peek. *No Place to Live.* Huntington, WV: University Editions. 1994. 174 p.

Time: late 1660's
Tribe: Potawatomie, Menominee
Place: Michigan and Wisconsin

As the White men pushed the Iroquois, the Iroquois pushed the Potawatomie further west, from Michigan to Wisconsin. White Eagle and Gray Bear are the leaders of two Potawatomie families moving west. White Eagle hates the French, but Gray Bear wants to live peacefully. The Seneca are also their enemies and kidnap Running Bird, White Eagle's daughter. The families stop traveling to allow young Stands Alone to have his vision quest, he realizes he must be a medicine man. Later the two families rescue a starving French trader, Gerard. The Potawatomies move to northern Wisconsin and join the Menominees. Gerard and some men go to the Soo to watch the French ceremonies claiming the lands for France. There they find Running Bird working in a trading post. Gerard marries her and they begin their own store at LaPointe where the tribe has settled in northern Wisconsin. Years go by, tribes fight each other, marry, have children, and then Gerard decides to take his family back to France. While they are gone, evil medicine exerts undue influence on the Potawatomies and the tribe breaks up again. The younger generation, sons and daughters of White Eagle and Gray Bear, head west again, looking for another new home. Not much has been written on these tribes or these years of French settlement along the Great Lakes. Although the novel is often awkward and full of misspellings, it does contain a great deal of relevant historical detail to add to our knowledge of these tribes.

303. Spence, Gerry. *Half-Moon and Empty Stars.* NY: Scribner. 2001. 409 p.

Time: 1969–1998
Tribe: Arapaho
Place: Wyoming

When Charlie Redtail is ten years old he is a witness to the brutal unprovoked beating and murder of his father by two sheriff's deputies. Left penniless, his White mother Mary Hamilton works hard to raise her twin sons, Billy and Charlie. Charlie spends his time with Henry Old Deer learning the ways of the Arapaho. Billy dedicates himself to studying and winning a scholarship to college, and he becomes an investment banker when he graduates calling himself William Hamilton. Attorney Abner Hill befriends the family and is in love with Mary but is afraid to declare himself. He acts as father to Charlie and protector of Mary against the attentions of Ronnie Cotler, a wealthy businessman who desires her. Cotler sets out to harass the family and the tribe in revenge, buying up Spirit Mountain, a sacred Arapaho site where he plans on building a development and resort. Charlie and his girlfriend Willow organize tribal resistance that ultimately discourages Eastern investors. When Cotler is found shot to death, Charlie is arrested for murder and put on trial. Abner Hill defends him, but very poorly, and Charlie is sentenced to the gas chamber. William/Billy pays for eight years of denied appeals and petitions. A psychotic gunman, Emmett Jones, comes to town to claim responsibility for Cotler's murder, with proof that he in fact shot the businessman. The state governor could free Charlie, but she was the prosecutor at his trial and is too embarrassed to expose her error. Charlie has a son, Henry, who now takes his place at the feet of Henry Old Deer, learning the ways of the tribe. A depressing novel, full of failed characters who are ineffectual but good-hearted, trying to fight evil, prejudiced people. The only character full of hope and internal peace is the convicted Charlie. Unfortunately the events that take place on the Shoshone/Arapaho reservation and in the small town between the Indians and the Whites are probably quite accurate, as the author is a lawyer who lives in Wyoming.

Reviewed in: Publishers Weekly 5/28/01; Kirkus Reviews 4/1/01; Library Journal 2/1/01.

304. Spinka, Penina Keen. *Picture Maker.* NY: Dutton. 2002. 464 p.

Time: 1300's
Tribe: Mohawk, Algonquin, Inuit
Place: Upper New York State, Canada, Greenland

As a little girl, Gahrahstah, Picture Maker, is stolen from her *Haudenosaunee*, Iroquis, home by the Algonquins. Made a slave to Hawk Feather, she becomes a woman, is raped and beaten continually. Finally she kills Hawk Feather and runs away, aided by an old storyteller. Found by the Naskapi people, related to the Algonquins, they take her in and care for her over the winter. Gahrahstah fears being returned to the Algonquins so insists her home is north with the Inuit. In spring the Naskapi take her to the Inuit at Trader Island, who accept her, calling her Mikisoq, or Little One. When the young leader Qisuk loses his wife in childbirth and Mikisoq gives birth to a daughter, her infant is killed so that Mikisoq can nurse Qisuk's son. Kept as a wetnurse, Mikisoq is taken to Greenland when a new home is sought for an expanding tribe in lean times. A minor ice age occurrs during this time period causing widespread famine. In Greenland the Inuit encounter *Qallunaat,* Big Eyebrows, the Norse settlers. Relations are not good between these peoples, but Qisuk rescues Halvard from the ocean and befriends him. Halvard asks for Mikisoq's hand, renaming her Astrid. Taking her back to the Greenlanders' settlements in the south, they encounter deep prejudice and religious hostility from the recently landed Christians. Famine spreads, winters are very harsh, and the villagers rise up against the priests. Halvard's father Gunther stands up to the priests, gets food and animals back from their tithes, and is murdered. The bishop demands that Halvard and his family leave. Together Astrid, Halvard and their children move west to start over. Quite the saga for a young girl from Mohawk village to Greenlander farm, Picture Maker has many good and bad experiences along the way. A fascinating history of the times and peoples in the late 1300's, Spinka has definitely done her historical and cultural research

Reviewed in: Kirkus Reviews 10/1/02; Library Journal 10/1/02; Publishers Weekly 11/5/02.

305. Stabenow, Dana. *A Cold Day for Murder.* NY: Berkley. 1992. 199 p.

Reviewed in: Armchair Detective/Fall 92.

Dead in the Water. NY: Berkley. 1993. 219 p.

Reviewed in: Publishers Weekly 6/14/93.

A Cold-blooded Business. NY: Berkley. 1994. 231 p.

Reviewed in: Booklist 3/1/94; New York Times 4/3/94; Library Journal 3/1/94.

A Fatal Thaw. NY: Berkley. 1994. 198 p.

Reviewed in: Publishers Weekly 12/28/94.

Play With Fire. NY: Berkley. 1995. 282 p.

Reviewed in: Booklist 3/15/95; Library Journal 2/1/95; Publishers Weekly 2/6/95.

Blood Will Tell. NY: Putnam. 1996. 241 p.

Reviewed in: Booklist 4/15/96; Library Journal 5/1/96; Publishers Weekly 4/1/96.

Breakup. NY: Putnam. 1997. 242 p.

Reviewed in: Booklist 5/15/97; Publishers Weekly 4/21/97.

Killing Grounds. NY: Penguin. 1998. 273 p.

Reviewed in: Library Journal 3/1/98; Booklist 2/15/98; Publishers Weekly 1/19/98.

Hunters Moon. NY: Putnam. 1999. 260 p.

Reviewed in: Publishers Weekly 4/19/99; Library Journal 4/1/99.

Midnight Come Again. NY: St. Martin's. 2000. 291 p.

Reviewed in: Publishers Weekly 4/10/2000.

The Singing of the Dead. NY: St. Martin's. 2001. 254 p.

Reviewed in: Library Journal 5/1/01; Booklist 5/1/01; Publishers Weekly 4/2/01.

A Fine and Bitter Snow. NY: St. Martin's. 2002. 211 p.

Reviewed in: Booklist 5/1/02; Publishers Weekly 5/27/02.

Time: Contemporary
Tribe: Aleut
Place: Alaska

Kate Shugak was an investigator for the Anchorage, Alaska, District Attorney's office until a near-fatal confrontation with a child molester caused her to resign and return to Niniltna, her hometown. Now she lives in the log cabin homestead inherited from her family in the Denali National Park, where she hunts, fishes and gardens to support herself and her half-wolf, Mutt. Kate's skills as an investigator keep dragging her back into cases, enticed by her lover Jack Morgan, still in the D.A.'s office. Her grandmother Ekaterina, "Emaa" lures Kate into tribal politics whenever the welfare of the native peoples is threatened. The mysteries are well written with recurring characters to build a sense of community. Cousins sent off to Anchorage are encountered later, FBI agents worked with on one case appear on another, people grow and change, and some, like Kate's grandmother Emaa and lover Jack, even die, but relationships last from title to title in the mystery series. The best part of the series is the sense of Alaska and the way of life of the Aleuts which is demonstrated by Kate and her numerous relatives. Everyone from the drunken teenager to the elderly subsistence hunter and fisherman is portrayed realistically and sympathetically. Kate is often caught in the conflict between preserving the best of the old ways and using the best of the new ways brought in by the Outsiders, the White people's culture which can often negatively impact traditional methods of Aleut lifestyles. Issues such as the Alaska Native Claims Settlement Act (ANSCA) and the Alaska Federation of Natives are thoroughly described and explored. Later entries in the series deal with drilling for oil in this pristine environment. This is an excellent series that offers not only well-plotted mysteries, but also a real sense of Alaska native peoples, their culture, and their conflicts with the demands of White society and its pressures to change and conform.

306. Stein, Garth. *Raven Stole the Moon.* NY: Pocket Books. 1998. 369 p.

Time: Contemporary
Tribe: Tlingit
Place: Alaska, Seattle

When investors decide to open a resort at Thunder Bay just outside Wrangell, Alaska, a Tlingit shaman, David Livingstone, is called in to investigate the spiritual health of the site. Livingstone discovers the site is full of *kushtaka,* the land otter spirits that steal the souls of lost or drowned victims and shape-change into people to lure the living to their deaths. Livingstone himself is almost sucked into their world, but is released and told to stop the resort. The investors refuse and soon vacationers Jenna and Robert Rosen's young son Bobbie is the next victim, drowned in the Bay while fishing with Jenna, who is herself a Tlingit from Seattle. Jenna is severly depressed for two years but finally decides to return to Wrangell and settle her tortured soul. She meets an old Tlingit woman who reminds her of the many Tlingit myths and stories Jenna had originally heard from her grandmother. Jenna tracks down the shaman Livingstone and enlists his help in settling the *kushtaka* spirits, including her son's, that are luring her into death. Jenna is initially protected by her *yek*, her spirit helper, Oscar, a dog she found in the woods. Oscar is eventually shot and killed and the *kushtaka* come in force for her. Jenna and Livingston prevail and Jenna takes Bobbie's spirit to his Tlingit grandmother in the Land of Dead Souls. The Tlingit myths are so interwoven in the story that they are totally believable, especially once one is in Alaska and among the Tlingit people. The characters are fully developed and the plot is very suspenseful. Many of the Tlingit myths are told in detail in the text of the novel and contribute to our knowledge and understanding of these Northwest Coast and Alaskan native peoples.

Reviewed in: Booklist 2/1/98; Library Journal 1/1/98; Publishers Weekly 12/8/97.

307. Stevenson, Melody Henion. *The Life Stone of Singing Bird.* Winchester, MA: Faber & Faber. 1996. 175 p.

Time: mid-1800's
Tribe: Unknown
Place: Kansas

Told through the eyes of India Walker as she watches her funeral procession, this is not only India's story, it is also the story of her mother Iris and the Native American woman Singing Bird. Iris is part of a wagon train heading to Oregon but when her husband is killed and their child stillborn, Iris is nearly mad with grief until she finds an Indian baby. Singing Bird has been mutilated and driven away from her tribe for sleeping with Runs Swiftly instead of her intended, Black-Faced Bear. Singing Bird abandons her daughter knowing Iris will find her. When Iris does, Singing Bird also gives her the life stone which is not an amulet or good-luck piece but which "grants its wearer the gift of Life. That's all. Not a good life; not a happy life; not even a long life. But a full life, filled to bursting, like an overblown carnival balloon, like a cow's belly stuffed with grain, like a compost heap left too long in the sun." Iris's life portrays that of the early pioneers and the hardships endured; India's life continues that story. And always Singing Bird (or her ghost) is present and her story, too, is woven into the fabric. Although a short novel, *The Life Stone of Singing Bird* can be read and reread on many levels and could be considered as an example of magical realism.

Reviewed in: Booklist 4/15/96; Christian Science Monitor 5/ 8/96; Kirkus Reviews 1/15/96; NYTBR 8/11/96; Publishers Weekly 2/26/96.

308. Stewart, Frank. *River Rising; a Cherokee Odyssey.* Las Vegas, NV: Waholi Press. 1997. 798 p.

Time: 1830's
Tribe: Cherokee
Place: South Central U.S.

Stewart has attempted a mammoth undertaking: to write a novel of the forgotten history of the Cherokees in the nineteenth century; of what was done to them and why; of the Trail of Tears and more. For the most part he has succeeded through the fictional family of the Drummonds. Wealthy attorney William is sympathetic to the Cherokee cause, his wife Elizabeth is frail but strong. Son Michael is in love with his Cherokee best friend James's sister Annie, and the spoiled, arrogant daughter Susanna is married to a weak Army officer, Peter Tanner, who rejects her after she bears him a daughter, not the desired son. The Drummonds see the beginning of the end for the Cherokees. The Treaty Party and the Ross Party are fighting over whether to leave for the West now or stay and fight for their land, only to have it stripped from them and given away in state lotteries. Michael and James kill the men who rape his sister and murder their mother. When James is captured he begs Michael to kill him rather than face the firing squad. Michael does so, but he and Annie must flee west. When the roundup of the Cherokee begins, one of William's enemies has discovered he had a part-Cherokee great-grandmother, so the Drummonds are caught in the net as well. They endure the terrible conditions at the internment camps, watching people die in the crowded and unsanitary conditions. Finally the long march gets underway with part of the party going by flatboat down the Tennessee River while others go overland along the Trail of Tears. Both parties encounter horrible conditions and treacherous behavior of Whites before reaching Indian Territory. Most books on the Trail of Tears end here, but *River Rising* goes beyond to relate the incompatibility of the two bands of Cherokee to get along and the murders of Major Ridge and others of the Treaty Party. Michael and Annie have turned into renegade outlaws, trying to protect the Cherokee travelers from the whisky peddlers and those trying to steal their allotment money, their equipment and food, and once again their land. This is a big, powerful novel which reads easily, although not pleasantly, as the reader discovers exactly what history has long covered up.

309. Stillwell, Larry. *Flash Point of Deceit: The U.S.–Dakota War of 1862*. Moorhead, MN: Gold Fire Publishing. 1999. 194 p.

Time: 1860's
Tribe: Sioux
Place: Minnesota

Stillwell has long been fascinated with the U.S.–Dakota War of 1862 and has done an enormous amount of research on it. Unfortunately, he does not have the skill to turn this knowledge into a novel. He attempts to tell the story of John Otherday and Little Paul, Christian Indians who helped save the lives of numerous Whites from the attacks of Little Crow and others. He is clear about what drove the Indians to war: the broken promises; the lack of food and annunities; the starving children. None of his characters come alive, the plot does not develop, and the reader gains little sense of what it might have been like to be at New Ulm or Fort Ridgely.

310. Stokes, Naomi M. (Cherokee). *The Listening Ones.* NY: Tom Doherty. 1997. 413 p.

Time: Contemporary
Tribe: Quinault
Place: Olympic Peninsula, Washington State

Jordan Tidewater is a U.S. deputy marshal and the Tribal Sheriff for the Quinault Nation on the Olympic Peninsula near Olympic National Park. Divorced from her husband, she lives with her great grandfather Ahcleet and her young son Tleyuk. Jordan is a shaman of her tribe and able to see the ancient spirit Klokwalle, who warns of danger to come. An elegant wealthy South American man, Lima Clemente, meets Jordan and they fall in love. Lima is from the same small Andean mountain village as a young boy found ritually murdered in the forest. He is also involved in mysterious business dealings and travels a great deal. Jordan is on many cases involving the poaching of bears to sell their parts on the Asian black market. Eventually Jordan discovers all these strings are attached, that ritual human sacrifice to the gods is still being practiced, and that Lima is involved in not only that, but also in the black market deals. After undergoing old Quinault rituals with members of her tribe, Jordan has the powers to deal with the evils she must. She saves her son from Lima and solves the mysteries of the murder and the poachers. Excellent descriptive atmosphere of the Olympic National Park and sympathetic treatment of the problems rangers must face in dealing with poaching make this an engrossing novel. The spiritual side of Quinault life is well incorporated to the story and to Jordan's role as a law officer and as a shaman. The author cites sources for her statements concerning contemporary human sacrifice and other rituals still performed in some areas of the world.

Reviewed in: Booklist 6/15/97; Publishers Weekly 6/9/97.

311. Stokes, Naomi M. (Cherokee). *The Tree People.* NY: Tom Doherty. 1995. 410 p.

Time: Contemporary
Tribe: Quinault
Place: Olympic Peninsula, Washington State

The MacTavish Lumber company has permission to log the old growth forest on the Quinault Indian reservation, so long as they respect the ancient cedar standing there. The witch Aminte moves the yellow tape, allows the cedar to be cut, and frees her ancestor, Xulk, buried beneath it for centuries. Xulk brings sickness and trouble into the world and even effects the family members of Jordan Tidewater, the Quinault Tribal Sheriff. Jordan and her twin brother Paul Prefontaine, another law enforcement officer, are investigating the deaths and disappearances of several people on the Olympic Peninsula. Are they linked to the strange northern tribal person Tuco Peters, the totem pole carver who follows the old ways? Hannah MacTavish tries to continue running the lumber company after her husband Michael is apparently killed and burned in an accident. Although Hannah loves the giant forest and its ancient trees, she is intent on logging them while she has time and permission from the tribe. Environmentalists try to prevent the loss of the old growth, but she pushes them aside and continues. Jordan has been resisting her preordained role as a tribal shaman, but the evil power of Xulk attacks her son Tleyuk, so she assumes her role, defeats Xult, frees the land from his evil diseases, discovers the murderer of the missing persons, and finds Michael MacTavish in Aminte's old cabin. Hannah and Michael are reunited, the environmentalists are exposed as nothing more than conniving marijuana growers out to distract the law, and the trees keep falling. There are many Quinault stories and legends told in this excellent novel, with good characters throughout. The witches and shamans are interwoven so well they are believable. Unfortunately the conflict between the love of the ancient cedars and the desire to log them quickly is not well explained. Turning environmentalists into drug dealers is particularly unjust, considering the value they place on old growth forest environments.

Reviewed in: Booklist 2/15/95; Library Journal 2/1/95; NYTBR 3/5/95; Publishers Weekly 1/23/95.

312. Strong, Albertine. (Chippewa). *Deluge.* NY: Harmony Books. 1997. 277 p.

Time: 1909–1993
Tribe: Chippewa
Place: Minnesota

This is a complex and fascinating multi-generational tale narrated by A'jawac' who is the family storyteller now that her grandfather Peke is gone. Peke had set off for Grinnell College in 1909 only to have a rainstorm sweep him into the arms of a beautiful Swedish girl, Isabel. Returning to the White Earth reservation in northern Minnesota, they raise their daughter Ninamuch, who later moves to the Twin Cities and meets and marries Roy, just before he sets off for war in the Pacific. Roy comes back severely disturbed, but is nonetheless sent off again to the Korean War after the birth of his children, A'jawac' and Jerry. Roy doesn't return for many years and by that time Aja is a teenager. Their relationship is deeply troubled and threatened with feelings of incestuous attraction. This attraction drives Roy over the edge and he becomes a Crazy Dog, walking backwards forever. Aja's genius brother, Jerry, goes off to medical school, becomes a doctor, and commits suicide. Aja meets and marries Myron from the Red Lake reservation, but he is also a deeply disturbed Vietnam veteran and she divorces him even though she is pregnant. Giving her son Prosper to her Aunt Betty, Aja goes off to college. When her grandmother Isabel dies, Aja returns to learn the stories of her grandfather, to fight for the legal rights to the land for the reservation, and to set up a school, Little Red, for the reservation children. She finds her salvation in helping her tribe regain their tribal lands, and in keeping the Chippewa tales alive, many of which are included in the novel. Finally Aja meets a Jewish lawyer, Benjamin, who wins her heart. They marry and have a daughter Nodin, although they are now in their forties. Prosper returns to live with them, completing the family. When they return to White Earth for Nodin's christening, they learn a long-lost relative has returned to claim his tribal inheritance and verifies the Chippewa's rights to their lands. Strong's first novel is beautifully written and makes very clear the troubled lives of the people on the northern reservations in Minnesota. The Chippewa tales are fascinating and give the story greater depth and meaning.

Reviewed in: Booklist 9/1/97; Publishers Weekly 7/7/97; Library Journal 7/1/97.

313. Sullivan, Mark T. *Ghost Dance.* NY: Avon. 1999. 339 p.

Time: 1998, 1891–1893
Tribe: Sioux
Place: Vermont

Documentary film maker Pat Gallagher comes to Lawton, Vermont, to research Father D'Angelo, up for sainthood for his miraculous cures of people sick with the Spanish influenza after World War I. Pat meets Angie Nightingale, a police sergeant, and soon finds a mutilated body in the local river. Angie's Aunt Olga is the next to be found murdered. The deaths appear to be linked to the sections of Sarah Many Horses' journal which were torn apart and distributed among several people in 1893. Pat and Angie work together and discover parts of the Sioux girl's journal, describing the Ghost Dance and the subsequent massacre at Wounded Knee, her family members including her uncle Sitting Bull, her escape and journey east with the Danby brothers, and her eventual arrival in Lawton. Pat begins to see Sarah Many Horses in dreams, trying to talk to him, and warn him. The murdered people all had parts of her journal and are being killed for them. Someone is collecting all the parts, perhaps to acquire her Ghost dance powers. Pat and Angie gradually discover the truth of Sarah's disappearance, murdered by the townspeople. Father D'Angelo had distributed her journal to keep the secret but also to keep her memory alive in Lawton. When the murderer is eventually exposed, the parts of her journal are restored and given to a Dartmouth Native American anthropologist, who is disappointed that exact descriptions of the Ghost Dance are still missing. Sarah Many Horses' bones are found buried in the churchyard and Pat and Angie take them back to Standing Rock reservation, where Sarah had learned to read and write before the Wounded Knee massacre. The novel ends with a very moving description of the traditional Sioux ceremony of releasing the soul, conducted by members of her tribe.

Reviewed in: Publishers Weekly 6/21/99; Kirkus Reviews 6/1/99; Booklist 5/15/99; Library Journal 3/15/99.

314. Sullivan, Mark T. *The Purification Ceremony.* NY: Avon. 1997. 335 p.

Time: Contemporary
Tribe: Micmac, Penobscot
Place: Maine, British Columbia

Diana Jackman was called Little Crow by her Micmac/Penobscot father and great uncle Mitchell as she grew up in Maine where they taught her to track and hunt deer and the ways of the forests. After her mother dies, apparently accidentally drowning in a fishing pond, Diana breaks off all contact with her father. She is convinced he murdered her mother, who was dying of Alzheimer's. When her father commits suicide, Diana has a nervous breakdown and her marriage falls apart. She signs up for a deer hunting expedition on a remote estate in British Columbia with a dozen other expert hunters. Once there, it becomes clear the hunters are being hunted and killed by someone who is deeply committed to the act. One by one they are shot with cedar arrows, scalped, gutted, and hung up like deer. Diana becomes one with the forest again, tracking and confronting the madman, a former University religion professor, Ryan, in his cave with a shrine to a dead woman. Diana discovers Ryan has a reason to kill, since his wife was shot and killed by one of the hunters in an accident years earlier. Turning to Huichol beliefs in his grief, Ryan has become a Huichol *Mara'akame*, or sorcerer, and can control wolves to do his bidding. Diana calls upon her own Micmac and Penobscot beliefs in the Power of all living things and finally defeats Ryan. An engrossing thriller, the novel slowly builds up suspense, moving from Diana's family conflicts to the setting in British Columbia and the dangers of the hunt and fears of the hunted. Diana finally realizes she will not become whole again until she accepts and forgives her father's actions, because they were based on the same set of beliefs in the six worlds of the Micmac, the underlying Power of all the worlds, which govern her own life.

Reviewed in: Publishers Weekly 4/28/97; Library Journal 4/15/97; Kirkus Reviews 4/1/97; Booklist 3/15/97.

315. Swonger, W. A. *The Trail of Tears*. Chicago: Moody Press. 1976. 288 p.

Time: 1838–1839
Tribe: Cherokee
Place: Georgia and Oklahoma

This novel of the Cherokee Trail of Tears is unusual in that it covers the time spent confined in the stockades of Georgia more than the trek west. John Ross, bound for Princeton, is surprised by Georgia militia taking over his family's wealthy Georgia estate, killing his father and imprisoning his mother and sister. A nephew of Chief John Ross, young John is more Scottish than Cherokee, more landed gentry than Native American. To the Georgia militia, however, they are all Indians. The summer spent in the stockades is dreadful, full of dysentery and small pox, heat, drought and starvation. Hundreds die including his little sister Priscilla. John meets Rachael Whiteswan, a beautiful full-blood Christian young woman and Bold Hunter, another full-blood who has willingly come to the stockade to be with Rachael. John also meets Pastor Worchester and his daughter Hope, who have come to preach and assist the Cherokee. The text contains some lengthy proselytizing sections, as John is eventually converted to Christianity. In October the Cherokee are finally given wagons and head off to Oklahoma, a trip that takes six months and kills more than 4,000 of the original 17,000 who were rounded up from Tennessee,

Georgia, Alabama and North and South Carolina. Bold Hunter has become a Christian in order to win Rachael's heart, but John realizes he really loves Hope, not Rachael. John has learned medicine from Dr. Smith and helps with the sick along the trail. Nothing helps with the freezing cold and Rachael dies before they reach Oklahoma, as does John's mother. Finally in March, 1839, John's wagon train reaches Oklahoma, although all of his family is dead. But John has learned to be a Christian and a doctor and has won Hope's hand. Best for its portrayal of life in the internment camps, better novels on the Trail of Tears are Glancy's *Pushing the Bear* and Stewart's *River Rising.*

316. Tabor, Doe. *Do Drums Beat There.* Norwich, VT: New Victoria. 2000. 236 p.

Time: late 1960's
Tribe: Sioux
Place: South Dakota, Montana, California

Fifteen-year-old Ritta Baker runs away from her South Dakota reservation fearing she has killed a tribal policeman after he raped her and beat her grandmother. She is taken in by a busload of hippies; two White men, a White woman and a Black woman. Free as the wind, they drive Ritta to Montana to an old friend of her grandfather's. Amos had died years ago, but his widow Gert takes them in and Ritta would be glad to stay there, but the law is on her trail. The hippies take her to Berkeley to Gert's daughter Jody, a half-breed and a lesbian, who is studying law at the university. Ritta and Jody become involved in the Red Power movement and are there when the Indians occupy Alcatraz. Through Ritta's eyes, the reader sees that what started as a strong, powerful movement has become corrupted. The dreams of Native American lands, schools, and cultural movements are lost in internal political struggles, alcohol and drugs. Ritta and Jody return to South Dakota to join with those trying to reclaim their land and the Black Hills. *Do Drums Beat There* is a compelling portrait of a young girl growing up, coming to terms with her sexuality, and finding her place in the world. It also depicts an event in contemporary Native American history, the occupation of Alcatraz, which has been neglected in other novels. This is definitely worth seeking out.

317. Taylor, Janelle. *Lakota Skies Series.*
Lakota Winds. NY: Kensington. 1997. 320 p. *Lakota Dawn.* NY: Kensington. 1999. 279 p.
Reviewed in: Publishers Weekly 12/14/98. *Lakota Flower.* NY: Zebra. 2003. *Lakota Nights* n.p. n.d.

Time: mid-1800's
Tribe: Sioux
Place: Northern Plains

These four romance novels each tell the story of one of the four children of Chief Rising Bear. *Lakota Winds* features his oldest son Wind Dancer and the Sioux woman Chumani/Dewdrops. Wind Dancer, as the eldest son of Chief Rising Bear, knows he will inherit the responsibility for the welfare of the tribe. When his wife and son are killed by the Crow, Wind Dancer becomes intent only on his obligations to his people. Chumani has also lost her husband and child to the Crow and lives only for revenge. Both Wind Dancer and Chumani resist their attraction to each other until their union is seen in a vision and the medicine man tells them their alliance will strengthen their tribes. *Lakota Dawn* tells of Cloud Chaser/Chase Martin, Rising Bear's son by a White slave woman. Cloud Chaser was born to Margaret Phillips and Rising Bear while she was his slave. He was raised as a Lakota until he was ten when he was injured during a hunt and left for dead. Found by Whites, Chase became the adopted son of the Martins who taught him the ways of the Whites and to read and write. Not until their deaths did he learn of his original heritage and has now returned to Rising Bear's band seeking acceptance by his father and brothers. His father does not want to accept Chase, his brothers believe he is their brother but fear he may also be a White spy, and his cousin Two Feathers hates him and tries to have him killed. Chase falls in love with Dawn and escapes with her, claiming the Great Spirit has destined that they be together. After stealing a copy of the Treaty of 1851 so he can determine what the rights of the Native Americans are, Cloud Chaser and Dawn return to Rising Bear's camp where his father now welcomes him. Both novels portray all Indians as good and pure, all Whites as either stupid or greedy. The language is very stilted and presents a highly idealized view of Native American society. *Lakota Flower* follows the third son War Eagle and White captive Caroline Sims/Kawa Cante, while *Lakota Nights* is about Rising Bear's daughter Hanmani and the Cheyenne warrior Red Wolf. Neither of these books can be identified in Books in Print or World Cat and may not have been published.

318. Thayer, Cynthia. *Strong for Potatoes.* NY: St. Martin's. 1998. 248 p.

Time: Contemporary
Tribe: Passamaquoddy
Place: Maine

Blue Willoughby had enough tragedy before she was five to last a lifetime. Her twin sister Berry died at birth and Blue was badly injured in a freak accident while filming a movie. She lost an eye and now walks with a limp. As she grows to adulthood, there is more. She sees her mother making love to an itinerant painter, while her father spends his life behind a viewfinder, taking pictures of everything, but interacting with no one. The one constant in Blue's life is her grandfather, who teaches Blue the ways of his Passamaquoddy ancestors. Blue is only one-quarter Native American, but she learns to weave baskets, first for sale and then as art. The baskets must be beautiful to look at and also strong, for potatoes. Blue herself is both beautiful and strong as she bears a child out of wedlock, comes to terms with her own sexuality, survives the suicide of her father, and finally the death of her beloved grandfather. The spirit of Blue's heritage and her own indomitable spirit shine through this book, making it a pleasure to read.

Reviewed in: Library Journal 1/1/98; Booklist 1/1/98; Publishers Weekly 11/17/97.

319. Thom, James Alexander. *The Red Heart.* NY: Ballantine. 1997. 454 p.

Time: 1778–1847
Tribe: Lenape and Miami
Place: Pennsylvania, New York, Indiana

When five-year Frances Slocum was stolen from her home, her life changed forever. Taken in by Neepah of the Lenapes to replace her own daughter killed by Whites, Frances is treated kindly and learns to love her Native American family. When the Town Destroyers come up the Susquehanna Valley, Frances, now called Good Face, is sent ahead to Neepah's aging parents near Niagara. Neepah does not return and Good Face is adopted by Tuck Horse and Flicker and is a good daughter to them. She marries, but her husband is consumed by the White man's spirit water and she sets him aside before he is killed in battle. Ever fleeing before the White invaders, Good Face and her people finally settle in Indiana where she marries Deaf Man, a Miami, and bears him four children. Although they live in relative peace, the Whites continue to break treaty after treaty and the Miami must move again. Maconakwa (Little Bear Woman) has never forgotten her White origins although she does not want to return to her birth family, for her heart has become Lenape. Nearing the end of her life and fearing death, she reveals her original name and her remaining Slocum sister and brothers make the long trip to see her. Her mother Ruth never gave up hope that her daughter was alive and her siblings finally realize that while she may have been born White, Maconakwa is forever an Indian. Ironically she does not have to move west with the rest of her people since her brothers have petitioned Congress for land in her name which can never be taken from her and which passed down through her descendants. This is a fascinating novel, covering much of the same ground as Thom's *Panther in the Sky* but from the point of view of a woman, not a warrior. Thom always tells a good story.

Reviewed in: Publishers Weekly 9/8/97.

320. Thurlo, Aimée and David Thurlo. *Blackening Song.* NY: Tom Doherty. 1995. 380 p.

Reviewed in: Kirkus Reviews 5/1/95; Library Journal 7/95; Publishers Weekly 5/1/95.

Death Walker. NY: Forge. 1996. 380 p.

Reviewed in: Armchair Detective Summer/96; Kirkus Reviews 5/15/96; Publishers Weekly 4/2/96.

Bad Medicine. NY: Tom Doherty. 1997. 350 p.

Reviewed in: Kirkus Reviews 10/1/97; Publishers Weekly 8/25/97.

Enemy Way. NY: Forge. 1998. 350 p.

Reviewed in: Booklist 9/15/98; Publishers Weekly 7/27/98.

Shooting Chant. NY: Tom Doherty. 2000. 349 p.

Reviewed in: Publishers Weekly 4/3/00; Library Journal 4/1/00.

Red Mesa. An Ella Clah novel. NY: Tom Doherty. 2001. 348 p.

Reviewed: Publishers Weekly 1/29/ 01; Library Journal 3/1/01; Booklist 12/15/00.

The Changing Woman. NY: Tom Doherty. 2002. 384 p.

Reviewed in: School Library Journal 6/1/02; Publishers Weekly 2/25/02; Booklist 2/15/02; Kirkus Reviews 2/1/02.

Time: Contemporary
Tribe: Navajo
Place: New Mexico

Ella Clah is an FBI agent and a Navajo woman who had moved away from the reservation and rejected her Navajo faith, but who has not become a Christian. A series of crimes and cases bring her back to the reservation where her brother, Clifford, is a traditionalist and a *hataalii,* a medicine man and healer. There is strong evidence of skinwalkers working their evil magic on the reservation. Ella has trouble believing in these supernatural beings because she has rejected the Navajo beliefs. However, since she has nothing with which to replace them, eventually she returns to her traditional faith and starts to follow her instincts. The use of skinwalkers in these novels is realistic, they are not figments of anyone's imagination. They change shape, appear and disappear, and work as a collective group. Ella resigns her FBI position to become a tribal policewoman, staying on the reservation where she now feels she belongs. In time she becomes pregnant but does not marry the father, Kevin Tolino, an attorney and Tribal Council member. Ella has a daughter, Dawn, and lives with her mother, Rose, who comes into her own in *The Changing Woman* when she fights against gambling on the reservation as a cure for unemployment. The Clah legacy says they will always have two children, one good, one bad. Ella knows the Navajo see her brother Clifford, the traditionalist healer, as the good Clah, and herself, the policewoman, as the bad Clah. The two siblings frequently work together on her cases, most of which involve skinwalkers in some aspect, and solve the crimes using Navajo spirituality in a common sense approach. The rivalry and the disruption it causes between Navajo progressives and traditionalists is a common theme in the Clah mysteries.

321. Thurlo, Aimée. *Night Wind.* Don Mills, Ontario: Harlequin. 1991. 250 p.

Time: Contemporary
Tribe: Navajo
Place: New Mexico

Belara Fuller is concerned about her Navajo uncle; not only is he ill, he appears to have gone back to his old ranch which is now part of the White Sands Missile Range. Determined to go after him, Belara enlists the help of Travis Hill to outfit her. Travis tries to persuade Belara not to undertake this dangerous mission; when he is unable to do so, he joins her. Other people are also looking for Jimmie Bowman: are they after the gold at Victorio

Peak or are there more sinister implications? Travis is ex-military and certain no woman could love a killer. Belara realizes he is not a killer; he will only protect what is his. There is some Navajo culture portrayed in this slight romance, but ultimately this is merely a typical Harlequin novel. It does represent the beginning of Thurlo's interest in the Navajo culture which culminates in the Ella Clah mysteries.

322. Thurlo, Aimée, and David Thurlo. *Second Shadow.* NY: Forge. 1993. 382 p.

Time: Contemporary
Tribe: Tewa
Place: New Mexico

Architect Irene Pobikan needs the job managing the restoration of the Mendoza hacienda high in the mountains outside Taos. Her firm doesn't think she is aggressive enough and is too tied in with the Indian belief of the individual being subservient to the group. She promises Raul Mendoza that not only will her plans restore the hacienda to its former splendor, they will do so with the finest of materials and on deadline. Irene hasn't reckoned with the animosity of the head contractor, John Cobb, with Raul's artist brother Gene who interferes at every step, or with his mentally handicapped sister Elena who sees many things clearly but who is hiding a terrifying secret. Irene also hadn't counted on being attracted to Raul, something she knows will lead to disaster, for there has been bad blood between the Spanish landowners and the Pueblo peoples for generations. Irene will need the help of her recently deceased grandfather and her spirit fetish the mountain lion to keep herself and others from being injured and to unravel the secrets of the past so the future can unfold.

Reviewed in: Library Journal 10/15/93; Publishers Weekly 10/4/93.

323. Thurlo, Aimée, and David Thurlo. *Second Sunrise: A Lee Nez Novel.* NY: Tom Doherty. 2002. 336 p.

Time: 1945–2002
Tribe: Navajo
Place: New Mexico

During World War II German spies attempt to steal a load of plutonium and are stopped by New Mexico policeman Lee Nez. One of the Germans,

Muller, is a vampire and infects Nez with his blood. Nez manages to find a *hataalii,* Bowlegs, to partially cure him but still is half-vampire, a nightwalker in the Navajo world, sensitive to the sun, equipped with extraordinary physical abilities and hated by skinwalkers. Vampires live forever and in 2002 Muller returns for the hidden plutonium. Bringing along two more vampires, the three attempt to force Nez to show them where the plutonium is buried so they can sell it on the world black market. Nez has a partner on the case, FBI agent Diane Lopez, to whom he has told the truth about being a nightwalker and his battle with skinwalkers. The Navajo skinwalkers can smell vampires and hate them for their immortality. Skinwalkers want the vampires' blood and powers. Together Nez and Lopez fight off the skinwalkers, fight off the vampires, and then set the skinwalkers on the vampires. Aided by John Buck, the *hataalii* nephew of Bowlegs, they even fight off Diane's poisoning with vampire blood to keep her a mortal. Finally the vampires are all dead, shot or stabbed through their hearts. Diane vows to continue the battle with Lee Nez against the skinwalkers. Clearly the start of a new series, readers will have to believe in Navajo skinwalkers and nightwalkers, both of which seem to fit into the New Mexico landscape just fine.

Reviewed in: Booklist 12/15/02; Library Journal 11/15/02; Kirkus Reviews 10/15/02.

324. Thurlo, Aimée. *Spirit Warrior.* Toronto: Harlequin. 1993. 250 p.

Time: Contemporary
Tribe: Navajo
Place: New Mexico

Marla Garret is an archeology professor in charge of a dig which might be Navajo or might be Anasazi; Sam Nez is an attorney and the tribe's representative at the site. Marla wants to learn all she can about the people who lived there and the artifacts they left, Sam and the tribe feel she is disturbing not only the bones of their ancestors but also the *chindi,* the evil spirit, forces which are best left alone. Although opposites in their feelings about the dig, both Marla and Sam witness mysterious happenings and ghostly occurrences and when one of Marla's graduate students is murdered, they join forces to find out exactly who is responsible. Basically a romance with a little Navajo lore thrown in for flavor, Marla and Sam are stock characters, which match the stock plot.

325. Thurlo, Aimée. *Timewalker.* Toronto: Harlequin. 1994. 250 p.

Time: Contemporary
Tribe: Navajo
Place: New Mexico

In 1864, knowing that the others of his band are dead, Benjamin Two Eagle uses the power of his agate amulet to escape capture. In 1993, FBI agent Julia Stevens is hunting down a gang on the Navajo reservation who have been buying and selling Indian artifacts to launder money. Trapped in an arroyo, she is saved by Benjamin who has awakened in a strange time and place. There once were two amulets, the agate known as Slayer and a turquoise Child-of-the-Water which had been passed down in Julia's family. In 1864 both had been in Benjamin's possession as a powerful medicine man, but he was forced to trade the turquoise one to an Army officer who promised his band safety and who betrayed them. Now in 1993, Julia and Benjamin join forces to locate the gang, determine their leader and get the amulets back. Although this is supposed to be a time-travel novel, Benjamin, who speaks fluent English and Spanish as well as Navajo, has little difficulty dealing with the technology of the twentieth century, and Julia easily accepts his explanation of traveling through time. The Navajo history and culture would enable a romance reader to learn something new, but otherwise there is little to recommend this novel.

326. Tilton, Jane, and Lynn Tilton. *Segundo.* Salt Lake City: Bookcraft. 1994. 185 p.

Time: 1870's–1880's
Tribe: Apache
Place: Arizona

Segundo is only eight years old when he sees his father tortured and killed by the outlaw Rafferty and his gang. Rescued by Hector Sanchez, Segundo clings to two beliefs: that "freedom is in the mountains" as his father had told him, and that he must avenge his father's death. Hector knows what revenge is, he had been a leader in the Mexican Revolution, saw his wife and son killed, and the goals of the revolution betrayed. Hector raises Segundo on their quiet farm, protecting him and trying to teach him that hate is not the way to live. Their Mormon neighbor Stanford Merrill also tries to teach Segundo this lesson, but as he becomes a man, Segundo is still convinced that this is something he must do. Only when he actually faces the cowardly Rafferty, does Segundo learn that killing is not the answer. Freedom does not lie in the mountains but in himself and how he lives his life. This novel is far more about the nature of evil than it is about the Apache.

327. Tooley, S. D. *When the Dead Speak.* Schererville, IN: Full Moon Publishing. 1999. 303 p.

Reviewed in: Booklist 1/1/99.

Nothing Else Matters; A Sam Casey Mystery. Schererville, IN: Full Moon Publishing. 2000. 288 p.

Reviewed in: Booklist 4/1/00.

Restless Spirit. Schererville, IN: Full Moon Publishing. 2002. 294 p.

Reviewed in: Library Journal 10/1/02.

Time: Contemporary
Tribe: Sioux
Place: Chicago, South Dakota

Samantha Casey is the daughter of Sam Casey, an investigative reporter killed years ago in a car accident, and Abby Two Eagles, a Sioux medicine woman, a *wicasa wakan*. Alex Red Cloud is Abby's protector, a Sioux healer also working as a groundskeeper on Sam's huge inherited estate in Illinois. Sam is a policewoman, able to "read" the thoughts and actions of the dead by touching objects they have held, a power that helps her solve her cases. Her Sioux mother Abby can "feel" the thoughts and emotions of the living. When Sam and Abby meet Jake Mitchell, another police detective, Abby knows he is the perfect man for Sam. In the first mystery Sam finds herself in trouble with the department when she is accused of the murder of a fellow policeman and ends up on suspension. That does not prevent Sam from exposing a State Representative as a murderer of African-American soldiers in the Korean War. In the second mystery, *Nothing Else Matters*, Sam is still suspended and working as a private detective. She encounters a mysterious hired killer, Sparrow, and determines who he really is and why he kills predominently evil persons. During the course of the first two mysteries, Sam and Jake realize their attraction for one another, marry, and Sam becomes pregnant. Abby works for the Bureau of Indian Affairs and is a leader of the Sioux community on the Eagle Ridge Reservation in South Dakota. She convinces the tribe to use gambling proceeds to further the welfare of the community as a whole, rather than parceling out revenues to individual families. Abby also succeeds in appointing women to the tribal council on the Reservation, a change from the past. One almost feels Abby's efforts with her Sioux people are more important than Sam's case solving. In the third mystery, *Restless Spirit*, Sam is still on suspension but working as a private investigator and quite pregnant. Finding an old button in a building site causes a vision of the murder of a young girl many years ago. Tracking down the culprit exposes Jake's childhood protector, Judge Wise, but brings peace to the restless spirit of the dead girl. A videotape is also found of the murder of the policeman which finally proves that Sam is innocent of the crime that caused her suspension.

328. Toombs, Jane. *Arapaho Spirit.* Wayne, PA: Dell/Banbury. 1983. 309 p.

Time: 1850's
Tribe: Arapaho
Place: Western U.S.

Hampton Abbott doesn't remember his childhood in the Arapaho tribe in the early 1800's, but has promised his White mother to exact revenge on his evil father, Bad Hawk. Coming west as an Indian Agent in the 1850's he meets Stands Shining, a warrior woman of the tribe who can lead raids, but not find a husband. They fall in love, even though Hampton also loves a girl in St. Louis. Hampton earns the name Fire Moon from the tribe and works on their behalf with Broken Hand Tom Fitzpatrick on a peace treaty. The Army brings Lieutenant Chambers, rival of Hampton's for the girl in St. Louis. Chambers and Hampton hate each other, eventually fighting almost to the death. Hampton's life is saved by One Claw, the kindly great uncle of Stands Shining. One Claw dies in the rescue, revealing himself to be Bad Hawk. Stands Shining and Hampton marry, hoping to live away from the White men encroaching on Arapaho territory. Accurate depiction of Arapaho customs and stories make this an above-average western.

329. Trainor, J. F. *Corona Blue: An Angela Biwaban Mystery.* NY: Kensington Books. 1994. 357 p.

Time: Contemporary
Tribe: Ojibwe
Place: South Dakota

Angie Biwaban is working as a farmhand on Josh Elderkin's farm when she finds a body in the field she is harvesting and runs the combine into a ditch. By the time she can get back to the body, it has disappeared. Does this current murder have a connection with the disappearance of eight-year-old Holly Larson thirty years ago? When Josh's aunt Miss Edna also dies, most accept her death as a heart attack; only Angie figures out that she was electrocuted. How did the killer tap into the power lines, what secret was Miss Edna hiding, and how can Angie save the farm from foreclosure? Angie must deal with racist local White police who view all Native Americans as drunks, a hydroelectric company ignoring safety rules, and a loan shark who profits from loans to farmers. Angie typically deals with greedy evil people by turning their greed back upon themselves. This is an intriguing mystery, although the only strong Native American connections are the character of Angie's grandfather, Chief, and a vision Angie has of her traditional Anishinabe grandmother tending her as a child.

Reviewed in: Library Journal 10/1/94; Publishers Weekly 10/10/94.

330. Trainor, J. F. *Dynamite Pass: An Angela Biwaban Mystery.* NY: Zebra Books. 1993. 380 p.

Time: Contemporary
Tribe: Ojibwe
Place: Utah

Angela's aunt married a *Nuche,* a Ute, and one of Angela's cousins, Billie Shavano, is a forest ranger in Utah. Billie is trying to save a unique stand of old growth aspen from being logged in Lodestone Canyon, which angers the local businessmen who want to harvest the lumber. Billie is found dead under a tree, an apparent victim of a logging accident, but Angela notices the traditional Ute offering of tobacco to the tree roots has not been made and concludes Billie was murdered. Angela goes *nandobani,* "on scout" for the killer. Assuming a false identity to hide her relationship to Billie, she befriends the local power brokers and engineers the deal that Billie had been working on before he died. Using the federal Section 206 to trade one parcel of land for another, Angela arranges for the Lodestone Canyon timber stand to be swapped for BIA Ute tribal land in the desert. Now the Ute tribe has say over the cutting of the aspen and they refuse to allow it. Native American influences appear throughout the text of the mystery and Angela frequently calls upon her early childhood training from Charlie Blackbear, her *Nimishoo*, grandfather, to help her figure out the mystery and survive an attack by Billie's killer. The mystery is engrossing; if only the relentless "cuteness" of Angela would cease, this series would win high praise.

331. Trainor, J. F. *High Country Murder: An Angela Biwaban Mystery.* NY: Kensington Books. 1995. 388 p.

Time: Contemporary
Tribe: Ojibwe
Place: Colorado

Anishinabe "princess" Angela is on probation and working for a lawyer, Sarah Sutton, whose family lives on a ranch near Crested Butte, Colorado. When Sarah's mother is killed in a car accident, Angela determines that it was not an accident and that Sarah's mother had quite a colorful and criminal past. The plot involves old robberies, including one by the Wild Bunch, with one of its members perhaps hiding the gold near the ranch. Sarah's ranch is in financial straits, her teenaged daughter is in trouble, and someone is trying to kill her. Angela is still wanted by the FBI for her own past criminal activities, but she decides to solve all the difficulties for everyone else without getting herself caught. With the assistance of her grandfather, Chief, Angela is able to rescue Sarah's teenaged daughter and expose the murderer. She is also able to find the Wild Bunch's saddlebags full of gold pieces and save the ranch. During the process Angela uses her Anishnabe skills to make snowshoes out of brooms and curtains and cross high mountain passes in howling blizzards, all while managing to keep her overly-cute sense of humor. No one loves Princess Angela more than she herself does. However, the description of the area around Crested Butte is good and the mystery is complex enough to keep one guessing until the end.

Reviewed in: Kirkus Reviews 9/15/95; Library Journal 11/1/95; Publishers Weekly 10/16/95.

332. Trainor, J. F. *Target for Murder: An Angela Biwaban Mystery.* NY: Kensington Books. 1993. 286 p.

Time: Contemporary
Tribe: Ojibwe
Place: Upper Peninsula, Michigan

Angela is fresh out of prison and on parole in South Dakota working at a circus when she sees her old childhood girlfriend looking hungry, lost and pregnant. Mary Beth's husband has been murdered and their farm confiscated by the bank back in Tilford, Michigan. Leaving Mary Beth in her grandfather Charlie Blackbear's care in Minnesota, Angela uses her *ikwekazo odaminowin,* her woman's make-believe, to trick the bankers and real estate brokers of Tilford into putting up a matching four million dollars to Angela's nonexistent four million. Once again Angie uses people's own greed to entrap them. Then

Angela electronically transfers the funds to Mary Beth, exposes the murderer of Mary Beth's husband, and returns to serve her parole in South Dakota. The mystery has the least connection to Angela's Anishinabe background or teachings of any of the Trainor mysteries and far more violence.

333. Trainor, J. F. *Whiskey Jack. An Angela Bibwaban Mystery.* NY: Kensington Books. 1993. 379 p.

Time: Contemporary
Tribe: Ojibwe
Place: Washington State

Mickey Grantz, an old attorney friend of Angela's, calls from prison in Washington State to ask for her help in finding the murderer of his ex-wife, Mona, in the San Juan Islands of Puget Sound. Angela sneaks away from South Dakota and with the help of her *Nimishoo,* her grandfather, Chief, is able to assume another identity in the town of Port Wyoochee on the Olympic Peninsula. Now she is Anne Marie Nahkeeta (Salish for "princess"), a financial investor looking for ways to bring economic health to a small dying lumber town. Angela/Anne, using many of the skills taught her by her father and grandfather back on the reservation, discovers the corruption behind the paper mill waste disposal, the secret support for the Aryan Nation fundamentalist preacher and his skinhead followers, and finally the real murderer, a drug running ex-boyfriend of Mona's. The description of the town and the problems between environmentalists and lumbermen in the Pacific Northwest is well done, as is the strong and supportive relationship between Angela and her grandfather. One only wishes Angela was not so enamored of her own appearance and behavior, because it mars what otherwise is an excellent story.

334. Treuer, David. (Ojibwe). *The Hiawatha.* NY: Picador USA. 1999. 310 p.

Time: 1940's–1980's
Tribe: Ojibwe
Place: Minnesota

Betty and Jacob marry on the Ojibwe reservation after World War II and have four children, two daughters and two sons, Simon and Lester. After Jacob is killed by a falling tree, Betty packs up her children and moves to Minneapolis as part of the 1950's Urban Relocation of Native Americans effort by the U.S. government. There she finds work as a hospital employee and is befriended by One-Two, a giant Winnebago high steel construction worker. Simon also goes to work as a high steel worker, when he realizes his mother is paying the rent to the landlord by prostituting herself. The description of the Native American high steel workers is excellent. Simon becomes physically strong but is full of anger, hating the life of poverty, feeling responsible for his father's death and the economic welfare of the family. Lester is the softer, quieter son. He and his girlfriend have sex on the abandoned train cars of *The Hiawatha*, a fabled passenger train now being cut up for scrap. When Lester's girlfriend Vera gets pregnant, Simon explodes and in a drunken rage kills Lester. Vera dumps the baby on Betty and disappears. Years later Simon returns from prison and finds Lester's son, his nephew Lincoln, living with Betty, One-Two living across the street, and Vera working in a jewelry store downtown. As the old buildings in Minneapolis are torn down, Betty loses her house and moves herself and Lincoln back to the reservation. Lincoln has never been told the family history, so when he finally learns it from his relatives on the reservation, he falls apart and goes into a life of drugs and bad companions. Lincoln returns to Minneapolis, finds Simon, learns the truth about his mother Vera, and robs the jewelry store, getting shot in the process. Simon frantically tries to save Lincoln by taking him back to the reservation, but it is too late. One-Two comes up to the reservation when he hears Betty has gone into a deep depression and the two finally find each other. Simon is emotionally destroyed, assuming the blame for all the miseries of the family, and he disappears. This is a heart-wrenching story of a young man who assumed the responsibility and blame imposed by a family caught in the economic disaster of all Native Americans during the Urban Relocation program. The relationship between Simon and One-Two is special, but the very close brotherly relationship between Simon and Lester was not to be duplicated or replaced. Simon deeply regrets his drunken rage and the murder of Lester and says "He not only took away Lester's life, he has had to do without it." One entire chapter poignantly describes how Simon remembers taking five-year-old Lester swimming on the reservation when they were both little boys, holding his hand on the trail to the swimming hole. "This is what he remembers, not the swim. . . . Just Lester's hand, his studied love. His hidden admiration. His little, little hands."

Reviewed in: Publishers Weekly 3/29/99; Kirkus Reviews 3/15/99.

335. Treuer, David. (Ojibwe). *Little.* St. Paul, MN: Graywolf Press. 1995. 248 p.

Time: 1968–1980
Tribe: Ojibwe
Place: Minnesota, Iowa

On a very poor reservation in Minnesota an extended family cares for a crippled child named Little, whose only vocabulary word is "You," a word both accusatory and personal. Little's mother is Celia, daughter of Jeanette, a woman now in her seventies but friend for many years to twin brothers, Duke and Ellis. Another family, the siblings Violet and Stan, and their cousins Lyle and Pick, also have a daughter, Jackie. Finally there is Donovan, a child found in a car on a bitter winter night by Duke and Ellis. Little can speak but refuses to do so and is an adventuresome and caring child. Each adult is given a turn in describing their past and each story is fascinating. Jeanette was sold as a young girl to two rich Iowa women to be their servant, was rescued by Duke and Ellis and brought back to Minnesota to be their wife. After their son is accidentally killed by the priest and the Indian Agent, who came to take the newborn baby away to be saved, Duke and Ellis murder the Agent and disappear for thirty years. They later return to father Celia and live beside the house in their Catalina automobile, having given up the confines of a house. Stan and Pick went off to Vietnam where Stan lost his right hand and Pick lost his life in the same fire fight. Stan returned to Celia and (he believes) fathered Little. Lyle is distraught when the Army sends him the letter about Pick's death and leaves the reservation for ten years, not realizing Violet is pregnant with his daughter, Jackie. This extended caring group of related Ojibwe live near each other and care for each other and the three young children. Thus when one night Little climbs the water tower and does not return, everyone of them grieves. An empty coffin is buried, since Little is floating above them all, shared in a sense now by all the community. Interwoven with the Ojibwe family stories is the life of Paul, the Catholic priest from Iowa sent to replace Father Gundesohn, killed in a fall against the baptismal font. The truth of the priest's death and the paternity of Little are finally revealed in one person's internal flashback thoughts. This novel, by a young Ojibwe who attended Princeton and was a Rhodes Scholar finalist, rivals the best Native American authors currently writing. The characters are fully developed, their individual stories are poignant, and each one's voice is authentic.

Reviewed in: Booklist 10/15/95; Choice 4/1/96; Library Journal 10/1/95; Publishers Weekly 8/21/95.

336. Turner, William O. *Blood Dance.* NY: Berkley. 1967. 142 p.

Time: 1880's
Tribe: Ute
Place: Colorado

Set in the 1880's a few years after Chief Ouray's death, this novel is concerned with the attempts of the Northern Utes to return to Colorado and reclaim reservation lands they lost in earlier years. Led by Coolisootkahn, a respected medicine man the White men call Spook, hundreds of Utes come together in southern Colorado, leaving their Utah reservations. Aided by school teacher Susan Gibson and half-breed Lloyd Finch who have robbed a stagecoach for money to buy guns, the uprising seems imminent. However Mort Colley, a friend of Ouray's and a former Army Scout, has been hired to retrieve the money and in doing so, thwarts the rebellion as well. Narrated by a young man, Charlie Magruder, this western is sympathetic to the Ute cause, but realistic in its probable failure. Included is information about the beliefs of the Utes and the rivalry between different tribal groups, Uncompaghres versus Northern Utes, which also defeats the effort. Ultimately the leaders are betrayed and the uprising is deflated with a minimal loss of life. The Utes lose once again and must return to Utah.

337. Udall, Brady. *The Miracle Life of Edgar Mint.* NY: Norton. 2001. 423 p.

Time: 1970's
Tribe: Apache
Place: Arizona

Little Edgar Mint was ignored by his alcoholic mother, abandoned by his father, and at seven, run over by the mail truck, crushing his skull. The mailman believes Edgar dead, but he is revived by Dr. Pinkley in the emergency room. Edgar is sent to a convalescent hospital where he is befriended by another patient, Alvin, who gives Edgar a typewriter which changes his life. Edgar has recovered all his mental faculties except the ability to write. He is considered a miracle for his survival after the accident but unfortunately no one wants him, so he is sent to Willie Sherman, an Indian school which takes all the Southwestern reservations' unwanted children. At school Edgar is submitted to horrible bullying by Norman, a giant Pima boy, and his evil friends. Edgar finally makes a friend in Cecil, a Havasupai boy, who stands up to Norman, trying to kill him with a bow and arrow. For this Cecil is sent to juvenile detention. Edgar decides to commit suicide, but is saved by Mormon missionaries, another miracle. Edgar is baptized, taken from the boarding school and sent to live with a kindly but sad Mormon family, the Madsens. When Edgar goes to visit Cecil in prison, he finds Cecil's life is not a succession of miracles. Cecil has died trying to escape. Edgar decides he needs to tell the mailman that he is alive, not killed by the mail truck. He finds the mailman's wife, Rosa, and hears an amazing story of his early childhood. He finally finds peace and the childhood he has missed with Rosa. This is a highly creative and often amusing story of a wretched childhood full of neglect, injury, bullying, misunderstanding, and finally the love a child needs.

Reviewed in: Publishers Weekly 5/28/01; Library Journal 6/1/01; Booklist 5/1/01; NYTBR 7/01/01; Kirkus Reviews 4/15/01.

338. Vernon, John. *The Last Canyon.* Boston: Houghton Mifflin. 2001. 336 p.

Time: 1869
Tribe: Paiute
Place: Utah, Arizona

Two stories overlap in this fictional account of John Wesley Powell's exploration of the Grand Canyon. Taking four boats and nine men to chart the course of this unknown river, Powell encounters endless hardships and setbacks, losing men, boats, and scientific equipment. Up on the top of the canyon, a small family band of Shivwits Paiutes have set out to rescue a young daughter from the Navajo and must cross the Colorado River, which they call the Pawhaw. In the Powell party, brother Walter Powell is suffering the aftereffects of the Civil War, with serious rages and mood swings. Other men are nothing more than mountain men and mule skinners, not scientists, and not particularly committed to the cause or to preserving each other's welfare. The quarreling is endless as are the heat, starvation, and portages past rapids. The Paiutes encounter some rough White miners, who shoot the woman Pooeechuts in the arm, causing her to sicken and die. Next the Paiutes meet Hopi and find they speak a shared language. Finally they find the Paiutes on the other side of the Pawhaw and learn the daughter is with Hoskininni, a powerful Navajo. Pangwits, a wealthy relative in the band, negotiates with the Navajo and rescues the daughter and they all start for home again. Meanwhile the flour has gone moldy and the bacon rancid, so three of Powell's men set off cross-country to find the Mormons and help. Instead they find the Paiutes, who think they are the miners responsible for Pooeechuts' death and kill them. Powell ends his river exploration with two boats and five men and vows to return. An excellent account of two sets of people exploring the same area and discovering amazing truths about geological and sociological history, Vernon's book succeeds on both levels. He includes many of the traditional rites and ceremonies of the Paiute and the Hopi and clearly has researched not only Powell, but also the native peoples of the southwest.

Reviewed in: Library Journal 10/1/01; NYTBR 11/11/01.

339. Vizenor, Gerald. (Chippewa). *Chancers.* Norman: University of Oklahoma Press. 2000. 159 p.

Time: Contemporary
Tribe: Ojibwe
Place: California

American Indian Literature and Critical Studies Series, v. 36.

The Provost and then several other faculty disappear on the Berkeley campus, dismembered and beheaded. Their skulls appear in the Phoebe Hearst Museum of Anthropology, replacements for Native American skulls that are rescued and reincarnated as Chancers. These murders are carried out by the Solar Dancers, a group of militant Native American students possessed by the spirit of *wiindigoo*. Token White, the one White woman allowed to be a member of the Solar Dancers, is their expert archer and shoots the victims with her bow and arrows, a gift taught to her by Ishi. Professor Peter Roses is also known as Round Dance and his mostly blonde and beautiful followers, whom he sexually entertains in his office, are called Round Dancers. He is thoroughly hated by the Solar Dancers. Before the victims are murdered, they are all marked with a blue character sign for death. During the final graduation ceremony at the end of the academic year, the Solar Dancers steal the ceremonial blankets, are marked with the blue symbol, and eventually meet their demise at the hands of Token White. Other guests at graduation include Pocahontas, the anthropologist Alfred Kroeber, Phoebe Hearst and more reincarnated others. The novel is short and entertaining, although not based at all in any semblance of reality. Characters appear from other Vizenor novels, including the Browne family, in what is essentially a critique of campus politics. The novel will probably appeal mostly to academicians.

Reviewed in: Booklist 10/15/00; Library Journal 8/1/00.

340. Vizenor, Gerald. (Chippewa). *Hotline Healers: An Almost Browne Novel.* Hanover: Wesleyan University Press. 1997. 172 p.

Time: Contemporary
Tribe: Ojibwe
Place: Minnesota

This novel is really a stream-of-consciousness rambling through the exploits of the narrator (who is unnamed) and his cousin, Almost Browne, almost born on the White Earth Reservation in Minnesota. Almost Browne has set up a system of hotline healers, so anyone can call over 1-900 numbers to reach their own healers: the best storytellers on the reservation and in native communities. Almost and his cousin also run a business of making calico covered handmade books full of blank pages, all the rage on university campuses, frequently assigned reading for courses. They are invited to give panel discussions across the United States, meeting famous authors, many of them Native Americans. Almost Browne and his cousin are frequently the source of trouble, through their actions or their proposed theories on these campuses. There are some other storylines, including that of Gesture, their great uncle, who runs a train all over the reservation, dispensing dental work, albeit without any dental school training. The names of cultural figures, from O. J. Simpson to Ishmael Reed to Gloria Steinem, pop up throughout the text. The object of the novel seems to be to poke holes in the sanctimoniousness of university intellectuals and those who revere Native Americans for no other reason than their ethnic backgrounds. Not an easy book to read, it is nonetheless a classic Vizenor work.

Reviewed in: Library Journal 4/15/97; Publishers Weekly 3/31/97; Kirkus Reviews 3/15/ 97.

For further criticism and interpretation of Vizenor's works see: Lee, A. Robert. *Loosening the Seams: Interpretations of Gerald Vizenor.* Bowling Green, OH: Bowling Green State University Popular Press. 2000.

341. Vollmann, William T. *Argall: Third Dream of Seven Dreams: A Book of North American Landscapes.* NY: Viking. 2001. 746 p.

Time: 1607–Present
Tribe: Powhatans, Pattawomecks, Pamunkeys
Place: Delaware, Virginia

Third in the author's series of Dreams, this history of the Chesapeake Bay tribes and their encounters with the early English settlers is densely written and complex, but with accompanying glossaries and a chronology to help one keep some things organized. Basically the story of "Sweet John" Smith and the Powhatan "princess" Pocahontas, the text includes great historical detail on the early governance of the Virigina colony, the eradication of the local tribes, the beginnings of the tobacco trade, and finally the present-day status of the remnants of the eastern tribes. Pocahontas is a tragic figure, rejected by Smith, married to a Powhatan, kidnapped, converted to Christianity with her name changed to Rebecca, and finally taken by her English husband John Rolfe back to his homeland where she dies at a young age of disease. Her son Thomas is rejected by his father, left behind in England, and when he finally returns to Virginia, is given no status due to his half-breed origins. Marriage between English and Indians or Negroes becomes illegal in Virginia in 1658. The history of the tribes as they try to help the English, then resist the English, then fight the English, then become overwhelmed and destroyed, their lands plowed under for tobacco, is also tragic. There is little sympathy for the English in this novel. They are cruel, oppressive people bound and determined to wipe out the Powhatans and all the other tribes to steal their rich estuary lands. More readable than earlier entries in the series, perhaps Vollmann will eventually write a reasonable length novel more accessible to more readers. His research certainly deserves a wider audience.

Reviewed in: Publishers Weekly 9/3/01; Kirkus Reviews 9/1/01; Library Journal 9/1/02; Booklist 8/1/01.

342. Vollmann, William T. *Fathers and Crows: Part Two of Seven Dreams.* NY: Viking. 1992. 990 p.

Time: 1534–1680
Tribe: Huron, Iroquois
Place: Eastern Canada

A densely written and complex historical novel about the Jesuits among the Iroquois and Huron in the early days of French exploration and settlement, this book contains a wealth of factual data and fascinating information. It will take time to read this thoroughly researched story of the Black Robes' attempts to convert these warlike tribes, but it will be worth it. The early part of the long novel concerns itself with Champlain in Quebec and the latter half is about the Black Robes among the Iroquois nations. Jesuit Jean de Brebeuf baptizes children as they die of European diseases, the only way he is able to save souls among a people who completely reject his creed. De Brebeuf's nemesis is Born Underwater, a woman with magical powers of her own. De Brebeuf is fascinated and attracted to her, and thus hates her as well. The Iroquois despise the French and their priests, but love the iron they can get in trade for their pelts. The iron is needed for arrow points to defeat their enemies and expand their territory. Ultimately the pursuit of iron defeats their own nation and their own Iroquois culture. This novel is almost more of a history book than a work of fiction, with glossaries, chronologies, diaries, footnotes and a list of sources. There will be little about the French and Jesuits among the Iroquois that one does not know when the book has been finished.

Reviewed in: NYTBR 9/6/92; Time 8/31/92; Times Literary Supplement 10/3/91; L.A. Times Book Review 8/23/92.

343. Walker, Robert W. *Cutting Edge.* NY: Jove. 1997. 424 p.

Double Edge. NY: Jove. 1998. 359 p.

Reviewed in: Publishers Weekly 10/12/98.

Cold Edge. NY: Jove. 2001. 326 p.

Reviewed in: Publishers Weekly 2/12/01

Time: Contemporary
Tribe: Cherokee
Place: Texas

Lucas Stonecoat suffers from constant pain as a result of injuries incurred in his job as a policeman and often turns to alcohol and native healing drugs, including peyote. He is short-tempered, rude and violent, not a calm, introspective, mellow Cherokee at all. Raised on the Coushatta Reservation in Texas, he has left the life of poverty, if not alcoholism, behind. Lucas is in charge of the Houston Police Department cold cases, unsolved murders. Dr. Meredyth Sanger, a psychoanalyst, works on these cases as well and frequently asks for Lucas's assistance. In *Double Edge* a Fox Indian, Miranda Roundpoint, was killed in 1948 and now her son has appeared asking for the crime to be solved. In *Cutting Edge* prominent people who attended Texas Christian University are being killed with a crossbow and then dismembered. Stonecoat must fall back upon his skills as a native tracker and hunter to survive being hunted down himself. Dr. Sanger must even turn into a modern Cherokee War Woman to save him. In *Cold Edge* someone is killing, scalping and beheading his victims. The murders are often gruesome, Stonecoat has his addictions and his obsessions and he certainly is not the kindly, wise sort of Cherokee often found in literature. However, the characters and plots are well developed and full of twists and turns.

344. Weibe, Rudy. *The Temptations of Big Bear.* Athens: Swallon Press/Ohio University Press. 1973. 423 p.

Time: 1876–1888
Tribe: Cree, Sioux, Blackfeet, Bloods
Place: Saskatchewan, Canada

Big Bear was a Cree chief who did not want to sign away his lands and hunting rights for a small "reserve" from the Canadian government. He and his band of Plains Cree tried to stay free and to create a resistance movement to include Sitting Bull and his Sioux, and Crowfoot and his Bloods, as well as Riel and the Metis. Little Bad Man was Big Bear's oldest son, Kingbird a younger son, and their personal stories are included. The novel follows the events of the signing of Treaty Number Six up to the Frog's Lake Massacre and the jailing of Big Bear. The Cree and Blackfeet are starving because the U.S. Army will not allow the buffalo herds to cross the border, hoping to starve those Sioux taking refuge in Canada. The Canadian government is just as poor in providing food for their native peoples and the Plains Cree, the Bloods and the Blackfeet are also suffering. Finally Wandering Spirit, the Cree war chief, takes command. He attacks the Indian Agent at Frog's Lake and demands food. When Wandering Spirit meets resistance, a massacre occurs. Men, women, two priests, and Metis, as well as the Agent Quinn, are murdered. Big Bear is arrested as the responsible party, although he had tried to stop the killing. He and Poundmaker, another influencial but peaceful Cree chief, are sentenced to three years in prison. Little Bad Man changes his name to Little Bear and takes the remainder of the Cree band to Montana where the U.S. government finally gives them a small reservation. This novel makes it clear that although Sitting Bull might have thought things were better in Canada, in fact that White government treated its native populations as badly as the U.S. did. The novel includes many details of Cree life and is an excellent account of the Canadian tribes in the late 1800's.

Reviewed in: Toronto Globe and Mail 6/19/99.

345. Welch, James. (Blackfeet/Gros Ventres). *The Heartsong of Charging Elk.* NY: Doubleday. 2000. 438 p.

Time: 1889–1905
Tribe: Sioux
Place: Marseille, France

Born at Pine Ridge, Charging Elk tries out for the Buffalo Bill Wild West Show and tours Europe in the late 1890's with the troupe. When he breaks his ribs and comes down with influenza, he is left behind in a hospital in Marseille. Charging Elk awakens to strangers and, unable to speak either English or French, is isolated and afraid. He sneaks out of the hospital and is arrested for vagrancy. The American Consul arranges his release and places him with kindly fishmongers, the Soulas. Charging Elk becomes a member of their family, who teach him French and give him food, clothes and work. Charging Elk is a man and wants his freedom and a job to make enough money to go home again. He moves out on his own, works in a soap factory, and falls in love with a prostitute, Marie. An unscrupulous homosexual young man falls in love with the strikingly handsome Charging Elk and bribes Marie to give him access to the Sioux. Tricked and drugged, Charging Elk awakens to find himself being sexually molested and kills the young man, who is a famous and respected Marseille chef. The public outcry sends Charging Elk to prison for ten years, even though he was the victim. Eventually he is released to a rural farmer, falls in love with his daughter, Natalie, and becomes a father. Buffalo Bill's troupe returns and his tribesmen ask Charging Elk to come back to the United States with them, but he refuses. He has made his life in France. This is a heart-rending story. Left behind by an uncaring Wild West Show, abandoned by the American Consulate, Charging Elk's lack of sophistication in dealing with the people of seamy Marseille causes him immeasurable suffering. Tricked, abused, given the most menial jobs because of his dark skin and halting French, he never complains and continues to strive to succeed. He truly loves Marie, who cheats and tricks him. He cannot make friends because his Sioux heritage is viewed with suspicion. It is only finally with Natalie in the rural areas of France that he finds happiness.

Reviewed in: Publishers Weekly 5/22/00; Library Journal 5/1/00; Booklist 5/1/00.

346. Westbrook, Robert. *Ghost Dancer.* NY: Signet. 1998. 308 p.
Warrior Circle. NY: Signet. 1999. 277 p.
Red Moon. NY: Signet. 2000. 283 p.
Ancient Enemies. NY: Signet. 2001. 308 p.

Time: Contemporary
Tribe: Sioux
Place: New Mexico

Perennial graduate student Howard Red Deer takes a job with blind, retired cop-turned-private investigator Jack Wilder just to pay the bills while finishing his dissertation. Howie is a very laid-back Indian, quietly surviving in a White man's world in the backwater town of San Geronimo, but the cases he and Jack investigate reflect contemporary issues. In *Ghost Dancer* their wealthy client, head of the San Geronimo Peak ski area, is murdered before they even meet him. Is the fact that the ski area wanted to expand onto reservation land responsible for his murder? *Warrior Circle* involves Howie in a New Age male bonding movement whose members are all involved in a proposed shopping center and perhaps several murders. *Red Moon* finds Howie and Jack on the trail of a Georgia O'Keefe painting stolen twenty-five years ago. *Ancient Enemies* is concerned with possible cannibalism among the Anasazi. Do the new murders have a ritual tie-in with ancient practices? Would someone kill to prevent the dissemination of this theory? Although there is little of Howie's Sioux heritage in these mysteries, Westbrook writes with sly humor and both Jack and Howie are engaging characters.

347. Whitson, Stephanie Grace. *Dakota Moons Book 1. Valley of the Shadow.* Nashville: Thomas Nelson. 2000. 295 p.

Time: 1861–1862
Tribe: Sioux
Place: Minnesota

Genevieve LaCroix, half Sioux, half French, is sent to the mission at Renville run by Simon Dane, to be educated. She lives with the Dane family, caring for the son Aaron and daughter Meg. When mother Ellen Dane dies in childbirth and Gen's father dies of an illness, her place in the Dane family becomes permanent. Simon Dane is a harsh, cold minister with no real love for the Dakota Sioux who are his flock. His mission is a failure. Losing his wife wakes him up emotionally and he begins to try harder to interact with people. Gen loves Two Stars, a young Sioux man. Two Stars is wounded in a horse raid, cared for by Gen and the Danes, and gradually learns to become a Christian, naming himself Daniel. Daniel's friend Otter hates Whites and starts the Sioux Uprising of 1862 in Minnesota. Hundreds of White families are killed or captured, including Gen and the Dane children. Daniel pretends to rejoin the warriors and rescues them. He takes them all the way from Chief Little Crow's camp to Fort Ridgely, where Simon also happens to be. Even friendly Sioux are arrested by vengeful Whites, determined to rid Minnesota of all the Sioux. Over 300 Sioux men are condemned to death, but President Lincoln intervenes, and only thirty-eight are hanged. Gen hears one of them is Daniel Two Stars and falls into a depression. Simon has found his calling in ministering to the Dakota and asks Gen to marry him. They watch as the captured Sioux are all loaded onto barges and sent to the Dakota Territory and the awful reservation on Crow Creek. Their lands in Minnesota are confiscated and their annuities are seized to pay Whites for losses suffered in the uprising. The Dakota are banned from their homelands forever. While this is Christian fiction, the author does not overload the text. The characters are well developed and the story can be enjoyed by those with little or no religious belief.

Reviewed in: Publishers Weekly 11/27/00.

348. Whitson, Stephanie Grace. *Dakota Moons Book 2. Edge of the Wilderness.* Nashville: Thomas Nelson. 2001. 263 p.

Time: 1862–1865
Tribe: Sioux
Place: Minnesota, New York

Daniel Two Stars was not hanged with the other Dakota men as Genevieve LaCroix and the Danes believed; he was arrested and with hundreds of other men in Mankato and suffers harsh prison conditions. The Army offers him better food and clothing if he will be one of General Sibley's scouts. Daniel and a few other Christian Dakota agree to track down roaming Dakota and bring them into Fort Ridgely. From there the Dakota are sent to Camp McClellan and then on to the Crow Creek reservation. At each place the Dakota prisoners suffer horribly from cold and bad food; their children and old people die. Simon has found his calling in ministering to these prisoners and when his brother-in-law Elliot Leighton arrives from New York to take the children back to their grandmother, Simon convinces Elliot to stay and help the Dakota. Eventually Simon encounters Daniel and discovers he is alive, but Daniel convinces Simon to not tell Genevieve. Daniel believes she would be better off married to the minister. Gen and Simon marry, but he dies of pneumonia brought on by his long hours ministering to the Dakota. In his Last Will and Testiment, Simon leaves his children to Elliot and tells Gen to go find her true love, Daniel Two Stars. A great deal of history of the Dakota in Minnesota is included in this series, which is often glossed over in other novels. What really happened at the Battle at Kildeer Mountain when General Sully's troops encountered thousands of Sioux families? The text is not overloaded with Christian piousness and is therefore accessible to non-religious readers.

349. Whitson, Stephanie Grace. *Dakota Moons Book 3. Heart of the Sandhills.* Nashville: Thomas Nelson. 2002. 296 p.

Time: 1865–1870's
Tribe: Sioux
Place: Minnesota, Wyoming

Daniel Two Stars and Genevieve are now married and working for the White farmer who took over Daniel's farm after the Minnesota Sioux Uprising. Local neighbors are uncomfortable with having Daniel and his Sioux friend, Robert Lawrence, living so close to them, since they are still afraid of the Dakota. After a series of nasty incidents, Daniel and Robert decide to become Army scouts for Captain Willets again. Willets hires them and Aaron Dane, now a young man. The company is moved to Fort Laramie in Wyoming and Willets, Daniel and Aaron are moved further to Fort Kearney. The Fetterman Massacre has recently occurred and Whites are afraid of the aggressive Lakota Sioux. The Lakota consider the Dakota cowards, losing in Minnesota and now working for their enemies, the Army. During the Wagon Box Fight of 1867, Daniel is severely wounded. Found by a widowed and grieving Lakota woman, Two Moons, he is taken back to her camp and cared for. When Two Moons realizes he will lose his leg, she drags him to Ft. Kearney for help. Captain Willets meets her and falls under her spell. Daniel does lose his lower leg, but recovers with the love and faith of Gen. Together they homestead a small valley and raise their children. The ending chapters of this third installment contain the most sermonizing and stilted dialogue. The Wagon Box Fight, led by Crazy Horse and Red Cloud, is portrayed from the perspective of the Dakota scouts, oddly unsympathetic to the plight of their Sioux brothers facing the same invasion of territory by Whites that they so recently experienced themselves in Minnesota.

Reviewed in: Publishers Weekly 12/3/01.

350. Wilkinson, David Marion. *Oblivion's Altar: A Novel of Courage*. NY: New American Library. 2002. 376 p.

Time: 1776–1839
Tribe: Cherokee, Creek
Place: Georgia, Arkansas, Oklahoma

This is probably the best novel written on the lives of Major Ridge, his son John Ridge, and John Ross, all chiefs of the Eastern Cherokee during the early 1830's when the Cherokee were forced off their lands in Georgia, Tennessee and Alabama. The novel begins with Man Who Walks the Mountain Tops, or Ridge Walker, as a young man, and follows him to his death at the hands of Ross's men in Indian Territory sixty years later. The education of Ridge's son John back east, his efforts to deal with the politicians in Washington, his friendship with John Ross, and finally his decision to sign the Treaty of New Echota that essentially seals his death warrant, are all covered in detail. Each character is fully developed, the historical events are well described and documented, and the reader is even given the perspectives in asides from other characters, such as Andrew Jackson. Major Ridge was a complex man and his decisions and political stands frequently had to change to reflect the reality of the situation facing the Cherokee. Some would say that John Ross's refusal to admit the Cherokee had lost their land to the Georgians caused the hardships of the Trail of Tears because the people were lulled into thinking they would never have to move West. The Ridges and Waties had recognized the inevitable and moved West earlier on their own terms, bringing their goods and livestock, without losing a single person. Once all the dispossessed families are in the Western Cherokee lands, the feuds continue, with multiple murders between the Ridge and the Ross parties. The feud continues today in many Cherokee hearts. This historical novel is highly recommended as an excellent source on the causes and events of the Cherokee Removal. The political nature of John Ross as he wrests power away from the Ridges is enlightening. The asides from Andrew Jackson show a man fully aware of what he is doing, but giving his own reasons why he felt right in doing so. Many books have been written on the Trail of Tears and years following, so this novel is a tremendous addition to the literature on all that led up to those events. Another excellent historical depiction of these trying times of the Cherokee Removal is Bolton's *Nancy Swimmer*.

351. Wilson, Tom. *Black Wolf.* NY: Signet. 1995. 440 p.

Time: Contemporary
Tribe: Blackfeet
Place: Montana, Washington, D.C.

Abraham Lincoln, "Link" Anderson is a retired Gulf War veteran working in a ski area in Montana. He meets Marie LeBecque, a Blackfeet woman, who introduces him to his past. Adopted as a small child, Link has dreams of "grandfather" and a role he is supposed to fulfill. A crazy woman wandering in Peshan, a deserted town on the Piegan reservation, is really Bright Flame, his mother. Link also has two half-brothers, Charlie "Little Crow" and Ghost. These brothers have become international terrorists, fighting back against the White Man and looking for revenge for the Treaty of 1855, the treaty that was a lie. Ghost and Charlie are counseled by the Bull Clan

Elders, a cult of militant Blackfeet. Link is finally convinced by dreams of Black Wolf, a Piegan medicine man and his grandfather helper, and by federal agents to try and stop his brothers. Link goes through the painful *Okan*, Sun Dance ceremony, and then goes on a Vision Quest, monitored by Dr. White Calf, Marie's uncle. Gradually he begins to accept and believe in his Blackfeet heritage and his mission to stop his criminal brothers. Ghost and Charlie come to Montana, kidnap Marie, and plan on a final attack against the U.S. Congress. Link finds their cabin, Charlie and Ghost wind up dead, and the final bombing plot is thwarted. While this is a fairly typical suspense novel, the Blackfeet history and ceremonies are accurate.

352. Wind, Ruth. (copyright held by Barbara Samuel) *Rainsinger.* NY: Silhouette. 1996. 248 p.

Time: Contemporary
Tribe: Navajo
Place: New Mexico

Half-Navajo Daniel Lynch has found the "Lost Orchard" of his ancestors, the only remaining peach trees to escape the destruction by the White soldiers. Apparently abandoned, Daniel has paid the last two years' back taxes and begun work on restoring the trees. In one more year it will be his. Winona Snow has inherited the land from her uncle but was out of the country in the Peace Corps when he died. She pays the current year's taxes and both are stunned to learn that the other feels the land is theirs. Since neither can afford to buy the other out, they grudgingly agree to share the house for a few months. Winona's young sister Joleen is suffering from the death of their parents in an automobile accident and needs the time to recover. Winona spent her childhood summers on the land and feels more than a legal ownership. Daniel feels it is part of his family's and his tribal heritage and should belong to him. Although they fall in love, they cannot acknowledge it to themselves or to each other, each feeling that possibly the driving motive is the ownership of the land. While this is a romance, the historical theme of the "Lost Orchard" makes it interesting. And it's very refreshing to find a romance heroine who is not only tall and strong but who can beat a man in basketball!

353. Wisler, G. Clifton. *Massacre at Powder River.* NY: Berkley. 1997. 259 p.

Time: 1860's
Tribe: Cheyenne, Sioux
Place: Northern Plains, Montana, Wyoming

Wolf Running has been married for ten years and has three sons when Red Cloud's War breaks out to stop the Bozeman Trail through prime buffalo hunting country. Wolf Running's brother-friend Stands Long Beside Him accompanies him on his numerous raids on the Army's pack trains and forts. Crazy Horse, Wolf Running's cousin, has become an effective leader of decoy raids. Wolf Running has taken up the warrior's road since the massacre at Sand Creek, but he is appalled by the mutilations which other Cheyenne perform on dead White men's bodies. He tries to get the young men to realize what they are doing is poisoning their own souls. Wolf Running still has powerful visions in his dreams and can foresee events. He foresees the little swaggering soldier, Captain Fetterman, lying dead in the snow, surrounded by his massacred soldiers. The Army and U.S. Government finally coerce the chiefs to come in and sign a new treaty at Fort Laramie, giving them back their lands and removing the troops. Red Cloud burns the forts and retires to a reservation, at peace. But Crazy Horse is not satisfied and fights on. This third in the series by Wisler is the most repetitive with endless skirmishes, battles, raids, and killings. It is, however, historically accurate in the account of Red Cloud's War and the Fetterman Massacre.

354. Wisler, G. Clifton. *The Medicine Trail. Dreaming Wolf.* NY: Zebra Books. 1992. 350 p.

Time: 1840's
Tribe: Cheyenne
Place: Northern Plains

Dreaming Wolf and his cousin Stone Lance are the young relatives of the Cheyenne Arrow Keeper, Stone Wolf, the man responsible for carrying the sacred arrows into battle and renewing them when they become tainted. Talking Stick is an angry Cheyenne warrior, more intent on killing the White settlers trying to cross the Plains than in hunting buffalo to prepare for winter. Gradually tribal politics demand that old Stone Wolf give up the sacred arrows to Talking Stick. Dreaming Wolf and Stone Lance are only in their teens, but swear to watch over the arrows while they are in Talking Stick's hands. Talking Stick and his followers bring cholera to the camp by robbing White graves. Stick also leads bands of warriors on disastrous raid after raid on the White wagon trains, losing many young men. Finally Talking Stick is killed in battle and Dreaming Wolf rescues the sacred arrows. With this brave deed to his credit, Dreaming Wolf is allowed to marry Singing Doe. The importance of the sacred arrows to the Cheyenne and the role of the Arrow Keeper in the tribe's life and ceremonies is well portrayed in what is otherwise a standard western.

355. Wisler, G. Clifton. *Warrior's Road.* NY: Berkley. 1994. 266 p.

Time: 1850–1860
Tribe: Cheyenne
Place: Northern and Southern Plains

When he is a young boy, Raven Feather saves the life of Walker Logan, the son of traders moving out west. As a man renamed Wolf Running, he again saves Walker's life at Fort Laramie. Wolf Running has dreams of prophecy in which future events are shown to him by the Snow Wolf. Wolf Running endures the New Life Lodge Ceremony, similar to the Sioux Sun Dance, and achieves great honors and wisdom as he matures through his teenage years. Wolf Running frequently rides with his Sioux cousin Curly, later to be more well known as Crazy Horse. The thorn in Wolf Running's side is Corn Dancer, another Cheyenne warrior about his age who is totally lacking in judgment. Time and again young men are killed by following Corn Dancer's lead. Corn Dancer breaks the peace made by the Cheyenne and enrages the Army. Traders are told not to sell any powder or lead to the Sioux or Cheyenne for their guns. Desperately in need of these things, Wolf Running and Curly go to the Logans, now running a trading post at Fort Laramie, and succeed in purchasing the powder and lead from Walker. After a successful pony raid against the Pawnee, their hated enemy, Wolf Running marries Sun Walker Maiden. By the age of eighteen, Wolf Running has already led a full life, but clearly has many more battles ahead of him. Wisler writes very well from the Native American perspective and gives all his characters fully developed personalities. He includes the details of Cheyenne ceremonies and his text contains many native Cheyenne words.

Reviewed in: Kliatt 9/94.

356. Wisler, G. Clifton. *The Weeping Moon.* NY: Jove. 1995. 311 p.

Time: 1850's
Tribe: Cheyenne
Place: Southern Plains

As a small boy, Buffalo Horn loses some of his toes in a steel trap, but is rescued by Black Kettle, who kills the trappers. Buffalo Horn's anger and hatred live on due to his crippling injury. Buffalo Horn is a dreamer who can see future events and can assist the Cheyenne in their hunting, as well as warn them of the coming of the Bluecoats. He wishes to marry Bright Swallow, but she insists he find his true self and calm his soul before she will agree. Buffalo Horn goes to live near White men, befriends Isaac Guthrie, a Kansas trapper half-breed who most believe is White. Guthrie is not accepted by the tribe, but tries to help them. Buffalo Horn learns English and goes with Black Kettle and other chiefs to Denver to talk peace with Governor Evans, to no avail. Told where to camp on Sand Creek, they do so. Buffalo Horn sees a vision of the coming massacre but is helpless to prevent it. Instead he is directly involved in it, nearly dying until Guthrie saves his life. The Medicine Lodge Treaty gives the Cheyenne their own lands and for a short time they are at peace, until renegade young Cheyenne men break it. Bright Swallow has married Buffalo Horn, who now dreams of another attack on their camp. Once again the Cheyenne are attacked in the Battle of the Washita, and their peace chief, Black Kettle killed. Buffalo Horn and his friend Otter and their families join a band of Arapaho and move on.

357. Womack, Craig S. (Muscogee/Cherokee). *Drowning in Fire.* Tucson: University of Arizona Press. 2001. 294 p.

Time: 1970's–1990's
Tribe: Creek
Place: Oklahoma

Sun Tracks, v. 48. An American Indian Literary Series.

Josh Henneha is caught between several worlds: gay and straight, Creek and White. As a young boy, he doesn't fit anywhere and lives mostly in his mind, sending thought messages to athlete Jimmy Alexander who is the only one of the town boys to befriend him. He imagines a physical closeness with Jimmy but when Jimmy turns out to be gay as well, Josh is repulsed by his overtures. Only as a grown man, meeting Jimmy again after twenty years, can Josh begin to understand his own nature. Josh's Creek heritage is harder to grasp for his parents have tried hard to assimilate into the White society. Through the tales of his grandfather and his great-aunt Lucille (the most engaging character in the novel), Josh understands how this all fits together as well. Womack has written a memorable coming-of-age story which deserves wide readership.

Reviewed in: Library Journal 10/15/01; Multicultural Review 3/02.

358. Wood, Barbara. *Sacred Ground.* NY: St. Martin's. 2001. 340 p.

Time: 1 A.D., 1542, 1775, 1792, 1830 and Present.
Tribe: Topaa (Gabrielino)
Place: Southern California

When First Mother comes to the seacoast from farther east, bringing her children and marrying into local tribes, she establishes a sacred cave and fills it with paintings. Later she is buried there and her descendents, all named Marimi as she was, are required to tend and protect the site. Each sacred woman is chosen because of her severe headaches which cause trances and visions. This genetic affliction is passed down through the generations and the story follows individuals. In 1542 the Marimi marries a Spanish man, who has been washed ashore from Juan Cabrillo's ships. In 1775 the Marimi, called Teresa at the Mission, has a child by a Francisian monk, Brother Felipe. In 1792, Angela, who has lost touch with her role as Guardian of the Cave, has a vision and names her daughter Marina. Marina and her cousin Angelique both have the headaches and visions they do not understand. Years later, an earthquake opens the cave, and archaeologist Erica Tyler finds the burial site of the First Mother. Bitter battles between homeowners and Native American rights groups over the cave site culminate in discovering who the orphan Erica is related to and her relationship to the tribe, called "Topaa" by themselves, but Gabrielinos by the Spanish. Well written and full of suspense, the novel includes a great deal of the history of the California tribes and their relationship to the Spanish and the gold miners.

Reviewed in: Booklist 10/1/01; Publishers Weekly 7/30/01; Kirkus Reviews 7/15/01.

359. Woodruff, Joan Leslie. (Shawnee/Cherokee). *Neighbors.* Berkeley: Third Woman Press. 1993. 154 p.

Time: Contemporary
Tribe: Zuni
Place: New Mexico

Dana Whitehawk leaves Los Angeles and heads east. She buys a house in the hills of New Mexico and Sam, the man who sold it, hopes she will like her neighbors. Since Dana's house sits on forty acres of land, she doesn't think she has neighbors nearby. But the house is clean and warm when she arrives and someone has left her a gift of eggs. Gradually she begins to know Kopeki who loves television and coffee; young Ben who brings the eggs and wants a horse; and Nakani who grumbles and complains and teaches Dana the traditional way of making pottery. Slowly Dana comes to realize that these people are ghost neighbors, she follows them to the ruined pueblo and sees them return to the underworld. Although they are not alive in the usual sense, they are alive in terms of personality, of caring and helping. Of mixed Choctaw ancestry herself, Dana finds peace in her house and with her neighbors. This is a lovely novel in which nothing much happens and much is revealed both to Dana and to the reader.

360. Wooley, Marilyn. *Jackpot Justice.* NY: Thomas Dunne Books. 2000. 311 p.

Time: Contemporary
Tribe: Modoc
Place: Northern California

Homer Johnson is a confused young Modoc, rejecting his heritage after his mother was killed by a drunk driver. His grandmother Winema raised Homer and tried to instill the tribal culture but without success. Now he is trying to join a White supremacist organization, the White People's Brigade, prejudiced men really only interested in Homer's trust fund. When Anerd Wood, a member of the WPB, is murdered, Homer is set-up for the crime. Cassandra Ringwald, a forensic psychologist, is called in to evaluate Homer before his trial. She finds a sweet boy trying to save Anerd's daughter Sally from the evil designs of her father. Mavis Wood, the wife and mother, appears initially to be a meek, beaten woman, but in fact is the one in total control of the situation. Cassie tries to prove Homer's innocence with the help of Tony, the cop next door, and Peck, the defense attorney. Ultimately the truth is exposed. Unfortunately Cassie is far more concerned with how attractive she is to Tony and Peck and even members of the WPB than she is interested in Homer's case. An unusual perspective, an American Indian attempting to seek his identity with White supremacists, is instead turned into a "girl-flirts-with-boy" plot.

Reviewed in: Publishers Weekly 4/3/00; Library Journal 3/1/00; Kirkus Reviews 2/15/00.

361. Wright, Sue Owens. *Howling Bloody Murder.* Vancouver, WA: Deadly Alibi Press. 2001. 181 p.

Time: Contemporary
Tribe: Washoe
Place: California

Subtitled "A Beanie and Cruiser Mystery," this slight volume is certainly more of a dog lover's story than a Native American one. Journalist Elsie MacBean "Beanie," who is part Washoe, lives happily in the Lake Tahoe area with her Basset Hound Cruiser, doing some freelance work and deploring the constant development which is ruining the land. When her daughter Nona arrives for Thanksgiving with her latest boyfriend who is heavily involved in the development of Cave Rock, a sacred place to the Washoe, more than fur will fly. There have already been a few murders, victims found with their throats ripped out and terror on their faces. Do these murders involve tribal politics as the Washoe try and stop the development or is the Native American element a smokescreen for financial problems? Deputy Sheriff Skip Cassidy also has troubles with his boss who's running for mayor. While the setting is pleasant, the characters don't grab one's attention and the Native American aspect is slight.

Reviewed in: Publishers Weekly 5/14/01.

362. Young, Scott. *Murder in a Cold Climate.* NY: Viking. 1988. 240 p.

Time: Contemporary
Tribe: Inuit
Place: Yukon Territory

Mountie Matteesie Kitologitak has been assigned to Northern Affairs, where he attends conferences instead of doing police work. His former boss asks him to investigate the disappearance of a small plane and its three occupants. When Morton Cavendish is murdered while he is being transported to the hospital in Edmonton in front of Matteesie, he knows he has to become involved, even if it means missing the conference in Leningrad. No one seems to know what happened to the plane or where Cavendish's son William is. Even if William were involved in drugs, would he have ordered his father's murder? By plane, snowmobile and dog team, Matteesie penetrates deeper into the frozen Arctic wilderness and deeper into the murder plot. Young gives the reader an excellent sense of place and shows the White and Inuit cultures as they live and work together.

Reviewed in: Booklist 9/1/89; Library Journal 9/1/89; Publishers Weekly 8/18/89.

363. Young, Scott. *The Shaman's Knife.* NY: Viking. 1993. 276 p.

Time: Contemporary
Tribe: Inuit
Place: Northern Canada

Matteesie Kitologitak, a RCMP inspector, flies to Sanirarsipaaq to investigate the murders of a young man and his grandmother. Another old woman has also been injured, Matteesie's own mother, who subsequently dies of her injuries and who was not able to identify her assailant. Matteesie must use modern detective methods, forensic science, and his knowledge of tribal ways to solve this crime. The sense of place is very well defined; one becomes chilled just reading about it. Matteesie is a likable detective, well anchored in both the contemporary White and the native worlds.

Reviewed in: Armchair Detective Fall/94; Booklist 5/15/93; NYTBR 5/16/93; Publishers Weekly 3/15/93.

364. Zimmer, Kay. *Bear Dance.* Redmond, WA: Goodfellow Press. 1994. 391 p.

Time: Contemporary
Tribe: Ute
Place: Colorado

Librarian Susannah O'Brien and Sheriff Daniel Jordan are made for each other, but they have a lot to work through before they can both accept that fact. Daniel is a Ute Indian, raising his eleven-year-old son Andy. His first marriage to an "outsider" failed and he feels Susannah will also tire of him and return to her privileged way of life. Susannah has an instinctive fear of men since she was abused by her stepfather, she abhors the violence in Daniel's profession, and feels he will leave her for a woman who can raise his son in traditional tribal ways. In trying to track down drug runners in the southwestern Colorado town, Daniel appears to have taken bribes. He cannot tell Susannah the truth and she flees to Denver. After Daniel allows himself to acknowledge what Susannah means to him, he comes for her, telling a story of Yellow Woman which she understands. Although this is a romance, the characters are fully developed, they actually work at their professions, and the situation they find themselves in is realistic. This is Zimmer's first novel, published by a regional press. It is hoped her work can gain a wider audience.

Novels Not Included

The following novels have not been included for one or more of the following reasons: they are not written from a Native American perspective, although they may contain Native American characters; they are poorly written, extremely difficult to read, or contain glaring inaccuracies; they are written for juveniles; or copies could not be obtained for our review. This list also contains titles whose literary format is not that of the novel.

Adams, Joyce. *Apache Pride*. NY: Zebra. 1999.
Aguilar, Paula. *Antiphon*. Nashville: Winston-Derek. 1992.
Aiken, Ginny. *Love Evergreen*. NY: Jove. 1993.
Archer, Jane. *Out of the West*. NY: Pocket. 1996.
Ariss, Bruce. *Full Circle*. NY: Avalon. 1963.
Armstrong, Jeannette C. *Slash*. Penticton, Canada: Theytus Books. 1985.
——. *Whispering in Shadows*. Penticton, Canada: Theytus. 2002.
Askew, Rita. *Mercy Seat*. NY: Penguin. 1997.
Aston, James. *Turquoise Talisman*. Hyrum, UT: Aston. 1996.
Baker, Madeline. *Apache Runaway*. NY: Leisure. 1995.
——. *Chase the Wind*. NY: Leisure. 1997.
——. *Cheyenne Surrender*. NY: Leisure. 1994.
——. *Feather in the Wind*. NY: Leisure. 1997.
——. *Hawk's Woman*. NY: Topaz. 1998.
——. *Love Forevermore*. NY: Leisure. 1997.
——. *Love in the Wind*. NY: Leisure. 1997.
——. *Midnight Fire*. NY: Leisure. 1992.
——. *Reckless Love*. NY: Leisure. 1995.
——. *Spirit Path*. NY: Leisure. 1993.
——. *Under a Prairie Moon*. NY: Leisure. 1998.
——. *Warrior's Lady*. NY: Leisure. 1993.

——. *A Whisper in the Wind*. NY: Leisure. 1993.
Baltz, Wayne. *Night of the Falling Stars*. Ft. Collins, CO: Prairie Divide. 1995.
Ballas, Jack. *Montana Breed*. NY: Jove. 1994.
Barreiro, Jose. *The Indian Chronicles*. Houston: Arte Publico. 1993.
Beckhard, Arthur J. *Black Hawk*. NY: Simon & Schuster. 1957.
Bennett, Constance. *Blossom*. NY: Diamond. 1991.
——. *Moonsong*. NY: Diamond. 1992.
Benson, Arnold. *A Count of Many Winters*. Scenic, SD: JH Production. 1992.
Berdine, William. *My Granddaddy was a Ramblin' Man*. Princeton, WV: Berdine. 1997.
Bittner, Rosanne. *Chase the Sun*. NY: Bantam. 1995.
——. *Comanche Sunset*. NY: Kensington. 1995.
——. *Unforgettable*. NY: Kensington. 1993.
——. *Tame the Wild Wind*. NY: Bantam. 1996.
Black, Michelle. *Solomon Spring*. NY: Forge. 2002.
Blakely, Mike. *Moon Medicine*. NY: Forge. 2001.
Bonander, Jane. *Heat of a Savage Moon*. NY: St. Martin's.
——. *Forbidden Moon*. NY: St. Martin's. 1993.
——. *Wild Heart*. NY: Simon & Schuster. 1995.
Bowen, Judith. *High Country Rancher*. NY: Silhouette. 1993.
Bowen, Peter. *Kelly & The 3-toed Horse*. NY: St. Martin's. 2001.
Boyle, Patten L. *Screaming Hawk; The Training of a Mystic Warrior*. NY: Station Hill Press. 1994.
Brackett, Leigh. *Follow the Free Wind*. NY: Doubleday. 1963.
Brand, John. *The Legend of Johnny Cloud*. London: Hale. 1998.
Brand, Max. *War Party*. NY: Dodd, Mead. 1934.
——. *Frontier Feud*. NY: Dodd, Mead. 1935.
——. *Cheyenne Gold*. NY: Dodd, Mead. 1935.
——. *Mountain Guns*. NY: Dodd, Mead. 1985.
Braun, Matthew. *Black Fox*. NY: St. Martin's. 1994.
Brick, John. *The Raid*. NY: Duell, Sloan & Pearce. 1951.
Bridges, Carol. *Secrets Shared in Ecstasy*. Nashville, IN: Earth Nation. 1991.
Brooks, Betty. *Comanche Passion*. NY: Zebra. 1992.
——. *Comanche Sunset*. NY: Kensington. 1998.
Brown, Sandra. *Hawk O'Toole's Hostage*. NY: Bantam. 1997.
Brown, Virginia. *Comanche Moon*. NY: Zebra. 1993.
Browner, Jesse. *Turnaway*. NY: Villard. 1996.
Browning, Sinclair. *The Last Song Dogs*. NY: Bantam. 1999.
Bryers, Paul. *Prayer of the Bone*. NY: Bloomsbury. 1998.
Bucheister, Pat. *Tame a Wildcat*. NY: Bantam. 1993.
Burleson, Frank. *Devil Dance*. NY: Penguin. 1997.
Camp, Deborah. *Cheyenne's Shadow*. NY: Avon. 1994.
——. *Lonewolf's Woman*. NY: Avon. 1995.
Camp, Will. *Comanche Trail*. NY: Harper. 1998.

Campbell, Thomas. *Oconee Dream Catcher*. Greensboro, GA: Emory. 1996.
Cantrell, Raine. *Desert Sunrise*. NY: Diamond. 1992.
Carey, Suzanne. *Bride Price*. NY: Silhouette. 1997.
Carter, Franklin. *Wyoming Testimony*. NY: Jove. 1994.
Champlin, Tim. *The Last Campaign*. Thorndike, ME: Five Star Western. 1996.
Charyn, Jerome. *Montezuma's Man*. NY: Mysterious. 1993.
Chase, Debra. *Child Crying Rock*. Falls Church, VA: Writers Club. 1999.
Cheshire, Gifford. *Stronghold*. Bath: Chivers. 1998.
Christiansen, Nancy. *Deadly Deep*. NY: Kensington. 1994.
Christopher, Amy. *Captive Kiss*. NY: Kensington. 1992.
Clayton, Paul. *Calling Crow National*. NY: Berkley. 1997.
Cockrell, Amanda. *The Deer Dancers*. 3 vols. NY: Avon. 1995-1996.
Coffman, Elaine. *Angel in Marble*. NY: Fawcett. 1991.
Coldsmith, Don. *Runestone*. NY: Bantam. 1995.
Combs, Harry. *Legend of the Painted Horse*. Accord, MA: Wheeler. 1996.
Compton, Katherine. *The Lady and the Outlaw*. NY: Avon. 1994.
Conley, Robert. *Incident at Buffalo Crossing*. NY: Leisure. 1998.
Conn, Phoebe. *Beloved*. NY: Kensington. 1994.
Cooper, Jamie Lee. *The Horn and the Forest*. Indianapolis: Bobbs-Merrill. 1963.
Cranford, Jack. *Sakeema*. Baltimore: American Literary Press. 1994.
Crews, Will. *Bones in Indian Country*. Tucker, GA: Chaps of Waleska. 1999.
Cutler, Bruce. *The Massacre at Sand Creek*. Norman: University Of Oklahoma Press. 1995.
Dailey, Janet. *The Proud and the Free*. NY: Little, Brown. 1994.
——. *Legacies*. NY: Little, Brown. 1995.
Dann, Jack. *Counting Coup*. NY: Forge. 2000.
Davidson, Sandra. *One Shining Moment*. NY: Kensington. 1995.
Dawkins, Cecil. *The Santa Fe Rembrandt*. NY: Ivy Books. 1993.
DeCourt, Ann. *Forbidden Love*. San Diego: Wabokat. 1998.
Dee, Kit. *Destiny's Warrior*. NY: Avon. 1997.
——. *Brit's Lady*. NY: Avon. 2000.
Deitz, Tom. *Stoneskin's Revenge*. NY: Avon. 1991.
Dellin, Geriell. *Comanche Flame*. NY: Avon. 1994.
——. *After the Thunder*. NY: Avon. 1998.
Donovan, Sandra. *Silver Seduction*. NY: Kensington. 1993.
Dorsey, Christine. *My Savage Heart*. NY: Kensington. 1994.
Drake, Shannon. *No Other Man*. NY: Avon. 1995.
Drymon, Kathleen. *Precious Amber*. NY: Kensington. 1996.
——. *Savage Heaven*. NY: Kensington. 1995.
——. *Warrior of the Sun*. NY: Kensington. 1992.
——. *Legend of Desire*. NY: Kensington. 1998.
Dunham, Tracy. *Train to Medicine Lodge*. NY: Avalon. 1994.
——. *Trail of Mythmaker*. NY: Avalon. 1995.
——. *Long Trail Home*. NY: Avalon. 1996.

——. *Ghost Trail.* NY: Avalon. 1997.
——. *Changing Trail.* NY: Avalon. 1998.
——. *Eureka Trail.* NY: Avalon. 1999.
Dyson, John. *Black Marshall.* London: Hale. 1996.
Eagle, Kathleen. *Fire and Rain.* NY: Avon. 1994.
——. *The Last Good Man.* NY: Morrow. 2000.
——. *The Night Remembers.* NY: Avon. 1997.
Edwards, Cassie. *Savage Pride.* NY: Leisure. 1995.
——. *Whitefire.* NY: Penguin. 1997.
Edwards, Hank. *Gray Warrior.* NY: Harper. 1995.
Edwards, Margaret. *Koom of the Tillamooks.* Portland, OR: Binford & Mort. 1996.
Eidson, Tom. *St. Agnes Stand.* NY: Putnam. 1994.
Elliott, Neel. *Eagle Dancer.* Birmingham, AL: Red Mountain. 1996.
Ellison, Suzanne. *Arrowpoint.* Toronto: Harlequin. 1992.
Englade, Ken. *Battle Cry.* NY: Harper. 1997.
Erdrich, Louise. *Tales of Burning Love.* NY: Holt. 1988.
Esely, Joyce. *Shining Star.* Unionville, NY: Royal Fireworks Press. 1995.
Evano, D. Charles. *Spirit Messenger.* Phoenix: Larkspur. 1995.
Faulkner, Colleen. *Fire Dance.* NY: Kensington. 1997.
——. *Captive.* NY: Kensington. 1994.
——. *Forever His.* NY: Zebra. 1993.
——. *Savage Surrender.* NY: Kensington. 1992.
Feagans, Carolyn. *In the Shadow of the Blue Ridge.* Lynchburg, VA: Warwick House. 1998.
Ferjutz, Kelly. *Secret Shores.* NY: Berkley. 1993.
——. *Windsong.* NY: Jove. 1994.
Ferrell, Olivia. *Secret Captive.* NY: Jove. 1993.
Finch, Carol. *Apache Knight.* NY: Kensington. 1994.
——. *Apache Wind.* NY: Zebra. 1993.
——. *Comanche Promise.* NY: Kensington. 1998.
Fitch, Ruth. *Heelstring Nation.* Independence, MO: International University Press. 1992.
Fontes, Montserrat. *Dreams of the Centaur.* NY: Norton. 1996.
Forrest, Pamela. *Renegade.* NY: Kensington. 1996.
Forster, Suzanne. *Night of the Panther.* NY: Bantam. 1992.
Fox, Kathryn. *Raven's Bride.* NY: Zebra. 2000.
——. *Bright Morning Star.* NY: Kensington. 1998.
Fox, Norman A. *Rope the Wind.* NY: Dodd, Mead. 1958.
Fox, Robert. *To Be a Warrior.* Santa Fe: Sunstone. 1997.
French, Judith. *Fire Hawk's Bride.* NY: Avon. 1997.
——. *Moon Dancer.* NY: Avon. 1992.
——. *This Fierce Loving.* NY: Avon. 1994.
French, Linda. *Talking Rain.* NY: Avon. 1998.
Gangi, Rayna. *Mary Jemison.* Santa Fe: Clear Light. 1996.

Garaway, Martin. *The Theft of the Anasazi Pots*. Tucson: Old Hogan. 1999.
Gentry, Georgina. *Eternal Outlaw*. NY: Kensington. 1999.
——. *Timeless Warrior*. NY: Kensington. 1996.
Gear, Kathleen O'Neal. *This Widowed Land*. NY: Tor. 1994.
Gear, Kathleen O'Neal, & Michael Gear. *People of the Lakes*. NY: Forge. 1994.
Gearhart, Sharon. *Seasons of the Enemies*. Chicago: Adams. 1993.
Gibbons, Reginald. *Sweetbitter.* Seattle: Broken Moon Press. 1994.
Gideon, Robin. *Loving Samantha.* NY: Kensington. 1996.
Gilfillian, Merrill. *Grasshopper Falls*. Brooklyn, NY: Hanging Loose Press. 2000.
Glancy, Diane. *Fuller Man.* Wakefield, RI: Moyer Bell. 2000.
——. *Monkey Secret*. Evanston, IL: TriQuarterly Books. 1995.
——. *The Man Who Heard the Land*. St. Paul, MN: Minnesota Historical Society. 2001.
Gorman, Edward. *Hawk Moon.* NY: St. Martin's. 1996.
Gottesfeld, Gary. *Tribal Shadows*. NY: Fawcett. 1994.
Graham, Heather. *Captive.* NY: Penguin. 1996.
——. *Runaway*. NY: Dell. 1995.
——. *Surrender*. NY: Penguin. 1998.
Gregg, Elizabeth. *Trail to Forever.* NY: Penguin. 1997.
Gregson, Frank. *The Man Who Killed Frank Slater.* London: Hale. 1997.
Griffith, Roslynn. *Shadows in the Mirror*. NY: Harper. 1995.
Hagan, Patricia. *Say You Love Me*. NY: Harper. 1995.
——. *Simply Heaven*. NY: Harper. 1995.
Hale, Janet Campbell. *Women on the Run*. Moscow: University of Idaho Press. 1999.
Hamilton, Donovan. *We Are Not Gathered Here Alone*. Tulsa: Champlin Pub. 1996.
Hanchar, Peggy. *Cheyenne Dreams*. NY: Fawcett. 1993.
——. *Swan Necklace*. NY: Fawcett. 1995.
——. *Wild Sage*. NY: Ballantine. 1994.
——. *Where Eagles Soar*. NY: Fawcett. 1992.
Harper, Karen. *River of Sky*. NY: Delacorte. 1994.
Harrington, Kathleen. *Dream Catcher*. NY: Avon 1996.
——. *Fly with the Eagle*. NY: Avon. 1997.
——. *Warrior Dreams.* NY: Avon. 1992.
Harrison, Jim. *The Road Home*. NY: Atlantic Monthly Press. 1999.
Hart, Catherine. *Charmed*. NY: Kensington. 1996.
——. *Summer Storm*. NY: Leisure. 1997.
Harte, Holly. *Texas Silver*. NY: Kensington. 1997.
Hassler, Jon. *Jemmy.* NY: Atheneum. 1980.
Hathaway, Robin. *The Doctor Digs a Grave.* NY: St. Martin's. 1998.
Hausman, Gerald. *Coyote Bead*. Charlottesville, VA: Hampton Roads. 1999.
——. *Tunkashila*. NY: St. Martin's. 1993.
Heisel, Edward. *Crazy Horse, the Boy*. Sun Lakes, AZ: Southwest. 1993.
Henke, Shirl. *White Apache's Woman*. NY: Leisure. 1993.
——. *Endless Sky*. NY: St Martin's. 1998.

——. *Fire in the Blood*. NY: Leisure. 1994.
——. *Night Wind's Woman*. NY: Leisure. 1993.
——. *Sundancer*. NY: St. Martin's. 1999.
Hirt, Douglas. *Brandish*. NY: Leisure. 1997.
Home, Montgomery. *Winterhawk, Winterhawk*. [n.p.] Spectrum. 1998.
Horsley, Kate. *Crazy Woman*. NY: Ivy. 1992.
Hudson, Janis. *Apache Legacy*. NY: Kensington. 1995.
——. *Apache Magic*. NY: Kensington. 1991.
——. *Long Way Home*. NY: Kensington. 2001.
——. *Apache Promise*. NY: Kensington. 1994.
——. *Hawk's Woman*. NY: Kensington. 1998.
——. *Warrior's Song*. NY: Kensington. 1997.
——. *Apache Heartsong*. NY: Kensington. 1995.
Humphreys, Josephine. *Nowhere Else on Earth*. NY: Viking. 2000.
Ihle, Sharon. *The Bride Wore Spurs*. NY: Harper. 1995.
Ingram, Hunter. *Fort Apache*. NY: Ballantine. 1975.
Ipellie, Alootook. *Arctic Dreams and Nightmares*. Penticton, Canada: Theytus. 1993.
Irgang, Frank. *The Wyandotte*. Nashville: Winston. 1997.
James, Deborah. *Beloved Warrior*. NY: Berkley. 1993.
Johnson, Charles Blake. *The Last Beloved Woman*. Townsend, TN: American Trail Books. 1994.
Johnson, Janice. *Winter of the Raven*. NY: Tor. 2000.
Johnston, Basil H. *Crazy Dave*. Toronto: Key Porter Books. 1999.
Jordan, Nicole. *The Savage*. NY: Avon. 1994.
Joseph, James. *Shadow of the Serpent*. Brunswick, ME: Audenreed. 1997.
Joynes, St. Leger. *Dead Water Rites*. Charlottesville, VA: Hampton Roads. 2000.
——. *Naked into the Night*. Charlottesville, VA: Hampton Roads. 1996.
Kay, Karen. *Night Thunder's Bride.* NY: Avon. 1999.
——. *Grey-Hawk's Lady.* NY: Avon. 1997.
——. *Lakota Princess.* NY: Avon. 1995.
——. *Lakota Surrender*. NY: Avon. 1994.
——. *Proud Wolf's Woman.* NY: Avon. 1996.
——. *White Eagle's Touch*. NY: Avon. 1998.
Keim, Charles. *Little Coyote*. Missoula, MT: Shining Mountains. 1996.
Kellerman, Faye. *Moon Music.* Rockland, MA: Wheeler. 1998.
Key, Samuel. *From a Whisper to a Scream.* NY: Berkley. 1992.
Kilgore, Katherine. *Tame the Wind*. NY: Harper. 1993.
Kincaid, Katharine. *Ride the Wind*. NY: Kensington. 1995.
Kinsella, W. P. *Born Indian*. Ottawa: Oberon Press. 1981.
Kirk, Charles. *Messin Man*. Raleigh, NC: Pentland. 1997.
Kraft, Louis. *The Final Showdown*. NY: Walker. 1992.
Krupat, Arnold. *Woodsmen*. NY: Letter Press. 1979.
Larson, Walt. *From the Wilderness*. Port St. Jo, FL: Karmichael Press. 1996.
Lee, Bernice. *Murder without Reservation.* Toronto: Worldwide. 1991.

Lee, Linda. *Texas Angel*. NY: Berkley. 1994.
Lee, Rachel. *Destination: Conrad County*. NY: Silhouette. 1999.
Legg, John. *Blackfoot Dawn*. NY: Berkley. 1993.
——. *Blood at Ft. Bridger*. NY: St. Martin's. 1995.
——. *Flintlock Trail*. NY: Harper. 1997.
——. *Frontiersman*. NY: Harper. 1995.
——. *Treaty at Ft. Laramie*. NY: St. Martin's. 1994.
Leigh, Catherine. *Rebel without a Bride*. Toronto: Harlequin. 1997.
Leppart, Jerry. *Headwaters*. Lakeville, MN: Galde. 1998.
Letts, Billie. *The Honk and Holler Opening Soon.* NY: Warner Books. 1995.
Longbow, Curt. *Warbuck*. London: Hale. 1999.
Lustbader, Eric. *Black Blade*. NY: Fawcett. 1993.
MacDonald, Elisabeth. *Bring Down the Sun*. NY: Avon. 1996.
Mack, Budd. *Undaunted Spirits*. NY: Carlton Press. 1994.
Manara, Milo, and Hugo Pratt. *Indian Summer*. NY: NBM. 1995.
Masci, Barbara. *Stolen Heritage*. Old Tappan, NJ: Revell. 1990.
Mason, Connie. *A Promise of Thunder*. NY: Leisure. 1993.
——. *Tears Like Rain*. NY: Leisure. 1994.
McAllister, Lee. *Squaw Dance*. Reno, NV: TJE. 1991.
McCain, Florence. *Visions of Murder*. St. Paul, MN: Llewellyn. 1996.
McCall, Dinah. *Dreamcatcher*. NY: Harper. 1996.
——. *Legend*. NY: Harper. 1998.
——. *Tallchief*. NY: Harper. 1997.
McCarthy, Candace. *Warrior's Caress.* NY: Kensington. 1992.
——. *White Bear's Woman*. NY: Kensington. 1998.
——. *Wild Innocence.* NY: Kensington. 1999.
McCauley, Barbara. *Whitehorn's Woman*. NY: Silhouette. 1993.
McGarrity, Michael. *Tularosa*. NY: Norton. 1996.
McGregor, Sheri. *Dream Catcher*. NY: Zebra. 1999.
McKee, Lynn. *Walks in Stardust*. NY: Diamond. 1994.
Meredith, Marilyn. *Deadly Omen*. Bakersfield, CA: Golden Eagle Press. 1999.
——. *Deadly Trail*. [n.p.] Hard Shell Word Factory. 2002.
——. *Unequally Yoked*. Bakersfield, CA: Golden Eagle Press. 2000.
——. *Intervention*. Bakersfield, CA: Golden Eagle Press. 2002.
Michaels, Kasey. *Promise*. NY: Pocket. 1997.
Mills, Anita. *Comanche Rose*. NY: Penguin. 1996.
——. *Comanche Moon*. NY: Topaz. 1995.
Mills, DiAnn. *Rehoboth*. Ulrichsville, OH: Heartsong. 1998.
Moen, Ruth. *Deadly Deceptions*. Sedro-Woolley, WA: Flying Swan. 1994.
Monfredo, Miriam. *Blackwater Spirits*. NY: St. Martin's. 2002.
Morgan, Mary. *Deeper Waters*. NY: Thomas Dunne. 2002.
Mulcahy, Lucille. *Dark Arrow*. Lincoln: University of Nebraska Press. 1995. c1953.
Munn, Vella. *Daughter of the Mountain.* NY: Tor. 1994.
——. *Navajo Nights*. NY: Silhouette. 1995.

Murphy, Barbara. *Fly Like an Eagle*. NY: Bantam. 1995.
Murray, E. P. *Savage Whisper*. NY: Doherty. 1995.
Nash, Clayton. *Dakota Wolf.* London: Hale. 1997.
Newcombe, Kerry. *Red Ripper*. NY: St. Martin's. 1999.
——. *In the Season of the Sun.* NY: Bantam. 1990.
Niswander, Adam. *Sand Dwellers*. Minneapolis: Fedagan & Bremer, 1998.
Oliver, Chad. *Cannibal Owl*. NY: Bantam. 1994.
Orwig, Sara. *Comanche Passion*. NY: Zebra. 1999.
——. *Comanche Temptation*. NY: Kensington. 1996.
——. *Warrior Moon*. NY: Kensington. 1995.
Owen, Wanda. *Savage Passion*. NY: Kensington. 1993.
Padgett, Abigail. *Child of Silence*. NY: Mysterious. 1993.
——. *Dollmaker's Daughter*. NY: Mysterious. 1997.
Page, Jake. *A Certain Malice*. NY: Ballantine. 1998.
——. *The Deadly Canyon*. NY: Ballantine. 1994.
——. *Operation Shatterhand*. NY: Ballantine. 1996.
Paine, Lauran. *The Running Iron*. Waterville, ME: Thorndike. 2000.
Palmer, Catherine. *Renegade Flame*. NY: Diamond. 1993.
Palmer, Jessica. *Shadow Dance*. NY: Pocket. 1994.
Parker, Trudy Ann. *Big Snow, Little Snow*. Lancaster, NH: Dawnland. 1999.
Parrish, Richard. *Defending the Truth*. NY: Onyx. 1998.
Pate, Albert. *Coree Treasure*. Pikeville, NC: A. Pate. 1995.
Patterson, Roy. *The Way Station*. London: Hale. 1999.
Patton, Oliver B. *My Heart Turns Back*. NY: Popular Library. 1978.
Pelton, Sonya. *Heaven Sent*. NY: Kensington. 1995.
Pesanda, F. J. *Sisters of the Black Moon*. NY: Penguin. 1994.
Powell, Neva. *The Long Crossing*. NY: Avocet. 1998.
Preston, Douglas. *Thunderhead*. NY: Warner. 1999.
Proctor, George. *Walks without a Soul*. NY: Bantam. 1995.
Quirk, Patrick. *When Spirits Touch the Red Path*. Salt Lake City: Northwest. 1993.
Ransom, Candice. *Between Two Worlds*. NY: Scholastic. 1994.
Ransom, Dana. *Dakota Desire*. NY: Kensington. 1992.
——. *Texas Renegade*. NY: Kensington. 1996.
Reavis, Cheryl. *Meggie's Baby*. NY: Silhouette. 1997.
——. *Mother to Be*. NY: Silhouette. 1997.
Red Eagle, Philip H. *Red Earth; a Viet Nam warrior's journey*. Duluth: Holy Cow Press. 1997.
Reed, Robert. *An Exaltation of Larks*. NY: Tor. 1995.
Reynolds, Brad. *Cruel Sanctuary*. NY: Avon. 1999.
——. *Story Knife*. NY: Avon. 1996.
——. *Deadly Harvest*. NY: Avon. 1999.
——. *Pull and Be Damned.* NY: Avon. 1997.
Richardson, Boyd. *Moroni's Camp*. Sandy, UT: Camden Court. 1998.
——. *White Thunder and Kokopelli*. Sandy, UT: Camden Court. 1996.

Riefe, Barbara. *Desperate Crossing*. NY: Doherty. 1997.
Ritz, Deanna. *Yellowbird*. [n.p.] Dorrance. 1997.
Robbins, Judith. *Coyote Woman*. NY: Onyx. 1996.
——. *Sun Priestess*. NY: Onyx. 1998.
——. *Moon Fire*. NY: NAL. 2000.
Robinson, Eden. *Monkey Beach*. Boston: Houghton Mifflin. 2000.
Rogers, Evelyn. *Hot Temper*. NY: Leisure. 1997.
Rollo, Naomi. *Goldy Lark*. Santa Barbara, CA: Fithian. 1992.
Romberg, Nina. *Spirit Stalker*. NY: Pinnacle. 1989.
——. *Shadow Walkers*. NY: Pinnacle. 1993.
Ross, David. *War Cries*. NY: Avon. 1995.
Russell, Sharman. *Last Matriarch*. Albuquerque: University of New Mexico Press. 2000.
Sage, Kathleen. *Many Fires*. NY: Jove. 1995.
Sandifer, Linda. *Embrace the Wind*. NY: Zebra. 1993.
——. *Firelight*. NY: Kensington. 1997.
Sans-te-wa-no-mens. *The Great Pueblo Revolt of 1996*. Santa Fe: Skunk & Melons Press. 1995.
Savage, Les. *Fire Dance at Spider Rock*. Thorndike, ME: Five Star Western. 1995.
Scott, Fela. *Ghost Dancer*. NY: Leisure. 1993.
——. *Spirit of the Mountain*. NY: Leisure. 1997.
Sherman, Jory. *South Platte*. NY: Bantam. 1998.
Shireffs, Gordon D. *Son of the Thunder People*. Philadelphia: Westminster Press. 1957.
Silvey, Diane. *Spirit Quest*. Vancouver: Beach Holme. 1997.
Simpson, Patricia. *Raven in Amber*. NY: Harper. 1993.
——. *Just Before Midnight*. NY: Harper. 1997.
——. *Mystic Moon*. NY: Harper. 1996.
Slipperjack, Ruby. *Honour the Sun*. Winnipeg: Pemmican Pub. 1987.
——. *Silent Words*. Saskatoon: Fifth House. 1992.
Smith, Bobbi. *Dream Warrior*. NY: Zebra. 1993.
——. *Half-breed's Lady*. NY: Leisure. 1998
——. *Renegade's Lady*. NY: Leisure. 1997.
Smith, Lawrence. *Map of Who We Are*. Norman: University of Oklahoma Press. 1997.
Sommerfield, Sylvie. *Night Walker*. NY: Leisure. 1998.
Stern, Richard. *Interloper*. NY: Pocket. 1990.
Stone, Ned. *Breed*. NY: Leisure. 1990.
Storm, Hyemeyohsts. *Lightning Bolt*. NY: Ballantine. 1991.
Stromberg, Stanley. *The Mesa*. [n.p.] Clark. 1993.
Summer Rain, Mary. *Seventh Mesa*. Norfolk, VA: Hampton Roads. 1994.
Sutcliffe, Ann. *Westering*. London: Janus. 1996.
Taylor, Janelle. *Chase the Wind*. NY: Kensington. 1994.
——. *Destiny Mine*. NY: Zebra. 1995.
——. *Wild Winds*. NY: Kensington. 1998.
Thom, James. *The Children of First Man*. NY: Ballantine. 1994.

Thompson, David. *Mountain Madness*. NY: Leisure. 1998.
Thompson, Lynn. *William Westerford*. Lavendar. 1991.
Thon, Melanie. *Sweet Hearts*. Boston: Houghton Mifflin. 2000.
Tobin, Greg. *Prairie*. NY: Book of the Month. 1997.
Turner, Vickery. *Testimony of Daniel Pagels*. NY: Scribners. 1991.
Van Camp, Richard. *The Lesser Blessed.* Vancouver: Douglas & McIntye. 1996.
Van Nuys, Joan. *Beloved Intruder*. NY: Avon. 1992.
——. *Beloved Pretender*. NY: Avon. 1992.
——. *Forever Beloved*. NY: Avon. 1996.
Veisel, Judy. *Untamed Love*. NY: Leisure. 1999.
Wahl, Jan. *Pocahontas in London*. NY: Delacorte. 1967.
Walsh, George. *Apache, My Son*. Okemos, MI: Deerfield. 1997.
Warfield, Teresa. *Cherokee Bride*. NY: Jove. 1994.
——. *Cherokee Rose*. NY: Jove. 1991.
Watters, Elsa. *Cherokee Woman*. Fowlerville, MI: Wilderness Adventure. 1992.
Wayne, Rochelle. *Captive Splendour*. NY: Pinnacle. 1993.
——. *Await the Wind.* NY: Kensington. 1996.
Waznis, Renee. *Under Cheyenne Skies*. Princeton, NJ: Xlibris. 1999.
Weatherwise, Wilma. *The Blue-eyed Chippewa*. Swartz Creek, MI: Broadblade. 1986.
Webb, Betty. *Desert Noir*. Scottsdale, AZ: Poisoned Pen. 2001.
Webb, Peggy. *Witch Dance*. NY: Bantam. 1994.
Werner, Patricia. *Warrior Bride*. NY: Zebra. 1992.
West, Charles. *Cheyenne Justice*. NY: Signet. 1999.
Wheeler, Richard. *Rendezvous*. NY: Tor. 1997.
Whipple, Dan. *Click*. Niwot: University Press Of Colorado. 2001.
Wilde, Lauren. *Beloved Captive*. NY: Kensington. 1997.
——. *Sweet Savage Splendor.* NY: Kensington. 1993.
Wilkinson, David Marion. *Not between Brothers*. Albany, CA: Boaz. 1996.
Williams, Bronwyn. *Bedeviled*. NY: Topaz. 1995.
Williams-Platt, Kathryn. *Forever Mine*. Orange, NJ: Bryant & Dillon. 1997.
Willman, Marianne. *Silver Shadows*. NY: Harper. 1993.
Wimberly, Clara. *Cherokee Wind*. NY: Zebra. 1997.
Wise, Noreen. *Morning Star*. Glastonbury, CT: Huckleberry. 1997.
Witt, Shirley. *El Indio Jesus*. Norman: University of Oklahoma Press. 2000.
Wolfe, Swain. *The Lake Dreams the Sky*. NY: Harper. 1999.
Woodruff, Joan. *The Shiloh Renewal*. Seattle: Black Heron Press. 1998.
Wright, Nancy. *Stolen Honey*. NY: Thomas Dunne. 2002.
Wyam, Michelle. *Night Singer*. NY: Kensington. 1995.
Yno, William. *From Out the Forest*. Stockton, OH: Valley Enterprises. 1998.
Young, Brittany. *Brave Heart*. NY: Silhouette. 1995.
Young Bear, Ray. *Remnants of the First Earth*. NY: Grove. 1996.
Zara, Louis. *This Land is Ours*. Boston: Houghton Mifflin. 1940.

Authors' Choice: Best Books of Native American Long Fiction

The following novels are what we, as the authors of this bibliography, found to be our personal favorites. Some have achieved wide public recognition; others have found a smaller audience and perhaps less fame. These are the novels we call our "Best Books" of this second annotated bibliography, 1995 to 2002.

Blevins, Win. *Stone Song: A Novel of the Life of Crazy Horse*. NY: Tom Doherty. 1995.

Chiaventone, Frederick J. *Moon of Bitter Cold.* NY: Tom Doherty. 2002.

———. *A Road We Do Not Know: A Novel of Custer at the Little Bighorn.* NY: Simon & Schuster. 1996.

Crummey, Michael. *River Thieves.* Boston: Houghton Mifflin. 2002.

Earling, Debra Magpie. (Salish/Kootenai). *Perma Red.* NY: BlueHen Books. 2002.

Erdrich, Louise. (Chippewa). *The Antelope Wife.* NY: HarperCollins. 1998.

———. (Chippewa). *The Last Report on the Miracles at Little No Horse.* NY: HarperCollins. 2001.

Glancy, Diane. (Cherokee). *Pushing the Bear: A Novel of the Trail of Tears.* NY: Harcourt Brace. 1996.

Hockenberry, John. *A River Out of Eden.* NY: Doubleday. 2001.

Hogan, Linda. *Solar Storms.* NY: Scribner. 1995.

House, Silas. *A Parchment of Leaves.* Chapel Hill, NC: Algonquin Books of Chapel Hill. 2002.

Johnston, Terry C. *Turn the Stars Upside Down: The Last Days and Tragic Death of Crazy Horse.* NY: St. Martin's. 2001.

King, Thomas. (Cherokee). *Truth and Bright Water.* NY: Atlantic Monthly Press. 1999.

La Duke, Winona. (Ojibwe). *Last Standing Woman.* Stillwater, MN: Voyager Press. 1997.

Lesley, Craig. *Storm Riders.* NY: Picador. 2000.

Maracle, Lee. (Metis). *Ravensong.* Vancouver: Press Gang Publishers. 1993.

Meyers, Harold Burton. *Reservations.* Niwot: University Press of Colorado. 1999.

Murphy, Garth. *The Indian Lover.* NY: Simon & Schuster. 2002.
O'Brien, Dan. *The Contract Surgeon.* NY: Lyons Press. 1999.
Power, Susan. (Sioux). *The Grass Dancer.* NY: Putnam. 1994.
Skimin, Robert. *The River and the Horsemen: A Novel of the Little Bighorn.* NY: Herodias. 1999.
Treuer, David. (Ojibwe). *The Hiawatha.* NY: Picador USA. 1999.
——. (Ojibwe). *Little.* St. Paul, MN: Graywolf Press. 1995.
Udall, Brady. *The Miracle Life of Edgar Mint.* NY: Norton. 2001.
Welch, James. (Blackfeet/Gros Ventres). *The Heartsong of Charging Elk.* NY: Doubleday. 2000.
Wilkinson, David Marion. *Oblivion's Altar: A Novel of Courage.* NY: New American Library. 2002.

Sources for Native American Fiction, Criticism and Interpretation

For a more extensive list, see The Native American in Long Fiction. *1996.*

Adamson, Joni. *American Indian Literature, Environmental Justice, and Ecocriticism: The Middle Place.* Tucson: University of Arizona Press. 2001.

Anderson, Eric Gary. *American Indian Literature and the Southwest: Contexts and Dispositions.* Austin: University of Texas Press. 1999.

Berner, Robert L. *Defining American Indian Literature: One Nation Divisible.* Lewiston, NY: Mellen. 1999.

Bloom, Harold. *Native American Writers.* Philadelphia: Chelsea House. 1998.

Brill de Ramirez, Susan Berry. *Contemporary American Indian Literatures and the Oral Tradition.* Tucson: University of Arizona Press. 1999.

Donovan, Kathleen M. *Feminist Readings of Native American Literature: Coming to Voice.* Tucson: University of Arizona Press. 1998.

Dreese, Donelle N. *Ecocriticism: Creating Self and Place in Environmental and American Indian Literatures.* NY: Peter Lang. 2002.

Glassman, Steve, and Maurice J. O'Sullivan. *Crime Fiction and Film in the Southwest.* Bowling Green, OH: Bowling Green State University Popular Press. 2001.

Heflin, Ruth J. *I Remain Alive: The Sioux Literary Renaissance.* Syracuse, NY: Syracuse University Press. 2000.

Horne, Dee Alyson. *Contemporary American Indian Writing: Unsettling Literature.* NY: Peter Lang. 1999.

Hulan, Renee, ed. *Native North America: Critical and Cultural Perspectives: Essays.* Toronto: ECW Press. 1999.

Isernhagen, Hartwig. *Momaday, Vizenor, Armstrong: Conversations on American Indian Writing.* Norman: University of Oklahoma Press. 1999.

King, Thomas, Cheryl Calver, and Helen Hoy. *The Native in Literature.* Toronto: ECW Press. 1987

Krupat, Arnold. *Red Matters: Native American Studies.* Philadelphia: University of Pennsylvania Press. 2002.

Krupat, Arnold. *The Turn to the Native: Studies in Criticism and Culture.* Lincoln: University of Nebraska Press. 1996.

Larson, Sidner [sic] J. *Captured in the Middle: Tradition and Experience in Contemporary Native American Writing.* Seattle: University of Washington Press. 2000.

Lincoln, Kenneth. *Indi'in Humor: Bicultural Play in Native America.* NY: Oxford University Press. 1993.

Nelson, Elizabeth Hoffman, and Malcolm Nelson. *Telling the Stories: Essays on American Indian Literatures and Cultures.* NY: Peter Lang. 2001.

Owens, Louis. *Other Destinies: Understanding the American Indian Novel.* Norman: University of Oklahoma Press. 1992.

Parker, Robert Dale. *The Invention of Native American Literature.* Ithaca, NY: Cornell University Press. 2003.

Vizenor, Gerald. *Fugitive Poses: Native American Scenes of Absence and Presence.* Lincoln: University of Nebraska Press. 1998.

Waldman, Carl. *Encyclopedia of Native American Tribes.* Rev. Ed. Facts on File. 1999.

Walker, Cheryl. *Indian Nation: Native American Literature and Nineteenth Century Nationalisms.* Durham, NC: Duke University Press. 1997.

Weaver, Jace. *That the People Might Live: Native American Literatures and Native American Community.* NY: Oxford University Press. 1997.

Welburn, Tom. *Roanoke and Wampum: Topics in Native American Heritage and Literatures.* NY: Peter Lang. 2001.

Wiget, Andrew. *Handbook of Native American Literature.* NY: Garland. 1996.

Womack, Craig S. *Red on Red: Native American Literary Separatism.* Minneapolis: University of Minnesota Press. 1999.

Index by Title

Index by Tribe

Index by Date

Index by Historical Events

Index by Historical Persons

About the Authors

Joan T. Beam received her B.A. in English Literature from the University of Washington and her M.S. in Library Science from Southern Connecticut State University. She is a member of the Library Faculty in the Reference Unit of Morgan Library at Colorado State University in Fort Collins, Colorado. Professor Beam has previously worked in both special and public libraries in the areas of reference, cataloging, collection development and instruction. She has published several articles in professional journals on a variety of topics and is currently active in the maintenance of the Library's public online catalog and the Colorado regional union catalog, Prospector. Professor Beam is also active in the American Library Association, Intellectual Freedom Round Table. Her research on Native Americans arose from her experience working with patrons utilizing electronic databases to locate relevant materials on this subject. As a result of the work leading up to the publication of the first bibliography, further interest has been generated in the historical, artistic, political and legal aspects of Native Americans in the United States. This interest resulted in the determination to continue the work and produce a second bibliography of fictional works with Native American themes published primarily since 1995.

Barbara Branstad is a graduate of Whitman College and earned her M.S. in Library Science from the University of Denver. She was Associate Professor at Colorado State University Libraries until her retirement in 2002. During her tenure in the Social Sciences and Humanities Department of Morgan Library her primary responsibilities involved collection development. Professor

Branstad has published several articles on serial publications and wrote the Golden Retriever column for *Pure-bred Dogs; the American Kennel Club Gazette.* She coauthored one other book, *Retriever Working Certificate Training* (Alpine Publications, 1986) and at present is working on a full-length annotated bibliography of Colorado fiction.